Governing the Japanese Economy

ASPECTS OF POLITICAL ECONOMY
Series Editor: Geoffrey Harcourt

Published

A. Asimakopulos, *Investment, Employment and Income Distribution*
Pat Devine, *Democracy and Economic Planning*
Paul Dunne (ed.), *Quantitative Marxism*
Richard M. Goodwin & Lionello F. Punzo, *The Dynamics of a Capitalist Economy*
Heinz Kurz, *Capital, Distribution and Effective Demand*
Marc Jarsulic, *Effective Demand and Income Distribution*
Peter Nolan, *The Political Economy of Collective Farms*
Bob Rowthorn & Naomi Wayne, *Northern Ireland: The Political Economy of Conflict*
Kyoko Sheridan, *Governing the Japanese Economy*
Ian Steedman, *From Exploitation to Altruism*
Christopher Torr, *Equilibrium, Expectations and Information*
Warren Young, *Interpreting Mr Keynes*
Grazia Ietto-Gillies, *International Production: Trends, Theories, Effects*

Forthcoming

Ravi Kanbur, *Risk Taking, Income Distribution and Poverty*
Jose Salazar, *Pricing Policy and Economic Development*

Governing the Japanese Economy

Kyoko Sheridan

Polity Press

First published in 1993 by Polity Press
in association with Blackwell Publishers

First published in paperback 1994

Editorial office:
Polity Press
65 Bridge Street
Cambridge CB2 1UR, UK

Marketing and production:
Blackwell Publishers
108 Cowley Road
Oxford OX4 1JF, UK

238 Main Street
Cambridge, Massachusetts 02142, USA

ISBN 0 7456 1060 9
ISBN 0 7456 1414 0

A CIP catalogue record for this book is available from the British Library and the Library of Congress.

Typeset in 10 on 11½pt Times
by Mathematical Composition Setters, Salisbury, Wiltshire.
Printed in Great Britain by T. J. Press (Padstow) Ltd, Cornwall

This book is printed on acid-free paper.

Contents

List of Figures

List of Tables

To my Mother and Father

Acknowledgements

In the course of writing this book I have accumulated debts to many people and organizations which I here wish to acknowledge. I wish to thank Nishikawa Shunsaku of Keio University, Bill Newell of Sydney University and Bruce McFarlane of Macquarie University for their valuable comments and encouragement. My thanks also go to Mizuno Satoshi of the Ministry of International Trade and Industry for introducing me to various representative officers in his and other ministries in Tokyo.

The Japan Foundation has awarded me financial assistance through its research fellowship and library assistance programmes and this I thankfully acknowledge. Keio University provided me with research facilities in Mita, where old friends and colleagues in its Department of Commerce and Business Administration made my visits to the common room most welcome and stimulating. The Japanese librarians at the National Library in Canberra have also generously aided me in my numerous searches for Japanese references.

Dawn Christopher of the University of South Australia has typed the manuscript several times and I thank her for her skill and reliability, as I do Helen Wickens and Paul Chapman who have read the proofs.

Finally, but not least by any means, my most sincere thanks go to Hugh Stretton of the University of Adelaide for his warm and professional support, interest and encouragement. He has given me great assistance in editing the whole text to make it more readable. I must however hasten to add that any mistakes which may remain are, of course, mine.

Polity Press has provided me with professional, high-quality assistance. Among their staff my special thanks must go to Geoff Palmer, Debbie Seymour, Jennifer Speake, Pam Thomas and John Thompson.

Introduction: The Past and Potential Role of Government in Japanese Economic Life

1 Two Purposes

This book recommends some new directions for Japan. Its proposals would conserve some threatened sources of Japan's high productivity as an 'achieving society'. They would improve the justice and quality of life, especially for women. They would introduce some new conditions of family life, some financial changes, and a radical land reform – which would be the third in Japan's modern history.

Such a programme might well be dismissed as Utopian in Western countries. Nevertheless, if it is workable in Japan it is because of that country's unusual capacity for making deliberate, effective choices of national direction. There are those who doubt if that capacity still exists, believing it to have died a natural death over the past 20 years, as Japan reached full economic maturity and government guidance gave way to market forces. It is true that a simple analysis of relations between government and business, at any one date, does not reveal a 'Japanese secret' in the form of permanent institutions through which a collective will, or the will of a ruling regime or class, gives direction to the nation's economic development. Instead there is a history of dominant purposes which have themselves changed from time to time, operating through frequently changing policies and instruments. To understand the nature, strength and limitations of the capacity for coherent national action it is necessary to see it at work, in changing forms, through the whole history of Japan's modernization.

Academic readers are advised that this is not another economic history of Japan. It does not add new detail to that history or review its current literature. I am a grateful user of, rather than contributor to, the work of economic historians. However, reading it as an outsider I believe that it discloses a sequence of policy cycles, within the long process of economic development. Many of the cycles come as the bureaucrats switch economic instruments and policies in order to pursue enduring purposes. It is in that pattern and sequence as a whole, observed over two centuries, that the 'Japanese secret' can best be discerned and understood.

That is the business of the first eight chapters. A ninth chapter distils what the record reveals about the capacity for concerted action, defends it against free marketeers and others who now want to dismantle it, and argues for conserving it as a valuable national capacity.

Informed by that analysis and arising out of it, the final chapter proposes the new directions which express the second and more important purpose of this book.

2   Western and Japanese Questions about Japan's Economic Achievement

Japan's prolonged and persistent efforts to industrialize and the resultant economic growth have aroused so much interest and comment from outsiders that we are reminded of the birth of a new star into the theatrical world. Patrick and Rosovsky, for example, remark that 'Japan's surge over the past quarter-century, seemingly from nowhere, to join the vanguard of the world's economies has been an unprecedented, exciting and at times, disruptive event.'[1] Here we may detect the curiosity and bewilderment of the outsider, particularly of the Westerner, wondering if this experience is at all explicable, given our established economic tools and models.

Why was Japan able to 'take-off' successfully and initiate modern economic growth? Why was Japan, both before and after the Second World War, able to achieve a more rapid rate of economic growth than many other economies? What is the probable future of the economy? How is Japan proposing to continue to improve social welfare, care for an ageing population, improve the quality of Japanese life, cope with environmental problems, maintain supplies of raw materials and energy sources, and reduce friction with her trading partners?[2] And what role is Japan going to play in the world economy? What will she contribute to the welfare of humankind beyond her own nationals?[3]

Western observers respond to those questions with Western answers, and three particular answers are commonplace. Japanese culture has allowed harsh exploitation of a hard-working and submissive workforce. The economic revolution has been driven by masterful government. And, because Japan has outperformed the West but lacks some of its welfare institutions, Westerners suspect that the excess of wealth comes from the neglect of welfare. So (in this view) the government should now aim to switch some margin of Japanese time, energy and economic surplus from saving to consumption, from work to leisure, from economic growth to public welfare provisions and environmental care, from industrial investment to investment in housing and public services, and from competitive national growth to international aid and co-operation.[4]

Some Japanese thinkers duplicate some or all of that advice. However, except for environmental anxiety, there still has been surprisingly little popular public debate in Japan about the future directions of economic development and national purpose. That is the more surprising because within government the single-minded devotion to growth has been troubled for 20 years now by considerable anxiety and uncertainty about the economic future and the government's role in it. Some of the uncertainty springs from a belief, held by some Japanese and many Westerners, that the time for government economic leadership has passed, and that the future of Japan's economy is now something for the government to follow rather than lead. They believe that as Japan has been overtaking Western technology and productivity she has also been in transition to an increasingly Western culture, and to a Western role, which means a diminished role for government. That would explain the declining importance of the Ministry of International Trade and Industry (MITI) in economic planning and direction since the 1960s.[5] In this view, when the economy arrives at full industrial maturity its direction naturally passes from government to market forces. Future directions of development will be determined as in the West, by the people's spending choices and by market relations with the world economy, rather than by political choices.

I do not agree. Unaided market forces did not determine Japan's economic development in the past, and they need not determine its future directions *unless there is a deliberate political decision that they should do so*. In its route to that conclusion this book differs from others of its kind in four main ways. It sees government not as intervening in Japan's economy from outside the economic system, but as an integral element in the system. As indicated above, it identifies a number of deliberate changes in the economic and national direction in the past; it argues that the capacity to make such changes still exists; and it proposes directions for the future, some familiar and some less so. The proposals for the future reflect a belief that although Japan and the West may well continue to teach lessons to each other, workable policies for Japan must generally be rooted in Japan's distinctive history, culture and political capacities.

On a personal note, to the extent that this book's lines of argument differ from those current in Japan or from the usual Western thoughts about Japan, this is no doubt because of its debt to both traditions, including the misgivings which each tradition has about the other. I, the author ('we' by convention hereafter in the book), am a Japanese economist who has lived half her life in Japan and half in the West. Being Japanese I am entitled to criticize my country's institutions as severely as I like. But I do not want

Japan to make the West its model, to become another 'Coca Cola clone'. I am bringing up bilingual children: I would like their living and working choices to lie between equally just and interesting and productive societies; but still different societies, each enjoying the best of its distinctive heritage and working to reform whatever remains of the worst of it.

3   Government's Role in Japan's Economy

It is not unusual to emphasize the importance of government leadership in the rapid industrialization of Japan. A commonplace explanation of Japan's economic modernization has the following essential ingredients.

From the seventeenth to the mid-nineteenth century, Japan was a secluded feudal society. At the time when Western force opened it to the trade of the industrializing world in the 1850s, the US western frontier and the European overseas empires were expanding rapidly. In that imperialist world Japan feared for her independence, and saw an urgent need to modernize her defences, and for that purpose, her economy. Members of the leading class created a strong central government through the Meiji Restoration of 1868. In contriving an economic revolution over the next 100 years, that government and its successors had two special advantages. One, peculiar to Japan, was the traditional culture which made Japanese people industrious, co-operative and submissive: they could be led to learn hard, work hard and save hard, and at low wages if necessary. The other advantage, available to all poor countries but until recently exploited by Japan alone among non-Western nations, was the advantage of the late developer. When advanced economic systems have created new industrial technology and business methods and institutions, latecomers can copy the new apparatus without the costs or the slow processes of inventing and developing it. In principle, they can thus develop their economics faster and at lower cost than older-established competitors, and there may be further benefits in having wholly up-to-date equipment, with no 'industrial museum', no inheritance of earlier vintages of less efficient plant.

However, to realize those potential advantages an undeveloped country must somehow educate the necessary human capital, build the physical infrastructure of power and water supply, ports and harbours, roads and bridges, post and telegraph services and basic urban services. It must develop the institutional apparatus of money and banking, company and commercial law, consular relations with trading partners, and so on, without which industrial production can scarcely begin. It is extremely difficult to create those necessary conditions in poor countries living on little but subsistence agriculture. If 'market forces' could do it, it would have been done widely through the nineteenth century; but in the non-Western world Japan alone managed it. Everywhere else in the non-Western world, a combination of market forces and Western power allowed Westerners to extract whatever raw materials they wanted from Asia and Africa and elsewhere, *without* initiating significant economic development in the territories concerned. The Japanese exception is commonly ascribed to four causes: (1) *external threats* to national independence prompted (2) *masterful government* to mobilize the productive potentialities of (3) the *traditional Japanese culture* to seize and exploit (4) the *late developer's advantages*, thus setting in motion what became in due course a self-sustaining, market-driven process of economic growth. The main contribution of government was to build the physical infrastructure and educate the human capital which market forces could not supply unaided. Thus government *intervened* in the economy to correct a *market failure*.[6]

We can agree with much of that account, except its beginning, its end and its implications for the future. In the first place, government did not assume an economic role because of external threats. In feudal form at central, provincial (*Han*) and village levels, government had been an integral 'working part' of the economic system for centuries.[7] When external dangers made it desirable to centralize government and modernize the economy, a group of the old ruling class responded accordingly with the Meiji Restoration. That transformed the government's economic role but by no means began it: one of the Meiji government's early acts, for example, was to allow farmers to decide for themselves, for the first time for centuries, what crops to grow.[8]

Similarly, at the latter end of the standard explanation, the retreat since the 1970s from the role played by MITI in the earlier postwar decades need not be seen as an inevitable passage 'from planning to market'. It is merely a response to changed conditions. It may signify some loss of conviction or direction, or some increase of capital owners' influence, in the national leadership. But it is a change of direction rather than a general withdrawal of government from economic leadership, as MITI's most recent publications make clear. Government is still active in the economy. It is increasing its efforts to clean up the physical environment by regulating or exporting pollutant industries. Japan's banking and financial system continues to be more strictly and prudently governed than most others. The parties of the Left are attracting increasing support and if they should be elected there is not much doubt that they will form a government capable, if required, of implementing substantial changes in tax, welfare, industrial, financial, trading and cultural policies. Thus the current retreat of government from some of the detailed resource-rationing, credit-rationing, import control and industrial planning of the 1950s and 1960s should be seen as one more change of direction, by a conservative government, in response to changing conditions and purposes.

In his renowned *Theory of Economic Growth* (1955), Arthur Lewis distinguishes nine categories of government functions which promote economic growth. They are:

1   maintaining public services,
2   influencing attitudes,
3   shaping economic institutions,
4   influencing the use of resources,
5   influencing the distribution of income,
6   controlling the quantity of money,
7   controlling fluctuations,
8   ensuring full employment, and
9   influencing the level of investment.[9]

The Japanese government has played an important role in all of these areas, although its level of involvement has differed from time to time according to its assessment of the needs of the economy. What is lacking in Lewis' list, in terms of the Japanese experience, is the importance of the government in guiding both the direction and the pace of economic development throughout the process of industrialization. It could be said that the economic function of the Japanese government has been consistently and continuously that of a skipper. If its attention to each of Lewis' nine categories of action has varied over time, that has been instrumental, as changing international conditions, government purposes and the stages of economic growth required. There have been two constant factors. The political approach to economics and the economic concerns of government have made 'economics' truly 'political economy' in Japan; and state planning and direction of economic development (albeit by changing means) has been continuous.

There is good reason to believe that the national capacity for single-minded economic direction is still there. Before suggesting what direction it might take through the coming decades, this book will explore the power itself by reviewing its history – its basic nature and its changing purposes – through the century and a half of Japan's economic modernization.

4   The Periodization of Economic Policy, 1830–1990

The historical chapters that follow focus on government's capacity to change the direction of economic development from time to time. However, there is an economic alternative to that political periodization. Historical studies of economic activity in Japan have identified cyclic fluctuations in growth rates. Some appear to conform to Kitchen cycles of 2–3 years, while others observe Juglar cycles of 7–8 years, and Kuznet cycles of about 20 years. Only Kondratieff cycles have not been identified.[10] Researchers have not discovered the causes of such cycles, but the duration of long swings, in which shorter swings are enclosed, has been agreed upon by most researchers in the field.[11]

In the light of our purposes, a political framework has been adopted. Chapter 1 sketches the economic role of government in feudal Japan, and then through the first years of the Meiji modernization from 1868 to 1882. Those first Meiji years saw innumerable outward-looking efforts to survey and understand the world's economic systems and technology, and at home a great many experiments and debates to decide how best to tackle Japan's modernization. The chapter could appropriately have been called 'What to do?', with the next chapter having the same title without the question mark; as a reconstructed government decided firmly what to do, and set about it from 1881 with financial reform, the sale of public enterprises and a coherent German/Japanese approach to modernization by state-supported private enterprise. At the turn of the century the achievement of a workable infrastructure for industrial development, together with military victory over China (and soon afterwards over Russia) brought changes of direction. Through the first third of the twentieth century there were further changes, some of them stimulated by war, riots, earthquakes and economic depression; but although we divide those years into two periods, it is convenient to treat them in two continuous chapters, one on investment and capital formation and one on labour and welfare policies, with each chapter trespassing at times to trace its themes back into the nineteenth century and forward beyond the 1930s. The chronological treatment is then resumed in chapter 5, on the war economy, chapter 6, on reconstruction (1946–55), chapter 7, on the period of high-speed economic growth (1956–72), and chapter 8, on the problems of the mature economy since 1970; as government faced – first – resource and environmental problems, and then uncertainties about the forms that 'welfare' should take in Japan. Since there will be reference to the periods as defined, it is convenient to tabulate them (see table 1.1). They are numbered to match the chapters that deal with them (except that chapter 8 covers periods VIII *and* IX).

5 Conclusions

Two final chapters will argue against any permanent surrender of economic direction to market forces, i.e. to the ungoverned uses of unequal bargaining strength and private financial power which Western economists are pleased to define as 'market forces'. Such an abdication of government would be likely to have ill effects on Japanese society, on the world economy, and consequently on Japan's relations with the West and her capacity to improve Western performance by example. Paradoxically, that would be a thoroughly Western solution, extinguishing a special Japanese advantage, and surrendering to some of the least admirable elements of

Western ideology and values. Better options are available in both worlds: in the alternative Western traditions of social-democratic and communitarian thought, and in the unique Japanese culture and capacity to give deliberate direction to a capitalist economy without damaging its capitalist efficiency. Some hybrid of the two might well provide the economic basis of a fairer and more enjoyable society than Japan's obsession with economic growth has yet allowed. It might be achieved by Japan's special ability to act with coherent national purpose, and it might surprise the West with a further 'Japanese miracle'.

Table 1.1 *Main economic plans and policies, 1868–1990*

Events and prevailing conditions	Main policy aims	State economic action	Income distribution and welfare
I. 1868–80, period of strong enterprise government			
Population = 34.8 m (1872)	Establishment of strong central government for national independence against foreign invasion	Ministry of Industry Development founded (1870)	Abolition of feudal class distinctions
Meiji Restoration (1868)		Ministry of Education founded (1871)	Commutation of samurai pensions
Establishment of central government (1871)	Economic growth and modernization for national strength	Establishment of public primary schools and universities (1872)	Reduction of land tax to 2.5% to counter increasing peasant riots (1877)
Seinan rebellion and end of civil turmoil (1877)		Uniform national taxation (1873)	
Hyper-inflation (1878–87)		State provides loan to *Hans* for promotion of industries	
		State takeover of *Han* public enterprises	
		Establishment of railway and communication networks (1872–3)	
		State ownership and operation of mining activities (1873)	
		Ministry of Home Affairs founded (1873)	
		Opening of state mining and agricultural technical school	
		Establishment of public model factories (1872–80)	

(continued)

Table 1.1 (continued)

Events and prevailing conditions	Main policy aims	State economic action	Income distribution and welfare
II. 1881–1900, period of transition to small government			
Population = 38.5 m(1886) *Economic indices* (1960 = 100.0): GNP = 16.1 (1886); production – manufacturing and mining = 2.0 (1886)	Establishment of high national status in international sphere	Establishment of Noshomu-sho (The Ministry of Agriculture and Commerce, MAC) (1881)	The trade union movement starts (1897)
	Economic modernization and growth, by state stimulation and protection of private enterprise	Establishment of public financial system: (1) establishment of (European model) central banking system; (2) creation of thrift institutions for small savers	Establishment of water service networks in Tokyo (1899)
Railway boom, encouraged by good performance in cotton spinning and state railway companies (1883)			Abortive attempt by government to sell state steel mill (1887)
Corporate boom (1885–90)		Establishment of Gunji Kogyo (defence) industry in Ministries of Army and Navy (1881)	Development of private business and entrepreneurship: (1) privatization of public model plants; (2) allocation of public finance to selected key industries and enterprises
Sino-Japanese War (1894–1905)		Steel production for defence purposes in Ministry of Navy (1882–96)	
		State initiative for purchase of steel mills in China (1899)	Further development of large combines (*zaibatsu*)
		Further public investment in state railway facilities	

III. 1901–16, period of 'take-off' and imperial expansion

Population = 44.4 m (1901) Economic indices (1960 = 100.0): GNP = 25.5 (1901); production – manufacturing and mining = 4.4 (1901)	To establish leadership in Asian economy to enter the world economic scene	Opening of state Yawata steel (the predecessor of the present Nippon steel) (1901)	Regulation to suppress industrial disputes and labour movements (1900)
Russo-Japanese War (1904)	Establishment of modern defence industry	Large-scale public investment in railway networks	Establishment of Shakai Minshu (Social Democratic) Party, only to be dissolved on the following day as an illegal organization (1901)
Depression in villages (1908–14)	Establishment of colonial economies in Korea and Manchuria	Public investment in Manchurian railways (1906)	Public support to foster longer working hours and cheap labour in textile mills
End of unequal trade treaty (1911)	Promotion of export industries	Nationalization of 17 railway companies (1906–7)	Labour dispute at Ashio and Besshi copper mines and Mitsubishi shipyard (1907)
Establishment of colonies in Korea, Taiwan and China		Government promotion of private investment in Korean railway (1907)	Factory Law (1911)
Rise of militaristic imperialism without full development of heavy industry		Public support of shipping industry (mid-1910s)	
First World War (1914)		Government monopoly of tobacco and salt manufacturing	

(*continued*)

Table 1.1   (continued)

IV.   1917–37, Taisho Democracy and social policy

Events and prevailing conditions	Main policy aims	State economic action	Income distribution and welfare
Population = 53.5 m (1916) Economic indices (1960 = 100.0): GNP = 36.4 (1916); production – manufacturing and mining = 9.0 (1916)	Further development of national status and economic power	Industrial development through public promotion of heavy construction investment: roads, bridges and other public works	Establishment of Nihon Shakai (Socialist) Party (1906)
Taisho Democracy (1918–22)	Promotion of capital–labour conciliation for harmonious social structure	Expansion and modernization of defence industry	Rice riot (1918)
Formation of Japan Labour Party		Development of nationwide transport network system	Numerous large-scale industrial disputes at Yawata steel and many manufacturing and mining companies (1919–20)
Economic boom (1918–20)		Promotion of education and industry training	Formation (illegal) of Nihon Kyosan-to (Japan Communist Party) (1922)
Collapse of Tokyo stock exchange and many bankruptcies (1920)		Establishment of Shoko-sho (the Ministry of Commerce and Industry, MCI) on the basis of MAC (1925)	Establishment of National Health Scheme (1922)
Kanto Great Earthquake (1923)			Improvement of labour code and introduction of Industrial Arbitration Act for public works (1922)
Manchurian Incident (1931)			
Road to recovery from the Depression (1932)			Achievement of manhood suffrage (1925); movements for woman's suffrage
Shanghai incident (1936)			
'2-26' incident			Wholesale arrest of communists (1929)

V. 1938–45, war economy

Population = 70.1 m (1936) *Economic indices (1960 = 100.0): GNP = 67.6 (1936); production – manufacturing and mining = 33.7 (1936)*	Directly controlled economy for war effort	Establishment of Kikaku-in (the Cabinet Planning Board)
Rise of fascism (1938–45)		Act of Total War and Electricity Power Act (1938)
Peking incident (1937)		Enforced co-operation between the military and business (*zaibatsu*) (1937)
Pacific War (1941–5)		Government-forced structural change in the *zaibatsu* system and their enterprise structure (1941–5)
Depreciation and destruction of capital stock (1942–5)		Key Industry Act (1941–2)
End of Second World War (1945)		Suppression of labour movement (1938)
		Fall in living standards of the population: real per capita consumption (1935 = 100.0) 91 in 1940; 65 in 1944

VI. 1946–55, postwar reconstruction

Population = 75.8 m (1946) *Economic indices (1960 = 100.0): GNP = 67.6 (1946); production – mining and manufacturing = 8.5 (1946)*	Recovery from wartime destruction	*US occupation policy:* democratic constitution, land reform, labour code liberalization, anti-monopoly measures (1945–6)
	Recovery of national independence	Introduction of Bukka Tosei (Price Control) Act (1946)
		Removal of fish and vegetables from ration listing (1950)

(continued)

Table 1.1 *(continued)*

Events and prevailing conditions	Main policy aims	State economic action	Income distribution and welfare
US occupation policies, (1945–51) and economic aid (1946–59)		*Postwar Japanese government policy:*	Red Purge (1950)
Hyper-inflation (1946–9)		Priority Production Formula (1946)	Large-scale industrial disputes across mining and manufacturing industries (1953–5)
Korean War boom (1950–52)		Reconversion Finance Bank (1947–52)	Establishment of Shunto (spring offensive) strategy (1955)
San Fransisco Peace Treaty (1951)		Introduction of fixed exchange rate of ¥360 = US$1 (1949)	
		Formulation of the basis of postwar industrial policy (1949–53)	
		Instigation of Anti-monopoly Act (1949–53)	
		Establishment of nine electric power corporations; establishment of five enterprise bases (1951)	
		Establishment of government banks (1951–3)	
		Industrial policy for capital accumulation (1951–3)	
		Corporate Tax Act (1952)	
		Law to promote industrial rationalization (1952)	

VII. 1956–70, period of high-speed economic growth

Population = 87 m (1953) *Economic indices* *(1960 = 100.0): GNP = 45.6* *(1953); production – mining* *and manufacturing = 40.3* *(1953)*	National efforts for economic prosperity	Promotion of *zaisei toyushi* (FILP) system (1953)	Public Housing Corporation established (1955)
		Relaxation of Anti-monopoly Law (1953)	Establishment of series of social security and welfare programmes
Economic recovery to the prewar peak level (1955)		5-year national programme for development of electricity generation capacity (1953)	
3–4-yearly economic cycle due to balance of trade industrial monetary policy (1953–70)		Development of the *keiretsu* business grouping system (1954)	
Japan joins GATT (1964)		Establishment of Keizai Kikaku-cho (EPA) (1955)	
Japan joins OECD (1964)		Public program for petro-chemical industry (establishment of Combinato) (1955–65)	
Student riots across many universities (1968)		Electrification of the whole Tokaido national railway network (1956)	
Large-scale demonstration and riots over Okinawa and US–Japan Security Treatment (1969–70)		Merger of Yawata and Fuji Steels to create giant monopoly, Shin Nihon Seitetsu (Nippon Steel), with MITI's blessing (1969)	
Expo'70 in Osaka (1970)			

(*continued*)

Table 1.1 *(continued)*

Events and prevailing conditions	Main policy aims	State economic action	Income distribution and welfare
VIII. 1971–85, decelerated growth and environmental concern			
Population = 110 m (1974) Economic indices (1960 = 100.0): GNP = 353.4 (1974); Production – mining and manufacturing = 430.7 (1974)	Stable and balanced economic growth with environmental safety	MITI publishes its first *Natural Resource White Paper* and proposes to establish public–private joint programme for resource/energy development programme overseas	Establishment of large-scale special hospitals for the aged.
Floating of yen (1971)			Introduction of Welfare Act for working women
Increase in value of yen: ¥264 = US$1 (1973)		Establishment of the Department of the Environment (1971)	General strike in transport industry (1972)
Ratio of students continuing secondary education at 16 yrs plus exceeds 90% (1974)		Anti-pollution law introduced against automobile exhausts (1971)	
Seven-nation economic summit meeting held in Tokyo (1975)		Postal savings deposits valued at highest record (1972)	
Sharp US criticism against Japanese export drive of steel, cars, coal etc. (1976)			
Huge accumulation of foreign currencies continued (1978–)			

IX. 1986–90, in search of a growth-based welfare state

Population = 122 m (1987) *Economic indices* *(1960 = 100.0):* *GNP = 1438.4 (1988);* *production – mining and* *manufacturing 2.4538 (1987)*	Use economic growth to improve welfare of the general population Formation of a Provisional Commission for Administration Reform – Rincho (1980)	Switch public effort from production aid to welfare aid: restructure government offices and sell public corporations	Active public investment to build infrastructure facilities, water, gas, parks, housing and health care facilities

1 Feudalism and Modernization, 1800–1880

1 The Feudal Political Economy[1]

Recent research has greatly improved our knowledge of Japan's economy and society in the seventeenth and eighteenth centuries.[2] First, it is generally acknowledged that despite its feudal form and conservative government the society was endowed with many conditions that were favourable for economic growth. Among them were low birth and death rates;[3] urban growth and commercialization in villages, which resulted in the development of some economic infrastructure; ethnic uniformity, which made the promotion of pragmatic education and the establishment of a mass culture economically viable; the development of irrigation, commercial and financial practices; and a system of land tax and land tenure which encouraged village and farm productivity.

However, Edo Japan was still essentially a pre-modern society, because its economic base was not 'industrial': it remained a 'revenue economy' in which the non-productive ruling class lived by exacting a land tax from the productive peasant population. The production of goods and services was *principally* based on tradition and social status rather than economic calculation.[4]

Second, although the tax burden borne by the peasants was heavy and they continued to live at a subsistence level, the commercialization of village activities led peasants' living standards to rise very slowly, but nonetheless steadily, throughout the Edo period. Thus farmers (in other words, most people) saw and personally experienced how economic development could come about due to their own efforts, and could bring about some improvement in their welfare – however small and slow in coming.

Third, most people still lived lives of extreme hardship. As the population-to-land ratio rose through the early Edo period the land-holding system led to the ownership of smaller sized tracts of land, and in the rice paddies extremely labour-intensive techniques were introduced to increase unit land yields. Farmers were forced to work longer hours in the fields, and in the slack seasons they worked late into the night to earn extra revenue by fishing, mining, spinning and weaving, making straw sandals and so on. A 'hard-working' ethic developed. However, those conditions did not generally encourage the introduction of draught animals or capital equipment as a source of energy, or other labour-substituting methods. Basically, throughout the Edo period the major source of energy was human. In fact, Hayami estimates that the labour : output ratio increased as the scale of GNP increased between 1660 and 1810.[5]

Fourth, the lack of interest in capital investment for productivity corresponded with the lack of modern industrialist–entrepreneurs to make devices to improve energy : capital : labour production ratios, which would lead to economies of scale in their operations. Although GNP was increasing in the Edo period, diseconomies of scale remained the norm, not only in villages but also in semi-manufacturing industries (processing agricultural products) and other sectors; instead of mass production, high-quality craft-type activities and products were developed for consumption by the wealthier classes. The breakaway from such trends had to wait, until the end of the *sakoku* (exclusion) policy opened up export markets to ambitious producers.

What does all this add up to? We would speculate that, on the eve of the Meiji Restoration, Japan had apparently reached the limits of economic development possible within the specific structure of her society. She was making the best use of her social and economic endowments, given the domestically available technologies, physical resources, traditional culture, thinking patterns and values. While those constraints continued, there remained little further scope for promoting the development of the material welfare of the mass of the people. However, in 1868, the door was opened to show the people an alternative. Some saw opportunities faster than others, seized them more eagerly than others, and wished and encouraged them to materialize more strongly than others: among these were the Meiji bureaucrats. To understand what had shaped their minds and purposes, it is important to know something of their previous experience of the role of government in the economic developments of the feudal period. For Western readers, we must first briefly sketch the structure of that government.

The *de facto* ruler of feudal Japan was the hereditary Tokugawa shogun, formally the Emperor's military deputy but effectively his captor. As a feudal lord the shogun ruled directly and taxed land estimated to yield about 15 per cent of Japan's farm output, and the great lords of his court held as much again. Those directly ruled Tokugawa territories included

Japan's main cities and most of her mines, yielding a further range of revenues. Japan's central government was financed by the taxation of these directly ruled lands.

Beyond the shogun's directly ruled territories, Japan was governed by 260 (or so) *daimyo*, feudal lords each with a domain which he held by grace of the shogun, but taxed and governed with considerable independence. The elaborate bureaucracies of the shogunate and provincial domains were staffed by samurai, warriors by tradition and increasingly civil servants, scholars or teachers by occupation: they comprised 6–8 per cent of the population. Of every 100 people at work in feudal Japan, more than 70 farmed; about 20 mined, fished, transported goods or were town-dwelling merchants or artisans; and six or eight governed. As feudal regimes go, the samurai were not a very economical ruling class, and through the eighteenth and into the nineteenth centuries the exploitation of the poorer farmers, by samurai and others, was often severe.

2   The Meiji Restoration: Establishment of an Integrated Society

The evaluation of the Meiji Restoration has changed considerably over the years. Both the dimensions and the purpose of the analyses made of it have altered as the Japanese economy has progressed from its semi-industrial status in Asia to being one of the industrial powers of the world. The greater the success, the more interest there is in the questions: Why did it happen?, Who provided the driving force in the reform and for what reasons?; and What have they gained from the reconstruction?

Scholastic debates are unresolved, but they tend – broadly – to veer between two conflicting views.[6] One sees the Meiji Restoration as the *coup d'état* through which a unified and modern nation–state was founded, as the basis for the development of a modern industrial capitalist economy. The way was thus cleared for an economic revolution comparable with any other Western industrial revolution: a business-led industrialization where initiative was taken by individual entrepreneurs.

The other locates the Restoration as an historical incident within the process of transition from Tokugawa feudalism to twentieth-century capitalism. Emphasis is placed on the increase in bureaucratic controls over major aspects of economic life, and on the generation of novel public industrial enterprises. In this interpretation, industrialization is seen as a more nationalist, government-led effort, and it relies on evidence from before as well as after the Restoration. Forced to open its ports to the West and fearful of worse intrusions, the Tokugawa shogunate and some of its larger *daimyo* administrations had begun major public works for both commercial and defence purposes, including dockyards and ironworks, before the political revolution began. Those initiatives helped to bring on the political changes: they ran the central and provincial governments further into debt, and made more obvious than ever the inadequacy, for modernizing purposes, of the feudal financial system and the decentralized multiplicity of domain governments on which it was based – hence the creation of effective central government through the 'Restoration'.

The *Fukoku–Kyohei* Slogan

The important framework for the future direction of industrialization was moulded in the period 1868–85. The basic social framework was called the 'economic super-infrastructure' (to distinguish educational and institutional from merely physical infrastructure) and was established in order to provide adequate working conditions for modern economic activity. The very first task of government in building such an economic super-infrastructure was to build the nation–state and set the future course for the relationship and the pattern of co-operation between the major sectors of the economy – state, labour and industry. The establishment of a nation–state with centralized financial resources was essential. The building of a nation–state and the securing of public revenue could be said to be technically separate objectives, the former 'political' and the latter 'economic', but the new Meiji government decided to identify the two objectives with each other by promoting the national slogan *fukoku–kyohei* (rich country – strong army).

The second source of the slogan is found in an idea which was coined and articulated as public policy in the Bakumatsu feudal domain (the latter part of the Edo period in the nineteenth century[7]). Industrial development (the expansion of manufacturing and mining activities) for the enrichment of society had been promoted in the *buiku*[8] policy in the pre-Restoration period in the domains of some feudal lords. It had social rather than national military purposes, being aimed at the well-being of the people in the community, along with the independence of the household of the lord concerned. How the development of the *fukoku–kyohei* policy came to the minds of the leaders of society at the end of the Tokugawa period should be explained in the light of the diplomatic and political crises which arose during a time of institutional and intellectual disagreement in the mid-nineteenth century. Let us briefly summarize the relevant conditions.

First, there was a series of famines in the years 1833–36. The effects spread rapidly and nation-wide from the original famine areas in north-eastern Japan, and disrupted the flow of rice, the major product and the basis of currency, to the cities where most samurai resided. Unsuccessful counter-famine action by the shogunal government only intensified the already mounting agrarian resistance. To make matters worse, news reached Japan of China's defeat at the hands of the West in the Opium War

(1839–42) and this, together with news of the other activities of Western countries, indicating their superiority in military power and knowledge, created a great fear of the West in society in general, and further weakened its confidence in the Tokugawa regime. Despite the *sakoku* (seclusion) policy, Japan was developing a keen interest and desire to learn about the West, this becoming evident from the beginning of the nineteenth century. First came Dutch books, then English, resulting in a direct confrontation between the loyalist *kokugaku* (nationalistic learning) and a group of Western-oriented scholars. The original idea of the slogan can be traced back to two different sources. The first is in the policy formula reported to have been proposed to government by Honda Toshiaki (1744–1821) and Sato Nobuhiro (1769–1850).[9] Opposing the conservative policy of national seclusion, these two scholars separately favoured positive defensive measures such as foreign trade and the colonization of overseas areas, and further proposed to increase production and develop industries by means of state control of industrial production and commerce. With this policy they hoped to transform Japan into 'the richest and strongest nation in the world'. However, in the *sakoku* period, their proposal was dismissed as a Utopian dream.[10] In 1837, when an American merchant ship attempted to approach the Japanese coast the Tokugawa shogunate government turned it away. A group of scholars of the West warned of the possible danger of inviting aggressive retaliation from the West: they were tried and convicted for criticizing the policy of the shogunate. Such confrontations increased in intensity in the late Edo period, with Western demands for a commercial treaty.[11]

Therefore, Maruyama observes that:

> The structural contradictions of Tokugawa society became more and more acute … [making] it difficult to strengthen military forces. As a result, the trend of thought emerged which sought to deal with the international threat by first to securing domestic economic stability and then strengthening the country's defenses on this basis. … And it was more or less realised that the social and economic difficulties were not the product of mistakes in specific policies or the negligence of certain individuals; they were deeply rooted in the Tokugawa social structure itself. Consequently, the solution to be sought lay not in the introduction of isolated measures, but in a considerable trans- formation of institutions. In order to make such a transformation possible it was essential to centralise political power.[12]

When Japan was actually confronted by foreign power in the mid-nineteenth century, both of the above-noted proposals put forward by Honda and Sato were resurrected. National unity became the most urgent concern, and it was to be sought by two means: political power must be retrieved from the scattered provincial domains and concentrated in the national government and national objectives must attract the commitment and support of the population. *For the first time, the common people were called upon to join willingly in the national enterprise.*

This meant a complete reshuffle in the social structure, starting from its foundation. Tokugawa feudalism involved a complete separation of the military (samurai) from the peasantry, and the world of the rulers was sharply distinct from that of the subjects. The common people existed to serve and feed the samurai; they had no rights, no responsibilities and no incentive to concern themselves with the fate of the state and the society. When, before as well as after the Restoration, national military and economic strength became the overriding concern, the situation of the common people had to change. However, although the change was in many respects a liberation, it was driven by nationalist concerns; and those concerns dictated the priorities, rather than priority being given to life, liberty and the pursuit of the happiness of the population in general.

The government began to promote the common people as being its 'agent', instead of their previous 'innately passive nothing-but-taxpayer' status, at about the turn of the nineteenth century, well before the political Restoration. However, as can be inferred from the fact that Fukuzawa Yukichi (1835–1901) devoted his whole life to 'implanting the concept of *nation* in the minds of the people of the entire country', this public call from the top did not have much effect at grass-roots level until the basic infrastructure for industrial development had been established and economic 'take-off' had been achieved, without common bonds to unite the economic and other interests and efforts.

Economic Reforms and the *Shokusan-Kogyo* (Industrial Development) Policy

On the basis of the *fukoku–kyohei* principle, numerous economic reforms took place. They were both large and small in terms of administrative input, the number of people affected and the breadth of their reference. These reforms involved not only technology, administration, government policy, business and industry decisions, but also economic tastes and attitudes, social values, and the lifestyle of the whole population.

As noted earlier, there were three public initiatives for the establishment of the 'super-infrastructure' necessary for industrialization: (1) the establishment of a nation–state with centralized financial resources allocated under the control of the new Meiji government; (2) economic devices to secure and increase public revenue for economic growth; and (3) a unique form of direct participation by the state through the establishment of public enterprises in various industries under the *shokusan kogyo* industry promotion policy.

The first two of these reforms were completed during the first half of this period of transition. The reforms included (1) the introduction of a new monetary system through the issue of a new standard currency, the yen, in place of various domain paper, metal and rice currencies; (2) the reform of the land tax by a comprehensive revaluation of all types of land, and the introduction of a standard tax rate across the nation, payable in currency; (3) compensation to the expropriated feudal lords and their retainers through the commutation of pensions; and (4) others such as abolition of the clans through the setting up of prefectures, to be administered by government-appointed governors, and the abolition of the feudal system of social rank, with individual freedom of occupation, residence, property possession and mortgage. Farmers were also given the freedom to select which crops to grow.[13]

Leaving detailed explanations of the actual procedure and evaluation of these reforms to other studies,[14] we would merely note here that the 264-year-old Tokugawa regime disintegrated in the first 10–12 years after the Restoration, and the effective preparation for building modern Japan had begun, at least in the sense of constitutional and public administration.

In the economic sphere, the reforms unavoidably created winners and losers in society. This was partly intentional and partly due to the efforts of the people involved. In general, it is fair to say that initially agriculture carried the main burden of industrialization, in that capital funds shifted from farming to industrial sectors, and interest rates gradually fell from 14.0 per cent in 1868 to 11 per cent by 1885.[15] In an economy such as Japan's, the pace and dimension of industrial development are regulated through the domestic accumulation of capital. Various ingenious policy measures to encourage saving by the population were applied throughout the process of industrialization. A form of 'forced saving' was imposed upon the economically weaker members of society when the Meiji government exercised its newly gained power to issue notes and currency to finance its own expenditure, thereby creating considerable inflationary pressure in Japan at the time.

To introduce Western technology and Western-style industrial organization, foreign experts were employed in factories, government offices, universities and schools, and many public servants were sent abroad to study.[16] Public enterprises in designated sectors and industries were established, owned and managed by the government in a direct and aggressive fashion, which was unusual in the history of public participation in Japan. The public investment and expenses for these activities during 1868–88 have been calculated as amounting to the equivalent of almost half of the government's total non-military capital expenditure. Most of this was financed out of ordinary revenue and through the public issue of paper currency; but at the beginning of 1880 the government began to phase out direct public participation in industrialization, and it was virtually discontinued by 1885.

Let us follow how public enterprises were established and how they came to be phased out from the centre of industrial policy. The question we seek to answer is: How was this unusual form of public enterprise conceived in this period, and how did it later develop into the distinctive Japanese form of public/private co-operation?

In order to realize the ideal of *fukoku–kyohei* (rich country–strong army), the government began by establishing Kobu-sho (the Ministry of Industrial Development) in 1870. This was an initiative of a group of leading bureaucrats known as the *Kaimei-ha* (the Enlightenment), who were committed to a vision of Japan as a modern industrial nation. The first decade saw three main innovations. The first was the establishment and development of the mining (coal and iron ore) and railway industries, for which modern Western production technology, tools and machines, and other essential facilities were imported. These two industries were given priority over all others in the allocation of whatever capital funds were available at the time. The mining of coal and iron ore was viewed as essential to building the strategic basis for industrial development. The mines had to be kept in Japanese ownership in order to make absolutely sure that their direction was in the public interest. In adopting this policy the government was quite aware of its logical implications. The railways, and the coal and iron ore industries were nominated infrastructure/target industries, the speedy development of which was expected to lay the foundation for the subsequent development of all other industries – first those most immediately related and then, gradually, a wide range of others – generated by private enterprises so as to eventually bring about the overall industrialization of the country. (This policy was to be resurrected in the *keisha seisan* priority industry approach of 1946, which saw steel and coal production as the key to the industrial recovery of postwar Japan.[17])

The ministry's second, more widely quoted, industrial policy of establishing public model enterprises and plants in strategic industrial sectors (such as steel, shipbuilding, textile and machine industries) was conceived later when the hoped-for private enterprises failed to materialize; first in order to alleviate looming balance of payments problems, and next to encourage export industries. By the mid-1870s, these policies had become almost as important as the promotion of the designated railway and mining industries. The focus of planning for industry shifted from designated infrastructure industries to wider areas of key industries, still with the ultimate purpose of stimulating the development of private industrial enterprise. It is also interesting to note that the major railway lines were connected to ports, as if every city was to be linked to Tokyo by both land and sea routes. In addition its industrial purposes, the network appears to have been designed to foster the centralization of the administrative network of the Meiji government and the spread of economic and cultural modernization into every corner of the nation.[18] The mining programme also had civic as well as industrial purposes: it was to raise government revenue, and to secure the supply of metal for coinage.

The Naimu-sho (the Ministry of Home Affairs) was established in 1873. Its special emphasis was on the modernization of agriculture through the introduction of Western technology and expertise, so that imports could be replaced and exports further developed in these sectors of the economy. The Ministry of Home Affairs also founded model cotton-spinning and silk-reeling factories.

In the official announcement explaining the purpose of the establishment of the ministries, there was an interesting shift of attention from English models and economic theory to the more mercantilist and technocratic practice of continental Europe. The government stated that it was only in England that industrial activities and development were left to individual entrepreneurs. Elsewhere in Europe such activities were all supervised by integrating the major ministries and departments so that the government could guide their development through an integrated public programme. The actual areas under direct government guidance included all manufacturing industries, and those industries from which goods and services for government activities were required.

In the first instance, the government took over the mines and armament and machinery factories which, in the Tokugawa period, had been founded and run by the central shogunate and various domain governments. Having initiated the development of the railways, pilot plants were built to produce and repair ships, weapons, machines and machine tools, motors and general machinery. Although the whole exercise was carried out within a relatively small budget, it became, as intended, a model for the private sector to imitate, and encouraged the emergence of adventurous entrepreneurs.[19] Unavoidable initial costs and losses were absorbed and many technical difficulties were solved. The programme also served as a symbol of the determination to make Japan a modern industrial nation.[20]

The first evaluation of the programme came in 1877. The operation of such a large-scale and general approach was checked, so that the revenue and expenditure of each plant and operation could be evaluated individually, instead of treating all public enterprises as one national operation under a common budget. A target approach was introduced, designating factories which could claim priority for the allocation of budgeted funds and other public resources. This rationalization was partly due to the government's need to reduce its budget after the Seinan rebellion in 1877,[21] but, more importantly, it raised the question of whether public plant should operate for 'industrial promotion' purposes only, or to make a profit.

The encouraging responses from the private sector continued, so that by 1879 – within the short span of 10 years – entrepreneurs had emerged to finance the construction of industrial plant in manufacturing, mining and transport. Their activities included shipbuilding and repair works, manufacturing of machines and tools, glass, cement and tiles, chemical products and fertilisers, sugar refining, paper and paper products, textiles and clothing, and power stations.

Such successes in the private sector, together with some losses in the model enterprises, provoked a public revision of the approach to, and operation of, the *shokusan* policy as a whole. In 1881 the government decided that no further establishment of new public plant was justified anywhere in the economy. Privatization of the plants followed shortly after: gradually at first, and then at a faster rate from 1884 through 1885, leading to the eventual dissolution of the Ministry of Home Affairs. The government had decided that all the intended aims and objectives of this ministry had been achieved by this time.[22] Step by step, the 'model plant' policy had given way to the co-operation between government and private enterprise which came to be known as the 'government–industry' relationship.[23]

3 Development of the Government–Industry Relationship

How did this relationship begin? Close relations between government and industry were not an immediate product of the Meiji Restoration. One of the first tasks of the new Meiji government was to find and support entrepreneurs who were willing and able to co-operate with the government in promoting the industrialization of the nation.[24] The government began its nationwide search for promising entrepreneurs as early as 1877, almost in parallel with the active promotion of public plants.[25] There were not many to be found, and in the early years the search proved to be extremely difficult, partly because the two policies were competing for very scarce talent. It was hard for any business or individual entrepreneur who had come to the attention of the bureaucrats as having good potential and/or a past track record to avoid being drawn into the state system. Their corporate efforts and profit-seeking motives were forced to conform to the 'national task' of the *fukoku–kyohei* policy.[26]

In the second process, government protégés were selected, and continuous assistance and encouragement was directed at those chosen few rather than at every agent and entrepreneur of the time. An insight into this process can be gained by studying the eventual sale (privatization) of public enterprises in the period 1882–4. The relationship between Iwasaki Yataro (1834–85), the founder of the House of Mitsubishi, and the government in their efforts to build up the shipping, and later the ship-building industries, offers an example. Japanese shipping services were, at that time, monopolized by foreigners (chiefly the English P&O Company). Government officials were eager to control the business for defence as well as industrial promotion purposes. Iwasaki and his business were selected to receive the government's favour and protection because of his long-established business record as a merchant working with the feudal Tosa domain (now the Kochi Prefecture) since the Bakumatsu period. Iwasaki had a proven business record and assets of his own, which the government saw as a viable basis on which to build the nation's modern shipping and ship-building and repairing industry. Government favours given to Iwasaki during the period took the form of: (1) 13 modern ships imported by the government from the US and Europe for the purpose of transporting arms and ammunition in and out of Japan; (2) an exclusive licence from 1875 for a regular ocean service from Yokohama to Shanghai, together with the eventual transfer to Iwasaki of the said 13 ships without charge; and (3) annual subsidies for 15 years from 1875 to cover part of the operational cost. In return, Iwasaki was duty-bound: (1) to provide the government with free mail and postal services; (2) to report revenue and expenses regularly to the government; and (3) not to mortgage the granted ships and subsidies for loan purposes,[27]

Iwasaki thus became one of the largest and most successful *seishos* (merchants by the grace of political connections). But there were not very many *seishos* or other entrepreneurs who were prepared to enter into such arrangements with the government. In those early days of industrialization Japan, without tariff autonomy,[28] found it extremely difficult to build private industry outside traditional fields. Lavish subsidies, privileges and markets guaranteed by the government for its fledgling products and services were not enough to ignite activity in new fields. As if to demonstrate the gravity of the situation, Iwasaki and his company Mitsubishi Steel reported in 1880 that they had to rely entirely on capital borrowed from foreign merchants to run the plant which government had given them for nothing, and to repair their ships.[29]

In the circumstances, the government–industry relationship seemed to officials to be the only possible way of promoting modern investment in the areas essential for national independence and welfare. The close links between government and the appointed firms existed only for the national interest; the profitability of the recipient business had to be secured, inasmuch as its survival and development as a going concern would clearly contribute to the achievement of the government's goals. By 1881 the method had performed well enough to attract quite wide understanding and public support. It was developed further when the government came to sell its public plant. Leaving aside discussion of the main reasons behind the government's decision to sell almost all public plant in this period,[30] it is important to observe that this privatization process again demonstrated the government's consistent efforts to select the entrepreneurs from inside Japan and not from abroad, as long as they had specific qualifications: they had to have proven managerial capability and a sufficient financial capacity to keep the privatized enterprises solvent.

4   'Enlightenment', Political Economy and the Meiji 14th Year Incident in 1881

In our discussion of the 'government–industry relationship', the word 'government' denotes the bureaucrats within the relevant economic departments and bureaux. The administrative structure and the appointment of senior bureaucrats in these offices were most frequently influenced by the relative political power of old *daimyo* domains (*hans*), particularly the four powerful Satsuma, Choshu, Tosa and Bizen Hans,[31] on the eve of the Restoration. This continued in a most exaggerated manner at least up to the eventual establishment of Kobu-sho (the Ministry of Industrial Development) in 1870. It also reflected the unresolved controversy between the advocates of 'Enlightenment' and the 'Nationalists'.[32] The former based their economic policy on English free-trade liberalism; in their view public enterprise should be limited to the provision of goods and service in railways, education and mining. The latter, on the other hand, threatened by the power and advanced technical capacity of the West, saw it as imperative that the government protect all of the nation's economic activities for the sake of economic growth.

An important turning point came in 1881 (the Meiji 14th year) when a group of Meiji leaders promoting liberal free-trade ideas were suddenly ousted from their policy-making offices. Before the 'coup' industrial policy was oriented, at least officially, towards mighty efforts to import modern knowledge, technology, skills and training into the Japanese economy, in order to facilitate their rapid and efficient diffusion into every corner of society. The whole exercise was promoted for the purpose of building the 'super-infrastructure' for speedy industrialisation; although much of the actual effort took the form of building a traditional economic infrastructure, by establishing transport and communication networks, building schools and training facilities, and improving forestry and agricultural land.

The economic thinking of those pro-free-trade policy-makers depended on accurate and carefully collated information about the international market.[33] It was as early as 1874 that government efforts to obtain a comprehensive list of domestically manufactured products and their costs led to the publication of *Bussanhyo*. Free trade was compatible with international competitiveness in light industries such as textiles and clothing.[34] The domestic market was also protected by consumers' traditional tastes, for which indigenous industries catered without any competitive threat from imported Western-style products.[35] However, in the case of machinery and other heavy industrial products, the disadvantages of domestic manufacturers were obvious, particularly while Japan could not protest her domestic market with tariff walls; and encouraged by German theory and practice, that consideration told in favour of the nationalist view of the economic role of government.

The sale of public plant was not the work of either the free-traders or the protectionists in particular. However, it marked a turn in industrial policy towards sharply focused target approaches. The successful buyers of public plant were, as previous research shows, mostly the *seisho* groups. We should not infer from this fact that privatization policy was formulated only to help the *seisho* entrepreneurs to grow into large monopolistic *zaibatsu* industrialists.[36] Rather, it should indicate that many of the *seisho* entrepreneurs had by then developed into modern industrialists, who were already planning to diversify their established production lines out into new and promising industries. With the government industrialization policy many heavy industrial sectors appeared to have good prospects, and recipient entrepreneurs took the opportunity to acquire public shipping, ship-building, steel and machine-making plant and integrate them into their organizations. Kobayashi's observation sums up this stage of development in Japan as follows:

> Modern industry had not yet been established at this stage [1882], but modern industrial enterprises with their financial and managerial skills and knowledge had already emerged to realise the opportunities offered by the privatisation policy.[37]

The 1881 incident took the form of personal dismissals of several Meiji leaders, but its causes lay in the industrialization process, and in the revision and transformation of government industrial policy. Basically, from this date, the pro-German currents were strengthened. Attention turned from English and French studies to German, and from liberalism and individualism to protectionism and nationalism, supporting the emergence of a strong, authoritative modern state as a late-comer with an imperialistic orientation.[38]

Why did this change of direction take place after 13 years of national effort to reconstruct the economy and society along Western lines? The conflict between the advocates of 'Enlightenment' and of protectionist nationalism may be seen as a controversy between individual human rights and the rights of the nation. This sort of controversy may be inevitable in the process of modernization of any underdeveloped country which has to catch up with advanced economies by bringing many resources under government control. The advocates of 'Enlightenment' were not all necessarily concerned with individual rights for their own sake, but they believed that individual freedom was necessary for the economic development and modernization of the society. However, their opponents insisted that underdeveloped national industries could not compete with those of advanced countries unless they were protected by the government.

By the 1880s, government initiative had set the stage for industrial development and had brought considerable success, with strong responses by private-sector entrepreneurs. Modern industries were established, and modernization of traditional industries was under way to such an extent that many were actively aiming to replace imports and even to grow to be export industries. Public servants saw government (as many in Germany did at that time) as leading and protecting the industrialization for twin economic and military purposes. With the successful achievement of the initial stage of industrialization the majority of the people began to feel that, considering the critical conditions in the Far East at the time, national independence had to be pursued first as a precondition for the independence of individuals: Fukuzawa loudly argued that 'there can be no rights for man if there are no rights for the state'.[39] He is reported to have advocated a *Laissez-faire* domestic policy and a foreign policy of imperialist expansion.[40] But even on the domestic scene, the nation began to develop in directions chosen by the state through centralized public administrative structures.[41]

The National University of Tokyo, founded in 1877, was amalgamated with other higher education institutions to form the Tokyo Imperial University, which was intended to educate most of the bureaucrats for the new era. Political economy, which had hitherto been taught in the Faculty of Arts, following the British model of the time, was transferred to the Faculty of Law and remodelled along German lines. The change in curriculum reflected a sharp shift from liberal free-trade principles to those of the German Historical School. Almost all of the earliest Western books on political economy imported into Japan had been English (J. S. Mill, W. S. Jevons and others). In 1881 the orientation turned 180 degrees towards German publications (F. List, W. G. F. Roscher and others). Lecturers invited to teach at the Imperial University followed the same trend; most English, American and French lecturers were replaced by Germans or by those with German Historical School training.[42]

The impact of liberal Western Enlightenment survived the 1881 incident through the continuous activities of Fuzukawa Yukichi and Okuma Shigenobu in the major private universities, Keio, Waseda and Senshu.[43] They were determined to devote themselves to the development of a business middle class by way of education in business and economics. Both refused to take up further government service, believing that the nation's future would depend on the rise of such a 'business middle class'. Since the establishment of an independent Faculty of Economics in public universities had to wait until as late as 1919, the training of business leaders and managers, both in the newly emerging heavy industries and in the development of the light industries from indigenous bases, was almost entirely undertaken in these private universities.

The influence of the 1881 incident, however, spread fast among the economic bureaucrats. It came at a time when senior bureaucrats were beginning to be replaced by a younger generation. Many of the former had experience in conducting *han* economic affairs before the Restoration, or had overseas training and experience. Most of the new generation had gained their education and training at one of the national universities and had served in government offices as economic 'technocrats'. Their training was directed towards providing the knowledge and skills necessary to understand and direct the national economy, to formulate effective industrial policy, to organize an adequate bureaucratic system, and to prepare public programmes so that the policy for the industrial development of the nation could be pursued. It was not a narrowly economic education, and its element of political economy had a strong orientation towards the thinking of the German Historical School, and the practice of the German government at the time.[44]

Beginning with primary schools in 1872, advanced provisions for public education through secondary school to university were in train by 1885. There was strong government control of the curriculum throughout, to combine a good technical education on Western lines with moral education in Confucian ethics and an emperor-centred nationalism. And economic policy was single-mindedly directed towards assisting key industries and enterprises to develop the national economy as far and as fast as possible. How much success the new generation of bureaucrats and businessmen had with that, through the remaining 20 years of the century, is the subject of the next chapter.

2 Developing the Principles and Institutions of Japanese Capitalism, 1881–1900

In this chapter we will see that, after three decades of trying to industrialize, Japan did in fact reach a new stage in its economic development at the turn of this century. We use the term 'take-off' to explain our understanding of this achievement; it does not mean that we support the specific hypothesis put forward earlier by Rostow in his discussion of the achievement of regular economic growth.[1] It is simply a convenient word to convey our understanding that the economy had finally emerged from its transitional stage into a process of steady industrialization: a successful passage from what T. Smith called a 'rural-centred industrialization' to sustained industrial development.[2]

It was from outside, from an observation of foreign models, that the urgent need for industrialization had been revealed to Tokugawa Japan and the most effective ways to pursue the task were subsequently sourced. The Tokugawa efforts at rural-centred industrialization used indigenous economic methods and administrative frameworks. In the 'Englightenment via Westernization' exercises the Meiji government used a different approach, and pursued industrialization more aggressively. In 1881 the drive for industrial progress changed its course again as it searched for its own Japanese formula based on the dialectic between economic growth and industrial development on the one hand, and traditional forms of economic organization (heavily influenced by cultural factors) on the other. Imported knowledge and skills were substantially revised before being integrated into the traditional style of economic management. By 1900 the government had developed a coherent, public/private, Western/Japanese mode of national economic planning and management, and at some point around 1900 the state economy 'took off' from its previous infantile and formative experimental stage.

For this chapter there are three main questions:

- First of all, what level and impetus of economic development had Japan reached by 1900?
- Second, in comparison with the industrialized economies of Europe, what economic characteristics had the public sector in Japan acquired? The public : private ratio changed continuously through the period, reflecting the process of industrialization.
- Finally, we must review the logic and reasons for the particular public/private mix which the policy-makers arrived at, both in the economy in general and within individual industrial sectors during the period concerned.

1 'Take-off'

The Base from which Growth Began

Kuznets argues that the starting date of modern economic growth (MEG) in Japan was around 1874–9, and views this period in Japan as roughly equivalent to 1765–85 in England in terms of the general stage of economic progress.[3] Officially accepted Japanese data on GNP only go back as far as 1885, despite attempts by some researchers to collect statistics covering the preceding years to 1870.[4] These researchers believe that the initial date of MEG should be placed at around 1870. However, the lack of reliable information about this period prevents an accurate assessment of the exact standard of economic development in Japan and a precise starting point for MEG, as measured by per capita GNP or by other similar indices. Some, like Kuznets, credit Japan with quite a humble starting level – not even a third of that of Britain in her initial stage of industrialization in 1760.[5] Compared to those economies with vast new frontiers, such as America, Canada and Australia, the figure can be reduced to as low as 9–15 per cent. This means, according to Kuznets, that Japan actually began her 'spurt' for industrialization from a lower income level than some currently less developed countries.[6] Others, however, revised Kuznets' estimates upwards, while considering the question from a different angle. Hanley, for example, suggests that little significant difference can be observed between the living standards of the Japanese and those of other developed Western economies during the initial stage of industrialization.[7]

Such differences in the estimation of the initial level of the economy lead us to ask another question: whether the performance of the Japanese economy in the early stages of industrialization – from, for example, 1870 to 1900 – was exceptionally high, or just ordinary.

Economic Growth up to 1900

Leaving the last question until additional information becomes available, and following progress only for the period for which reliable figures exist (1885–1900), we observe that the economy had reached a watershed in its development at the turn of the century. By this time, the old stumbling blocks had been removed, leaving the way open for Japan's industrialization.

The change of command in 1881 was an expression of dissatisfaction with a number of Meiji policies, especially with an unsatisfactory national financial system and performance. Nevertheless, the government leaders could look back at the first 13 years of the Meiji era with relative contentment. The government had built a modern nation–state, powerful enough to survive on the world political stage, out of a feudal culture.[8] In the process, the power and authority of the new government against internal opposition had been consolidated. With the suppression of the Satsuma rebellion in 1877 (the Seinan Civil War), the government had proved to the population that its political supremacy had been finally established, leaving no possibility of a return to the old regime. As for the nation's capacity to withstand foreign pressure, despite energetic efforts to modernize the army and navy, and to support them with modern transport, communications and industry, the years to 1880 had seen little more than a promising start. It was through the 20 years to 1900 that the government arrived at effective policies which bore fruit on a sufficient scale to provide the economic infrastructure for a competitive national economy, able to hold its own against the more advanced countries of the world.

A National Financial System

Matsukata Masayashi became Minister of Finance towards the end of 1881, and the government immediately began to introduce order into the financial sector. The so-called 'Matsukata deflationary policy' began with the aims of (1) balancing the budget, (2) halting price inflation, and (3) restoring parity between the silver yen and silver itself.[9]

For these purposes, vital administrative restructuring was swiftly undertaken and grants for public works and private enterprise were curtailed. The sale of public enterprises, which had already commenced under the preceding Okuma government, was hastened. The amount of money in circulation was reduced through the withdrawal of large sums (said to have been as much as 30 per cent of the total at one stage) of money from the market in favour of new convertible notes. Within the next five years the effects became visible in the decline of prices, the stabilization of the national debt and a rapid decrease in the current account deficit. Wages also came down, encouraging industrial activity, particularly in the textile sector. By 1886 the disorderly state of public finances had been successfully remedied. This was achieved by two new instruments: a national budget system, and a modern central bank.

Draft proposals for the National Budget were formulated in 1881, and were further revised before being finalized in 1885. Throughout those years the bureaucrats gradually succeeded in establishing a public finance system under the control of the central government. It was designed to strengthen central control both over local government and (as far as possible) against any future national parliament. By 1880 the Meiji leaders were under such pressure from the 'Jiyu Minkeu Undo' (freedom and people's rights movement) that they decided to create a form of parliamentary assembly; it was to conciliate popular pressure, to encourage compliance with taxation, and to equip Japan with parliamentary institutions comparable with those of most leading nations. As in imperial Germany at the time, the Diet, which was eventually created by the Meiji Constitution of 1890, did not give the elected assembly control of the government. However, the assembly did have to approve changes in law and taxation, and therefore – before the introduction of the Constitution – the financial system was designed to be insulated, as far as possible, from democratic interference at either national or local level. Considerable financial control was given to public banks, which answered to the government rather than the Diet. The government drew up the annual budget, which included budget allocations to local government. The representative local government officers were obliged to follow the decisions of central bureaucrats and, as a result, the finance officers of prefectures, cities and villages were reduced in practice to little more than administrative officers of the central government for the purpose of keeping budget accounts in order.[10] With the creation of the Diet in 1890, the Standing Committee of Budget was established to ensure that the national budget was adequately scrutinized, and to obtain approval from the Diet before government could spend its budget.[11]

The tax structure was also reformed to improve equity among the population. The minimum income tax exemption level was lifted from ¥800 to ¥1200 per annum, and a tax on income from asset holdings and capital gains was introduced, together with an increase in the rate of death duties.[12] But at the same time indirect tax was to be levied more widely and heavily so as, in effect, to spread the burden of tax among the general population as a whole. Land tax and sales tax on sake and tobacco represented the major part of government tax revenue, while corporate tax contributed an insignificant portion.

Leaving aside any moral judgement, we should note that the drastic change from high inflation in the second half of the 1870s to sudden deflation in the following five years caused numerous bankruptcies and considerable hardship in business and on farms. The smaller the operators, the harder they were hit. Small peasant proprietors were forced to sell their land, becoming tenants who eventually migrated to become urban factory workers and miners.[13]

The government designed the financial system in the strong belief that the banking system is the nation's most important means of channelling individual savings into investment by firms. Accordingly, it built a modern financial system with a central bank and trading banks along Western lines, although the quality and scale of operations at this stage were rudimentary by the Western standards of the time.[14]

When the Bank of Japan was established in 1882 it was to be nominally independent from the government. This was achieved through 50 per cent of its shares being held by private financial institutions. Initially the discounting of commercial bills was the Bank's main lending activity, and the issue of bank notes its main source of funds. This structure was introduced using the model of the Banque Nationale de Belgique. However, through the need for active public promotion of industrial development and economic growth, the structure and function of the Bank were altered, to become a more integral part of the financial activities of the government than was the case with many central banks in the West.[15] The government deposited its national revenue with the Bank, thus considerably increasing its capacity to lend to commercial banks. Its asset holdings indicate its close connection with the Ministry of Finance. Loans to the government and holdings of government securities were almost 20 per cent of the total assets.[16] Such close ties between the government and the Bank in its public finance and banking activities have come to be a distinctive feature of the mixed economic system that has developed in Japan.

Meanwhile, the government actively promoted the development of a network of national and local, general and special-purpose banks, many of them indebted in one way or another to the central bank. By 1900 the system included:

1   Savings banks, through the national postal service. These were designed to encourage the whole population to save, and (unlike their Western counterparts, which divided their lending between government and housing) they lent mainly to industry. The first was established in 1880, and 21 more had been formed by 1883.
2   Specialized banks to deal in foreign exchange were formed on government initiative. The first was the Yokohama Specie Bank (the forerunner of the bank of Tokyo), established in 1880. The government subscribed its capital and deposited funds in it to foster its rapid development.
3   For long-term financing of industrial firms, the government sponsored many long-term credit banks. The first of these was the Nihon Kangyo Bank, established in 1897 to extend development loans to agriculture and industry. In addition, *noko ginko* (agricultural and industrial

banks) were established in each prefecture to provide development loans on a regional basis.

4   The Hokkaido Takushoku Bank was established by the government in 1900, to assist the rapid development of the underdeveloped northern territory of Japan–Hokkaido.

5   In the same year, Nihon Kogyo Ginko (The Industrial Bank of Japan) was established by the government to provide long-term funds to government-promoted heavy industry. The borrowing of foreign capital was also promoted through this bank.

The result of the policy was a range of banks, each with specific functions for the promotion of industrialization. The government thus created a comprehensive set of financial institutions with an advanced modern outlook as part of its overall industrial policy.[17] Contrary to Western precedents, these institutions were created before there was very much industrial development of the kind that they were designed to support. Later, when private industrial growth had gained its own momentum and could well have looked to other sources for its capital, the dependence on banks persisted – and, with it, government influence over the flows of capital. This will be seen in the further development of the public-sector economy in the years after the turn of the century.

Industrial and Trade Development

The institutional development of the banking and monetary sectors was designed to encourage savings, which would then effectively be directed to industrial development. This included the savings not only of well-to-do middle-class people, but also of smaller savers in villages and newly emerging cities.

Under comparatively stable economic conditions,[18] steady economic growth was achieved from 1885 to 1900. There is still some disagreement about the rate of growth, but real national product appears to have increased at between 2.3 and 4 per cent annually, while population growth was only slightly more than 1 per cent, giving an annual increase in real national product per head of 1.5 per cent or more. The extent to which this improved the standard of living of the Japanese population cannot accurately be assessed, although keen observers trace some improvement from a study of the available information.[19] We can speculate, from looking at official statistics on national income and personal and household income, that people began to save, albeit slowly and in extremely small amounts.

Agriculture continued to account for almost half of the national income, although its share of both production and the labour force began to fall. During this period agricultural output is estimated to have risen by 1.5–1.8

per cent annually, a rise attributed mostly to improvements in productivity rather than to larger inputs.[20]

A larger contribution to economic growth came from increases in the output of traditional light industries, such as textiles, food processing and other miscellaneous manufacturing, to which modernization had been applied. The establishment of modern manufacturing, power and transport industries contributed a large share. Manufacturing output increased at an average annual rate of 5 per cent, doubling the size of the sector during this period. But manufacturing output, particularly in the heavy industries, was still very moderate when compared with the world's advanced economies.

Large-scale enterprises had only begun to develop in the manufacturing sector. New techniques and machinery had been introduced during the *Bummei Kaika* (civilization and enlightenment) era, but they had mostly been accommodated in small-scale operations organized along traditional lines. Some of the first modernization was in the domestic cotton-spinning industry, with the utilization of imported yarns that were much finer and cheaper than those available domestically. Cotton-weaving, silk and later woollen and other industries followed, and soon made the textile industries by far the most important sector of the nation's manufacturing activity. Their rapid expansion was soon to become considerably dependent on foreign markets.

Japan began to take initiatives to integrate herself into the world economy by developing the mechanisms of foreign trade. An important step was the adoption of the gold standard in 1897. Until then, Japan held to silver, a policy which had led to a considerable depreciation in the yen in comparison with the currencies of the economies with which Japan was increasingly trading. The disparity between the yen and silver stood at about 15 per cent in 1885 when Matsukata's policy to re-establish parity began but, despite the policy, the gap continued to widen, peaking about 50 per cent during this period. However, this depreciation of the yen worked to the advantage of Japan's exporters. There were no strong economic reasons for the government hastily to redress the situation. Given that Japan and China were the only major countries trading without links to the gold standard, the government policy should be understood to have been prompted mainly by a desire to achieve some kind of equal status with advanced nations in the international arena.[21] The shift to the gold standard and the stabilization of foreign exchange rates probably helped to keep the rate of inflation at a minimum during the buoyant economic conditions of the two investment booms of the 1890s.[22]

At this time, business in Japan enjoyed a sudden growth in new plants, factories and enterprises of all sizes in various industries in 1886–90 and again after 1895 – a remarkable phenomenon recorded as the *kigyo-bokko* (new enterprise boom), and not yet fully analysed by researchers. Throughout the two booms, the capital invested and the number of corporations expanded considerably. Total paid capital grew by a factor of 2.3 in the first boom and by a factor of 1.9 in the second, and the number of incorporated establishments rose from 2400 in 1884 to 5600 in 1892. The expansion began in the transportation sector, particularly in railways, and spread into the spinning and weaving industries, and then the mining sector.[23]

The first boom lasted for four years, from 1886 to 1890. It seems to have been sparked by simple speculation by the public, who were suddenly moved to invest in the railways, in the belief that their development potential would be limitless and that such opportunity should be secured by Japanese nationals. Many railway companies were able to sell shares before they actually obtained government approval for their projects. Widespread speculation on the futures market accelerated.[24] Numerous enterprises and plants were formed, but many disappeared as the boom subsided. The aftermath was a sudden drop in investment and production, resulting in bankruptcies and falling share prices which hit many small speculators very hard. However, another investment boom occurred five years later, in 1895. This came about as a result of the expansion of public investment after the Sino-Japanese War, when victory brought the government a windfall war indemnity payment.[25]

The expansionist booms and the periods of severe deflation and retrenchment in the 1880s and 1890s created winners and losers in the economy. But through such drastic fluctuations the economy steadily formed the outline of an industrial system. There was a rapid rise in industrial output. Although much investment was speculative, without any real consequences for long-term industrial growth, enough of it was sufficiently real to transform the economy from one with a heavily agrarian bias into an economy oriented significantly towards textiles, other consumer goods and manufacturing.

The available statistics allow us to outline the industrial progress which had been made during the formative years of the early Meiji period, and the structure of the economy at the turn of the century when it 'took off' into substantial industrialization:

1   In Tokugawa times, between 70 and 80 per cent of the workforce were peasants, and by 1872 the heavy reliance on primary activities – agriculture, forestry and fishery – had not changed much. A steady, gradual decline in agriculture's proportional importance began from that time. Between 1872 and 1900 the national workforce expanded by 3 million, almost all of them (2.6 million) in sectors outside traditional agriculture, forestry and fishery. The proportion of the workforce in the agricultural sector had fallen to 65 per cent by 1900. However, we must not take such a trend as indicating a speedy transformation of the economy's industrial base. There was still a heavy dependence on the traditional village-based processing of agricultural products, and only a very small portion (4 per cent) of the total workforce was effectively engaged in modern

industrial activities in factories. The importance of the industrial development up to 1900 lies in the speed with which industrial activities began to replace the traditional primary-based economy, rather than in their extent. The net production index of the industrial sectors – steel, metals, machinery, cement, chemicals, food processing, textiles and printing – rose by a factor of 2.8 in the period 1875–1900.[26]

2 The transition from traditional village-based industries to modern industry took place in a variety of ways:

(a) In cases such as silk reeling and match production, imported modern techniques were observed and adapted, to be combined with traditional ones, in rural conditions with the use of capital-saving devices.

(b) Traditional industries were modernized. For example, in the steel industry, traditional furnacing methods were gradually replaced by Western techniques.

(c) Government-led industrialization began by developing industries for consumer goods (sugar, woollen cloth, and so on), and then progressed through finance, transportation and communications to the establishment of heavy industries such as coal and pig iron.

By 1900, Japan had reached the eve of its last stage in the foundation of heavy industry. The successful development of a modern industrial economy depended not only on establishing effective ways of assimilating borrowed technology and increasing saving and capital formation. It was equally important to relate the activities of modern industry to the development of consumer tastes and domestic demand. Industrial development came about only through social change and, accordingly, the leaders of the Meiji enlightenment promoted the modernization of industry as a vehicle for the modernization of society as a whole.

3 Structural change emerged earlier in areas of international trade than in the overall industrial structure of the economy. It became obvious by the end of the 1880s that the production of value-added export products should be Japan's priority, and subsequently the export of raw materials (raw silk, coal and copper) and semi-processed foodstuffs (tea and marine products) was replaced by fully processed consumer products (straw mats, ceramics and silk cloth) and manufactured products for industrial use (silk yarn, silk and cotton cloth). In statistical terms, the export of raw and semi-processed products represented almost 60 per cent of total exports in 1870–4 and declined to 30 per cent by the end of the 1880s. At the same time, imports of machinery and finished products, both for consumer and industrial use, declined rapidly, to be replaced by a predominance of raw materials such as coal and raw cotton. The contribution of exports in generating national economic

activity increased during this period. In 1885 exports represented only 6 per cent of Gross National Expenditure (GNE), but they soon grew to represent over 10 per cent. The characteristic economic pattern in which raw materials were imported from overseas, then processed into added-value products for export (*kako-boeki*) was adopted during this period, and became the basic strategic pattern of Japanese trade and industrialization in the years that followed. This national choice pushed Japan into strengthening her ties with the world economy. It came about partly due to the fact that Japan was poorly endowed with natural resources, but also through the conscious implementation of public policy.

2 Economic Policy and its Structure

Arthus Lewis suggests that there are three principal causes of economic growth: (a) increasing knowledge; (b) economic activity; and (c) increasing capital.[27]

Government policy in periods I and II, 1868–80 and 1881–1900, concentrated on the first two causes. The *fukoku–kyohei* government policy under the 'civilization and enlightenment' principle tried to promote economic growth and industrial development by increasing technological and social knowledge. It was promoted via three channels: the public provision and encouragement of general education and training; the education of a selected few to become competent public servants; and the education of entrepreneurs through the *shokusan kogyo* (production and industry) policies.[28] The importance attached to this was symbolized by the creation of Monbusho (the Ministry of Education) in 1871, before the formation of any other government departments.

The Japanese government has been an innovator in accumulating knowledge and disseminating it to industry – a characteristic which presents us with one of the most important areas for our study. The earlier efforts of the government concentrated mostly on traditional areas, using established methods known to other industrializing economies. Knowledge – not only technical but also economic and managerial – was earnestly and energetically imported from Europe and the US through publicly sponsored study missions by Japanese scholars, as well as by the appointment of foreign lecturers and researchers to universities, schools and other institutions. Imported knowledge and skills were adapted to establish, organize and operate public plants so as to provide examples and models for the education of businessmen, and for the general population.[29]

Many researchers stress the importance of government efforts in providing education and training services as well as in encouraging people to take advantage of these newly emerging opportunities. Compulsory primary education was introduced as early as 1872, providing basic schooling to as great a proportion of the population as in any of the leading nations of Europe.[30] This undoubtedly helped to increase the speed and extent to which new knowledge and training permeated the society. Meiji bureaucrats agreed to see the cost of education and training as an investment and granted it the same priority, in terms of budget allocation, as public works.

Public efforts to increase the invisible assets of knowledge and training extended to the creation of public institutions and bureaucratic organizations. We noted earlier that an important turning point occurred at the beginning of the 1880s. Its political manifestation was the 1881 public administrative reorganization, in which 'free-trade enlightenment' leaders were replaced by protectionist–nationalist bureaucrats. This came about with the change in the decision-making system and in the membership of the top echelons of government. Hitherto, most major government decisions had been negotiated within a closed circle of oligarchs. The system changed rapidly with the opening of the Diet in 1890 and the formation of political parties, which led to the emergence of several political and business pressure groups. We have also noted the change that took place in the training of bureaucrats for economic management in this period. Public institutions modelled on Western counterparts had to be revised in structure and administrative method in order to respond more effectively to the needs of the newly developed industries, which sought and won more influence over government. The economic systems which the Meiji leaders had derived from Western models and grafted on to indigenous society now began to reveal their weaknesses and unsuitability.

The establishment of the Noshomu-sho, or Ministry of Agriculture and Commerce (MAC), in 1881, provides a point of reference for the transformation of the understanding of bureaucratic needs. The ministry's establishment was in response to emerging changes in the general course of economic policy, as a result of the agreement made between the two most senior government leaders, Itoh Hirobumi and Okuma Shigenobu, on the future direction of industrial policy on the eve of the 1881 coup. Appointments to the ministry began to come increasingly from those groups with academic training in the national universities and colleges that were newly established following the founding of Tokyo University in 1877. Subsequently, appointees rose to positions of status and responsibility in the ministerial hierarchy.

A more extensive development of higher education began in the mid-1880s, and was closely parallelled by the establishment of public institutions responsible for the promotion of the economic and social infrastructure needed for industrialization. We have already noted the establishment of the Bank of Japan as the nation's central bank. Government offices were also established for the study of industrial policy (Kogyo Iken), for a military general staff and for a military police force. The old domains were consolidated into a smaller number of prefectures, each with a (fairly powerless) elective assembly. In 1890 the Meiji Constitution created two houses of parliament, also with limited franchise and limited powers. A strong reason for introducing them was to impress Western governments with Japan's modernity, as part of the continuing effort to be rid of the 'Unequal Treaties' imposed on Japan in the 1850s, and finally terminated in 1911.[31]

In addition to the education offered in the newly established universities and colleges, on-the-job training was extensively promoted in these new public institutions and government offices. Effective new public policy and administrative measures, relevant to the needs of a rapidly industrializing economy, were most energetically sought. The importation of new knowledge and technology through enlightenment and efforts at Westernization had to be replaced by a specifically Japanese formula, itself the result of informed study and research.

Among the *shokusan* production and industry policies, the establishment and later sale of public-sector factories, and the lending and sale of equipment, enhanced the accumulation of knowledge among entrepreneurs in the private sector. The visible effects of such public efforts took the form of the successful sale of public corporations to the private sector through the 1880s, and the emergence of the two investment booms noted above. But where private investment failed to meet national needs, the government itself continued to be a willing investor. The publicly owned and operated Yawata steel mills were planned in 1896 and operational by 1901.

Lewis remarked that '... it is seldom the case that a large proportion of any community is keenly sensitive to its chances, and neither is it necessary for growth that the masses of the people should be so inclined'.[32] We conclude that the Meiji *shokusan kogyo* production and industry policies helped to educate and inspire a few willing pioneers, an enterprising few whose success eventually convinced the general public to make the economic efforts that became apparent during the two investment booms in 1888–1900.

Let us turn to Lewis's second cause of economic growth: the people's will and effort to increase their economic welfare.[32] Both the extent and the nature of such a will and effort (directed towards economic activity in search of improved material welfare) differ considerably between countries, between different stages of the history of the same country, and between groups and individuals in the same country. The popular determination to succeed in the economic sphere is associated most frequently with a stronger inclination (on the part of individuals and society) to 'manoeuvre economically', so as to achieve economic growth. On the one hand, this tendency creates competition between individuals. On the other hand, it prompts collective action to establish various institutions and organizations for the encouragement of economic growth and the removal of perceived obstacles. The most important and powerful of such institutions is, of course, government. Our observation in Japan of the coexistence of, and co-operation between, two apparently contradictory impulses – 'competition' and 'state intervention', for the purpose of economic growth – reveals their common basis in this strong wish to 'manoeuvre economically', on both the social and individual levels.

What, then, is the relationship between an individual willingness to work and a social aspiration for economic growth? This is the central question of industrial/economic policy. It cannot be answered simply by a study of 'social, cultural and historical backgrounds'. Lewis's study does not offer any decisive discussion but provides us with a rough line of argument. Our basic question is: What motivates some people to make more economic effort, individually and socially, than others? Precisely why have the Japanese devoted such considerable effort to economic growth in the century since the Meiji modernization? We will return to this question from time to time, but it is opportune to reflect on it at this point, as the elements of a coherent and effective policy of economic growth come together towards the turn of the century.

3 Public versus Private Relations in Japanese Society

In order to study government intervention in economic affairs in European countries, Kirschen and others have suggested a particular framework.[34] As we will show below, Japan presents distinct differences from European countries, in both the purpose and the mechanisms of economic policy. According to Kirschen and others, the analysis of economic policy may be pursued by dividing the process of policy formation into four steps, to identify policy 'aims', 'objectives', 'instruments' and 'measures'.[35]

The term 'policy' embraces all forms of action taken by the government in pursuit of certain *aims*. The aims of government policy are often expressed in a single phrase such as 'the general good' or 'the welfare' of the population. However, in order for government to actually promote such 'general good' or 'welfare', those notions must be given some concrete form. Specific *objectives* can be expressed as various maximizing goals such as 'pursuing law and order', 'reducing social tensions', 'defending the country from external threat and influence', 'raising the living standard of the population', and 'building a unified "nation–state"'.

In order to implement economic policies, government must find means by which it can influence economic quantities (such as investment, interest rates or taxation rates), or make changes in the economic structure (such as establishing public corporations and introducing tariff protection policies). We can call these forms of government economic intervention *economic instruments*. The selection of relevant economic instruments (and in the absence of suitable ones, their formulation) is important for the effective achievement of policy objectives. The particular form of optimum intervention differs from time to time, depending on the economic and social conditions of the particular occasion. The selection and use of particular instruments for particular occasions is referred to as an economic *measure*.

From the preceding observations of government activities in periods I and II, let us see what specific characteristics can be observed in the structure of economic policy in Japan. It was during period I (1868–80) that Japanese government struggled to relate its 'aims' to actual public 'action', and sought the economic directions and means to pursue them. These efforts are illustrated in table 2.1.

In period II the aims and objectives stood, while a number of the instruments and measures were reformed or replaced.

Lewis spoke of the importance of 'the will to economize' on the part of a society as one of the permanent causes of economic growth. We are discussing the same phenomenon, although our study is confined to state activities, while Lewis' view extends over the attitude of the whole society concerned.[36] The case of Japan may be seen as one in which the government translated the greater portion of its national aims directly into economic terms, and consequently pursued economic development to the maximum extent.

Once the search for effective government action begins, focusing on the 'aim', the optimum 'economic objective' clearly emerges from the list of applicable economic instruments in the minds of the bureaucrats. They scrutinize national economic activity in those areas which the government itself can change directly in order to produce the desired economic effects. This may be an economic variable, such as the quantity of bank notes, or it may be a part of the institutional framework, such as the regulations governing and encouraging new investment. Because industrial develop-

Table 2.1   *The structure of economic policy: period I, 1868–80*

Policy dimension	Policy measures
National aim	National independence (defending the country from the threat of colonization by the West)
Economic objective	*Fukoku–kyohei* (building a strong economic basis for industrial development and independence)
Economic instrument	Direct control (direct government participation in investment and production activities in selected industries)
Economic measure	Pilot plant (government ownership and management of key enterprises to promote and motivate industrialization)

ment was at such a primitive stage in period I, the government's shopping list of 'economic interventions' was limited almost entirely to those in which direct public involvement was required. In order to pursue the national aims, the government saw it as necessary to participate directly in the production of goods and services.

Public enterprises (model plants) were established to provide mineral resources along with processing and transport and communication facilities, and foreign teachers, advisers and technologists were employed to introduce Western education, knowledge and skills. Some reseachers see this direct action alone as the basis of Japan's 'government-led industrialization'. But this view ignores the other dimensions of government leadership – the setting of national aims and economic objectives. Studies of the economic role and effectiveness of government have so far been almost exclusively directed towards the government's selection of economic instruments and measures. Economic policy and the role of government have been discussed as a subject for research within the limited context of particular objectives such as full employment, price stability or economic growth. In studies of that orthodox kind two basic functions are neglected: setting or (democratically speaking) articulating national aims and economic objectives, and leading (or failing to lead) the mass of people to harmonize their private ambitions with those public purposes.

4   Understanding the Relations Between Public Purpose and Private Enterprise in Japan

Examination of the role of government only in terms of its activities in selecting economic instruments and measures has led to an imperfect appreciation of the extent and nature of the role of government in Japan, and has obscured from sight one main foundation of the Japanese economic system.

The difficulties which orthodox economists[37] find in their attempts to explain the Japanese experience may be summarized under the following three headings:

1   *The problem of economic theory.* While, in general, the case of Japan is viewed as an example of a successful economic performance – a successful transition from an underdeveloped stage to an advanced industrial one – it is not clear how far it can be explained by purely 'economic' analytical tools. Many economists feel that some parts can be reasonably well understood and explained in terms of ordinary economic causes, but other elements appear to require explanations from sociological, political or other disciplines. However, the boundaries of the areas in which economic explanations suffice are neither clear nor

definable, so that in the end economists are forced to leave large and nebulous parts of Japan's experience in the catch-all category of 'beyond measurement'.[38] A plea for interdisciplinary study is not new. What embarrasses orthodox economists is the fact that they cannot explain the relationship between the 'economically explainable areas' and the other, more mysterious areas.

2   *Issues of 'efficiency' and 'equity'*. In an effort to understand the 'economically explainable areas', some researchers study Japan as an example in which economic growth is maximized without pursuing economic welfare.[39] Furthermore, to these researchers growth appears to have been promoted unequally, resulting in discrepancies between villages and cities, and between small firms and large corporations.[40] The economic achievements of Japan should accordingly be discounted in comparisons with other Western economies.[41] Such characteristics make Japanese and Western economic achievements difficult to compare (in this view) until such time as Japan's economy solves all of the equity and welfare problems stemming from economic growth.

3   *Cultural effects*. Even if we accept that the Japanese example can be approached with conventional economic analytical tools, others believe that the importance of the 'specific' and 'unique' circumstances surrounding her economic management make her case an especially difficult one to explain and her experience not valid as a general example. But these theorists rarely agree among themselves as to the extent and nature of such 'specific' factors and their relationship with other, economically explainable factors. Broadly speaking, Japan's specific culture and history, and her exceptional dependence on imported natural resources for her industrial activities, have led many researchers to question her suitability for study by mainstream methods. Her case belongs instead to 'area' studies, as an exotic (non-Western) exception.[42]

How are we to interpret those three approaches in our attempt to understand the role and function of government in Japan? How do we assess them in the specific framework of the structure of economic policy presented in table 2.1?

As for the first point, our question is different from theirs. Where they ask 'Why and where does the Japanese experience not fit in with orthodox economic theory?' we see more point in asking what is wrong with orthodox theory, in that it cannot explain the Japanese reality. A first fault is the custom of dividing all economic systems into two types: one being the planned economy, in which what is produced is determined by the planning authority; and the other being the 'free-enterprise economy', in which production is carried out by private businesses and individuals who produce whatever they think will make them a profit. In this type of economy, the efficient role of government would be confined strictly to the maintenance of the conditions necessary for both producers and consumers to make free choices. Public participation in production is justified only in the provision of those goods and services which the market fails to supply adequately. In order to carry out such functions, the free-enterprise economy establishes two distinct sectors, referred to as the 'public sector' and the 'private sector'. Public goods and services are by definition supplied by the 'public sector' of the economy.

In actual fact, very few economies fit neatly into either of these simple classifications, and a paradigm called the 'mixed economy' is created in order to explain the cases that fall in between. However, the Japanese case does not appear to fit into this third category, let alone the first two. Why not? Let us review again the major areas of government activity undertaken, for example, in period I, in an effort to identify those particular government activities which prevent Japan from falling into any one of these three classifications. First of all, with the free-enterprise economy, we can discuss only those government economic activities which can be considered to be 'economic instruments' or 'economic measures'. Out of all forms of public economic activity, only those efforts by government to seek ways and means of producing goods and services for national defence purposes appear as study material for economists. With the help of the 'planned economy' paradigm, we can encompass further government activities in our analysis, by recognizing the areas in which it determines the order of priority in allocating resources. Such activities are subsumed under the heading of 'economic objectives' in table 2.1. But government efforts to express the national aims in terms of economic philosophy, to connect such aims to workable economic objectives, and to convince the citizens that they will prosper rather than suffer by concurring with those aims and objectives and investing in accordance with them, escape the researchers' attention, even with the introduction of the 'mixed economy' paradigm. In orthodox economic studies, this whole mode of choice and coordination is left to other disciplines within the social sciences.

The omission of this specific area of government activity leads us not only to an incorrect evaluation of the role of government in Japan at any stage of its economic development, but also to a distorted picture of the Japanese economic system. The second and third difficulties for the economists – issues of 'efficiency' and of 'equity and welfare' and cultural effects – are the direct outcome of the first problem, of the failure of conventional economic theory. How this occurs will be explained when we question the prejudice of economists who assume that all aims of government policy have, of necessity, an economic aspect and require national resources to be diverted from directly productive uses. Instead, we argue the need for the study of the aims of government – their systematic classification in the context of the political administrative framework – and the explanation of how particular aims are selected, and served by particular objectives, at a specific stage of industrial development.

What has been the role of the government in Japan in promoting the nation's industrial development? How and where have cultural, historical and social elements influenced the determination and dimension of government activities, and their effective management and implementation in economic affairs? In the following pages we attempt to explore some of these questions.

Characteristics of Government Activities

In order to explain the foundation of the modern Japanese economic system in period II, it may be useful to introduce distinctions between individual, communal and state needs, and to reflect on the state's role in articulating individual and communal wants. Based on his observation of Germany 'in the most desperate straits', Hans Ritschl proposes the concept of a communal/state economy which can be distinguished from a traditional market economy.[43] He sees the economy of the state as having its own peculiar properties. He suggests that orthodox economic principles are only partially valid in his 'state' economy, because the state must use its resources efficiently: to that extent it is in the market economy, but beyond that it differs. In short, the rule of self-interest, in the sense expounded by Adam Smith, cannot be applied. The state identifies its economic goals, raises funds (tax revenue), and uses them and its economic resources in quite different ways and for different purposes. Writing in the early 1930s in Germany, Ritschl may have exaggerated the importance of the government. But his observation is still relevant to our study because it asserts the need to study the nature of the state. Social wants are not merely a set (or aggregation) of individual wants which may be characterized by a technical feature of indivisibility, so that they have to be served by public goods. Social wants derive from the needs of the group as such, and the state (as opposed to any aggregation of individual wants) is commonly the voice which articulates the needs of the group.

There is no unavoidable conflict between that view of communal life and a liberal view of individual life, but there are vital links between the two. People may be understood as having dual experience. On the one hand, we have individual wants. They are met by individual choice and market exchange (or, where there is market failure, by public supply) just as orthodox economists describe. On the other hand, those individual wants are not exhaustive, because we are at the same time members of communities. We need and value our communal membership. We share the communal needs, desire that they be met, and willingly work or pay to meet them. Finally, even as individuals with individual needs, we ourselves are communal creations: our personalities, tastes and consumer demands are shaped by family, village, nation and shared culture. One of our interests, a vital one in which we are simultaneously individual and communal, is this:

to the extent that our individuality is shaped by the communal culture and institutions, we want the culture and institutions to be such as to encourage better rather than worse individual and communal characteristics. The institution with most influence on those effects (for better or worse, depending on the quality and morality of the prevailing purposes) is commonly the state.

If we accept that the Japanese economic system includes a strong communal element, we are able to discuss the role of government in its entirety, from 'aim' through 'economic objectives' to 'economic instruments' and 'economic measures' as illustrated in table 2.1. This leads us to argue that the government's role, and the reasons for its economic activities, should be sought beyond the confines of the terms 'public goods' and 'market failure'. In addition to the things that it does to supply public goods, meet market demands and support private enterprise, government also has its own specific role which is independent of market considerations. To the extent that social unity is desired, its task is to unify the activities of the members of the community and identify the communal goals, and find ways to pursue such goals most effectively. This task is essential for the survival and maintenance of the communal society and state.

Given this task, it is possible to argue that the government requires certain 'publicly required' goods and services for its purpose, and government economic policy must secure an adequate supply. In contrast to 'public goods', 'publicly required goods' can be supplied either directly by government or indirectly through the market with government intervention. The list of such 'publicly required goods' overlaps to some extent with that of 'public goods', but this should not distract us from seeing the real reason for the government involvement in providing them. The main 'publicly required goods' are orthodox economic infrastructure facilities such as science, education, housing, roads and railways. However, an important point to be made here is that the components of the list vary, by necessity, from period to period, depending on the nature and extent of the government's role in meeting communal needs, and the ability of the economy to provide them, which reflects its stage of development.

Issues of Efficiency, Equity and Welfare

The above argument leads us to question the relevance of the hitherto-practised ways of evaluating the size and direction of government in Japan. It is often claimed that Japan's government has been kept small compared to most European countries, an assertion has been based on the low ratio of government budgetary expenditure of GNP. The low ratio comes about mainly due to the low level of government payments to households for social security purposes. As for government investment, most of it has been directed to the promotion of industrial activities through the building of economic infrastructure and promotion of the education and training of the population, leaving their general welfare to the efforts of individuals.

Questions about the comparative 'size' of the Japanese government have led to unresolved debates among economists because of difficulties of measurement. It is not easy to quantify the effects of public policy interventions such as fiscal and loan programmes, the regulation of monetary, fiscal and trading activities, the control of capital inflow from overseas, and a wide range of forms of public administrative guidance. Those issues remain to be examined in the rest of this book. The point to make now is that the small size of national expenditure on social security payments should not be taken as the basis for a view of Japanese government as relatively small, geared towards 'growth and efficiency' only, and thus neglecting 'equity and welfare' issues.

The equity and welfare issue is one which can only be understood by looking at Japanese state, communal and individual activity as a whole. Japanese governments have not – at least, until very recently – regarded welfare as something that should be provided independently of the system of production. Like some recent Western neo-conservatives – but from a much earlier date – they have expected the economic system itself to provide for the people's welfare by enabling them to meet their own material needs. Where market forces fail to do that unaided, Japanese governments (unlike Western 'market-worshippers') have been ready and willing to act, not outside the system of production but in it and on it. They have typically acted on the productive system to make it grow, to keep it stable and fully employed, to diversify the range of employment that it offers, to stimulate investment in backward regions, and to enable people to get the best out of it individually by nourishing their skills and propensities to work and save. This contrasts with the common Western practice of leaving the growth and structure of the productive system to market forces (with or without some macroeconomic aids to stability and full employment), and then redistributing some of its product through welfare institutions. A hostile view of the Japanese approach may regard Japanese governments as mistaken in believing that they can shape their capitalist system to enable the people to provide for their own welfare. But that is not the same as the common but, we believe, erroneous view that Japan has consciously sought economic growth 'instead of', 'regardless of' or 'at the expense of' the people's welfare.

Such criticisms commonly focus on the small size of the public budget, but that conceals a large public contribution to economic development. We will see later that Japanese government expenditure in capital formation was high by international standards. It was high in relation to private capital formation, and it was high in relation to public consumption goods. It was thus unusually productive per unit of expenditure: a great deal of the fiscal activity in Japan has been assigned to the improvement of the economic infrastructure for the sake of growth. In turn, such public investment influenced the pattern of distribution of income and wealth. Thus policies for 'growth' 'efficiency' and 'equity' and 'welfare' have been pursued simultaneously. Whatever its shortcomings in Japanese practice, we agree with this in principle. It is wrong to approach economic development by aiming first at economic growth, and afterwards seeking ways of distributing the fruits of growth among the citizens. Education provides a good example. Public education brings immediate material and spiritual benefits to individuals. Nationally it promotes economic growth, and if it is universal it enables each member of society to seek employment on an equal basis with any other member, and to receive a fair share of income in the labour market, thus promoting equity.

What we are suggesting here is not that the issue of 'equity and welfare' has been dealt with effectively in Japan in the process of the deliberate maximization of 'growth', but that economic policy for growth cannot be studied separately from problems of income distribution and social and individual welfare. Government economic policies and activities should be examined as integrated efforts at achieving growth, equity and welfare together, and should be judged by their effects on all three. Growth can be sought by more or less efficient and more or less equitable means; welfare objectives can be pursued by means which either help or hinder growth. There is no necessary or invariable trade-off between those effects, and the best policies are those which integrate them. There may be little relevance in a comment such as '... it is tempting to say that a few percentage points of the growth rate might well have been sacrificed for greater social welfare'.[44]

Competent Public Authorities

Much thought and experiment went into the development of the institutions which make and implement public economic policy. That was understandable, given the persistent trend of allocating a remarkably high proportion of national income to capital formation in various fields and for various purposes. From the public enterprises of the shogunate and the domains before the Restoration, the list of public infrastructure developments has expanded from irrigation to include transport and communication facilities, education, training and information services, and organizational skills and services for the business community. In this kind of intervention the government cannot merely react to group demands. It must formulate national strategies which protect and promote general economic activity. Public guidance of public and private investment involves long-term economic thinking and planning. It requires competent public authorities to discriminate between members of the community on the basis of subtle and complex judgements of the community's collective needs, now and in the future. A designated target approach is employed in Japan so as to nurture and develop those economic activities selected as important by competent public authorities. It is fashionable for Western economists to insist that 'government cannot pick winners'. Japanese governments have been picking winners for 100 years now, in two senses: *deciding* which industries to develop, and often also *predicting* which entrepreneurs and corporations would prove to be skilled enough to be worth supporting.

Market Principles

It has been widely acknowledged that the success of industrial policy, at least in the postwar years in Japan, may be due partly to its effectiveness in co-operating with the market. The importance of 'administrative guidance' in industry policy and 'over-the-counter guidance of city banks' in monetary policy has been examined by many researchers,[45] but the actual working of the 'invisible hand' has yet to be explained. The 'mixed economy' is the rule throughout the world except, of course, in orthodox socialist countries, where the state did not see any need, until recently, to be apologetic about conducting economic affairs. In Japan the government has never shrunk from forming the 'state' economy in Ritschl's sense, but the academic community has been reluctant to recognize the fact, and has seemed embarrassed about studying it, while those outside Japan have speculated naively on the link between public–private relations and 'cultural' traits. Economic backwardness, in the Gerschenkronian sense, and the national need and desire to catch up with the West, have always been heavily relied on as the analytic basis in both cases.

However, our observations tell us that planning for industrialization had begun before Japan woke up to discover her backwardness and to find herself under pressure from the West. An important implication of this fact is that the state economy in Japan should not be seen as an instrumental device developed for specific political or military purposes (although it has, of course, been adapted for military purposes at particular times). Even during periods of great external political pressure in the Bakumatsu and Meiji eras, and during the days of military ambition, Japan has continued to pursue distinctive communal aims; and a distinctive feature of those aims is that they have been articulated predominantly in economic terms. This is one heritage of the Tokugawa industrial policy. Without carefully dissecting and analysing the means of government intervention, and the private responses from business and other members of the community, the Japanese economy cannot be explained.

In concluding our observations of the above four basic aspects of government intervention in Japan (the state economy; integrated policies for growth, equity and welfare; competent public authorities who can and do pick winners; and an influential and co-operative relationship between the planners and the market), let us speculate as to where and in what ways 'cultural traits and specific historical factors' present themselves as influences on the economic activities of the government. We postulate that cultural traits should be studied carefully in order to understand the government's role in the industrial development of Japan, in both the formulation of objectives and the choice of measures throughout the different stages of economic development. But culture is not a convenient carpet under which to sweep everything about the Japanese success that cannot be explained by orthodox economic theory. We can be more precise than that: cultural factors are important in two particular areas in our breakdown of economic policy in table 2.1, (i) where the national 'aim' is translated into 'economic objectives' and (ii) in the making of 'economic instruments'.

First, it has often been observed that Japan is a business-oriented society, and that the Japanese are industrious and strongly motivated by materialistic desires.[46] Although it is too general to be more than an impression, there is an element of truth in this claim. In our study of periods I and II, we discovered that the national aim of military defence was expressed in economic terms as *fukoku–kyohei*, and that the same *fukoku–kyohei* economic objective was adopted in order to build a nation–state. The practice of stating a national aim in economic terms and pursuing it through the economic activities of government emerges as a distinctive characteristic of Japanese society.

Lewis observes that societies differ widely from each other in the extent to which the members seek and exploit economic opportunities. He discerns these differences in the will to economize, in the valuation of material goods relative to the effort required to obtain them (as noted above by Patrick and Rosovsky), and in the available opportunities and the extent to which institutions encourage effort.[47] In the Japanese case we view the third explanation as being most important, taking government as the core of such institutions. But the extent to which government has attempted in its economic policy to orient the society towards economic activities poses intricate questions of causation. To a degree, their elite culture and values may have disposed the members of government to choose as they did. But at the same time the culture of the population as a whole was one of the resources that they could draw upon. Even an alien authority, itself untouched by Japanese culture, might have chosen objectives which the society's culture made achievable, and designed measures which took maximum advantage of the industrious, co-operative, frugal or submissive qualities implanted by the culture. To the extent that the culture shaped the values and aims of Japanese leaders, the culture could claim to have industrialized Japan. But the same culture shaped other aims in other would-be leaders, including some very conservative aims which would have prevented *any* modernization. To the extent that particular policy-makers *discerned and mobilized the productive potentialities rather than the conservative potentialities of the culture* and used them with competence and precision, the leaders' choices do much to explain the industrialization, and the culture was more a 'resource' than an active cause.

Thus the culture cannot be seen as the single or main determining factor of economic policy. Like many institutional devices in management, such as the life employment system and enterprise training schemes, many of the institutional organizations and regulatory formulae set up by government reflect unique Japanese culture traits and specific historical influences. For example, in MITI's administrative guidance and the Ministry of Finance's 'FILP' (Financial Investment and Loan Program) systems, we will clearly see, later in this book, that traditional customs and unique Japanese cultural elements are critical factors in explaining their structure, effectiveness and working mechanisms. The important point, however, is that the invention of particular economic instruments, whether they be public institutions or rules and regulations, needs to be explained by reference to more than merely Japanese culture. In particular, one must argue that if specific economic instruments contribute to the successful administration of economic policies, this is due to the effectiveness of the policy-makers who identify and make use of specific cultural elements, harnessing them for particular economic purposes.

3 Capital Accumulation and Economic Growth, 1901–1936

The years from 1900 to 1937 could be 'periodized' in a number of ways. There were significant events and turning points in: 1910–11, with the annexation of Korea, the achievement of tariff autonomy and a major factory law; 1918–20, with social confrontations and democratic initiatives under the liberal mood of the Taisho period;[1] 1923, with the Great Earthquake; and 1931, with the Manchurian incident and policies to cope with the World Depression. Our table 1.1 on pp. 9–17 divides period III from period IV in 1917. But for narrative and analytical purposes it is convenient to treat the 36 years continuously, with one chapter on the government's role in capital formation and growth, followed by one on its troubled and indecisive approaches to labour and welfare.

Between 1900 and 1939 the population (including only those residing in Japan) grew from 44 million to more than 71 million; that is, by more than 60 per cent. At the same time, the real national income increased by a factor of 2.8.[2] A great national effort was continuously directed in this period to build up the nation's industrial equipment, as is evident from the large proportion of the national income (15–23 per cent) which was invested annually.[3] In industrial development there was at first little sign that Japan's main industrial strength would shift from light industry to government-designated heavy industry. Much of the early expansion took place in fishery products, silkworm cocoons and various agricultural raw materials and later in cotton and silk textiles. New techniques tended to be concentrated at this stage in those sectors and in other consumer goods industries such as woollen and worsted, with chemicals, engineering, iron and steel still lagging behind. Consumer spending and an expanding export trade were together moving the economy towards specialization in textiles.

However, the government began to lay the foundations in the 1920s for a large expansion of heavy industry, and when the economy emerged from the depression of the 1930s a new course had been set for it.[4] This is indicated clearly by contrasting the composition of industrial production, the export trade and the workforce in 1930 with that of 1940. The expansion of industrial output in this decade came mainly from capital goods manufacturing: steel and other metals, chemicals and machinery. By the late 1930s the industrial sector was producing more than one third of the national product, half of which – a sixth or more of national product – was generated in the heavy industrial sectors: a great change from the pattern a decade earlier, when metals, machinery and chemical products represented only a meagre 5–6 per cent of national product.[5]

What caused such industrial progress, and then such a shift from light to heavy industry, through this period?

The following sections approach this question in a number of ways. How did investment relate to other generators of economic growth through the period? In what causal way were public and private investment related? That relation being difficult to prove, we explore – with some unavoidable repetition – three approaches to it, through the sequential timing of public and private investment, the changing composition of the capital stock, and the institutional history of the government's banking and financial controls.

1 Capital Formation and Economic Growth

Capital Input

Total capital formation, and the public and private shares of it, from 1890 to 1935, is shown in table 3.1.

Earlier we observed that, in the years before 1900, investment in modern economic activities had to be added to the resources and capital assets of a feudal agricultural economy. If the estimates of capital formation now available are accepted, investment during the first decade of the Meiji (period I) must have been modest – approximately 6 per cent of national expenditure.[6] That was not abnormally low for a country at such an early stage of development, when capital-intensive sectors such as manufacturing, railroads and power scarcely existed. National savings are estimated to have been even lower than the investment level – around 4 per cent of national product.[7] Rapid capital accumulation became possible only after 1900 or thereabouts, when GNP reached a higher level from which significant savings – both public and private – could be derived. The change was then dramatic. In appendix table A.1 (C_p's share in GNE in section D), we see that in 1907 the proportion of consumption to national income had fallen from its previous high level to less than 75 per cent. From that point on it continued to stay at around this level, except for the Depression years.

Table 3.1 *Public and private capital formation, 1890–1935. Capital formation as a percentage of gross national expenditure*

Year	Total	Government	Private	Government as a percentage of total capital formation
1890	14.5	2.4	12.1	16.6
1895	16.2	3.2	13.0	19.8
1900	16.2	5.9	10.3	36.4
1905	16.8	4.9	11.8	29.2
1910	17.6	6.2	11.4	35.2
1915	15.9	5.1	10.8	32.1
1920	22.6	6.5	16.1	28.8
1925	16.6	6.9	9.8	41.6
1930	15.8	6.9	9.1	43.7
1935	18.3	7.4	11.0	40.4

Source: figures are originally from Ohokawa and Takamatsu (1974) and quoted in Ando (1978, p. 7).

This observation is important for three reasons. First, it implies that the economy had reached a stage in its development where consumption had to be curtailed if production was to increase any further. Available resources were now fully employed through the expansion of economic activity, and further growth could come only from the accumulation of more capital resources. The days of a semi-industrial rural economy, in which additional production could come about through better use of existing resources, were gone; capital building had now to be promoted in a systematic way. Second, the standard of living had risen a little above subsistence so that the general population could begin to save. Third, although the Meiji government had been determined to take the lead in industrialization, its financial means of doing so were very limited. That constraint was lifted by three means: the development of a national financial system through the 1880s; the windfall of the war indemnity after 1895; and a sharp fall in the transfer payments which had to be met from the government's budget, freeing more of its revenue for investment. (The Meiji budgets had included compensation payments to ex-samurai families, and subsidies to marine transport industries and to flood and landslide relief, all of which had ceased or diminished by the turn of the century.) Government expenditure, which had increased only in proportion to national expenditure up to the 1890s, rose sharply from 1900. While GNE grew at an average of 3 per cent annually to 1938, government economic activity grew by an average of 5.5 per cent.

Among the wealth of research and survey results now available for Japan's economic history, the three volumes of *Estimates of Long-term Economic Statistics of Japan Since 1868* (LTES) cover the study fields of 'Public Finance', 'Capital Stock' and 'Investment'.[8] The study shows how earnestly and persistently the Japanese worked at building capital stock through the present century. Every year an increasing portion of the national income is allocated to investment,[9] with its growth rate rising in 'wavelike movements'.[10] Previous studies[11] have observed some characteristic aspects of the investment patterns, which we may summarize as follows:

1   All forms of capital formation – gross and net capital investment, and fixed capital formation as well as inventory build-up – increased faster than the growth rate of the GNP.[12]

2   This rapid increase in capital formation exhibits a long-swing investment wave, consisting of periods of relatively rapid capital formation followed by a number of years of lower growth. Ohokawa and Rosovsky described the initial movement of such upswings as an 'investment spurt' and sought the driving force of economic growth in this mechanism.[13] They noted investment spurts in 1901, 1931 and 1956.

3   Active investment by the public sector has contributed to this high capital formation. Much public investment has, of course, been for military purposes; but excluding that element and counting only non-military investment in transport, telecommunication facilities and networks, public engineering works and public buildings and schools, the public-sector contribution has ranged between 28 and 40 per cent of annual capital formation, and accounted for more than half of capital accumulation, throughout the period. This is a high level by international standards.

4   The business sector also accumulated capital, and the behaviour of the two sectors was complementary. A lower rate of increase in capital formation in the private sector in any period was met by accelerated growth in the public sector. This meant that the total gross domestic capital formation (GDCF) grew fairly continuously except in the worst years of the World Depression. The pattern of cyclic fluctuation in the GDCF is derived from the ups and downs of private GDCF, with counter-movements in the public sector working to reduce the fluctuation.[14]

5   Shinohara's earlier study shows that there were several economic cyclic fluctuations. The cycles in the period before the Second World War seemed to be primarily due to plant and equipment investment (7–8-year 'Juglar cycles') whereas those in the postwar period seem to have been caused by inventory cycles (2–3-year 'Kitchen cycles'). Shinohara also observes that in GNE movements there were no absolute cycles, but rather growth rate cycles. How does this compare with the cycles in investment? Minami observes several cycles of real capital formation of various scales and of varying durations of longer than 7–8 years.[15] It seems, therefore, that cycles due to 'construction investment' – 'Kuznets cycles' – also existed during this period.

Economic Growth

How was the rate of investment related to the rate of economic growth throughout this period?

There is no doubt that capital is required for economic growth. But how much capital is required? What is the relationship between the growth of capital and income? And by what means and to what extent has government influenced the rate and composition of Japan's capital accumulation?

Rapid expansion of capital formation in Japan is not a post Second World War phenomenon. Real fixed capital formation also increased very rapidly in the prewar period: its annual growth rate is estimated at 5.4 per cent – a much higher rate than the rate of economic growth.[16]

From 1900 to 1937 the proportion of national income directed towards net capital formation averaged 18–19 per cent annually.[17] The five-year-average annual rate fluctuated between 15.8 and 22.6 per cent. It rose further, to exceed 30 per cent, in the postwar years of high-speed growth, and thus brought about the general trend of a rising share of investment in aggregate demand. It is on this statistical observation that Ohokawa and Rosovsky base their hypothesis that investment activity has been the driving force behind economic growth in Japan, and that consumption, both personal and public, has played a more passive role.[18]

Periods of high investment have occurred in several countries other than Japan. For example, the US in 1869–1913, Germany in 1891–1913, and Canada, Norway, Sweden and Australia in 1950–60 have all recorded rates of investment comparable with those in Japan.[19]

Two factors distinguish the Japanese experience from the others: (i) the high-investment period has lasted longer than in any other economy, having continued throughout the present century; and (ii) the high level of investment is associated with an active and accelerating rate of public investment.[20] Moreover, public investment has generally been linked to a long-term growth strategy for industry. At the same time, in the short term it has also been promoted, as we will presently see, as an anti-cyclic economic measure by creating effective demand when investment activity in business is depressed: the idea, a 'Keynesian' approach to fiscal policy, occurred to Japanese policy-makers as a natural way of maximizing industrial growth long before the World Depression in the 1930s.

Military Requirements

High investment and comparatively fast growth did not improve the well-being of the mass of the people as much as economic growth generally did in the West. A significant share of the benefits of industrialization went to finance military aggression abroad. The wars, or 'military incidents', in which Japan managed to involve herself after the Meiji Restoration were

Table 3.2 Gross national expenditure by purpose (per cent), 1885–1986

	(1) GNE (current prices)[b] (¥)	(2)[a] Personal consumption, C_p	(3)[a] Government expenditure, C_g	(4)[a] Capital formation, I	of which (a) Private, I_p	of which (b) Government, I_g	(5)[a] Public share of total capital formation, I_g/I
1885	806	80.9	7.4	12.1	9.2	2.9	24.0
1890	1 056	82.2	6.3	14.5	12.1	2.4	16.6
1895	1 552	74.7	9.5	16.2	13.0	3.2	19.8
1900	2 414	79.3	7.6	16.2	10.3	5.9	36.4
1905	3 084	73.8	20.3	16.8	11.8	4.9	29.2
1910	3 925	75.5	8.6	17.6	11.4	6.2	35.2
1915	4 991	72.5	7.3	15.9	10.8	5.1	21.1
1920	15 896	71.3	6.8	22.6	16.1	6.5	28.8
1925	16 265	78.4	6.6	16.6	9.8	6.9	41.6
1930	14 671	76.3 / 74.0	11.7 / 9.9	8.6 / 15.8	5.0 / 9.1	3.6 / 6.9	41.9 / 43.7
1935	18 298	64.7 / 69.2	15.8 / 11.6	14.2 / 18.3	11.1 / 11.0	3.0 / 7.4	21.1 / 20.4
1940	36 851	48.6 / 55.1	24.5 / 13.1	21.7 / 31.7	18.0 / 17.2	3.7 / 14.6	17.1 / 46.1
1944	74 503	35.6	37.1	23.3	18.5	4.9	21.0
1950	3 947	60.7	11.1	16.2	11.4	4.8	29.6
1955	8 623	64.1	10.4	19.8	13.3	6.5	32.8
1960	15 487	57.0	8.9	30.2	22.8	7.4	24.5
1965	31 954	56.6	9.2	30.6	21.6	9.0	29.4
1970	75 152	51.3	9.2	35.0	26.9	8.2	23.4
1975	152 209	56.6	11.1	30.8	21.4	9.4	30.5
1980	245 163	58.5	9.8	32.2	22.6	9.5	29.5
1986	334 652	57.7	9.8	27.6	21.1	6.8	24.6

(For 1930, 1935 and 1940 two sets of figures appear; the first and second sets are shown separated by "/".)

[a] When two sets of figures appear, the first (for 1885–1940) are from EPA, *Kokumin Shotoku Hakusho*, while the second (for 1930–1965) are from EPA, *Kokumin Shotoku Tokei Nenpo*, 1966 and 1967, and (for 1970–86) *Annual Report on National Accounts*, 1988.

[b] ¥ million for 1885–1940, and ¥100 million after 1945. For 1885–1940, LTES, *Kokumin Shotoku*, pp. 178 and 184–5; for 1944 and 1950, EPA, *Kokumin Shotoku Hakusho*, 1962; for 1955–75, EPA, *Kokumin Shotoku Nenpo*, 1977; for 1980 and 1986, EPA, *Annual Report on National Accounts*, 1988.

Sources: same as for appendix table A.1.

numerous, occurring on average every three or four years, with the nation at war during 15 of the 50 years 1895–1945.

Between 1900 and 1940 an average of 20–25 per cent of total government purchases were for immediate military purposes. The figures were of course much higher in actual war years, rising to 70–75 per cent of the total. These expenses mostly comprised government purchases of goods and services for the defence forces. This underestimates the real extent of government financial commitment to defence activities. As indicated in table 3.2, a large and annually increasing proportion of GNP was allocated by the government for investment in the establishment of economic infrastructure. In the official statistics, most public spending on construction works, which absorbed the major part of government investment (I_g), is classified as 'non-military'. But given the fact that these works were undertaken primarily to give the nation a strong defence basis, we estimate that an additional 15 per cent or so of government expenditure was directed towards military ends. In all, it could be said that throughout the prewar years no less than a third, and perhaps as much as a half, of government expenditure was for military purposes. That substantially reduced what might otherwise have been the welfare effects of economic growth. At the same time, because of the means by which it was enforced, it further extended the government's influence over the structure and working of the economic system.

What effect the military spending had on economic growth itself is harder to judge, because it depends on hypothetical assumptions. On the one hand, the defence budget might alternatively have been used to augment the rate of investment and therefore of growth. On the other hand, those funds might not have been withheld from consumption at all and, furthermore, some of the investment in infrastructure might not have been undertaken if there had been no military motivation – so gross investment and growth might conceivably have been *less* without the military motivation.

2 Public Investment and Capital Formation

Before relating public investment to total capital formation, it is as well to remember that the government share of annual capital formation is no measure of the government's whole contribution to capital accumulation and economic growth, for a number of reasons. First, public capital (roads, bridges, railway lines, public buildings, school and university buildings) tend to last longer than most private capital (machinery, equipment and vehicles), so if government contributes a quarter or a third of annual investment it eventually possesses half or more of the society's accumulated capital. Second, much of the public capital (roads, bridges, harbours and railways) is used mostly for private rather than public production, so that separate capital: output ratios for the two sectors exaggerate the productivity of private capital and underrate that of public capital. Third, new public investment commonly stimulates private investment, as private producers equip themselves to supply public demand for capital goods. Fourth, from the development of the national system in the 1880s until at least the 1960s, the Japanese government used its public banks and its power to control private banks, to channel private saving heavily into private industry, rather than to housing, household equipment, farm credit and consumer credit; which received larger shares, especially of household savings, elsewhere in the world. Finally (and a recurring theme of this book), the government did a good deal to influence private investment decisions directly, by persuasion, demonstration and indicative planning.

To try to estimate the government's effect on the whole pattern of capital formation and economic growth, we will look in turn at the history and composition of capital formation as a whole; at the functional relations between public and private investment; and at the banking system as a second means of public influence on the volume and direction of private investment.

The first Meiji government had aimed to provide both the infrastructure which new industries would need, and a number of the industries themselves, by public investment. It may be argued that less industrialized economies can benefit from that public approach: once factory industries exist they can make immediate contributions to national output, and at the same time create a flow of profit which can be invested to increase factory production, thus starting a production–saving–investment–production cycle. Thus direct government investment in plant may be justified in less developed economies in order to initiate capital accumulation in manufacturing industries at a time when both savings and knowhow for industrialization are likely to be scarce.

However, such an argument does not appear to find much support in the Japanese experience, at least in the early Meiji years. Ohokawa and Rosovsky have suggested that the growth in production after the Restoration represented merely a continuation of the improvement in agricultural efficiency.[21] Throughout that period the flow of new capital was from the traditional agricultural sector to industry, not from industry back into industry. The factories established by the government during the 1870s may well have had demonstration and educational effects and helped to develop some entrepreneurs, but they failed to play the generative part in capital accumulation which the above argument would assign to them.

As a direct employer of labour, the government stayed comparatively small throughout.[22] The ratio of public expenditure to national income was also low, rising only as the defence budget swelled in the approach to the Second World War.[23] However, especially after the turn of the century, a large part of the small budget was for investment. The areas of public investment changed over the different stages of industrial development. First and most extensively, the government built roads, bridges, harbours, water and embankment facilities throughout the years before and after the First World War; next in order of importance were schools and administrative facilities for government services in the early years of industrial development; then railways and other transport facilities began to claim larger portions of public investment, so that well over half of total public-sector investment was in engineering, road and railway facilities through the 1920s and 1930s. These public efforts brought about a rapid increase in labour productivity in the economy in general. Minami estimated that it increased by a factor of 1.5 between 1907 and 1920, and by a further factor of 1.3 from the 1920s to the outbreak of the Second World War. The achievement was not so spectacular in the agricultural sector, but it was even faster in service sectors such as transport, telecommunications and public utilities, where growth was most highly concentrated.[24]

Minami also reports that the rise in both the capital : labour ratio (K/L) and labour productivity (Y/L) is most obvious in the so-called 'M' industries, which comprise manufacturing and mining, construction, transport, communications and public works.[25] Information about the age structure of capital assets tells us that government-owned infrastructure industries appear to have had larger proportions of modern and more recently acquired capital assets than many private-sector enterprises.[26]

In summary, we may argue that public industries brought about, directly and indirectly, most of the general increase in the capital : labour ratio of the national economy as a whole, from its relatively low level in 1900 to a level almost 1.4 times higher by 1938. The result was a considerable increase in labour productivity, as private as well as public-sector labour worked with the benefit of improved education, transport and communications. We estimate that the increase in labour productivity of the Japanese economy was in the region of 23–40 per cent every ten years, so that its level in 1938 stood at almost three times that of 1900. Public-sector efforts to develop infrastructure facilities for industrial development were largely responsible for achieving this aim.

There is another dimension to be considered when studying the effective contribution of public capital formation to industrial development. The public investors were preoccupied with what they perceived as productive investment only. In sectors such as gas, water and electricity supplies and social services to households, for the welfare of the general population, we cannot help but notice a considerable lag in the establishment of modern services. We will return to this subject in the following chapter on the welfare and distributional aspects of prewar growth.

3 Composition of Capital Stock

The increase in the real fixed capital stock of the economy was accompanied by considerable changes in its composition. Based on the results of the

LTES study on 'Capital Formation', the overall trend in changes in the composition of capital stock can be followed.[27] There were changes in the types of capital stock and in the ratio of public and private ownership of capital stock.

To begin with, let us consider capital stock, as grouped in figure 3.1.

This classification has been constructed in order to improve our understanding of the LTES data and to enable us to compare and relate the growth of:

● infrastructure and other public capital
● producers' capital, and
● capital for livelihood.

The classification summarizes the changes in proportion between the three groups of capital formation in Japan in the period from 1868 to 1940. It may be helpful for several reasons. First of all, we note that investment in public works is the most important kind of capital formation by the government throughout the period. It took the form of roads and bridges, harbours, riparian and water works and other works for improving agricultural land and urban areas. In the early years of industrialization the construction of government offices and other facilities for public administration claimed the second largest share of government capital funds.[28] Railways (National Railways, local railways and street railways) and electric utilities began to claim larger shares in later years.[29]

The general term 'buildings' includes factory and commercial buildings and farmhouses, schools (public and private) and residential buildings (houses). Since schools built privately, houses built by the government and private construction works for transportation represented comparatively small proportions of the total, we may deduce that the total value of

1. Building and construction

    (a) Government offices

    (b) Schools $\begin{cases} \text{Public sector} \\ \text{Private sector} \end{cases}$

    (c) Housing $\begin{cases} \text{Public sector} \\ \text{Private sector} \end{cases}$

    (d) Other construction work

1.1 Buildings $\begin{cases} 1.1.1 \quad \text{Public} \\ 1.1.2 \quad \text{Private} \end{cases}$

1.2 Public works

1.3 Public utilities

1.4 Transportation $\begin{cases} 1.4.1 \quad \text{Public} \\ 1.4.2 \quad \text{Private} \end{cases}$

2. Equipment

    (e) Equipment $\begin{cases} 2.1 \quad \text{Furniture, machinery and tools} \\ 2.2 \quad \text{Transport equipment (rolling stock and so on)} \end{cases}$

Figure 3.1   *Classification of the capital stock*

'construction' less houses $(1.1.1 + 1.2 + 1.3 + 1.4$ in figure 3.1) was promoted by public investment. Similarly, we may take 'equipment' to be an indication of the size of 'producers' capital', assuming that the proportion owned by the public was not significant enough to upset this approximation. Capital formation in 'residential houses' is interpreted as 'capital for livelihood'. When we approximate 'construction' with public infrastructure, government investment for military purposes should be excluded. Capital formation for military purposes was mostly in the form of warships and armories, and is included in 'equipment'. The contribution of these investments to the promotion of industrial development is negligible compared with 'infrastructure' and 'producers' capital'. Thus this section will concentrate on capital stock for non-military purposes only.

The LTES study of capital *stock*, that is accumulated capital, shows that there was a general trend in the economy to accumulate more 'construction' than 'equipment' in most of the years before the First World War (figure 3.2). We see in the figure strong surges of 'construction' in new capital stock in 1900, 1912 and 1926, with the consequent increase in the stock of 'equipment' coming two and four years later. But the importance

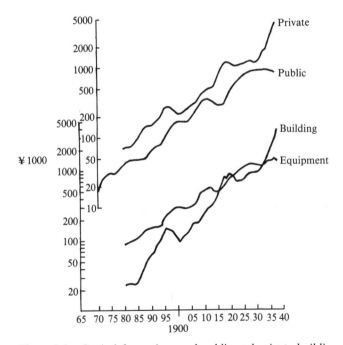

Figure 3.2 *Capital formation, and public and private building and equipment, 1870–1940 (at 1934–6 prices). Capital formation is for civilian purposes only, and figures are for five-year moving averages.*
Source: Emi (1971).

Table 3.3 *Capital formation by different type, 1886–1940*

		(1) Infrastructure and other public capital	(2) Producer's capital	(3) Capital for livelihood	(4) Total
1	1886–1890	128 (26.7)	170 (35.4)	182 (37.9)	480 (100.0)
2	1891–1895	187 (26.5)	307 (43.5)	212 (30.0)	706 (100.0)
3	1896–1900	462 (33.0)	538 (38.4)	401 (28.6)	1 401 (100.0)
4	1901–1905	511 (35.3)	559 (38.7)	376 (26.0)	1 446 (100.0)
5	1906–1910	973 (39.8)	1 026 (41.9)	447 (18.3)	2 446 (100.0)
6	1911–1915	1 295 (37.3)	1 581 (45.5)	599 (17.2)	3 475 (100.0)
7	1916–1920	3 043 (29.0)	6 225 (59.4)	1 214 (11.6)	10 482 (100.0)
8	1921–1925	6 009 (50.7)	3 918 (33.1)	1 917 (16.2)	11 844 (100.0)
9	1926–1930	6 870 (56.8)	3 808 (31.5)	1 412 (11.7)	12 090 (100.0)
10	1931–1935	5 122 (47.9)	4 322 (11.7)	1 256 (11.7)	10 700 (100.0)
11	1936–1940	7 369 (29.4)	15 949 (63.6)	1 761 (7.0)	25 079 (100.0)

Source: Iida and Yamada (1976, table 8–6).

of 'construction' in the total capital stock gradually declined, so that its relative share fell from the peak of 80–85 per cent in the years before the First World War to 60 per cent of the total by the late 1930s.

To examine the implications of this observation, Iida and Yamada rearranged the LTES statistics as in table 3.3.[30] In the table they trace the cyclic changes in the relative importance of infrastructure and other 'public capital' and 'producers' capital' in the years 1886–90 and 1936–40. What they observe is that there was considerable public infrastructure investment in the early Meiji years. They presume that this promoted capital formation by the private sector and brought about the increase in 'producers' capital' in periods (1) and (2) in the table.

Since active investment in producers' capital is expected to generate production activities and increase the size of the GNP, this will result in heavier demand for, and use of, infrastructure facilities in this period. The government is accordingly pressed to increase infrastructure and other public capital[31] to catch up with the level of producers' capital. The levelling of the ratio in periods (3)–(5) between 'infrastructure' and 'producers' (columns 1 and 2 in table 3.3) may be taken as a sign of the government response. Further efforts by the public sector to build infrastructure would eventually lead to an ample supply of it in periods (6)–(8) which, in turn, as indicated earlier, stimulates yet another increase in producers' capital formation in periods (8)–(10); and thus the process creates cyclic changes in the relative size of the two different forms of capital stock. Following this logic, Iida and Yamada argue the case for effective government-led industrialization in the period concerned.[32]

How plausible is this argument? What exactly has taken place to produce the observed changes in the ratios between the two forms of capital stock? How do we interpret these changes in order to explain Japan's process of industrialization? The available publications on capital information do not adequately answer these questions. However, a recent survey by NIRA on social capital formation discusses the reaction of the general public to government activities in the provision of social capital.[33] Using newspaper reports from the Meiji period to the present day, this survey discusses the responses of the population to government investment policy on building roads and railways, communication facilities, schools, hospitals, houses and water, gas and electricity services. A further report, giving a descriptive explanation of government activities in the building of infrastructure, was compiled by a government officer in the Ministry of Construction.[34] With the help of this information, plus statistical information concerning public capital formation, how can the effect of public investment activities in generating capital formation in industry be evaluated?

We will begin by restating our previous statistical observation of the trend in public investment activity in the long historical period from the Restoration to 1940 and in the period after the Second World War in the following manner.

Table 3.4 Public capital formation for infrastructure facilities and GNP, 1877–1963

	Annual growth rates								
	1877–1901	1901–6	1906–12	1912–17	1917–34	1934–40	1877–1940	1948–1963	1877–1963
(i) Infrastructure (%)[a]	9.4	−5.1	10.0	−7.8	8.0	−3.3	5.1	10.9	6.0
(ii) GNP (%)	3.5	2.1	3.9	5.9	3.4	4.9	3.7	10.1	4.0
(iii)[b] (i)/(ii)	2.7	2.6	2.8	2.3	3.2	2.6	2.8	4.6	3.0

[a] Infrastructure facilities include: water supply; city and national parks; public housing; hospitals and other health service facilities; schools and other educational and training facilities such as libraries; road, railway, subway and tram networks; airport and other transport facilities; harbours; telecommunications; forestry; river and sea improvement; fishing grounds; repair works following national disasters; and dam and electricity generation facilities.
[b] The proportional share of the value of public capital formation for building infrastructure facilities to GNP.
Source: Sawamoto (1982, table 5).

First, there has been a steady rate of increase in public capital formation for non-military purposes, with the result that the ratio of the value of public capital formation to GNE (I_g/GNE) has grown from an initial level of 6 per cent in the mid–1880s to 8–10 per cent in the mid–1960s, since when there has been a slight decline to a level of 7–8 per cent in the 1980s. This is indicated in figure 3.3.

Second, underlying this general trend there appears to be a time lag between public capital formation (I_g) and that of the private sector (I_p). The investment activity in the private sector, I_p, did not follow the same growth path as I_g. However, we have also noted earlier that if we combine I_g with I_p the total capital formation of the economy as a whole follows a steady growth trend.

Third, the share of public capital formation in the total has fluctuated over time, so as to prevent us from observing any continuous trend in the change of the ratio of public to private (I_p/I_g) capital formation (see column 5 in table 3.2).

We have already observed that in the early Meiji period before 1885 public capital formation grew at a faster rate than did private capital formation, and that this experience was repeated in the 1930s when public spending was increased to offset the decline in private investment to counter the problems of the World Depression.

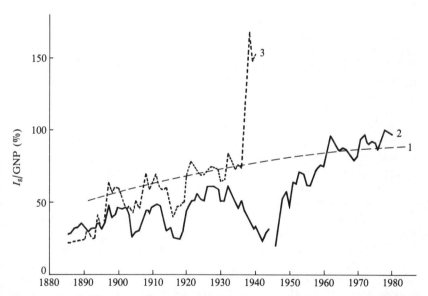

Figure 3.3 *Public capital formation and GNP, 1880–1980 (at current prices). Curve 1, long-run trend (Azuma); curve 2, EPA estimate (civilian purposes only); curve 3, Emi and Rosovsky estimate (including military purposes). Source:* Azuma (1984, figure 5).

Fourth, as a result of public-sector activity, fluctuations emerged in the value of I_g and its ratio of GNE on a yearly and three to four yearly short-run basis. Downswings of I_g have also occurred in the years when Japan was involved in wars and pseudo-war activities.

From these observations it can certainly be said that the government has acted *as if* it aimed to manipulate its public investment in order to allocate a fixed proportion of GNP to capital formation for the continuous industrial development of the economy. The attempt has failed only when large shares of public revenue have had to be used for military purposes.

In order to see the relationship between major economic policy and public investment and capital formation on the one hand, and private-sector activity on the other, in the prewar years, we will consider the historical sequence of events in more detail.

Before 1885

We observed earlier that until 1885 public capital formation continued to increase at a faster rate than that of private industry. Most of the public investment was in public works for farming and urban areas, and government offices and public administration facilities. Such developments took place, according to the NIRA survey mentioned earlier, with little attention to the internal needs of the society. The purpose was international, to establish Japan as a 'modern industrial state' equal to its Western counterparts.[35] We also noted earlier that government investment in infrastructure grew by 6 per cent annually, considerably faster than GNP, from 1880 to 1900. The main works were harbours, coastal and river works, and roads and bridges, often repairing and expanding facilities inherited from the Tokugawa period. Before 1885 such public efforts were unable to generate a corresponding investment by the private sector.

This means that it was not until after two decades of solo efforts by the government that private enterprise began to invest in capital formation, by establishing local railways and railway services to supplement the national railway networks. That long lag motivated 'the state as entrepreneur', and is the reason why the Meiji government had to found and run its own 'model plants' in the 1870s.

As a direct investment, the construction of public plant was not an economic success. It was indeed direct industrial investment, but it was conducted in the same manner as was infrastructure construction. Most of the public enterprises in which the government was directly engaged were capital-intensive, whereas the majority of private factories had remained labour-intensive for some time and made little demand on new capital supplies.[36] In those traditional areas of private enterprise, capital resources could be spread quite thinly while maintaining the widespread use of established labour-intensive production techniques. In those areas, an infusion of comparatively small amounts of new capital, and minor improvements in production and administrative methods, could often bring about a marked improvement in productivity. That was also true of some of the public works,[37] but although the government needed to economize on capital, it was also determined to demonstrate to the population in general a strong determination to promote industrialization; and so some of the public factories were more heavily capitalized than simple profit-seeking required.

Publicly owned factories and enterprises were not financed by importing foreign capital, as was the case in Australia, Canada and elsewhere. Needing to economize on what savings there were, the Japanese government tried to find economical uses for capital in as many trades and industries as possible, so as to leave adequate resources for the new large-scale industries, the technology of which was imported from the West, with no alternative but to use capital-intensive methods.

The government sought to determine what the most economical proportions of infrastructure and producer's capital to labour and to output were, in order to produce the required level of capital stock. However, the NIRA survey notes that the problems of industrialization in the early Meiji economy were not actually caused by shortage of capital accumulation. It suggests that, before the first enterprise boom in 1890, there were considerable capital funds lying idle in the household savings of wealthy merchants, farmers and upper class ex-samurais.[38] The holders of this idle money were apparently waiting to see what direction industrial development would take before committing their funds to specific investment projects, and government commitment was important to them. Ten or twenty years of public investment in infrastructure facilities and model plants and enterprises eventually convinced them that the publicly designated direction of industrialization would provide safe and profitable investment opportunities. Thus public capital formation before and during period 1 in table 3.3 successfully encouraged entrepreneurial activity and private investment in the following period 2 (in table 3.3), as argued by Iida and others.

1886–1900

In this period there was a remarkable expansion of modern industry, which it seems reasonable to see as a direct result of the preceding decades of public investment. To symbolize the relationship, the government founded the Japan Railway Company in 1881 and private railways followed, expanding most rapidly in the next few years.[39] The rise in Japan's international status enabled her to raise foreign loans after the wars against China and later Russia, and the government found it easier to find capital for large-scale public works and industrial development.

1901–1916

It was in such a mood of economic expansion that the state steel mill, Yawata Steel (later to be developed into Nippon Steel), was founded in 1901 to produce steel for industry, thus allowing an expansion of light industry and laying the foundations for future expansion into heavy industry. The government's high investment activity stimulated modern industry, but it also increased imports and created a trade imbalance. While the government hesitated to invest further in infrastructure the private sector continued to expand through the enterprise boom. Private investment began to expand faster than public investment at an increasing speed, so that by 1910 the shortage of infrastructure facilities, the extent of urban slums and the excessive use and exploitation of land, forestry, fishing and other natural resources emerged as serious problems. As a result the country became more susceptible than ever to natural disasters (landslides, floods, and so on), all of which contributed to increases in public unrest and labour protests during the Taisho period.

This phenomenon, of public capital formation occurring ahead of private investment activity, is not unique to Japan. Economic history provides us with various examples of countries in which the government provided essential capital formation as 'seed' money for economic growth in the early stages of industrialization. Large-scale public works funded by the federal and state governments in America and by colonial governments in Australia in the nineteenth century offer such examples. But in Japan the shift in the relative sizes of public and producers' capital stock in table 3.3 in periods 3 and 5 (1896–1900 and 1906–10) should not simply be interpreted as increasing public efforts to provide social capital in response to the expanded production activity of the economy in the preceding periods. The NIRA survey vividly portrays how the population recognized the role played by the railway networks in opening up the physical infrastructure of the country, at all levels and between all communities. People's tastes, lifestyles, philosophies and values were affected by this modern technology. The result was that the hitherto carefully maintained balance between the continued progress of many of the older industries and the preservation of traditional techniques, which were supported by the people's faithfulness to habits of consumption inherited from the past, began to crumble. In fact, this was the essence of the public capital formation of the period. The government aimed to modernize the lifestyle of the population along with their values and thinking habits by effective and swift industrialization. The modernization of private industry and production techniques was expected to follow from the *social* effects of public investment in these areas. Nakamura's careful study[40] of this aspect warns that the role of the government in capital formation in this period should not be discussed simply in terms of the demand–supply relations of infrastructure and producer's capital.

1917–1932

The relative shortage of infrastructure facilities as compared with industrial capital continued. The Great Earthquake of 1923 exacerbated the situation; as did the developing shift from light industry to heavy industry, which demanded different quantities and kinds of public infrastructure. As a post-earthquake recovery programme, the government began to invest in four major industrial development sites around Tokyo, Osaka, Nagoya and Northern Kyushu (the Big Four Industrial Complex), for the promotion of the steel and chemical industries. This not only helped the development of these designated heavy industries, but also promoted rapid expansion of cities and urban areas around the sites.

1933–1937

Government investment rose substantially in this period under Finance Minister Takahashi Korekiyo's expansion policy. Public capital formation through the building of infrastructure increased on average by 8 per cent annually in this period, much faster than the 3.4 per cent growth in GNP. In 1932, Takahashi proposed a policy of reflation to make use of unemployed people and resources, and to engender economic recovery following the World Depression. Government expenditure was increased, and public works were undertaken in villages and cities. The aim of the policy was principally 'full employment', but the results were considerable increases in capital formation in river, road and harbour facilities. Public investment in urban public works and non-military plant and equipment was helped by the fall in the relative prices of investment goods in this period, so that large-scale investment was achieved with relatively little money.

(Takahashi's approach to *private* capital formation was just as masterful; public control was extended to the lending practices of private as well as public banks, and used to direct resources predominantly into industrial investment. We will return to this aspect of his work in the following section.)

We may now briefly review the prewar history of public investment as a whole.

Between 1885 and 1934 public capital formation for the building of infrastructure is estimated to have increased by 6.1 per cent annually, while total non-military public investment increased by 7.1 per cent in the same period. The difference is due to increased construction for purposes such as schools, government and other public offices, public housing and sewerage facilities in residential areas.[41] We may note that public investment in these 'non-productive' areas had expanded relatively quickly in the Taisho years before and after 1920,[42] but from a low base; even in the turbulent period of the Taisho years, the government seems to have managed to legitimate industrial development by spending quite small sums on residential and the related services. Therefore, when the economy emerged from the shock of the Great Earthquake, the government was able to direct its capital formation single-mindedly into production purposes only. Net capital formation in housing per capita is estimated to have deteriorated from 1930 to 1940.[43] Meanwhile, annual public investment in infrastructure rose from 2.6 per cent in the 1901–17 period to exceed 3 per cent of GNP in 1918–37.[44]

In the period from 1917 to the outbreak of the Second World War (roughly periods 7–10 in table 3.3) the general aims of public investment changed substantially. Much of the necessary infrastructure was in place, and the educational and demonstration purposes of earlier public activity had been accomplished: there appeared to be general enthusiasm in the population for industrialization and modernization. The size, composition and direction of government capital formation changed accordingly: most of it could now be focused directly on industrial productivity. It continued to be directed towards infrastructure facilities, but investment decisions by policy-makers were now based on an overall calculation of industrial productivity. Heavy industry – a few large factories controlled by the *zaibatsu* and other large-scale enterprises – became the main beneficiary of public investment in this period, even though manufacturing expansion continued to come principally from light industries such as cotton and silk, and spinning and weaving in the period 1914–29.[45] The expansion in light industries caused an expanding demand for industrial equipment, so that the markets awaited the heavy engineering industries which the government was encouraging. By 1939 Japan was able to reduce its imports of equipment, and supply a major portion of domestic demand for steel, machinery and chemical products. Thus, in terms of the fecundity of public investment, Japan was able to justify the switch to heavy industries, even though conventional calculations of 'greatest comparative advantage' or 'return on capital invested' would not have justified the switch at the time when the government forced it to happen.

From 1931 the government's comprehensive approach to recovery from the World Depression makes it difficult to separate the effects of public investment from the effects of other public policies. The government's first response to the World Depression in 1930 was to compound the problem, as many Western governments were doing, by applying severely restrictive policies. But Takahashi Korekiyo, Finance Minister from 1931, quickly reversed course. He reasoned that the Japanese (Showa) and World Depressions had left much slack in the economy, which could be taken up quickly without any inflationary effects.[46] Expansive public and private investment were fuelled by a rapid increase in public spending and an expansion of bank credit, with large public deficits. The gold standard was abandoned and the yen devalued about 40 per cent in a successful campaign to expand exports to world markets.[47] Public investment, financed by the deficit, enabled new roads, bridges, ports, waterworks and other public works to be completed, aimed primarily at creating public and private employment but incidentally improving living conditions and the industrial infrastructure.[48]

In two directions – one social and one military – Takahashi refused, or tried to refuse, to spend as others wanted him to do. Industry recovered more quickly than agriculture, and the Ministry of Agriculture and others wanted public spending on rural relief. But Takahashi would spend only on reactivating and expanding the productive economy, not on rescuing 'lame ducks'. For a time, public spending was well dispersed through all sectors of the economy, and the 'productive' strategy worked quite well as the factory labour force swelled by nearly a million new workers, most of them from country areas, between 1930 and 1936. New manufacturing industries brought new income to many farming families from wages sent home by members who had emigrated to the cities.[49] Therefore the 'productive' spending did somewhat reduce the harsh effects of the refusal to spend on direct social relief.

Most of the private-sector economic recovery took place in light industries. Government stimulation of heavy industry continued, increasingly to meet orders for public engineering and military purposes. Takahashi's basic success was in applying what would later be called Keynesian stimulants to revive and expand economic activity as a whole, with an emphasis on civilian rather than military benefits. He tried to restrain the growth of military spending, with some success at first, but fatally in the end. In what became known as the '2–26 incident' he was assassinated in February 1936 – ironically, within days of the publication of Keynes' *General Theory*. His death opened the way for faster military expansion, and fascist government. Army planners and young economic bureaucrats wanted heavier military spending, in an economy directed by a stronger central government. For those purposes they believed that many of the mechanisms of the free-market economy needed to be replaced. Thereafter, the whole margin of growth each year, and soon a rising proportion of the whole national product, went for military use, at the cost of falling living standards.[50]

Before Takahashi's death, the government was committing a record 7.4 per cent of national product to public investment; which was 40 per cent of all annual investment, and had accumulated to account for more than half of Japan's capital stock. However, as noted earlier, although public investment appears to have been the strongest public influence on national economic activity, it was by no means the only one. Next in importance was the government's design and use of the national financial system, to which we now turn.

4   Public Financial Influence on Private Capital Formation

Until the outbreak of the Second World War, the financial system created between 1882 and 1890 worked sufficiently well. The government was able to meet its expenditure from taxation. However, the Russian and then the World War imposed stress, as the government had to meet direct military costs, new costs of colonial acquisition and exploitation, and the cost of establishing further industries that were considered to be of 'national importance for military purposes'. Expenses in the interests of national power began to exceed the growth of the economy. The government borrowed heavily, adding domestic and foreign debt to its problems. Under these pressures it began to restructure public and private banks in a bid to increase savings, and increase capital accumulation in industry, especially heavy industry. It developed closer ties with the Bank of Japan, and between the Bank of Japan and the commercial banks, and began to guarantee bank debentures. The overall effect was an increase in the already considerable public control of private capital sources. Some of the features of this process were as follows.

Our period II (1881–1900) had equipped Japan with its central bank (the Bank of Japan), a network of post office savings banks, a national Industrial Bank for government-sponsored heavy industries, long-term credit banks, and agricultural and industrial banks in each prefecture to fund regional developments. There was also growth in private commercial banking. Although many of the European models from which the government-sponsored banks were derived funded housing and other non-industrial developments, the Japanese banks were almost all designed to direct most savings into industrial investment, or into the infrastructure that industry needed.

Under the new pressures the long-term credit banks, the European models for which had provided mortgage finance for housing, developed the mortgage instrument chiefly for long-term lending to industry and agriculture.

The main source of financing consisted of long-term debentures backed by mortgages which were not guaranteed by the government. They were secured on immovable property of various forms, such as paddy fields, upland fields, salt fields, forests and fishing waters and rights. Issues were initially small, but grew rapidly to almost one-sixth of all private fixed non-housing capital expenditure by 1910. This substantial amount was absorbed by the Deposit Bureau of the Ministry of Finance. Since the Bureau's funds were sourced almost exclusively from the postal savings system, we can see how government policy to encourage small savers to contribute to capital formation was promoted through these banking channels.[51]

The commercial banks underwent extraordinary expansion during this period, and their pattern of development again followed a trend peculiar to

Japan. The expansion developed through increasingly tight relationships with specific industrial enterprises, which allowed large-scale business houses to create 'in-house' banks. This was caused by the fact that most of the private commercial banks had to expand their lending activities before they had time to accumulate an adequate level of capital. The resources of financial institutions, particularly of private commercial banks, expanded much more rapidly than national production.[52] This brought two peculiar factors into the commercial banking system. The first was the phenomenon known as 'over-borrowing', a trend of the recipient enterprises as well as of the banks concerned. The comparatively small proportion of deposits in the total assets of commercial banks had already become apparent by 1890. Compared with commercial banks in England, where deposits represent the majority of the total capital, the Japanese counterparts were reported to have operated with deposits accounting for only 40–60 per cent of the total assets. As a result, commercial banks in Japan implemented policies to select limited numbers of enterprises, to which they then extended large-scale credit. They developed specific lender–borrower relationships with these enterprises, and became, in effect, 'in-house' banks for them. The beginnings of the *zaibatsu* and other enterprise groupings can be observed at this time. Those firms which were left out of such credit arrangements were forced to seek credit from lesser banks at higher costs; leading to the formation of a dual financial structure, for large-scale enterprises on the one hand and small to medium firms on the other.

Behind the development of these features stood the Bank of Japan, which provided continuous credit to the commercial banks and guaranteed their loan activities. This public support enabled the commercial banks to fulfil their assigned role of providing cheap and easy money to businesses for industrial growth.

In our period IV, from 1917, the financial institutions had a rough ride. Although Japan joined the First World War, its actual military expenses were kept to a minimum, while it reaped all the economic benefits of the war. A rapid expansion of exports took place, while most of Japan's competitors were preoccupied by the fighting and were withdrawing from their international markets. Gaining from such windfall opportunities, Japan succeeded in accelerating her industrialization for a time. However, the end of the war was followed, as in most other countries, by a sharp recession: then, to make matters worse, the Great Earthquake disrupted the public programme of industrial development. The activity and economic role of the government differed sharply in the two halves of this period; but, in general, the importance of the public sector in the process of investment, saving and economic development expanded further through the period of expansion, and continued to expand through the subsequent decade of economic setbacks and depression.

Throughout that second phase, economic policy was directed most intensively towards countering depression: the postwar Japanese depression of 1920–7, and the World Depression of 1930–1. All available resources and networks of financial and banking institutions were mobilized for the administration of counter-depression policies, with increasing public influence in business decision-making.

The postwar World Depression began in March 1920 as a reaction to the preceding extraordinary expansion of investment in industry, particularly in the heavy industrial sectors. Easy money had been provided by banks to enterprises wishing to increase their capacity. Real gross national production increased on average by more than 8 per cent annually from 1916 to 1918. The share of manufactures in the net domestic product rose above 25 per cent, as compared with 20 per cent in 1913. All of this achievement was carried out on the back of the 'over-loan' practice. Excessive gearing ratios were most evident among enterprises to whom capital was extended by the 'in-house' banks.

With the end of the postwar boom, the economy plunged into a sharp recession. Financially, the problem began with the collapse of share prices, first of industrial firms and then of small regional banking corporations. The government advised the Bank of Japan to take measures to squeeze credit by lifting its discount rate. The damage done through the easy money policy of the war boom was too great to remedy by ordinary monetary manipulation. The Bank undertook rescue operations by extending loans to all banks with difficulties. Soon the main preoccupation of the Bank became simply to prevent or mitigate the crisis in the credit and banking system. The difficulties originated in an over-expansion of credit during the war and the immediate postwar boom, and were compounded by losses suffered by business in the Great Earthquake. The Bank continued to discount a substantial volume of bills representing all those doubtful commitments, in order to save numerous small and poorly managed commercial banks from bankruptcy. This eventually led the Bank itself into financial difficulties. The government finally decided to provide loans to the Bank of Japan from its Deposit Bureau in the Ministry of Finance, as well as ordering the Bank to write off most of the doubtful bills that the Bank had previously discounted. This caused considerable losses to banks, many of which were subsequently forced into liquidation. One of the better remembered incidents in the period was the collapse of a large combine (the Suzuki Group) due to its heavy debt to one of the large banks. The group's collapse led to widespread effects in fields beyond those directly connected with Suzuki's trade. Many closed, and some barely managed to survive even with the assistance of the Bank of Japan.[53] In addition to the Bank of Japan, the government ordered the special banks, such as the long-term credit banks established by government capital and/or sponsorship to direct their capital towards financial rescue. By early 1928 the Bank of Japan and all the publicly controlled special banks found themselves barely managing to operate even with the support of capital and guarantees provided by the government's Deposit Bureau.[54] The period between 1922 and 1931 thus saw considerable consolidation and concentration of the government's direct influence over the nation's financial and banking system.

How did the government finance such rescue expenses? It sourced them mainly from increased tax revenue and the issue of bonds. The tax increases were principally in income tax, and sales tax on sake: roughly 40 per cent of the increase in revenue is reported to have come from those sources in 1920.[55] Between 1919 and 1921 the government bond issue increased by almost 33 per cent. This heavy reliance on the issue of government bonds increased as the depression continued into the latter part of the 1920s, resulting in a sharp decline in the market value of these bonds,[56] to the point where it became obvious to the government that its debt could not be further promoted. As an alternative source, early in 1924 a loan was floated in New York and another in London, mainly to meet the extraordinary import requirements caused by the Great Earthquake. The loan was raised at the extremely disadvantageous rate of 6.97 per cent, said to have been equivalent to that floated by the Austrian government in its attempt to resurrect the economy after defeat in the First World War.[57] Having judged that banks and other overseas financial institutions were unlikely to buy much more of its bonds, the government launched a nation-wide campaign in 1925 to induce Japanese households and other small savers to absorb, through the post office outlets, what remained unsold.[58]

Japan's recovery from depression after 1931 was engineered by policies which further extended public control over the financial institutions. The public financial networks of the Bank of Japan and the special long-term credit banks were placed under direct government control, so as to enable the government to provide ready credit. Commercial banks also became engines for the government's spending policy: they increasingly lost their autonomy in determining their own lending or liquidity policies. Nationally, the policy of a balanced budget was abandoned and no attempt was made to control the government deficit. All banks, from the Bank of Japan through to the publicly controlled banks and the commercial banks, became mere executors of government instructions. Controls extended for purposes of economic recovery became available for other uses when the government's interest switched to mobilizing economic resources for war.

5 Surveys of National Wealth

The development of the public and private proportions of capital stock in the economy can be studied further in the changing trend of capital accumulation which emerges from surveys of national wealth. In this regard we are fortunate in being able to reference the many observations made regularly during the pre- and postwar years: this is because, as early as 1907, Japan had a strong interest in estimating her total economic assets, as a

Table 3.5 *National wealth (in ¥m), 1905–35*

	(1) 1905	(2) 1910	(3) 1913	(4) 1917	(5) 1919	(6) 1924	(7) 1930	(8) 1935	(9) 1917/1905	(10) 1935/1924
1. Harbours and canals	51 (1.0)	97 (1.2)	150 (1.6)	106 (0.8)	209 (0.9)	352 (0.7)	343 (0.8)	454 (0.8)	2.07	1.28
2. Forestry	932 (17.7)	1 414 (18.2)	1 760 (19.0)	2 127 (15.6)	4 534 (20.4)	9 530 (18.0)	6 707 (15.0)	7 086 (13.0)	2.28	0.74
3. Building	2 331 (44.4)	3 535 (45.4)	3 632 (39.3)	5 317 (39.0)	8 560 (38.4)	27 806 (52.6)	22 843 (52.6)	26 211 (48.1)	2.28	0.94
4. Household furniture	120 (2.3)	175 (2.2)	250 (2.7)	275 (2.0)	594 (2.7)	1 447 (2.7)	1 180 (2.4)	1 285 (2.4)	2.29	0.88
5. Machinery	208 (4.0)	343 (4.4)	399 (4.3)	533 (4.1)	1 102 (4.9)	1 956 (3.7)	1 809 (4.0)	2 921 (5.4)	2.65	1.49
6. Livestock	115 (2.2)	161 (2.1)	154 (1.7)	229 (1.7)	503 (2.3)	588 (1.1)	346 (0.8)	431 (0.8)	1.99	0.77
7. Railways	687 (13.1)	970 (12.5)	299 (3.2)	2 092 (15.4)	1 111 (5.0)	3 241 (6.1)	3 598 (6.1)	3 746 (8.0)	3.04	1.15
8. Railway rolling stock	11 (0.2)	15 (0.2)	47 (0.5)	56 (0.4)	182 (0.8)	779 (1.5)	660 (1.5)	846 (1.6)	5.09	1.09
9. Ships	143 (2.7)	157 (2.0)	471 (5.1)	1 051 (7.7)	1 182 (5.3)	1 896 (3.6)	2 060 (3.6)	3 035 (5.6)	7.34	1.60
10. Water supply	45 (0.9)	56 (0.7)	77 (0.8)	128 (0.9)	1 874 (4.0)	2 522 (5.5)	3 967 (7.5)	583 (1.1)	8.05	1.39
11. Bridges	51 (1.0)	56 (0.7)	95 (1.0)	222 (1.6)	234 (1.1)	589 (1.1)	483 (1.1)	786 (1.4)	4.35	1.33
12. Public assets	n.a.	n.a.	881 (9.5)	1 461 (10.7)	1 237 (5.6)	n.a.	n.a.	n.a.	n.a.	n.a.
13. Others	557 (10.6)	809 (10.4)	1 030 (11.1)	1 461 (10.7)	2 681 (12.0)	2 522 (4.8)	2 250 (5.0)	3 547 (6.5)	2.62	1.40
Total (1–13)	5 251 (100.0)	7 787 (100.0)	9 245 (100.0)	13 617 (100.0)	22 278 (100.0)	52 819 (100.0)	44 741 (100.0)	54 545 (100.0)	2.59	1.03
(i) Social overheads	1 375 (29.3)	1 900 (27.2)	1 971 (26.9)	4 183 (34.4)	5 031 (25.7)	13 902 (27.6)	12 787 (30.1)	16 336 (32.0)	3.04	1.17
(ii) Producers' capital	2 150 (45.8)	3 312 (47.5)	3 479 (47.6)	5 305 (43.6)	10 120 (51.6)	22 435 (44.6)	18 245 (42.9)	21 582 (42.3)	2.46	0.96
(iii) Capital for livelihood	1 169 (24.9)	1 766 (25.3)	1 884 (25.7)	2 668 (21.9)	4 446 (22.7)	13 960 (27.8)	11 459 (27.0)	13 080 (25.6)	2.28	0.93
Total (i)–(iii)	4 694 (100.0)	6 978 (100.0)	7 334 (100.0)	12 156 (100.0)	19 597 (100.0)	50 297 (100.0)	42 291 (100.0)	50 998 (100.0)	2.58	1.01

n.a. denotes 'not available'.
Sources: for 1–13, Bank of Japan, *Hundred-year Statistics of the Japanese Economy* (1971, pp. 18–27); for (i)–(iii), Iida and Yamada (1976 pp. 8 and 9).

measure of national power. The aim of these surveys was to assess the effectiveness of her policy to promote national enrichment and security (the *fukoku–kyohei* policy).

However, in the era after the Second World War, public interest shifted, and the survey was restructured to evaluate how effectively the economic resources of the nation were being utilized to produce the maximum GNP. One result was that the prewar surveys included 'non-renewable' land and resources, while postwar national wealth was assessed only in terms of renewable assets.[59] Bearing in mind that inconsistency in the data, tables 3.3 and 3.4 are compiled:

- to show an estimate of national wealth in terms of renewable assets only, and
- generally to gauge the wealth of the nation, taking into account total renewable and non-renewable assets.

We have shown earlier that the period covering 1886–1917, periods 1–6 in table 3.3, saw the eventual acceptance of modern development by many entrepreneurs, who were responding both to government leadership and to buoyant economic conditions as a result of war activities against China, Russia and Germany. The increase in capital formation was rapid in the 1905–17 period and national wealth increased by a factor of 2.58 (total of 1–13 in column (9) of table 3.5). The rate of accumulation varied marginally between different types of capital stock, with public capital growing faster than the other two (producers' capital, and capital stock for livelihood, in other words community and household use). However, the annual growth rate of social overhead capital, based on the increase in capital stock in public works, railways and electricity supply facilities, is estimated at 4–5 per cent in the period,[60] a slightly lower rate than that of the preceding years of 1880–1900, and less than the rate of expansion of GNP.

We know, however, that public investment was extremely high, and that it increased throughout the prewar years. There had been continuous public investment throughout the period, so that capital formation for non-military purposes and infrastructure build-up by the government grew at the following rates:[61]

1886–1900	9–10 per cent
1901–10	7 per cent
1911–20	3 per cent (approximately)
1921–30	8 per cent (approximately)
1931–8	> 10 per cent (includes military)

The overall trend in the prewar years in general was, as noted above, that capital formation by the government ranged between 29 and 40 per cent of all capital formation, and grew at a faster rate than that of capital

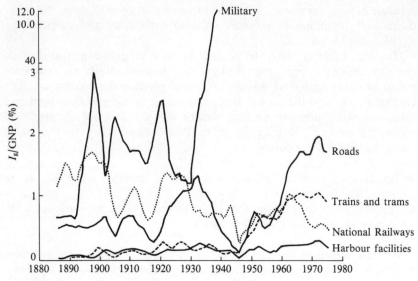

Figure 3.4 *Government capital formation (I_g) by purpose, 1880–1980 (at current prices). GNP = gross national product.*
Sources: Azuma (1984, figure 7) and Sawamoto (1982, table 27).

formation by private enterprise, even when the considerable investment made for defence purposes was excluded from government activities (see column 5 in table 3.2; see also figure 3.4).

What is the reason for this discrepancy? The discrepancy between the extremely high public performance in investment and the not so high public performance in capital formation, as compared with those of the private sector, lies in the fact that much of the government effort in capital formation was directed to increasing non-renewable assets (see table 3.6). The government did not make a great effort to create 'social capital' in the commonly accepted sense of building transport facilities, parks, hospitals and schools. Given Japan's ambition and strong desire for economic expansion, and the fact that she had a limited supply of land and natural resources, the government directed its efforts towards *creating* land and natural resources, even though these could not really be created or reproduced.

How could the government have produced non-reproducible (non-renewable) assets? The question may sound absurd, but it deserves careful attention once we clarify what is meant by 'non-reproducible' as against 'reproducible' assets.[62]

Economists have argued for some time about how to measure national wealth. If it is defined as the total stock of goods accumulated over time for production and consumption, national wealth is a measure of the assets which generate national income. 'Land and natural resources' ought to be

Table 3.6 *Increase in national assets, 1905–83*

	Between 1935 and 1905		Between 1983 and 1955	
	Nominal factor	Real factor	Nominal factor	Real factor
1. Stock and fixed assets	8.8	4.0	43.7	10.3
2. Land (urban)	4.4	1.6	72.6	1.8
3. Forestry and farmland	2.8	1.0	56.4	6.0
4. Financial assets	16.1	7.3	88.9	21.0
5. National total assets (1–4)	7.5	3.0	68.8	11.9
6. GNP (in 1934–6 prices)	5.4	2.5	31.9	7.6

Source: Shinohara (1986, p. 295).

included in such an accumulation of stocks, because they are clearly a factor of production. However, once we try to estimate the value of land and national resources we soon run into difficulties in assessing their value in terms of market prices that are consistent with the assessment of other stock. Traditional methods have been to distinguish stocks of goods which are man-made (renewable/reproducible) from those which are endowed to society by God or nature (non-renewable/non-reproducible).

In the West, it has been customary to base the estimate of national wealth only on the basis of reproducible assets. However, for Japan's situation this practice is felt to be unsatisfactory, for the following reasons.

First, land and natural resources represent a very high proportion of any nation's stock for production and consumption, and in Japan these natural resources are in short supply. They are in short supply in Japan because both the nature and the speed of expansion of the economy have proceeded in such a way as to create an acute shortage. Accordingly, industrialization is based on the extensive use of raw materials – 'land' products – imported from abroad.[63]

Compared with other industrial economies, the high and rising proportion of GNP generated per square kilometre of domestic land and per unit of such imports throughout the period of industrialization indicates the economy's response to the growing inadequacy of Japan's agricultural, industrial and urban land, forests, fishing grounds and mining deposits to sustain the growing population and the rising level of production and income.[64] Consequently, among total capital assets, land and natural resources have been so priced as to comprise the major form of productive wealth in Japan.

Second, we must note that the public response to this problem has taken the form of public investment for the improvement of land and natural resources, at a rate much faster than that directed into other (renewable) forms of real capital. Much of the capital formation by the government has taken the form of maintaining and improving this non-renewable stock: draining and irrigating it, banking it against floods and landslides, increasing its cultivatable area and its fertility, and so on.

These observations may be applicable to some extent to other over-populated Asian economies. The factor that has made the Japanese experience distinct from others is that in Japan large-scale agricultural and industrial public works have been promoted in ways that increase the value of the productive stock in private farm and business ownership. Such public efforts were not adequately reflected in the increase in value of publicly held non-renewable assets. The actual increase in the value of publicly owned land, mines and forests was a very small part of the expansive effect that the public activities had on capital formation in the economy as a whole. Public investment in public works, railway facilities, harbours, water supply and other infrastructure facilities increased the productive capacity of the economy in general, and the value of the private stock of capital in particular, in ways which should properly be ascribed to public investment when estimating national wealth.

6   Social Costs of Selective Growth

The concentration of public and private capital resources on industrial growth limited the resources available for public welfare provisions and for housing. The central government, intent on economizing on available capital and directing it to its most productive uses, made minimal allocations for local government services, and for transfer payments to households. Housing was starved partly by deliberate choice and partly as a market effect of the success of the industrializing policies. We have noted how public infrastructure investment stimulated private industrial development, which in turn increased the demand for industrially oriented infrastructure and services, in a cyclic way. One effect was simply to squeeze or pre-empt resources from alternative uses as 'capital for livelihood'.

In the early 1900s, house-building was already failing to keep abreast of the increase in population. It also failed to keep abreast of the migration of population, as industrialization brought about a massive and rapid shift of population out of the villages into the cities. Lack of housing and welfare investment meant that the shift from farm to factory brought an actual decline in living standards for many.

The lack of capital formation for community and household use (such as housing, sewerage and other facilities) is obvious both in absolute terms and relative to developing stages of industrialization and the other forms of capital accumulation. The standard of living of the population had increased considerably by the late 1930s, but this was principally a result of the increased availability of consumer goods and services, and not of any noticeable improvement in housing, living and recreation space and associated facilities.[65] Capital formation by public works was high throughout the 1920s and 1930s, particularly in the early 1930s under the Takahashi public finance policy in the World Depression period. Between 1926 and 1940 almost half of public capital formation took place in the form of public works for industrial and farm production.[66] Private capital responded with large increases in producers' capital stock (equipment and machinery) at the cost of a deterioration in housing and related facilities for the general population. For example, we note little development of water supply facilities in residential areas in proportion to other forms of capital accumulation, despite the industrial development and level of urbanization achieved. As for the relative share of capital accumulation, there seems to be no change in the composition of the accumulation of different types of fixed assets – social (infrastructure) capital, producers capital and household capital – throughout the dynamic *sturm und drang* of industrial development across the three decades from 1905 to 1935. Why do we see no improvement in housing? Is it not one of the conditions of industrialization and economic progress, as well as one of its obvious benefits? Why did it not take place in Japan? Other countries have managed to improve their housing while at the same time developing their industries and increasing their national income. West Germany did so throughout her postwar recovery; Japan herself did so through the later years of her postwar high-speed growth. So why was it not attempted in prewar Japan? The next chapter will explore the reasons for that and other welfare shortcomings.

7 Retrospect

It is worthwhile pausing for a brief review of Japan's 'planned progress' as it stood before the catastrophe of the Pacific War. Hindsight as of 1937 offered a different perspective from that of the longer-term view that we now have of those same years.

When the Meiji government was established in 1867, its task and ambition was to save the nation from colonization by the Western powers. The band of Western-oriented samurai who comprised the new elite decided almost immediately after taking power that rapid and thorough industrialization would have to be undertaken: but they had little background for this, except for the widespread development of government-owned arsenals in the Bakumatsu period. As discussed in the previous chapters, they began to improvise policies to deal with the situation facing them. The first official statistics on the size and organization of the Japanese central government tell us that it was manned by 37 000 officials – only 0.19 per cent of the total gainfully occupied population.[67] From these small beginnings, the government expanded its activities to the point at which every researcher of the

Japanese economy today acknowledges the importance of the government contribution in the industrialization and economic development of the nation.

In this chapter we have discussed how the government organized the nation's economic activities. A consistent and continuous pattern of public intervention and private dependence developed to create a public policy responsive to changing economic, political and social circumstances, but unwavering in its devotion to economic growth. Government developed the necessary policy to ensure rapid industrialization, directed its own substantial investment to that purpose, and integrated public finance activities with banking networks so as to accelerate the creation of capital and its effective use for economic growth. Whatever its mistakes, shortcomings and adaptable changes of direction, the effort was deliberate and persistent.

There was, and perhaps still is, a view that the whole enterprise was accidentally knocked off course by the external events of 1923–31. In this view, the government's special economic role was a response to the nation's economic backwardness and its justified fear of foreign interference at the time of the Meiji Restoration. Westernizing rapidly, in democratic temper and institutions as well as industrial growth, Japan was approaching the economic and political maturity that would allow a final change to full democracy, a small government and a market economy, when her society was overwhelmed by the Great Earthquake, the Showa Depression of the 1920s and the World Depression of 1930–31. Those disasters destroyed the liberal mood of the time and brought about the hardship, frustration and disillusion from which fascism was generated, and with it a further generation or two of state control of the economy.[68]

As we have argued, we do not take such a view. From the very beginning of industrialization in 1868, Japan has put her public efforts into finding the most effective ways of promoting industrial growth, building on the basis of her indigenous values and methods. Her forms of government, social organization and economic systems were gradually developed to achieve the national aim. Seen from the 1930s, the achievement could well be judged to justify the methods employed. In the 1930s the government launched what is called a *jun-senji-keizai* (quasi-wartime) economic system to test its newly found technical skill, to secure critical resources on the Asian mainland, and to prepare the nation's economic capacity for the next great leap. These new techniques and the supporting structure of the public-sector economy were, as its preceding success indicates, a double-edged weapon. Japan discarded 'sound finance' and rescued herself from the post-First World War depression, from disaster following the Great Earthquake and from the World Depression by adroitly employing reflationary policy. The force and imagination of the leaders who had continuously promoted national economic expansion since 1868 should be taken as the inspiration behind the development of such a strong public-sector economy. The catastrophic murder in 1936 of the Finance Minister and subsequently the destruction of the material welfare of people both inside and outside Japan from 1937 to 1945 was not due to any failure of the government-led economy, nor to administrative inefficiency or corruption, nor even to internal social conflicts. The collapse of the economic system in its transformation from the *jun-senji-keizai* to *senji keizai* (from a quasi-wartime economy in 1936–7 to a total war economy in 1938–45) was due to the political ambitions of fascism; in other words, from a national change of direction, one of many in the past 150 years, and the only one to have been generally and bitterly regretted.

The economy went through radical reform and restructuring at the end of the Second World War. It is true that in the process it experienced many changes. However, it is most important to grasp the fact that the postwar economic development which saw Japan become one of the world industrial powers was founded on the economic system built in the prewar years, with its unique structures and its mechanism for government to influence all of the significant decision-making processes of the national economy.

4 Social Policy in Economic Policy, 1901–1936

By 1900 the official *fukoku–kyohei* national objective began to bring concrete material changes to the everyday lives of the people. As the aspirations of the word *bunmei-kaika* (efforts for civilization and enlightenment in the Meiji period) implies, the population began to experience the fruits of industrialization and development widely in villages, cities, factories and households. Gas and, later, electric light began to replace candles in metropolitan houses and buildings. The 19-day journey between Tokyo and Osaka by palanquin was shortened to less than half a day by rail. Modern medicine and hygiene increased life expectancy and drastically reduced infant mortality. Public works – the building of roads and bridges, the improvement of river and irrigation facilities, and the building of schools and government offices and other public facilities – created jobs for even the least skilled labourers, besides improving living and travelling conditions for many. Rising income enabled more people to direct their expenditure beyond life's bare essentials. But the cost of progress was high. Many hard-working peasants were transformed into hard-working factory hands, driven to work long hours on night shifts, destined to suffer from tuberculosis and other industry-related diseases and to live in dwellings below the standard of the sheds in which they had formerly housed their farm animals.[1]

Government policy-makers had always acknowledged responsibility for the people's welfare, but not as separate from their other economic responsibilities. Where as Western theorists tend to see the economic system generating income, and government then providing welfare through public services and income transfers, Japanese policy-makers saw their role differently: it was to develop an economic system which would itself provide for the people's welfare. In the tradition of the *keisei–saimin* philosophy, writing industrial and welfare policy was one task, not two. That integrated approach, and its degree of success, are the subject of this chapter.[2]

1 The Growth of Income

There is disagreement about the actual rate of Japanese economic growth before the Pacific War. T. Nakamura,[3] for example, estimates the growth of GNP for 1870–1913 and 1913–1938 to be somewhere between 2.4 and 3.6 per cent and 3.9 and 4.6 per cent respectively. Ohokawa and Takamatsu[4] speculate that a more conservative estimate of 2.0 per cent for the Meiji period (1870–1911) would be more realistic. The problem lies primarily in the lack of accurate and comprehensive data for the calculation of the initial level of GNP and its deflator in the early Meiji period. Production statistics for the farming sector are particularly unreliable.[5] Given the available information and its constraints, it is possible to note the general trend of economic growth and performance in the prewar years only in the following general terms:

1 Japan's performance should be viewed as comparable with that of the USA, Canada, Australia, Belgium, France and the UK. It should not be taken as extraordinarily high, as some researchers have suggested.
2 Population growth in Japan was relatively low during the period. As a result, growth per capita was comparable to the high performances of Sweden, Norway and Italy.[6]
3 The rate of growth of both total GNP and per capita GNP fluctuated considerably. Industrial structures also changed considerably, so that production in some industries grew while others declined. On the whole, however, the scale of economic activity grew throughout the period to record a long-term path of steady upward growth.[7]
4 To what extent has such growth and industrial development brought material welfare to the population? Unfortunately, we do not have sufficient quantitative evidence about the level and changes in the standard of living of the Japanese people in the prewar period.[8] What can be said with reasonable confidence, however, is that both disposable income and consumption per head in constant prices increased at about the same rate as the increase of GNP per capita.[9] Contrary to the theories of some researchers, who postulate a lack of economic justice in the Japanese economy, the increase in income and consumption did not lag behind GNP to any significant extent. If the increase in consumption did lag a little behind the increase in income, Minami ascribes at least some of the lag to persisting tastes, habits and customs which constrained the consumption of new products during the prewar years.[10]

It is estimated that in 1913 consumption per head was in the order of ¥75, or nearly $40 at the then current exchange rate, a figure which should be compared with $300 in the USA, $270 in England and about $100 in Italy.[11] Although the domestic purchasing power of the yen may have been higher than indicated by the exchange rate, the ¥75 statistic leaves little doubt about the low level of the Japanese standard of living at that time. Taking income and consumption as the basic determinants of welfare, economists generally agree that there has been steady improvement throughout the economic development of Japan, but the distribution of income is held to have become more unequal in the prewar period.[12] According to NIRA's recent survey, economic growth has brought benefits to the living conditions of ordinary Japanese people by expanding life expectancy and providing better health care, better education, higher income and consumption, while other aids to the quality of life (leisure time, parks and other recreation spaces, housing and others) still lag behind those of many other industrial economies.[13] Environmental and working conditions also affect the quality of life. Final judgements of the level of welfare must depend on judgements about the relative weight to be given to the components of economic welfare, a subject on which economists are by no means agreed.[14]

2 Efficiency, Equity and the Welfare of the Population

How do we evaluate the government's contribution to welfare? The question has so far rarely been discussed systematically by economists in Japan. Most students of Japan's industrialization have been interested primarily in analysing high-speed growth and forced industrialization. Questions of 'efficiency, equity and welfare' have traditionally been confined to the area of labour economics and the special economic problems arising from 'the dual economic structure' and subcontracting systems of production.

Such an inadequate approach has resulted in conflicting judgements of the welfare outcomes of modern economic growth. We observe the following contrasting positions on this topic in Japan:

1 Growth at the cost of equity: Ohokawa and Rosovsky[15] suggest that Japan's successful industrialization and subsequent high economic growth, both in pre- and postwar periods, have only been possible because welfare policy has been ignored and sacrificed. They interpret government activities as 'the all-out growth effort' and comment, as quoted earlier, that '... it is tempting to say that a few percentage points of the growth rate might well have been sacrificed for greater social welfare'.[16] A similar observation is made by Bennett and Levine, who see Japan in a particular class of nation '... which chose a pathway toward economic growth described by the phrase "production first"' and in

which '...all capital has to be plowed back into production in order to achieve a high level of economic growth'.[17]

2   Growth without welfare: in 1954, Reischauer called Japan '...an industrialized nation supported by the toil of people living not far above the subsistence level.'[18]

In contrast to the above views, other observers highlight more positive aspects of Japan:

3   GNP growth with an increase in disposable income: Gleason's careful study[19] of consumption, from the Meiji period to the mid-1960s, argues that the benefits of economic growth have been passed on to the population as much as in other Western nations (including the USA and England) over their periods of industrialization. Therefore, he argues against the view that it must have taken public coercion to force the public to save as much as they did as a means to faster growth than would otherwise have occurred.

4   The need for a better welfare index: Gleason also warns researchers into welfare and living standards in Japan, particularly in the prewar period, that the definition of 'economic welfare' needs to be approached in a different way from accepted notions of the term in relation to Western societies. Nakagawa and Vogel[20] observe positive welfare effects of the economy's performance which would escape notice in studies of welfare as a separate product of public welfare services.

5   Welfare superpower: Nakagawa called Japan a 'welfare superpower' equal to any in the West. Vogel comments that Japan's potential for welfare advancement is so great that it offers 'lessons for America' to follow. A similar view is expressed more recently by Dore,[21] who attempted to highlight various economic (and other) aspects of Japanese society which have most frequently misled researchers, leading them to incorrect evaluations of Japan's economic and social performance.

The first three observations above are principally based on the pre-1973 period, before welfare issues were officially incorporated into public policy. Although we are discussing perspectives on different stages of economic development, popular journalistic interpretations over the century of industrialization have ranged from the image of 'workaholics in rabbit hutches',[22] on the one hand, to that of a 'welfare superpower' on the other.

These conflicting portrayals of Japanese society suggest not only the difficulty in evaluating 'efficiency, equity and welfare' but also some failure of economists to understand the Japanese economic system. In the West the economic rationale for social policy has, so far, been approached either from a Marxist orientation, or neoclassical or Keynesian frameworks. In either case, the problem is considered as a compromise between citizens' rights and property rights. According to neoclassical thinking, the allocation of economic rewards – whether for individual work or for society's overall industrial development – is determined by market forces, without reference to welfare and social policy. We observed earlier that in the traditional *keisei–saimin* approach[23] to economic policy and, earlier, in the industrial policies of the feudal domains, the promotion of industry was designed for a range of military, economic and welfare purposes. It must be emphasized that in Japan this logical compound of 'efficiency and welfare' means more than a simple aggregation of the two terms 'growth' and 'welfare', and it is therefore wrong to conclude that a 'growth first' policy is an innate characteristic of economic management in Japan. If government policy has at times taken the 'growth first' approach, for example, for urgent military reasons, the inclination towards such thinking should be explained within the context of the economic and political conditions prevailing at the time. It has not been a general or characteristic purpose of those concerned. As will be argued later, both 'efficiency without welfare' and 'welfare for purposes of legitimizing efficiency' are foreign concepts to the bureaucrats who have planned Japanese industrial development since the Meiji restoration.[24]

In Japan Dore sees mechanisms '... which allow for a little give and take and make sure that the powerful do not drive their bargains so hard for short-term advantage that they destroy the relations of trust and cooperation which may be necessary for their own and others' long-term benefit ... I argue for the virtues of such mechanisms ... partly because [they] also seem to promote greater economic efficiency.'[25]

The crucial point of this argument is that Japanese policies for industrial growth and popular welfare are combined as policies with a single comprehensive economic objective. Growth is sought not instead of welfare, or even to allow some welfare later when the country is richer, but as the direct source of improving welfare.[26] Economic development has been pursued with the integral goal of achieving desirable social and welfare objectives. The level of public welfare expenditure, therefore, is not an adequate measure of public efforts to achieve 'equity and welfare' in Japan. Instead of increasing the transfer of resources from government, as is seen in the West, government in Japan has developed its own institutional devices and structures to approach the 'efficiency-welfare' problem. It is essential to recognize this: but recognizing it does not necessarily compel the researcher either to agree with such policies, or to assume that they have always been successful.

How effective has this Japanese approach, with its associated public institutional devices, been? Where do we place Japan between the twin poles of 'workaholics in rabbit hutches' and 'welfare superpower'? We can begin by tracing the policies and their developing effects through the changing phases of industrialization in 1901–16, 1917–23, then after the Great Earthquake, from 1924 to 1937.

3 Early Debates on Welfare Policy, 1901–1916

Japan won two wars, one with China in 1894–5 and the other with Russia in 1904–5. Some observers see the two conflicts as Japan's most effective operations in terms of the benefits that accrued to the industrializing nation.[27] But although the wars may have shown good results on the national balance sheet, they contributed nothing in welfare terms. The waging of the wars diverted resources and economic planning away from welfare considerations and in fact created a number of negative social results.[28]

First, as a consequence of the successful military campaigns the government revised national objectives and decided to build Japan as an internationally strong power equal to the leading nations of the West such as Britain, the USA, France and Germany. The new goals were more ambitious than the previous objective of building an independent nation safe from foreign invasion. The economic objectives for fulfilling the revised aim were rewritten as three specific goals: (a) to build a strong army; (b) to own colonial territories; and (c) to build and develop heavy industries for defence purposes.[29] Government policy-makers saw the international status of the leading Western powers as stemming from the possession of those three factors: Japan must therefore acquire them as quickly as possible. In the coup of 1881, the liberal thinking of the early Meiji government had already been replaced by more aggressive nationalist ambitions. Industrial planning began to be based more on international political considerations than on domestic economic needs, with the result that policy diverged increasingly from the *keisei–saimin* wealth-for-welfare policy.

The increase in the factory labour force was explosive in the early Meiji period. Industrial (non-farming) labour increased from 61 000 in 1882 to 294 000 in 1892, and it doubled again by 1905.[30] The new labourers came mostly from villages where their low levels of subsistence drove them to emigrate to fast-growing urban areas. In addition, over 400 000 households of lower-ranking ex-samurais – two million people, all told – were reported to have been turned into wage earners in the transformation of feudal to modern society.[31] Workers in privately owned factories worked under primitive conditions, with long hours and meagre pay. There appeared to be limitless supplies of cheap labour; yet, as Dorothy Orchard wrote in 1929, 'labour in Japan has neither been very abundant nor very cheap for industrial purposes.'[32] Many workers lacked adequate mechanical and other relevant skills, and the poor working conditions and low pay resulted in a high rate of turnover. Acute labour shortages emerged as soon as the transformation to an industrial economy began. Employers competed fiercely with each other, but by methods other than offering high wages, and there was some forceful suppression of labour movements. There were frequent disputes at mining sites in the first years after the Restoration.

Organized labour protests began around 1890 and spread rapidly in textile mills. Industrial disputes reached a peak of 43 in 1898 when 6300 protesters were involved.[33] The government's first reaction to these problems was to introduce the Public Order and Police Law of 1900, which empowered the police to suppress disputes by force. That reduced the number of disputes, helped no doubt by the primitive state of the workers' consciousness and organization.

The government also decided to give workers in private factories some public protection; but that took much longer. It was in developing the first factory legislation that, for the first time, government officials began to view welfare as a separate issue from industrial development. Preoccupied with 'modernization and enlightenment', bureaucrats forgot their traditional ways of managing economic and welfare matters and imported foreign approaches instead. 'Welfare' thus came to mean, in Western technical terms, such things as limiting working hours and the use of child and female labour. Such policies came to be conceived as aspects of modernization and industrialization. 'Welfare' did not mean rescuing the victims of the economic system; it meant getting the economic system to serve all its members satisfactorily, by operating (where necessary) in an enlightened, paternalist way.

This early attempt may be examined by looking at the 1911 Kojo-ho (Factory Act), the first legislation to protect labour in private industry.[34] Although it was enacted in 1911 and proclaimed in 1916, the government had understood the need for some sort of labour legislation as early as 1883, when an investigation documented appalling working conditions in textile factories and their workers' dormitories. The 1911 Act, the result of close observation of existing legislation in Western nations, established a minimum age of 12 for child labour, limited working hours to 12 per day, outlawed night labour for women and children under 16, and established guidelines for workers' accident compensation. It had taken a quarter of a century for the government's good intentions to take effect: every year from 1895 the proposed law was blocked by Diet spokesmen for the textile industry. Public outrage at the conditions in textile mills eventually brought about enactment of the 1911 Act, but it suffered not only from such a long delay but also from a myriad of compromises and loopholes.[35] The result was a mutilated and ineffectual law which lasted until 1923, when it was marginally strengthened. It was eventually replaced by the more effective Labour Standards Law of 1947.[36]

The more humanitarian and traditional philosophy of Meiji Japan is best seen in the efforts of Fukuzawa Yukichi, whose greatly misunderstood 1896 proposal in the area of labour legislation illustrates the rift between the traditional Japanese and imported Western approaches to labour relations.

Fukuzawa opposed the introduction of the labour legislation at that stage of Japanese industrial development. He argued that (i) the Act would reduce the working hours of labourers, limit their employment opportunities and reduce their earning capacities, and (ii) it was inappropriate

Western legislation which did not take note of specific customs and practices traditionally followed in Japan. Fukuzawa wanted the Act rewritten to build on the best potentialities of indigenous Japanese employer–employee relations and working conditions: the traditional benevolent and affectionate (*onjo*) relationship between landlords and tenant farmers should be the model for the new industrial relations, to provide pay and working conditions more appropriate to Japan's traditional culture as well as her stage of industrialization.[37]

The intent of Fukuzawa's approach was mistaken by most government officials as a conservative reaction against national 'modernization'. Business leaders and employers twisted it to their advantage and argued that the introduction of such legislation was 'too early' for the textile industry. Given the infant stage of the industry's development, critics argued, the law would reduce its cost competitiveness in the export market. Fukuzawa died in 1901.

Despite the eventual enactment of the Factory Act in 1916, the working conditions in factories continued to deteriorate as the industrial sector expanded. An acute shortage of workers, in the cotton-spinning and silk mills in particular, promoted the increasing misuse of what competent workers there were. Night work and generally poor working conditions fostered tuberculosis and other diseases in factories and company dormitories. Workers, mostly young females from villages, were unable to turn the labour shortage into a bargaining advantage due to a lack of organization and the inhibitions and traditions of an older Japan.

Although the beginnings of modern social welfare came with the start of modern government in the Meiji period, the fundamental assumptions about the government's responsibility for its citizens' well-being hardly changed from their traditional basis until the development of the ideals of the Taisho democracy in the 1920s.

We may look at the Meiji bureaucrats' resort to labour law as a naive and ineffective attempt to imitate the advanced West; but, equally, we must note what the workers were demanding at the time. T. C. Smith observes that workers from the 1890s to the 1920s demanded roughly what the bureaucrats tried to give them, 'improved treatment' and 'higher status' rather than higher pay.[38] Nevertheless, the approach to social welfare by way of a factory act remained little more than a token effort at civilization and englightenment.

4 In Search of a Home-grown Social Policy, 1917–1937

1917–1923

In this period we see an intensive welfare effort, springing from different motives in the public and private sectors. Four decades of industrialization and urban growth since the Restoration had brought about steady economic expansion, and changes in productive, administrative and managerial techniques and organizational structures which pointed to a promising future. The progress was substantial but irregular, not equal or evenly spread across all fields of endeavour. Conflicts of interest and tension developed between employers and employees, between large enterprises and subcontractors, and between industrial and village sectors. The problems of the 'dual economy' emerged as a serious social and economic concern. The bureaucrats' monopoly of intellectual leadership provoked protests and debates, and those who had been denied a fair share of the benefits of industrialisation stepped forward to voice their protests.

In this period we will examine (i) how a campaign for greater social justice came to be mounted by the public, (ii) the development of public policy for both social purposes and industrial growth, and (iii) the influence of culture on the making of economic policy.

The data are more reliable and comprehensive for the period after the First World War. The national censuses of 1920 and 1930 record the occupational distribution of the population.[39] National Wealth surveys were organized in 1913, 1917, 1919 and 1924 (twice), and there were various other surveys of the effects of industrialization.[40] The inquisitive mind of the government not only reflects its pride in estimating the raw extent of the progress of modernization, but gives important insight into the thinking of the so-called 'Taisho democracy' in the 1920s.[41]

Between 1914 and 1930 the population grew from 51 to 64 million (an increase of more than 25 per cent), and gross national income increased twofold in real terms. A faster growth occurred in the first part of the period (before 1924), with increases in export activities and a sharp increase in government investment in infrastructure, industrial equipment and defence.[42] The effects of this on the various social and economic classes of Japan are difficult to assess. In general terms, however, we can say that workers' real income appears to have grown by between 50 and 60 per cent from 1914 to 1929. For the peasants, real income growth may have been much more modest.[43]

The First World War created enormous opportunities for industrial expansion. Demand over the period 1914–20 is comparable with that of the Korean war of the 1950s in its effect on expansion and structural changes in industry. Production in heavy industries, such as iron and steel, cement, chemical fertilisers, ship-building and engineering, rose significantly. The government supported and encouraged further expansion of these sectors through the introduction of favourable regulations and tax laws. The number of steel mills, for example, rose from 21 in 1913 to 208 in 1918, raising national self-sufficiency in iron and steel to 47 per cent and 73 per cent respectively over the five-year period.[44]

In the 1920s Japanese industry was still dominated by light industries – small factories and cottage industries. But the expansion of the light and heavy industries together marked the beginning of a new stage of industrialization. It brought about a sudden and massive increase in the number of factory workers. Between 1914 and 1921 the number of workers in manufacturing factories increased from 948 000 to 1 636 000 (an increase of 70 per cent), with expansion in mining (from 272 000 to 330 000), in government factories (from 41 000 to 54 000), and in transport industries (from 115 000 to 185 000). The factory growth gave Japan, in a relatively short space of time, a large and mainly permanent 'working class' population. The proportion of workers in large plants increased: those in factories of more than 5 000 hands were 22.7 per cent of the total factory workers in 1914 and 30.1 per cent by 1921.[45]

As their numbers and concentration grew, workers began to identify themselves as belonging to a particular social class, and to organize labour unions to protect and represent their interests against employers. Although still technically illegal, the number of labour unions increased from 40 in 1911 to 107 in 1918, to 187 in 1919 and to 273 in 1920. Official records also estimate that the number of industrial disputes increased from 50 in 1914 to 497 in 1919 (involving 63 137 workers), 333 in 1924 and 495 in 1926.[46] A series of civil disturbances, housewives' 'rice riots' and tenants' disputes developed within the same context of rising social discontent. Between the liberal mood of the Taisho democracy on the one hand, and the increasing commitment of the nation to militaristic aggression in neighbouring Asia on the other, the government response was by no means uniform, and was complicated by a heavy reliance on the German Historical School in inventing a policy of social regulation and control. German social welfare models were imported to the Japanese government through academics who persuaded officials that the government's role was to legitimize industrialization by public action to reduce its social costs and conflicts.

The making of public policy for social purposes in this period is best understood in two stages. From 1917, buoyant postwar economic conditions coincided with the politically and socially liberal mood of the Taisho democracy. This happy period ended abruptly in 1923 with the Great Earthquake.[47] The years from 1924 to 1932 are known as the time of the Showa recession, the later part of which coincided with the World Depression of the 1930s. In this climate of severe depression, social policy continued to grope its way toward an indigenous Japanese formula.

A common interpretation of the period is that 40 or 50 years of persistent national effort to industrialize and modernize Japan had yielded its results. The productive capacity of a supposedly 'backward' people had risen, and been matched with democracy and peace in the 'Taisho' period. The growth of the labour movement, the citizens' protests and the introduction of public regulations for the protection of people's rights, even to a limited extent, are proof of the tolerance and genuine liberalism of the period.

The short duration of Taisho liberalism – a decade between 1914 and 1923 – is often explained by mentioning Japan's authoritarian heritage. The liberal trend was checked when, under the parliamentary constitution, the plutocratic alliance of *zaibatsu* monopolistic capital and the political parties coincided with the hardship of depression, and the nation's growing and successful military involvement in the Asian mainland.[48]

There are conflicting views and interpretations of the emergence of liberal trends in this period. What was desired, demanded and attempted, and what was actually achieved? The whole picture of the observed liberal attempts of the period troubles us for the following reasons. First, we have noted the short duration of the liberal trend between 1914 and 1923. Second, the liberal phase was ended suddenly by an earthquake, and not by accumulating economic and political forces. Third, only a few of the public policies and activities created in this period survived the following years to form the basis of the subsequent social policy. Many welfare policies introduced since 1945 cannot trace their origin to this Taisho period.

What actually happened in the years between 1917 and 1923? In the area of labour, the newly emergent working class gained some improvement in living standards through their own efforts and the industrial development of the period. The gains were modest but they were clear enough to show the population that the organization of labour unions, the pressure of industrial disputes and even citizens' riots could bring positive rewards. Statistics show that (a) the index of real wages of factory workers increased from 100 in its base year in 1900 to 121 in 1914 and 169 in 1921. Over the same period labour hours were shortened from 12–13 hours per day in 1900 to 11 hours in 1914 to less than 10.5 hours in 1921. In 1921 workers were provided with an individual bed in a factory dormitory, rather than day and night shift workers sharing beds, as in previous years.[49]

Employers were opposed to government intervention as well as labour aggression: they thought that government initiatives to regulate conditions in the workplace were unnecessary. Regardless of whether intervention was motivated by a desire for industrial peace or by more enlightened social goals, business leaders, particularly in textile industries, feared the loss of autonomy and the reduction of cost competitiveness in the expanding export market. But industrial disputes and strikes were frequent enough to prompt employers to a careful study of exactly what it was that labour was demanding, and what was required for an effective relationship between management and labour. The fear of unions and government intervention and the need to reduce labour turnover and industrial stoppages spurred management to greater efforts to control the workforce. A cost-effective employment system had to be found urgently; and a range of issues, such as the employers' responsibility to provide training, education, work clothes and tools, had to be resolved. In addition, the state of the working environment, the length and distribution of working hours, communication between managers and workers in office and factory, payment systems and an appropriate rewards structure emerged as issues demanding some resolution as industrialization accelerated in the boom that followed the First

World War. Neither government legislation and regulations formulated on imported Western models nor police intervention appeared to offer useful answers. Traditional employment systems as practised in villages were unworkable without some modification for the new industrial conditions. So rapidly did industrial modernization change the nature of work in Japan that by 1920 traditional 'benevolent' models for workplace practices and relations had become anachronistic. Nevertheless, it was from that indigenous tradition rather than from Western models that the employers developed their own solution to the problem.[50]

By the late 1920s the intensified efforts of management in heavy industries and the larger textile mills had developed a package of workable principles that would later be developed into a corporate welfare and management system specific to Japan. The system aimed to provide workers with greater job security, semi-annual bonuses, separation pay, regular rises, factory committees and internal training systems. Smith observes[51] that, by 1907 at the latest, some managers were aware of the seriousness of the labour problem; during the next decade the larger companies began to meet the demands of workers; and by 1930 the union movement had lost its aggression and its influence had begun to fade fast in the larger enterprises.

The Government's record through the same years presents a conflicting and puzzling picture, both through enacted and proposed legislation. Among researchers, a lack of information has fuelled conflicting interpretations. Many see a liberal leaning in the Taisho government, which introduced legislation on industry, farming and education as well as putting into operation the Labour Act of 1911. Economic historians with a Marxist viewpoint see in the Japan of the 1920s the beginnings of a government role as the legitimizer of industrialization. One of these researchers, Miwa, cites this period as the beginning of a modern capitalist economy in Japan.[52]

We see neither view as acceptable. To put forward our view, we have to go back to the creation of the previously mentioned Labour Act of 1911. According to Iida,[53] the Act was written following closely the recommendations of a report presented by the Japan Social Policy Association (Shakaiseisaku Gakkai)[54] – the only academic study association in the field of social policy in Japan.

The association consisted of distinguished and influential university professors whose opinions and guidance were most frequently sought and adopted in the policy-making offices of government. What did the association stand for and what were the basic government philosophies in the making of social policy? Iida sees the basic direction of the association's ideology in its Inaugurating Regulation in 1899 in the following terms:

The Association believes the members should support the development of industries in Japan by way of amicable development and cooperation between government efforts and those of individual citizens so as to produce the maximum possible prosperity for the nation. In order to bring such cooperation,

Government regulations and legislation should be written in the spirit of enhancing the national aims and goals of the time. Individual benefit should be subordinate to the national task given the economic and cultural development stage of the country.[55]

The association continued to have a strong influence on the thinking of government bureaucrats in the making of industrial and social policies, until its sudden dissolution in 1924. Its manifesto, above, suggests neither Western liberalism – with government arbitrating the industrial disputes which are natural to *laissez-faire* capitalism – nor a Marxist picture of government as a single-minded servant of monopoly capital. Instead, it suggests that government should act (i) to subordinate all group interests to the pursuit of national wealth and growth, and (ii) to induce active co-operation between all concerned, for those national purposes. That is a distinctly Japanese concept of the economic role of government, but it was far from clear how such a role should be enacted in the conditions of 1917–24. The government lacked an understanding of the adverse effects of rapid industrialization on the life and welfare of the population. This is why we observe many conflicting and inconsistent motives behind the series of social policies introduced in this period.

The search for social security eventually followed an industry-led pattern. Employment systems characterized by paternalism and benevolence had been developed by Muto Sanji of the Kanegafuchi Cotton Textile Mills at the beginning of the 1920s, and they were widely practised in public plants as soon as their effectiveness had been demonstrated in the private sector.

It was in the farming sector, however, that a public policy recognizing both industrial and social conditions had first become apparent. During the First World War and the immediate postwar boom, the economy experienced a sharp inflationary trend. The rise in prices stimulated industrial activity but the effects on the farming sector were negative. The sector suffered a fall in real income, and when the postwar boom receded towards the end of 1920, the prices of rice and silk, two major sources of income for peasants, collapsed. The silk valorization scheme and the Rice Control Act had proved ineffectual in arresting the decline. In parallel with industrial disputes and labour strikes, tenants' disputes and other forms of unrest increased dramatically in villages as early as 1917, becoming a serious concern to the government.[56] The annual production of rice in the later 1920s was only slightly above the prewar average, and the economic status of the peasantry failed to improve substantially during the period when that of the urban population was increasing very fast. As a result, Japan was forced to rely to a growing extent on the import of rice from Korea and Formosa to supply her rising population.[57]

The government's response to these troubles was not to side with landlords, tenants or consumers in their conflicts. Instead, it used public aid to make private agriculture more efficient, so that the productive system itself could provide for the welfare of those concerned. Special banks were established by the government to provide cheaper capital to farms.[58] There was public action to increase the area of cultivable land from 1919 onwards, and a relatively large portion of the budget was allocated to public works such as improvements in irrigation facilities and the improvement of arable land. Research and education programmes continued to improve the productivity of rice crops and silk rearing. Thus, to rescue farmers from the hardship caused by deteriorating incomes, the government selected investment policies which would increase agricultural productivity, rather than income transfers.

Investment in public works and economic infrastructure emerged in this period as the government's main economic approach to welfare. In principle, the public investment should be directed to increasing production in specific industries and sectors which have flow-on effects, either furthering welfare directly, or increasing the productivity of other sectors. Economic growth through public capital formation was thus selected as the main form of social policy.[59] The formula was only experimental in this period and had its early trial in the farming sector. During the World Depression of the 1930s we will see that the experiment was extended to more of the economy, so that growth via public capital formation become the key economic strategy in Japan. This observation is important when we discuss the distributional and welfare aspects of economic growth. The Japanese experience should not be taken simply as a case in which growth is pursued without equity or welfare considerations, although there were lapses in Japan's record in the 1940s, and practical shortcomings at other times. The development of an integrated industrial and social policy is best seen in a study of the activities of the Ministry of Agriculture and Commerce (MAC) in the latter part of the 1920s.

1924–1937

Despite the opportunities that the First World War brought to the industrial sector, approximately half of the national income was still derived from farming and farm-related activities. To promote industrialization, particularly heavy industry, imports of machines, new materials and energy resources increased considerably. They were financed almost exclusively from exports of silk, tea, food-processing activities and the cotton textile industry. This trade placed a great strain on farming and other indigenous traditional industries. Government policy began to cause various skewed and unbalanced patterns in the development of the economy. In the heavy industries designated by the government, modern technology was actively introduced in the production, employment and management fields. In light industries, however, which carried the burden of earning foreign currencies, traditional technology and employment systems still dominated, and cheap labour, long hours and poor working conditions remained the norm. Critics accused the cotton textile industry, for example, of 'social dumping' in the export markets. The economic phenomenon generally described in Japan as a 'dual structure' or 'differential structure'[60] became a characteristic feature of the economy as a whole.[61]

With the development of the 'dual structure', the welfare benefits of Japan's industrialization were distributed with increasing inequality.

Statistically, the 'dual structure' in manufacturing began to emerge about 1909 in the form of wage differences between smaller enterprises and larger concerns employing 500 or more workers. The gap widened slowly for some years, and then increased dramatically between the First World War, and the Pacific War.[62]

Nations which move rapidly from a traditional base into modern economic growth tend to develop such differentials – a reflection of the difficulties in mustering technical and economic knowledge, patterns of entrepreneurship, and an ability to accumulate capital. Rapid economic development must lead to some degree of dualism between the capital-intensive, knowledge-intensive modern sector with high productivity, and the traditional labour-intensive sector with low productivity. What is specific to Japan is that the government itself was responsible for developing the duality of the economy. Furthermore, we suspect that the government also took advantage of some of the features of the dual economy it had created. This is certainly the case in the period between the wars.

Compared with the rapid economic expansion and the general optimism of the first postwar years, the years from 1924 to 1932 saw slow growth with severe economic, financial and political difficulties. Foremost among these problems was the economic damage caused by the Great Earthquake. The loss was estimated as equal to one-third of one year's national product, almost two years' gross capital formation, and about one-tenth of the value of the reproducible tangible assets of the nation.[63] The depressed state of the economy may be indicated statistically. From 1920 to the mid–1930s, despite an increase in the area of arable land, agricultural output increased at less than 1 per cent per annum. Investment activity declined considerably in both the industrial and farming sectors, with the result that gross domestic capital formation fell, dragging with it the net stock of fixed capital to a level below that of 1913. The labour force suffered a reduction of more than 10 per cent in the agricultural sector, while the non-agricultural sector recorded a mere 1.7 per cent increase. At the same time the population increased by almost 1.1 per cent annually, the highest rate since the Restoration. These figures suggest that the increase in productivity virtually came to a standstill. The deterioration of economic welfare from these causes worsened conditions for a population that was still coming to terms with the uneven process of industrialization.[64]

Why did the recession persist for so long? To be precise, the postwar Japanese recession began in the spring of 1920 and lasted throughout the

1920s until the World Depression of the 1930s accelerated it further. The government had little idea of what it should do. In search of the causes of the recession, bureaucrats and academics tried several theoretical postulations. Was Japan experiencing an 'overproduction crisis' because of the war boom in the years 1916–23? Was she suffering from excessive (and destructive) competition caused by the sudden and explosive growth in the numbers of banks and corporations in the second enterprise boom of 1919? Was Japan entering the stage of monopoly capitalism as the marxian hypothesis predicts? Was the 'dual structure of the economy' (which at this stage was conceived as the gap in productivity between large-scale *zaibatsu* and other modern corporations and the smaller enterprises with traditional labour-intensive production methods) causing problems specific to the Japanese economy?

The government had no answers to these questions. No policies systematically addressing the problems and hardships of the period were ever formulated. What the government did in the period was nothing but a collection of temporary relief and subsidy measures and devices on an *ad hoc* basis. However, as is seen in the financial relief policy for the Great Earthquake, in which the government provided special credit to banks and trading companies, government assistance clearly saw its direction as favouring large *zaibatsu* companies.[65] This amounted, in effect, to a large subsidy to big business which left smaller firms and farmers to their own devices to avoid bankruptcy. After the earthquake crisis the government continued its established policy of inducing industrialization primarily by assisting large enterprises in heavy industries. However, the failure to revitalize the economy caused leading bureaucrats, particularly those in Shoko-sho (the Ministry of Commerce and Industry – MCI), to pay some attention to the rest of the economy, to smaller firms in traditional light industries such as textiles and food-processing. Johnson reports his observations of the efforts of the MCI and the introduction of two new laws in 1925, the Exporters Association Law and the Major Export Industries Association Law (EAL and MEIA), which encouraged the export activities of the textile and food-processing industries.[66] The MCI observed that: (i) despite the government understanding that the modern *zaibatsu* enterprises were strategically important to Japan's industrialization, it was a fact that medium and smaller factories (employing less than 500 workers) employed the overwhelming majority of the nation's industrial workers; (ii) exports were generated almost exclusively by those medium to small factories, while the *zaibatsu* firms produced primarily for the domestic market (to be more specific, 50–65 per cent of Japan's total exports came from medium and smaller manufacturers of products such as bicycles, pottery, enamelware, canned goods, hats, silk and textiles, and the remaining exports – rayon, silk yarns and cotton textiles – were also from light industries); (iii) most of those export activities barely covered their production costs, or made losses.[67]

The MCI's observations became more pronounced through the later 1920s and the early 1930s as smaller to medium size enterprises continued to increase in importance in terms of the 'number in employment',[68] and their 'contributory share of exports – exports which inadequately covered total costs'.

Why were these small exporters forced to export at below cost price? The MCI saw that there were too many small firms operating on the basis of an overabundance of cheap labour – labour forced to work for subsistence wages – and with inadequate means of distribution and marketing. The large *zaibatsu* trading companies exploited the medium- and small-scale manufacturing exporting firms in two ways through their export and import marketing activities: (1) they imported raw materials from overseas and supplied them to small and medium sized manufacturers at high prices, using their monopoly advantages; and (2) they took the consignments of finished products from those (small and medium sized) manufacturers at low prices, using their monopsonist advantages. This mechanism resulted in small export manufacturers actually earning very small net amounts of foreign exchange, while affording their workers an extremely low standard of living.[69]

How was this observation interpreted by policy-makers in the MCI? What we do know is that the government, particularly the MCI officers, thought it essential and urgent to reform the marketing structure. The exploitation of small exporting manufacturers by monopolist *zaibatsu* trading companies needed attention, because the practice was clearly hindering the national economy from earning the amount of foreign currency that it needed for further industrial growth. The two 1925 laws noted above were drafted by the MCI with the main aim of eliminating the cut-throat competition among smaller manufacturers: competition which was leading them to (a) form associations which accepted members' export products on consignment for sale to *zaibatsu* trading companies and (b) impose central control of quantities, qualities and prices of products for export. In addition to the introduction of the laws, the MCI officials sought effective policy measures for increasing the cost competitiveness of exports without unduly exploiting cheap labour in the smaller export manufacturing factories.[70] They saw a special need to build an adequate industrial structure to achieve economies of scale, and they believed that the introduction of new technologies was necessary for any increase in productivity. Their efforts culminated in the drafting of the Juyosangyo Tosei-ho (Important Industries Control Law – IICL) of 1931.

Whether the attempts of the MCI in formulating these three laws – the EAL, the MEIA and the IICL – actually resulted in an increase in economic productivity and an improvement in the welfare of the population cannot be assessed accurately at this stage. The important point, however, lies in our observation of these early government efforts to arrive at policy measures, whether they be public corporations, laws or regulations, which would advance growth, equity and welfare simultaneously, as in the measures designed to rescue farmers from financial difficulties after the First World War.

To summarize we may reiterate a few important points. The long economic recession after the First World War led policy-makers to build modern forms of government intervention on the basis of their traditional '*keisei–saimin*' ideals, in which economic growth is pursued as a means of advancing the welfare of the population. The early attempts of the government and its 'enlightened paternalism' proved to be unworkable. Welfare measures up to and including the Taisho period were not integrated into the general process of industrial growth, and at the same time ignored traditional Japanese solutions which could have supplied better social policies in the period of fast modernization. Employers were ahead of the government in giving birth to a 'corporate welfare' system in the 1920s. Such an approach in business led the government to build new forms of state intervention in the late 1920s. They were forms which were different in critical ways from both the German and the other Western examples which had previously served as models to the Japanese.

At this stage we need only notice two general characteristics of the new approach. First, Tokugawa thinking on political economy, crystallized as '*keisei–saimin*', the compound of '*keisei*' (ordering the social world) and '*saimin*' (saving the people), emerged clearly in the building of new forms of state economic intervention. Integral to this philosophy was the notion that economic and industrial development would simultaneously promote the welfare of the population. Because of this, public policy for economic and industrial development cannot be taken as simply policy for the 'GNP machine', as Johnson suggests – as action comparable with the tariff policies, export promotion devices and industrial development subsidies of the West. Our earlier observation, that the Japanese always tend to translate their national aims into economic objectives, is consistent with this observation of the integral approach to 'growth, equity and welfare'.

Second, the early attempts of the government and the prototype industrial policy of the 1920s were not free from contradictions and inconsistencies in purpose and consequence. In search of effective means of promoting 'efficiency–equity–welfare' objectives, many economic measures were tried – and they were not all successful. Even those which were successful did little for people not directly involved in production, or for people with no access to 'corporate welfare' who needed protection against retirement, health hazards, urban congestion and poor housing. In the transition from a pre-industrial stage to modernism in the 1920s and early 1930s, the concept of citizens' economic rights was not clearly recognized among the population.[71] The government did eventually come to accept that it had a responsibility to provide all the citizens with basic security, but that acceptance was slow. In the 1930s the hardships of the World Depression and the subsequent national preoccupation with war severely restricted the search for a public policy that could effectively balance or integrate rapid industrialization with social concerns. The government came to formulate industrial policy forgetting that social improvement was the very purpose of the exercise, and moved away from the traditional '*keisei–saimin*' approach. The resulting policies were generally less efficient, as the next chapter will seek to show.

5 Economic Conduct of the Pacific War, 1937–1945

1 Organization of the *Senji Keizai* (Wartime Economy)

To the Japanese, the Pacific War[1] was literally a 'total war', and all efforts – government, industry and household – were directed to winning it. Taking the war with China as the starting point of the new aggression, the war effort lasted for a full eight years from July 1937 to August 1945, during which time Japan poured all her strength into military activities and, in so doing, destroyed a great part of what she had built during the preceding period of modern economic growth. During these wars the government increased military spending and strengthened its control over the economy, the labour movement and civilian life, while further developing strategic industries, especially heavy industry. The industrial structure of the country was distorted to accommodate a swollen military production sector. Production of commodities for civilian consumption was gradually curtailed so as to transfer all resources to the support of the armed services and to the production of war goods. By 1943 the production of consumer goods, beyond the bare necessities of life, had come to a halt.

GNP began to shrink as soon as the aggression expanded into the Pacific in 1942. The consumption of war materials continued to rise, and as a result defeat came to the nation's economy long before the national surrender.

Both wars were fought with considerable disregard for economic logic and, as a result, national bankruptcy was only to be expected. The best workers and the most dedicated managers were conscripted, usually for less skilled tasks in the front line; so were the best materials, as industrial engines and transport locomotives were left to run on oil pressed out of pine roots.

Those times were in many ways devoid of economic rationality and common sense. This seems to have led some economists in Japan to ignore the wartime economic experience as not worthy of their analytical efforts. Some others gravely doubt the reliability of the very limited sources of information that are available for the period, and have decided to omit the war years from discussion altogether. This has resulted in a tendency to treat the modern development of the Japanese economy as distinct 'prewar' and 'postwar' histories, to be studied independently of each other.[2] In contrast to this, there are others who treat the prewar and postwar years continuously, as if little change took place in the economic system between 1937 and 1945.[3] Minami, for example, takes the view that the postwar growth which continued up to the late 1960s can be explained partly as an extension of the accelerating trend of the prewar period.[4] He sees the growth rates of investment and productivity in the 1950s as carry-overs from the acceleration of the prewar years, and sees in the year 1960 the turning point when the economy embarked on a new period of postwar development.

Some of these arguments can be interpreted to imply that the very fast economic growth from 1955 to 1972 was driven wholly or predominantly by newly emerged factors peculiar to the postwar economy, factors which can be understood independently of the prewar experiences of the economy. It is true that a quick glance at economic performance – growth rates of investment and their public and private components, returns to capital, savings ratios, productivity growth rates, and economic growth in general – consistently indicates that the postwar period provides the economy with higher performance than the prewar years, by a wide margin. And it is true that many distinct facts and features differentiated the postwar from the prewar economy. Yet it is our strong belief that neither of the above approaches is acceptable. The war economy and the development of economic controls should be studied in the context of the long economic history of the country. The Japanese economy was already a quasi-wartime economy in 1936. In 1940 there appeared to be no settlement in the war with China, and Japan concluded the Tripartite Alliance with Germany and Italy in September of that year, only to encounter the US imposition of an embargo on scrap iron and machine tool exports to Japan. A subsequent shift into a fully controlled wartime economy was unavoidable. Towards the end of the year the 'New Economic Order' was introduced into the national economy, whereby production was to come first in order to pour all of the nation's economic strength into the inevitable war against the US. Government officials had important functions throughout the war, in formulating and then administering public control measures to concentrate all possible economic capacity on to the military priorities. Many important elements of Japan's industrial development after 1945 arose from the organization and leadership experience of the wartime bureaucracy.

The aims of this chapter are twofold: first, to identify the above-mentioned elements; and, second, to argue that they did not *originate* in the abnormal conditions of national expansion and war, although they developed strongly in those conditions. They were not temporary phenomena which were transformed when the economy returned to normal peacetime conditions. We will explore the elements of national purpose and policy which were present before the war, were further developed by the wartime experience of the bureaucracy, and survived to propel the high-speed growth of the 1950s and 1960s, and then the decelerated course of the 1970s and 1980s. We will acknowledge a debt to some researchers who see the origin of many public policy measures in the set of economic administrative measures developed in wartime. Finally, we will try to understand how and why it was that the wartime experience had such significant effects on the postwar achievements – and what may be learned from it about the enduring character and driving force of the Japanese economy in peace as well as at war.

2   From the Marco Polo Bridge Incident in September 1937 to August 1945

The Japan–Manchuria–China Trade Block

In 1937 Japan established a trade block,[5] originally involving Manchuria (China's three northeastern provinces) and subsequently Northern China (five northern provinces).[6] The aim of this was to counter the trade restrictions enforced by Britain, which had imposed its own imperial tariff in 1932 in order to check – among other things – the rapidly expanding exports of Japanese-manufactured products into British colonies in Asia. Under a strong military influence, the South Manchurian Railway Company was used to spearhead Japan's interests by penetrating and expanding into Manchuria, and further into neighbouring areas of China, so that its holdings and operation were spread over wide areas of the colony. Public transport facilities became the target of such military ambition, as did mining, agriculture and the general administration of the areas near the Manchurian railways.[7]

The Control Law of May 1937 stipulated that industries in Manchuria be integrated into Japan's five-year programme of national mobilization. Direct investment in Manchuria by Japan was promoted by establishing one Japanese-affiliated company in every major industry. Manchurian industry, and indeed the Manchurian economy as a whole, came to be dominated by Japanese capital.[8]

The outbreak of Japan's war with China in July 1937 further hastened the building of the railway empire. Many of the Japanese-affiliated companies, which numbered over 80, were combined with Nissan (*zaibatsu*) to form the Manchuria Heavy Industry Company (Manchuria Jukogyo Kaihatsu

Kaisha). This company expanded until it became a leading industrial force in Manchukuo in 1943. In return for the considerable government assistance given to it, the company secured supplies of coal, iron ore and industrial salt for heavy industrial activities back home in Japan.

The Kokusaku Kaisha (Government Policy Company)

In addition to the Manchuria Heavy Industry Company, the army's ever growing desire to strengthen the economic supply base for defence purposes prompted further large-scale development of mining and other resource industries in Manchuria and China.[9] A programme to build a series of companies called the Kokusaku Kaisha (Government Policy Company) was established in 1938, with capital from the established Mitsui and Mitsubishi *zaibatsu* groups.

The Government Policy Company comprised partly government-owned enterprises, most of which were for offshore operations. The very first of these was established as early as 1895, immediately after the Sino-Japanese war. The main aim of this first Government Policy Company was the rapid industrialization of the occupied territories. However, it was not until the depression of the 1930s that many such companies emerged. Most of them were established by legislation, so that government authorities could retain final approval in the selection and appointment of management. Their activities were mostly in the fields of transport, the generation and transmission of electricity, natural resource development and coal and petroleum supply facilities. After the Second World War they were either dissolved or, if they were located inside Japan, transformed into government-chartered companies (*tokushu gaisha*) – a type of public corporation – such as Japan Air Lines and Kokusai Denshin Denwa (KDD).[10]

Nanshin-Ron (the Southern Expansion Doctrine)

Japan's military expansion into South-East Asia and the Pacific Islands led her to establish semi-colonial territories in South-East Asia following the so-called 'Nanshin Southern Expansion Doctrine'.[11] Although in fact the army and the navy came to fight bitterly over the exact direction of military operations, the doctrine called generally for the extension of Japanese interests in South-East Asia and the Pacific, and saw the US as the potential enemy.[12] It held that the whole of South-East Asia was destined to come within Japan's sphere of influence. In July 1940 it was incorporated into the larger plan to establish a *Dai Toa Kyoeiken* (Greater East Asia co-prosperity Sphere), the aim of which was to promote the idea of a politically and economically integrated Asia, free of Western domination. The basis of the doctrine lay in the government's belief that expansion into South-

East Asia would have greater potential value for Japan's industrial development than expansion in any other direction (north into Russia, Korea or China, for example). This was precisely because, according to the doctrine, the South-East was *economically less developed and culturally backward* because it had escaped Western influence; therefore the benefit of Japanese guidance would be greatest.[13]

Before the doctrine could be adopted, it provoked the USA, which decided in 1941 to ban the export of fuel, oil and other war materials to Japan. Thus, the doctrine remained a doctrine without ever becoming the foundation of an economic empire.

Kokka Sodoin Ho (the National General Mobilization Law)

At home, in order to develop heavy industrial production for military purposes, a programme of industrial rationalization was considered. It followed the German school in seeking to improve efficiency in industries designated as important for national purposes, by means of government-sponsored cartel agreements and public controls of economic resources. Competition and market mechanisms had to be replaced by co-operative public–private planning. Individual profit-seeking motives were reinforced or replaced by stronger national motives for achieving lower production costs, and the National General Mobilization Law of 1937 was introduced.

An earlier law in 1931 had brought the volume of production of selected industries under voluntary control by representatives of the firms concerned. The 1937 law replaced those representatives by bureaucrats, and provided the government with the overall legal authority for deploying both manpower and material resources for the highest and most efficient development of the total power of the state in time of war.[14] Public planning replaced the market mechanism in determining the allocation of national economic resources. Public decision-making replaced private decision-making wherever the government thought necessary; in civilian organization, labour, industry, consumer sovereignty, price-setting, contractual obligations, the news media, and even economic activities within private households.

Wartime attempts at economic expansion did not bring about the planned expansion. However, the composition of manufacturing industry was changed as planned, with heavy industry expanding to replace textiles and food-processing. Economies of scale were promoted: large enterprises and factories with modern technology replaced many smaller operations which relied on traditional techniques and skills. Wartime government control succeeded in restructuring industry but not in increasing the total output of the economy.[15] To expand the total output, further ingenious measures were required to enable the government to expel not only the 'market mechanism' but also 'entrepreneurs' from the economy.

The State-planned Economy

Industrial production began to fall from 1940. There was a sharp decline in the production of foodstuffs, textiles, paper and pulp, and chemicals, which were not war products themselves, but were essential to the war effort in one way or another. The shortage of such inputs was a serious hindrance to the production of arms, ammunition, aircraft and warships. There were shortages of raw materials, such as coal, iron ore and fuel oil, due to the disruption of transport from North China. There were labour and skill shortages as national conscription exhausted the supply of manpower, and many production targets were not met.[16]

What were the reasons for such a failure? Government leaders were inclined to seek the basic reason somewhere in the working mechanisms of the capitalist economic system in Japan, as it had developed since the Meiji era. To them, the public planning of all production activities, by way of public ownership of resources, appeared to be the only sensible alternative. To extend the National General Mobilization Law, the Ministry of Commerce and Industry came up with a formula to create 'true' public corporations: 'true' in the sense that they were to be formed with capital subscribed by the government and a board of directors appointed by a ministry. The *eidanren* (meaning 'management foundation') was created as a bureaucratic device to bring a selected part of economic activity under direct, official control.[17]

The *eidanren* public corporations were expected to maximize production and minimize costs, with rates of profit and dividend determined in accord with the national aims of the time.

Munition Companies Law (Gunji Kaisha Ho) and Ministry of Munitions

Additional efforts were made by the army to separate public management from private business ownership by the introduction of the Munitions Companies Law in November 1943.[18] The law authorized government to 'conscript' the top managers of selected companies and factories, and transform them into public servants under the title of 'munitions supervisors'. Their appointed task was to supervise all of the industrial activities of the selected companies and factories, to ensure that the production rules for achieving targets were strictly followed. In all, 600 companies and factories were placed under such supervision.[19]

As far as the state challenge to the basic foundation of the capitalist system is concerned, this law proved to be less important than the introduction of the *eidanren* public corporation. The Munitions Company Law marked the last serious effort by the government at state control of the economy. The new Ministry of Munitions absorbed and integrated some of the functions of the Planning Board and the Ministry of Commerce and Industry (MCI), which until then had direct responsibility for the war economy and the production of munitions. The remaining functions of the MCI – which were principally civilian – were merged with the Ministry of Agriculture. Thus the Noshomu-sho (Ministry of Agriculture and Industry), the predecessor of the postwar Ministry of International Trade and Industry (MITI), was formed.

3 In Search of a State-led Economic System

Two features of the public management of the war economy, although related, should be distinguished from one another.[20] One is the specific activity of the 'economic bureaucrats' in organizing war production, and the other is the more general attempt to find an alternative economic system to market-oriented capitalism. It has been suggested that wartime needs were the origin of various public service structures and administrative methods, which were further developed to form the basis of postwar industrial policy.[21] Our aim in this section is not to discover those links between wartime and postwar performance; that will be done in later chapters. Here we are concerned with earlier continuities. Deliberate, directive industrial policy was not born of the economic crises of depression and war: it has earlier origins and a longer history. The purpose of this section is to recall enough of that history to show that the pressures of war accelerated, rather than initiated, Japanese efforts to build effective forms of state direction of the economy.

In the development of economic control, Ando stresses the special importance of (i) the establishment of the Shigen Kyoku (Resource Bureau) in May 1927 and (ii) a series of economic policies formulated in the 1926–31 period for economic rationalization (the reduction of production costs) and industry protection from import competition.[22] The Resource Bureau was established to collect and collate all necessary information concerning the nation's productive resources – human, natural, mineral and energy resources – on a most comprehensive basis, so that such information could readily be mobilized when the time came to plan the total national economic activity for a particular purpose.

Under the Shigen Chosa Ho (Resources Investigation Law) of 1929, all factories and enterprises, both public and private, were requested to report to the Bureau on their productive and financial capacities. The Bureau inspected factories and mines to determine their resource potential and, by 1931, it was ready to provide the government with comprehensive and up-to-date information on which it could base 'plans for the controlled operation' of enterprises and industries. Through the process of the survey, the officers of the Bureau had accumulated considerable knowledge and expertise in assessing the productive capacity of the national economy as a whole, and in planning for its expansion. Many of them took an active part in planning the war economy later, in the army, navy and business sectors.[23]

However, those economic policies were not introduced as a preliminary to war, or even with expected wartime uses in mind. They were introduced to remedy the economic hardships of the Depression, and they subsequently proved to be adaptable to wartime purposes. In the development of public controls for two distinctly different purposes and circumstances, we will now study how and why the Japanese came to build their specific form of state intervention.

We noticed in chapter 3 that under the leadership of Takahashi Korekiyo, the government believed that the key to economic recovery from the Depression would be found in providing business with markets of adequate size. Before the Keynesian revolution, the Takahashi spending policy was an attempt to provide markets to industries on a national macroeconomic scale.

A general trading policy to restrict imports while increasing exports through government subsidies, as well as the promotion of a yen-based trade block in the South-East Asian market, were pursued. For industrial development there were two basic policy components: the so-called *sangyo gorika*, an industrial rationalization policy, and *sangyo tosei*, an industrial control policy.

The first component (industrial rationalization policy) was, in essence, aimed at cutting the costs of industrial production. In practice, how this was pursued changed from time to time. Public efforts at cost-cutting were not applied on an individual enterprise basis, but through broad state policies. However, there was some intrusion into the detailed financial and operational activities of factories and enterprises, as the bureaucrats informed themselves about the business and considered the best means of intervention.

They expected that after they had investigated the operations of individual factories and enterprises, they would find a general formula to guide all enterprises to achieve the desired cost reductions, so that both industry and the nation as a whole would benefit from the exercise. Depending on the economic and social circumstances of the time, the public formula might involve new technical know-how, up-to-date equipment, quality control, new management techniques, or public action to improve the economic and social environment of business generally.

At times this might require public investment in infrastructure facilities; at other times it might involve the restructuring of distribution and market structures through, for example, laws against restrictive practices or, by contrast, encouragement of inter-firm co-operation. In the 1930s the cost-cutting was mostly directed at the workers. In the face of a contracting market and a considerable reduction in the size of operations, few enterprises could afford much in the way of technological modernization and re-equipment. Enterprises were not able to find capital funds for new investment and, more importantly, could not be persuaded by government to risk new investment. Therefore, workers – particularly those in export industries such as textiles and food-processing – were expected to work longer hours in order to cut costs and thus increase access to export markets outside the depressed home market. [24]

The second component (industrial structure policy) shared the same national aim of reducing production costs. In good times it encouraged enterprises to grow or amalgamate to achieve economies of scale. In the Depression, when the market was shrinking, the only way to achieve economies of scale was to control the total output of each industry. Therefore the government organized and administered control agreements for various selected industries. The agreements were designed to utilize idle capacity, with minimum profit to member companies, in order to secure their continuous operation in the industries concerned.

When the economy recovered from its depressed state, and was transformed into a wartime economy in which production could be expanded to the maximum, the industrial policy measures of the 1930s had to be revised. The government had to find a policy formula to satisfy two not always consistent aims at the same time. The national benefit was still seen to be achieved through an increase in total output (GNP). However, in wartime what the nation needed most urgently was a sudden and considerable expansion in the productive capacity of war industries, and therefore also in the other sectors which contributed to the planned increase in war industries. Allocation of resources had to be planned so as to obtain maximum output with the desired proportions of military and other goods. The whole of the nation's economic power had to be mobilized to maximize its military power. The government therefore had to estimate the optimum proportions of agriculture, mining, manufacturing and services for that purpose. It had to control the ratios between light and heavy industries, labour-intensive smaller operations, and capital- and knowledge-intensive enterprises, large established *zaibatsu* firms and others in order to achieve the maximum output of the optimum proportions of war products.

To this end the industrial structure was forcibly distorted into a swollen military production sector and a reduced subsistence sector, at the cost of lower living standards for the working people of the country. It was a strategy in which conflicts between economic interest groups were expected to raise bitter controversy. The task of 'integrating' conflicting activities, interests and motivations emerged clearly as the central function of government. At the heart or this 'integration' was the promotion of systems of production which could respond most efficiently to the needs of government. Instead of the productive 'efficiency' of individual firms and economic organizations, 'effectiveness' in mobilizing every sector of the nation – business, workforce and household – emerged to claim priority in contributing to the appointed national goal of maximum production of war products. For government to carry out its function during the war (1937–45) the supply of coordinators for tasks of integration became its most crucial service. Government offices (economic bureaux) emerged as the most important 'public goods'.

Following the establishment of the Resource Bureau, as noted above, various public organizations were created, restructured and developed in order to house increased numbers of economic officials and administrators. An elite body called Naikaku Chosa Kyoku (Cabinet Research Bureau – CRB) was established in 1935, with bureaucrats detached on temporary duty from the main industries. By merging with the Resource Bureau, the CRB was later developed into the yet larger and more prestigious Kikakuin (Cabinet Planning Board – CPB) which became known as Keizai Sanbo Honbu (Economic General Staff).

The CRB immediately attracted many able and ambitious economic bureaucrats. Many came from colonial offices in Manchuria, with experience in public economic control.[25] There was a sudden and rapid increase in the influence of economic bureaucrats in the decision-making network of government. Unfortunately, no comprehensive study is available of the characteristics of the 'new bureaucrats' or their relationship with the rise of the postwar economic bureaucrats (*kancho* economists).[26]

The rise of economic bureaucrats resulted from the government's needs and also from their own self-promotion campaign. They were not a homogeneous group of people with common characteristics: Rather, they were people with varying ideological beliefs, professional training and experience. Indeed, their success in gaining an influential role in government can be traced to this complex and varied background. However, they all shared a strong belief in the national need to strengthen public economic control, and this was the common element binding them all. Through this they rose to the top in government, and put their shared beliefs into practice. Therefore, it is important to clarify the basis of their beliefs, and the ways in which they proposed to promote the strengthening of public economic control.

4   Showa Kenkyukai (Showa Study Group)

During the Depression, serious doubts emerged in government circles about the relevance of economic policies and other public activities. The doubts grew into a general mistrust of market-oriented capitalism as an economic system, the seeds of which lay in the failure of the world economy to recover from the Depression.

The hardship experienced by the West during the Depression was widely reported in Japan in order to discredit the effectiveness of economic management in most of the industrialized economies of Europe and the USA, on which Japan's efforts at industrialization had been modelled. To many public policy-makers it was rather a shock to learn that these model economies were suffering from the hardship of the Depression more seriously and for longer periods than Japan.

In contrast to the poor performance of the West, some viewed the performance of the Soviet leadership in formulating the first five-year economic Plan in the midst of world Depression as a remarkable success, since it appeared to prove the superiority of public planning over market mechanisms. Even the performance of Fascist Italy in the 1920s and Nazi Germany in the 1930s seemed to support an extension of state control. Such a general distrust of *laissez-faire* capitalism found solid theoretical support among Marxist-oriented academic and intellectual thinkers.

Having experimented with closely guided public control of the economy in Manchuria, many public servants who had worked closely with the army in the colony now argued confidently that Japan was ready for a publicly controlled economic system in the homeland. The tide turned in Japan from 'following the West' to an alternative economic system of a state-controlled capitalist economy.

During the general upheaval of anti-*laissez-faire* sentiments there developed a political study group called the Showa Kenkyukai (Showa Research Association), which was originally founded in 1933.[27] It expanded its membership and its influence in government, until its eventual disbandment in November 1940. Its influence continued in varying forms in organizations which took differing directions, from proposals of state control to national support of the war. The original vision of the association was as an informal organization, the major intent of which was to reassess Japan's constitutional policies in the light of the demise of party-political government, which began in 1932. It soon became the permanent and most influential adviser to the Prime Minister on general policies and administrative strategies for the war. In 1938 the press dubbed it the 'Prime Minister's brains trust'. At its peak, membership swelled to 3000, including almost all senior economic bureaucrats and leading academics, and many important business leaders, politicians and journalists.[28] Each year the association undertook research for the government. Specialists with different backgrounds were invited to form study groups. At one time, for example, 130 different participants formed ten major task forces covering issues such as foreign affairs, politics, culture and education. The most notable results came from the research on implementing a state-planned economy.[29] This task force urged the importance of 'co-operation' among all members of the economy – farmers, industrialists, miners, workers and households – under government guidance. Thus the philosophical framework for mobilizing national support and a commitment to a national goal was a deliberate blend of socialist, liberal and fascist ideas. The proposal was made in order to organize the war economy, but it drew on earlier studies and practices, and it was projected to provide the foundation of the national economic system beyond the immediate requirements of the war. The concept of Ritschl's[30] communal/state economy appeared as the basis of industrial policy in the postwar years.

Thus the idea and practice of state control of the economy did not originate in wartime, or purely in preparation for war. Many writers have observed that control of the economy under the Kokka Sodoin Ho (National General Mobilization Law) found little justification on economic grounds.[31] Government control expanded into the wider sphere of society because of the strong interest of government officials, most of all the influential economic bureaucrats, in promoting and strengthening control of the national economy.

6 Reconstruction, 1946–1955

On 15 August 1945, the Second World War in the Pacific finally ended, and within two weeks, on 30 August, the occupation of Japan by the Allied Forces began. The humiliating experience of the occupation distinctly marked in Japanese minds the 'beginning of her modern era' (*gendai*). It was viewed as an era which was more than just a postwar period: it was a new epoch, different in nature from the preceding 70 or so years of modernization, Westernization and industrialization (*kindai*) since the Meiji Restoration in 1868. The occupation lasted for six years, until shortly after the signing of the San Francisco Peace Treaty in September 1951.

In this chapter we discuss the first decade of Japan's postwar economic history. It was a period without war, a period in which – for the first time since the Meiji Restoration – Japan made its industrial development efforts without either actually being involved in or preparing for military aggression. We see this decade as the period of 'postwar reconstruction', during which the economy made a new start and progressed from its devastated condition in 1945 to the beginning of the so-called 'miracle' which took it through the high-speed growth of the 1960s to the point in the 1980s when Japan succeeded in surpassing the West in industrial and living standards. Economic growth continued steadily through the immediate postwar years to the high-speed growth of the 1960s, as if to suggest that the economy followed a smooth continuous upward trend. Based on this, Nakamura, for example, suggests that the economy had taken off on its high-speed era as early as 1955.[1]

However, as will be shown below, the driving forces and economic and social environment in which the national efforts at growth took place changed considerably through the years after 1945. Government control, both American and Japanese, was pervasive in effecting a drastic transformation in the economic system through the early years. After 1947 the American influence diminished, and after 1955 the direct industrial influence of Government receded quickly as economic recovery progressed.

Section 1 covers the economic conditions inherited by the postwar economy from prewar efforts at industrialization and wartime state control. Section 2 describes how various radical reforms were introduced from outside to change the basic sociopolitical and economic infrastructure of the country. During this period the government carefully evaluated the direction and the magnitude of economic reforms. Based on the evaluation of the early occupation policies, a set of new postwar industrial and macroeconomic policies were formulated. In section 3 the process of economic recovery with foreign aid and special procurement from the USA will be studied, together with the process that gave birth to the Economic White Paper of 1955. Throughout the period we observe the emergence of major policies which were implemented, and also major policy proposals which were not adopted or were abandoned in midstream. The non-adoption of some policies was as important as the adoption of others, and had substantial effects on future events. We will sketch out the characteristics of government intervention and its contribution in leading the economy towards a high-speed growth path.

1   Making a New Start

As K. Hara observed:

> Economic losses resulting from World War II were approximately five times greater than those incurred during World War I, even if only direct military expenditure is considered. ... War casualties, including civilians, are estimated to have claimed 56 million victims ... [To look at this differently] it has been said that the number of lives taken during World War I exceeded the number of people killed in the entire one-thousand-year history of warfare up to that time. Yet the victims of World War II were seven times those of World War I.[2]

What was Japan's share of these horrific statistics? Official estimates put the number of those killed as a direct result of enemy action during the 1937–45 period at 1.7 million military personnel and 289 000 civilians. Total casualties, including the indirect results of war, were estimated at 2.7 million. The overall impact of war on the Japanese population was that there were 2.3 million fewer males and 534 000 fewer females in 1950 than would have been expected given the demographic structure in 1940.[3]

Of course, the destruction was not limited to loss of human life. The ratio of war losses to total national wealth in 1944 was as high as 35 per cent.

Even subtracting losses of military equipment, the rate still stood at over 25 per cent, a figure almost equal to the entire gross national product in 1946. This is why, at the time, many thought that it would take more than ten years to make up the losses, even if the economic recovery were achieved smoothly following a normal course of reconstruction.[4]

The general state of the economy at the end of the war cannot be sufficientiy expressed by statistics alone.[5] Four general facts must be taken into account:

Economic infrastructure.   As a result of directing all its attention to the war effort, the government neglected forestation projects for flood control and the repair and maintenance of water control facilities. Therefore the country suffered massive floods in 1946. Forests were stripped for timber without any effort at reforestation. The total acreage under cultivation also dropped, and the agricultural land in continuing use suffered a great decline in productivity due to over-use and neglect of fertility.

Loss of empire.   Manchuria, China and South-East Asia left the Japanese Empire, thus reducing it to about half the size that it was at its peak. These lost territories left a legacy of six million demobilized soldiers and repatriated civilians, who returned to Japan to swell the ranks of the unemployed by 4 million, joining 8–9 million already out of work due to the physical destruction and the closing of the defence industries.

Cessation of trade.   The loss of the empire also resulted in the abrupt cessation of trade with areas which had been in Japan's former sphere of influence, thus denying her supplies of raw materials, food and energy resources.

Railways and hydro-electric facilities.   These facilities survived the war more or less intact, but they were by no means sufficient to meet the sudden and rapid increase in demand placed on them during the postwar recovery of economic activity.

Although the Occupation Authority pursued the line of 'indirect rule', its directions were in effect direct orders and no opposition from within Japan was possible. In addition, the Occupation Authority enforced a rigid system of internal censorship, so that the Japanese government was not free either to seek news from abroad or to appeal directly to public opinion for support of its own initiatives.

In the name of democracy, various important reforms were introduced into all spheres of the social, political and economic structure of Japan.[6] Freedom of speech, rights to health and welfare and freedom from discrimination according to race, creed, sex and social status were only a few of the principles proclaimed at the time. Then there was the famous peace provision, under which Japan renounced warfare and armaments forever. The American education system was rapidly introduced, and many private schools, colleges and universities were founded in order to replace the traditional style of 'thinking nation first' with more 'individualistic' ways.

However, not all of the reforms were effectively implemented. They went through in a series of fits and starts due to American ignorance of the frame of mind of the people and the structure of Japanese society. In order to understand this, the occupation period may be subdivided into five main sections according to the changing direction of reform and economic recovery:

1   *August to end of 1945.* Various manoeuvres were made to form a co-operative alliance between the USA and Japan.
2   *Beginning of 1946 to beginning of 1947.* Social and economic reforms were passed by the Allied Forces under heavy American pressure. On the national economic scene, crisis, confusion and extreme hardship were experienced in every sector and every field.
3   *1947 to early 1950.* The direction of American policy-makers began to shift, although still pressing for reforms in some areas. In 1947, the drive to both democratize and weaken Japan came into sharp conflict when the Cold War led the USA to new perceptions of Russian power, the Chinese revolution and new movements in Asia. The American emphasis switched to rebuilding the Japanese economy and some signs of recovery began to emerge.
4   *1950 to mid–1952.* Discussions focusing most sharply upon Japan's future security requirements took place between Allied Headquarters in Tokyo and Washington.
5   *Mid–1950 to 1956.* American policy continued to shift, and the outbreak of the Korean War helped Japan to achieve further economic recovery and move towards her prewar level of independence. By 1951, various economic indices stressed that industrial production had recovered.[7]

In order to promote democracy in industry, labour and agriculture, the main reforms were: (i) economic decentralization in the modern industrial and banking sectors, with the dissolution of the *zaibatsu*, the huge financial combines: (ii) the establishment of a viable labour movement; and (iii) reform of agriculture with the introduction of the Land Reform Law. New tax laws and business and labour codes were also introduced.

Generally speaking, the economic reforms intended by the Allied GHQ were more radical than the social and political changes. First, they involved the very concept of property rights and, second, they were introduced to weaken Japan's economic capacity as a potential military power and to shape Japan into being forever a 'second-rate nation'. The idea was to create a new economic system with a democratic, competitive nature, and widely diffused ownership, and through the first years of the occupation it was coupled with the idea that Japan should remain a relatively undeveloped country, with agriculture and small local industries. There was to be no revival of heavy industry.

Leaving the detailed discussion of these reforms to previous studies,[8] the nature of these reforms may be summarized as follows:

1 Various pieces of 'trust-busting' legislation were passed, and *zaibatsu* family members were banned from employment in their firms. Their holding companies were broken up, so that ownership was widely dispersed, and the size of firms in Japan in general was reduced to decrease their market share. Instead of oligopolistic forms, competitive markets were introduced in all industries in the economy.

2 The new Labour Union Act, modelled upon the US Wagner Act, was introduced to give workers in Japan the right to form unions, bargain collectively, set minimum pay rates and establish arbitration procedures.

3 A land reform act abolished absentee ownership of farmland and turned most tenant farmers into owners, to minimize conflict and distress in the villages.

4 Educational reforms were introduced to guarantee academic freedom, although not at first the freedom to teach children nationalistic or undemocratic principles. Compulsory education was extended from six to nine years, and was modelled on the American pattern of general education in pursuit of what the Occupation Authority hoped would be a more pacifistic and generally pro-American government and society.

Whatever their merits in later years, these reforms were seen at the time as nothing but a hindrance to economic recovery. It is no exaggeration to say that at this time 80 million Japanese people were driven to feel extreme pessimism for their future. The official repatriation policy, the Pauley Report, was drafted early in 1945. Its aim was to inflict punishment on Japan, and it recommended the removal from Japan of more than 1000 existing sets of plant and equipment which had managed to survive air raids. Another report, from the Brookings Institute, recommended that the standard of living allowed to the Japanese people should be that of 1930. News of these reports produced a great fear and pessimism among the people. They perceived the Occupation Authority carrying out sweeping changes without any compassion for the Japanese people, to punish them and to destroy the industrial capacity which their national efforts had built up over the past 80 years.[9]

Within government, there were some corresponding crises of spirit. The forced retirement of much of the business elite, the loss of property rights by the *zaibatsu* and the rural landowners, and the effective default of government bonds through the postwar hyper-inflation shook the very foundation of the nation's capitalism. In the confusion of the immediate postwar years, the government was tempted to wash its hands of such developments. Economic planners had an opportunity to contemplate alignment with a popular ideal of the time: to reverse course 180 degrees and re-direct the planning devices, rationale and organization which they had built up over the past long period of industrial growth, to establish in Japan a frugal 'Switzerland of the Orient' or a 'nation of culture'.[10] Policy for growth was to be abandoned entirely.

However, a reorientation of American policy came suddenly in April 1947, as the Cold War led to new perceptions of Russian power, the Chinese revolution and other insurgent movements in Asia. The USA now helped Japan to regain her prewar economic position as the workshop of East Asia. Obsessed with Russia and communism, the USA desired a strong and prosperous Japan. American loans and credits poured into Japan and Japanese leaders were quick to exploit the situation.

2   First Steps to Postwar Reconstruction, 1945–1951

In August 1946, Keizai Antei Honbu (the Economic Stabilization Board) was established to formulate a national policy of economic reconstruction. The board had extensive and peremptory powers, which made it the most influential economic planning body in the history of the postwar economy.

The most serious bottleneck in the rehabilitation of manufacturing industry, and thus the economy as a whole, was the shortage of coal, the basic energy source at the time. Numerous plans were formulated, evaluated and implemented, until Professor Arisawa Hiromi's proposal, Keisha Seisan Hoshiki, (the Priority Production Concept),[11] was finally employed by the newly formed Stabilization Board. In essence, the concept sought to have the coal and steel industries nourish each other. Every effort of economic policy was to be directed at increasing coal production. Then the increased output of coal was to be directed to the steel industry to generate steel output which, in turn, would be thrown back into the coal industry to increase coal production, and so on. Shortages of coal at the initial stage of the proposed cycle would be made up by imported crude oil. As the production of coal gradually increased, coal supply to other basic industries such as chemical fertilisers, railways and other transportation services, could be expected to increase.

The allocation of resources was strictly controlled, and the coal and steel industries were given first priority. The Reconstruction Finance Bank[12] (later, the Industrial Bank of Japan)[13] was established for the specific purpose of channelling available funds to those two industries. The system began to bring about the expected result, and in 1947 the planned goal of 30 million tons of coal production was attained. The economic recovery appeared to have been initiated, but not without an unprecedented bout of inflation during which consumer prices increased by a factor of 40 by mid-1947.

The Economic Stabilization Board was strengthened in March 1947 by the transfer of all economic planning tasks to the board, with the backing of the relevant economic planning staff engaged in each ministry. [14] In addition, able economists in the academic and business fields were transferred to the board. Recognizing the severity of the general economic crisis, the board made a comprehensive study of the nation's economy, reviewing every important economic activity: food supply, distribution systems, wage and price determination mechanisms, money supply, detailed factors of production in various industries, working conditions and plans to improve them, potential export markets, and various proposals for improving the administrative structures of government ministries to ensure fast and effective economic recovery. In June 1947 the board announced a comprehensive national plan called the 'Emergency Economic Policy'.

This was followed a month later by the First Economic White Paper, subtitled, 'A Report on Actual Conditions in the Economy'. [15] It is also referred to as the 'Tsuru White Paper' named after its chief editor, Professor Tsuru Shigeto. Its purpose was to analyse accurately and comprehensively the exact economic situation that the nation was facing at the time. It aimed first, to present the theoretical basis of the Emergency Economic Policy and, second, to appeal to the people of Japan for their full understanding of the current problems and difficulties of the economy, and to request their whole-hearted co-operation for the sake of the very survival and recovery of the economy. The appeal was made in straightforward language, with the slogan 'Economy under a grave deficit – the finances of nation, business and household are all in the red', a slogan which was often quoted with nostalgia in later times of economic prosperity.

The scope of the paper was not restricted to industrial policy. It extended into wider areas of general economic activity. Its character is important because, in our view, it laid the foundation for the planning of the economy in postwar Japan, both in terms of macroeconomic and industrial (sectoral) planning. It set enduring trends in the following respects at least.

Economic Messages and the People

In the paper, the government took pains to establish an effective way of communicating with people in business, industry, households and trades unions. The Tsuru White Paper paved the way for such communications by presenting the population with three important economic messages: (i) 'facts and figures', which presented an overview of the actual economic situation and painted the picture of an ideal and desirable economy to be pursued; (ii) 'policy', which explained the measures and policies which government was to employ for the purpose of attaining that desirable form; and (iii) 'direction', which guided the private sector to concentrate their efforts in order to help the economy to transform itself into that ideal form. The Tsuru White Paper set the pattern from which Japan's unique style of indicative planning developed through the following four decades.

Policy Emphasis of the White Paper

Despite the social reforms enforced by the Occupation Authority to 'democratize and uproot the ultra-nationalism in Japan', one may already detect a nationalistic current in the basic thinking underlying the policy emphasis of the paper. This may sound strange: after all, in 1948 people were certainly opposed to the emergence of the centrally controlled economy from which they had just freed themselves. Nevertheless, the paper advocated active government involvement and the guidance of business and industry. Its ideology was not based on neoclassical or Keynesian ways of thinking but, rather, it advocated a government-led economy that reflected the actual situation of the time, of 'strong government and weak industry', which resulted from the *zaibatsu* dissolution and other postwar reforms discussed earlier. Some direct governmental guidance and assistance to industry was assumed to be desirable by both government and big business, as early as the publication of this paper in 1947.

Economic Issues: Planning

As Tsuru reiterated in 1964, the message from the government in the 1947 paper was clear: '... the task of adjustment which the defeated country was called upon to make was mainly economic in character'. Economic questions, in particular those directly concerned with production and productive efficiencies, became the number one issue, as against those related to civil welfare in general. This remained the general trend at least until 1970, when the new problem to be confronted was that of equity in the context of environmental pollution, consumer interests and the concentration of economic power among large firms. The planning of the society had in effect meant the planning of economic activities, and the non-economic aspects of national life had been neglected. We do not mean to say that this growth-oriented bias was caused by the Tsuru White Paper. What we note here is the importance of questions which arise out of that bias: To what extent was the distinctive character and power of growth-oriented economic planning in postwar Japan a function of the social system? To what extent was it influenced by the more temporary circumstance that the very first plan was conceived during a time when economic matters had an obvious, overriding urgency for the survival of the people and the nation? These questions will be discussed later in the light of the long-term continuities and changes in the process of industrialization.

Role and Status of Economists

Upon publication, the paper gave a larger role and a higher status to economists in Japan – particularly to economic bureaucrats in government offices – than had been the case in the prewar period. To many economists the problems of postwar Japan presented a challenge.[16] Between 1946 and 1949 consumer prices rose by over 1000 per cent, and in 1948 the price levels stood at about 200 times those of 1934–5. There were tasks of adjustment which the defeated nation had to attend to promptly. There was the need to absorb into the workforce 6 million repatriates returning from Manchuria and other countries which Japan had relinquished. There was the need to reorient the economic structure from one which depended on international trade to one of a more autarchic character. Besides these, there were, of course, the tasks of economic reform for democracy. As far as these are concerned, it is not difficult to see the urgency and magnitude of the tasks which economists were called upon to perform. Since that time economists have gained further influence within the bureaucracy, whereas previously an elite group of officials with legal training dominated. Academic economists began to gain a greater voice and a higher status through their involvement in formulating economic policy with the expanding Economic Stabilization Board.

Nevertheless, as we will see later, this did not bring about an 'academic takeover' of national policy-making. Economists who joined in government tended to be those willing to adopt the broad interventionist style of political economy that had been traditional in the government's direction of the economy, rather than the strictly theoretical, analytical discipline which prevailed in the universities. In prewar Japan, the profession of economics was roughly divided into two groups of equal size, those with Marxist training and those with neoclassical and Keynesian inclinations. The majority of the scholars in both groups tended to depend on derived authority recognized in the West. In interpreting the problems of their own economy, methods of analysis imported from abroad were followed submissively.[17] These economists were faced with a considerable challenge in 1947, when the Tsuru White Paper presented a clear picture of postwar economic problems and demanded a response from the economics profession. It is no exaggeration to say that the majority, well-versed in the formalities of Western Marxist or neoclassical theory, found themselves quite unable to understand the real-life situation and problems of the war-damaged nation, let alone offer their professional services effectively to the board and other policy advisers. However, they rapidly took up the challenge and soon began to produce their own study results, paying special attention to postwar reforms and the potential growth rate of the economy. The status and the standard of the economics profession in Japan rose hand-in-hand with an increase in expectations of the role of economic planning.

The Statistics Act

The Tsuru paper set the trend among economic ministries of issuing regular factual survey reports, and led to successful legislative enactment of the Statistics Act of 1947. As a result of the Act all statistical data produced by government agencies was gathered and reported to the Bureau of Statistics Standards for publication. This encouraged all spheres of economic research which, in turn, have been incorporated extensively into the planning of the nation's economy and industry.

The economic plans of the period 1945–50 were in fact little more than simple estimates of Japan's needs and capabilities. They included a very crude estimation of future trends in productivity, investment and supply from abroad. Nevertheless, it should be noted that the people at large received from those plans the strong message that Japan could hope to return to her prewar standard of living. In this way the plans helped to generate a positive, and even hopeful, outlook towards rehabilitation and industrialization, despite the rubble and ruin of the war. As the forerunners of a series of more detailed economic and industrial plans, these at first relatively crude efforts nevertheless had important 'demonstration effects', teaching people to expect useful economic information and leadership from the government.

The San Francisco Peace Treaty of September 1951 ended the occupation of Japan. The regaining of political independence coincided with the successful recovery of economic independence. Economic recovery in production and investment was considerably faster than planned, especially in the industrial and mining sectors, but levels of per capita national income and consumption lagged behind. These trends are illustrated in table 6.1.

The recovery was assisted in the first stage by special procurement income from the US Army, which enabled Japan to import foodstuffs and other necessities for people's daily lives as well as new material for Japan's industrial activities. The outbreak of the Korean War in January 1950 and the ensuing war boom further helped the Japanese economy to recover from war damage. Many progressive firms, of various sizes and strengths, emerged which were quick to take up opportunities. The war boom gave a further push to their entrepreneurship. The struggle and painstaking efforts by such firms as Toyota Motors[18] displayed the dynamic entrepreneurial spirit of Japanese industry at that time. Rapid economic reconstruction began in many sectors of manufacturing industry, as much of the available investment capital concentrated on increasing the supply of raw materials

Table 6.1 *Level of economic activity: planned and actual levels as at the end of 1951 (1933–6 level = 100)*

	A Planned	B Actual	B/A
Production			
industrial and mining	87	131	151
farming	n.a.	100	n.a.
Imports	29	49	169
Exports	24	36	150
Per capita national income	n.a.	93	n.a.
Per capita consumption	86	86	99.5

n.a. indicates 'not available'.
Source: EPA, *Shiryo Keizai Hakusho* (1972, pp. 10–11).

so as to fully employ plant and equipment which had survived the Second World War. By the mid-1950s productive facilities had depreciated, and were grossly outdated by international standards. Modernization of industry became essential, and the problem of increased capital requirements became acute.

3 Development as a 'Semi-industrialized' Economy, 1951–1955

On 25 June, 1950 war broke out in Korea. Uchino states that 'the economic boom resulting from the Korean War was the largest and the most important in Japan's postwar economic history'.[19] As noted above, economic expansion during the war boom was promoted principally through concentrating investment capital on increased supplies of materials. The productivity of plant which had survived the war was raised to the maximum by extending working hours and overtime and, in the case of larger firms, increasing the use of subcontractors and temporary workers. As the boom continued, such makeshift measures proved to be inadequate, but the boom also brought high profit margins, and many companies began to draw up plans to undertake new investment for expansion with lifetime employees. This change in the private sector demanded a shift in government guidance from 'direct control' to 'assistance'.

Until 1950 the main state activity consisted of allocating materials and other production resources to state-designated industries such as coal and steel. Thereby the price mechanism was ignored. In the Korean War boom, entrepreneurial activities began to emerge. The separation of ownership from management brought about by the *zaibatsu* dissolution and other occupation reforms initiated a 'managerial revolution' in which skilful managers and ambitious enterprises were able to seek opportunities with a new freedom.

The First Rationalization Plan of 1950–1 was drafted for the purpose of upgrading production techniques and capacity. It was clear that, after the conclusion of the Korean War, new policies would have to be developed if Japan was to achieve complete economic independence without US aid. The government saw a need to promote several export industries. Modernization and rationalization were essential to promote cost competitiveness in the international market. To achieve this, the economic planners had to deal with the grave problem of promoting capital accumulation in a poor, capital-starved economy.

The steel and coal industries were chosen as target industries to attract special attention and assistance from the government.[20] The logic of the choice of these two industries was the same as that of the preceding 'priority concept' in the immediate postwar years: by giving them privileged access to resources the government would contrive the expansion of these two and some other strategic industries, and their growth would both allow and stimulate an eventual expansion in the production of all industry and in the national economy as a whole. In the same logical manner, the government tried again for rationalization in those same coal and steel industries in order to effect a reduction in the production costs of the domestic economy as a whole so that it could become competitive internationally. This time, the aim of the policy was to achieve growth in export industries, and not a simple growth in the size of the national economy. The policies adopted were mainly: tax exemptions from exports, of up to 50 per cent of a firm's export income; a special depreciation system for investment in rationalization; and considerable tax deductions on royalty payments for imported technology. Additional policies were designed to mobilize the government's own capital to promote capital accumulation via the Japan Development Bank, the Export–Import Bank and other banks established by the government.

These policies did not work as smoothly as planned. However, the essential pattern of the strategy which led the economy's rapid growth from 1955 onwards can be traced back to them, so we will briefly comment on them. First of all, given the significance of the role assigned to the steel and coal industries, the government saw it as essential and urgent to solve the problem of high prices. To reduce the price of steel to international levels, it was thought necessary to reduce the price of coal in the domestic market by half. A Coal Shaft Development Plan was introduced to achieve structural modernization by closing inefficient mines and exploiting new coal sources. In addition, the import of advanced mining technology from Germany was encouraged, mainly by tax exemptions. The measures failed because of the poor quality of Japan's coal deposits. The coal-mining industry was never able to reduce costs sufficiently to become internationally competitive; but the misjudgement was soon outdated by the emergence of oil to replace coal in the global energy revolution, following the discovery of large new oil reserves in the Middle East in this period.

In contrast to the coal industry, the steel industry was able to achieve considerable structural modernization, as planned. The original three-year rationalization plan was extended into a five-year plan, in which new technology in the hot rolled steel sector progressed at unprecedented speed. Output rose and costs fell with the introduction of automation and high-speed operations. By the end of the five-year plan the industry is reported to have increased its production capacity by as much as 100 per cent.[21] The production costs of major producers were reduced by as much as 15–20 per cent in the period 1950–5, although several years were to pass before the industry became fully competitive internationally.[22]

Government assistance to the industry was not confined to tax measures. It included improvements in the economic infrastructure of the steel industry. Uchino reports how the Keiyo (Tokyo–Chiba) industrial belt was built by the Government.[23] This was a public works programme, the result of which was a huge industrial park in Chiba Prefecture on land reclaimed from Tokyo Bay. Kawasaki steel, a new entry to the industry, received 3 million square metres of this land, including a modern harbour built by the government, enabling them to open the most modern integrated steel facility in the world at the time, and to build one continuous production line from dockside delivery of raw materials to blast furnace to steel production to rolling. Moreover, three of the established steel producers – Yawata and Fuji (now merged to become Nippon Steel) and Nihon Kokan (NKK) – were encouraged to launch modernization projects of their own to initiate fierce competition in the industry.

Other industries, such as synthetic fibre manufacturing and textiles, chemical fertilizers and ship-building, many of them new to the economy, were soon added to the government's list of 'target industries'. They were to gain public assistance and encouragement as they demonstrated aggressive expansion into the export market.

Nominal private investment rose by nearly 10 per cent during the first half of the 1950s. This is in contrast to a 20 per cent increase in the second half of the 1950s, which was only to be further outperformed in the period 1965–70. Sales and profit levels of the Matsushita Electrical Industry, for example, were reported to have increased as much as 13 times in the years 1954–63. Similar performances were reported by Sony, Sanyo and other electrical goods manufacturing firms, as well as by the Toyota and Nissan Motor Companies.[24]

Behind this spectacular growth, there had been fierce competition for market shares. Market concentration ratios declined in almost every industry, and the ranking of firms by turnover and profit changed frequently in many target industries through the 1950s.[25] The term *kato-kyoso* ('excessive competition') was coined during this period:[26] the policy makers in MITI saw this excessive competition as 'highly undesirable' and feared that it would cause many of the target industries to operate below optimal scale, thus rendering them internationally uncompetitive. Despite this fear, investment competition in plant and equipment and new entries into MITI's target industries continued vigorously.

The ineffectiveness of government policy in the coal industry was overshadowed by overall success in other sectors of industry which, as explained above, were added to the target list. Political credit was attributed to the government, particularly to MITI as the ministry in charge of the plan. The remarkable growth in plant and equipment investment and the consequent increase in productivity and cost reduction in the designated industries led outsiders such as McRae to suggest the Japan Inc. concept as a way of capturing the spirit of the successful industrial policy pursued.[27] The Japan Inc. concept should be applied, if at all, to this specific period of postwar reconstruction, before the economy returned to more normal conditions in the mid-1950s.

In the years 1951–5 the economy had emerged from immediate postwar confusion and hardship. The recovery process was helped by the Korean War. Uchino's observation of the war boom as '...the largest and the most important in Japan's postwar economic history' is correct, but it means that through those years Japanese growth depended considerably on the US special procurement demand in Korea. In this abnormal situation economic activities in Japan took a peculiar form in order to gain maximum benefit from the war activity. The government was therefore concerned to redirect the economy in directions which could sustain continuing growth after the end of the war and the special demands that it created. Economic policy, particularly that promoted under the Rationalization Plan, was designed almost exclusively to find effective ways of channelling windfall revenue from the war boom into industrial investment, to reduce the production costs of designated companies and industries. From 1951–5, policy was geared to the control and guidance of industry at the micro industrial and corporate level. On the macro level, the government was preoccupied with the problem of balancing import and export activities, given the newly established exchange level of $1 to ¥360 in April 1949. In the minds of economic bureaucrats the macro balance of payments problem was to be solved by micro policies, on the basis of their awareness of the 'international backwardness' of Japanese industry as a whole. Thus the most urgent state initiative was to improve the cost competitiveness of industries and industrial companies, and thereby help them become export industries and companies. As T. Nawa says, 'the reasoning behind this initiative was the desire to discover what it is that the best individual enterprises are already doing to produce the greatest benefits for the least cost, and then, in the interest of the nation as a whole, to cause all the enterprises of an industry to adopt these preferred procedures and techniques.'[28]

The interest of the nation as a whole in this period was conceived to be economic independence of US aid and US special procurement spending.

The 'Japan Inc.' concept captures the role of state policy at the micro level; that is, state leadership exercised in the detailed operations of individual enterprises and the other associated public measures intended to improve these operations.

Despite such efforts, a large balance of payments deficit forced the government to take emergency steps to dampen domestic demand. The results were a sharp decrease in inventory investment, then in plant and equipment investment, and then in productivity in such key industries as steel and machinery. The Industrial Rationalization Plan needed to be reconstructed and integrated with other industrial policy measures and with macroeconomic policies. A new mix of public economic measures was sought, in order to respond swiftly and effectively to the changing needs of the economy.

The government's Industrial Rationalization Plan and the responding investment boom in industry, together with the effects of the *zaibatsu* dissolution, created considerable changes in inter-firm trade relations. The networks of supply of production materials, and processing and distribution of products at each production stage, developed new patterns, quite distinct from the established channels and structures of the prewar *zaibatsu* networks. In the 1953–4 slump, bankruptcies threatened many firms, including some large ones. As shown by the labour dispute at Nissan, which was one of the longest and most militant strikes in postwar history, we should not forget that many labour problems stemmed from large-scale rationalization programmes.[29] Efforts at industrial rationalization did not remain at the level of cost minimization exercises inside individual firms, but developed further into cut-throat competition between firms, leading to restructuring of the industries involved. Rationalization of industry as a whole was considered, and an effective industrial structure policy was needed. After eight years of direct state control in wartime plus another decade of government intervention in postwar reconstruction Japan's economy in the mid-1950s stood at a crossroads, looking for a 'market-conforming' formula for state intervention for a new phase of growth in new conditions.

7 High-speed Economic Growth, 1956–1972

Early in 1956, a leading literary critic, Nakano Yoshio, called on the population of Japan to free themselves from the binding and standard-setting influence of the occupation experience, using the famous catchphrase 'the immediate postwar period is over'. The prewar levels of economic activity had long been regained. Real GNP and GNP per capita had regained their prewar levels by 1951 and 1955 respectively, and industrial investment and output had made even larger and faster gains. Following Nakano's initiative, the 1956 Economic White Paper announced that 'It is no longer postwar',[1] which also became a catchphrase, indicating that the special conditions of the postwar period no longer applied. The economy had fully recovered, and future economic growth had to be achieved by modernizing and transforming it.

With this public manifesto for the future, the year 1956 marked the beginning of two extraordinary decades, which witnessed a rise in real national product of more than 530 per cent, or an average of nearly 10 per cent per annum, and the consequent shift in Japan's position in the world economy.[2] Whatever the quality of the White Paper's economic analysis, it succeeded in delivering a message to people's minds that a new phase of economic development had replaced the previous philosophy of recovery to prewar levels. In the White Paper the economic planners declared their belief that Japan should discard her fatalistic view of herself as an over-populated poor country without resources or accumulated capital.

Foreigners also began to discard that view. From September 1962, when *The Economist* in London published a special issue entitled 'Consider Japan' which praised Japan's high-speed economic growth, we may trace how images of Japanese society and economy changed in the titles of various publications. In another special issue of *The Economist* in 1967, entitled 'The Rising Sun' many of the articles read like success stories.[3] These were carried further by H. Kahn in 1970 and E. Vogel in 1979, then in 1982 by Johnson's 'MITI and the Japanese Miracle'.[4]

In these publications the words 'miracle', 'success', 'super' and 'high performance' were most generously used to praise the economic performance of this industrial latecomer. But was the Japanese performance worthy of such praise? We are hesitant to accept this view without first reviewing the policies of economic management that were actually adopted in the period, and then setting the national effort into the long historical perspective of industrial development since the Meiji Restoration. The second task is deferred to the closing chapters of this book, after the developments of two further decades have been considered. In this present chapter we will review the major policies which were proposed but rejected, those that were adopted but later abandoned, and those that were implemented as planned, through the period of very fast growth.

The influence of economic policy and the various forms of government participation in economic activity should be neither exaggerated nor underestimated.[5] This is important because, despite the many studies that have been undertaken to analyse the period, there is still confusion and disagreement as to how to evaluate the contribution of the public sector to the economic performance. The problem stems not so much from any lack of reliable information but, rather, from the difficulty in interpreting correctly the extent to which public policy contributed to achieving the observed result without being overly mesmerised by statistical figures of high performance. In this chapter our major attention is directed towards the Shotoku Baizo Keikaku (the National Income-doubling Plan) of 1960 (table 7.1). The chapter has three sections: the first is a study of the economic performance of the period; the second covers economic policy and other public influences on the economy as a whole; and public-sector activities are studied in the third section.

1 The Measure of Growth

In 1955, where we locate the starting point of high-speed economic growth, the economy celebrated its success for the first time in balancing export and import activities without relying on revenue from US special procurements programmes. It could thus be said that the aim of public policy in the preceding ten years had been met through the successful promotion of export industries.

In broad statistical terms, the economic achievements of the period may be summarized as follows. Having regained the prewar levels, many economic indices began to show a continuous climb before 1955, and by 1960 they had doubled their prewar levels. The progress from then on is even

Table 7.1　*Comparisons of targets set by the National Income-doubling Plan and actual economic performance*

	National Income-doubling Plan		Actual performance	
	Target levels for 1970	*Targeted growth rate (%)*	*Actual levels for 1970*	*Actual growth rate (%)*
Total population (tens of thousands)	10 222	0.9	10 372	1.0
Persons employed (tens of thousands)	4 869	1.2	5 094	1.5
Employers (tens of thousands)	3 235	4.1	3 306	4.3
GNP (1958 prices, ¥100 millions)	260 000	8.8	405 812	11.6
Gross national income (1958 prices, ¥100 millions)	213 232	7.8	328 516	11.5
Per capita income (1958 prices, ¥)	208 601	6.9	317 678	10.4
Personal consumption expenditure (1958 prices, ¥100 millions)	151 166	7.6	207 863	10.3
Per capita personal consumption expenditures (1958 prices, ¥)	147 883	6.7	204 079	9.4
Structural components of the national income				
Primary industry		10.1		7.4
Secondary industry		38.6		38.5
Tertiary industry		51.3		54.1
Mining and manufacturing production	431.7	11.9	539.4	13.9
Agricultural, marine and forestry production	144.1	2.8	130.3	2.1
Total demand for energy (unit = 1000 tons of coal)	302 760	7.8	574 095	12.0
Value of exports (customs clearing basis, $100 millions)	93.2	10.0	202.5	16.8
Value of imports (customs clearing basis, $100 millions)	98.9	9.3	195.3	15.5

Notes: (1) Growth rates are in comparison to the average for 1956–8. (2) Figures are based on 1958 prices. (3) For all indices, 1958 = 100.
Source: Reprinted by permission from Uchino, *Japan's Postwar Economy*, published by Kodansha International Ltd. © 1983. All rights reserved.

faster, leading Johnson to remark that 'the miracle was actually only beginning in 1962, when production was just a third of what it would be by 1975'.[6] Japan's share of the world's economic activity increased rapidly from 1960 onwards. Japanese GNP in 1960, for example, was equivalent to only 3 per cent of that of the whole world (as against 33 per cent and 15 per cent for the USA and USSR) but it grew to exceed 10 per cent of the world total by the late 1970s.[7] Considerable progress was seen not only in per capita net income but also in various social indicators. By 1982 Japan could claim to have transformed itself into one of the most advanced industrial and welfare societies in the world, equal to if not better than the USA, West Germany, France and the Scandinavian countries.[8]

The reasons for economic growth varied considerably through the 1955–72 period. In 1955 the economy was still in its 'semi-industrialized' stage, with over 40 per cent of the work force still engaged in farming and other primary sector activities, and 65 per cent of its industrial production consisting of textiles and food-processing. By 1970 the demand for workers by the heavy industrial and chemical sectors had led to an exodus of younger workers from villages to factories, thus transforming the economy into a fully industrialized one, with the ratio of the work-force employed in the industrial sector reaching its highest level in history, at 35.2 per cent. The statistics presented in tables 7.2 and 7.3 below indicate this transformation of the economy.

The rate of growth of the national economy as a whole was continuously high throughout the 1955–72 period, but the growth path can be understood more clearly when we follow the performance through two stages, 1955–65 and 1965–72. In the first stage economic growth was pursued in a single-minded way, as though the rapid increase in GNP were the panacea for every economic problem. But in the following years several specific

Table 7.2 *Percentage proportion of national income and employment in various industries, 1960–87*

	1960	*1965*	*1970*	*1975*	*1980*	*1985*	*1987*
National income							
Primary industry	14.9	11.2	7.8	6.6	4.2	3.1	2.9[a]
Secondary industry[b]	36.3	35.8	38.1	35.5	38.5	37.5	37.1
Tertiary industry	48.9	53.0	54.1	57.9	57.3	59.4	60.0
Employment							
Primary industry	30.2	23.5	17.4	12.7	10.4	8.8	8.3
Secondary industry	28.0	31.9	35.1	35.2	34.8	34.3	33.3
Tertiary industry	41.8	44.6	47.5	52.1	54.8	56.9	58.5

[a] Figures are for 1986.
[b] Includes mining, manufacturing and construction industries.
Sources: EPA, *Keizai Hakusho* (1978, table 4-1-1), *2000 Nen no Nihon* (Series 10, 1984, p. 30) and Yanokota, *Nihon Kokuzei Zue* (1983; 1988, appendix table 1).

Table 7.3 *Percentage proportion of factory production and value of exports in various manufacturing industries, 1930–83*

	1930	1950	1955	1960	1965	1970	1975	1983[a]
Factory production								
Food-processing	16.1	13.5	17.9	12.4	12.5	10.3	11.9	11.0
Textiles	38.0	23.2	17.5	12.4	12.3	7.7	6.8	4.6
Wood products	2.8	4.6	5.1	4.5	5.0	4.2	4.3	n.a.
Machinery	10.6	13.9	14.7	25.8	26.6	32.3	29.8	39.6
Metals	9.6	26.0	17.0	18.8	17.7	19.3	17.1	14.0
Chemicals	15.3	12.9	11.0	9.4	9.5	8.1	8.2	12.5
Others	7.6	5.9	16.8	16.7	16.4	18.1	21.9	n.a.
Factory production – total	100.0	100.0	100.0	100.0	100.0	100.0	100.0	100.0
Exports								
Food-processing	9.0	6.3	6.8	6.3	4.1	3.4	1.4	0.9
Textiles	63.9	48.4	37.4	30.3	18.8	12.6	6.8	4.5
Other light industries	5.1	6.9	3.2	2.2	1.5	1.0	1.1	5.2
} (light industries grouped total)	76.5	56.0	57.2	47.3	32.0	22.6	13.1	
Machinery	3.1	10.4	13.8	25.6	35.4	46.7	54.5	63.1
Metals	3.8	18.9	19.3	14.1	20.5	19.9	22.8	13.6
Chemical	2.5	1.5	4.7	4.5	6.5	6.4	7.1	4.7
} (heavy industries grouped total)	9.4	30.8	37.8	40.2	62.4	73.0	83.4	
Others	12.6	7.6	14.8	17.0	13.2	10.0	6.3	8.0
Exports – total	100.0	100.0	100.0	100.0	100.0	100.0	100.0	100.0

[a] Factory production figures are for 1985.

n.a. indicates 'not available'.

Source: EPA, *Keizai Hakusho* (1976, table 4-1-2; 1978, table 4-1-1; 1984, appendix table 1-2).

economic issues emerged that needed to be highlighted and addressed. Achieving full employment and reducing inequalities in industrial development and income between large and smaller enterprises, agricultural and industrial sectors and between regions – in other words, resolving the problems of 'dual structure' in the economy – became a main aim of government economic policy. [9] At the beginning of the 1960s, Japan was still seen by the West as a country whose exports depended on cheap labour and dumping and whose domestic market was heavily protected by various devices. This stigma had to be shed, and the economy developed to full maturity.

Full employment was achieved. Workers began to move from firm to firm and industry to industry. The announcement of the National Income-doubling Plan, in November 1960, brought about rapid increases in confidence, and in plant and equipment investment. A tremendous growth in the construction industry followed the decision to hold the 1964 Olympics in Tokyo. The so-called Iwato boom (1959–62) brought virtually full employment for the first time in the country's modern history. The demand for labour during the Iwato years created 3.4 million new jobs and the number of permanent employees increased by 44 per cent. Overall unemployment fell from 2 per cent to 1.4 per cent, and labour shortages became a serious problem, affecting every sector of the economy. Large enterprises were forced to hire their lifetime employees from those already employed in small enterprises and to upgrade their temporary workers to the status of lifetime employees. This served to narrow wage differentials between large enterprises and small and medium firms. The dual structure began to be eroded and the wide productivity and wage differentials which were observed between different parts of the manufacturing and agricultural sectors, and between lifetime employees and temporary workers in large enterprises, were all narrowed considerably (see table 7.4).

Externally, as an important part of trade policy, a plan for trade liberalization was introduced in 1960. This was necessary because Japan had to meet growing pressure from abroad to open her domestic market to foreign products and investment, so that she could participate in the free trade system advocated by the General Agreement on Tariffs and Trade (GATT) and the International Monetary Fund (IMF). [10] Until then it was estimated that 84 per cent of Japan's total imports had been subject to import restrictions through tariff and foreign currency allocation systems. The comparative figure in 1961 was still 74 per cent, which was reduced to 20 per cent by late 1963. It was 1964 when Japan finally gained Article 8 status in GATT, and officially joined the club of advanced nations by obtaining membership of the Organisation for Economic Co-operation and Development (OECD). To achieve this, Japan had to discard government subsidies for exports, as well as measures of protection and import control. Capital liberalization was introduced more slowly: it began in 1967 and was completed by 1973. [11]

Table 7.4 Labour supply and demand, price trends and wage increases in the period of high-speed growth, 1956–73

	1956	1957	1961	1965	1967	1973
A. Price increases per annum						
Wholesale (%)	4.4	3.0	3.0	0.7	10.1	13.1
Consumer (%)	0.3	3.0	5.3	6.7	11.5	12.2
B. Wage increases per annum[a]	5.0	8.4	13.8	10.6	12.5	24.1
C. Effective ratio of job offers to applicants	0.35[c]	0.48	0.73	0.61	1.05	1.74
D. Ratio of job offers to applicants for new school graduates						
Middle school graduates	1.06[c]	1.18	2.73	n.a.	3.45	5.79
High school graduates	0.69	1.07	2.04	n.a.	3.05	3.13
E. Wage differentials between large and small enterprises[b]	60.4[c]	56.1	61.7	72.6	67.7	70.9

n.a. indicates 'not available'.

[a] Wage increase after spring wage offensives.

[b] Wage differentials are expressed as the index in smaller enterprises with 30–97 employees when wages in larger enterprises with more than 500 employees are given the value 100.

[c] 1953 figures.

Sources: For A, B and C Yanokota, *Nihon Kokuzei Zue* (1988, appendix table 1), Kosai (1986, table 8.5). For D and E Uchino, *Japan's Postwar Economy*, published by Kodansha International Ltd. © 1983. Reprinted by permission. All rights reserved.

What benefits have these two decades of high-speed economic growth brought to the Japanese people? The economy expanded at high speed – more than twice the speed of other advanced nations – without the serious problem of high price increases, which other advanced economies were unable to avoid. The National Income-doubling Plan was not simply a paper moon. The rise in household income was so fast that the wave of modernization affected almost every family. Under the 'consumer revolution' the popularization of electric household appliances such as the vacuum cleaner, fridge, washing machine and television resulted in a general modernization and Westernization of lifestyles, as well as making Matsushita a giant company by international standards. We noted earlier that in 1955, the starting date of high-speed economic growth, Japan was viewed – by outsiders and more importantly, by itself – as a second-rate nation, located somewhere between Europe and America on one hand and the underdeveloped countries of the Third World on the other. Despite long efforts to shift its industrial structure from one depending heavily on light industries such as textiles and the manufacture of toys to one depending on heavy and chemical industries and high technology, Japan's inability to achieve internationally cost-competitive high-quality production methods meant that Japanese enterprises were doomed to remain 'marginal suppliers', which repeatedly lost out to Western competitors in bids for contracts. Despite the national efforts since 1868 to industrialize and modernize the economy, by the mid-1950s the status of the economy was still that of a 'semi-developed country'. Ten years later, in GATT and the OECD, Japan had joined the Western club; and after a further ten years, she was among its leaders! Of all the high-performance economic indicators, the most significant was the message that the Japanese economy had successfully been transformed into one equal to any in the West. What role had government played in that achievement?

2   Economic Policy for Growth

Staging Growth Policy

The aim of economic policy in this period can be summed up as one of maximum economic growth while maintaining the balance of payments.[12] Through much of the 1950s, the goal of economic growth was pursued using capital equipment which had survived the war, and the still-abundant supply of labour.[13] As we noted earlier, much plant and equipment had been outmoded by international standards, and industry saw an urgent need to replace it; to invest in technical innovation to raise productive capacity to postwar standards. However, on its part the government saw securing the supply of raw materials from abroad as the primary use for scarce foreign exchange. The balance of payments ceiling was seen as the most important constraint on economic growth.[14] Various fiscal and monetary policies were administered to guide the expansion of industrial activities, and of GNP, without running into exchange deficit. Hence, despite the optimism that pervaded this period of high-speed growth, the macroeconomic policy adopted by the government during most of the period was 'deflationary' in nature. It was entrepreneurial spirit and aggressive driving force which, after the isolation from technical progress in the West in 1938–45, led Japan's private sector to yearn for new technology to modernize industry, and propelled her rapid economic growth from 1955 to 1965. Given such enthusiastic entrepreneurial activities, the government's macroeconomic concern was to avoid foreign deficit and domestic inflation.[15] General price levels had to be kept stable to keep the export industries cost-competitive. At the same time industrial policies were formulated for individual sectors of the economy in order to identify and promote export industries. The ultimate aim of both the macro- and microeconomic policies, therefore, was the lifting of the balance of payments ceiling of the nation's economy. Rapid growth tended to raise the ceiling which, in turn, allowed an increase in the growth rate. However, the remarkable performance of the economy through this period was plagued by frequent and sudden balance of payments deficits, almost as if the problem was inherent in the economic structure and its mode of growth, so that public policy could do little to alleviate it, let alone solve it.[16]

The first attempt to deal with the deficit was a straightforward short-term deflationary measure in late 1955. This curbed domestic demand through a general credit squeeze, because the government had identified the main cause as being excessive investment in plant and equipment, leading to a surge in imports of capital equipment, in addition to an increase in consumption of imported raw materials and energy. The deflationary policy did not succeed in suppressing investment demand, and an unprecedented international payments and foreign currency crisis followed in 1957. The government was forced to apply for IMF loans twice in July and August of the same year. The loans were given on condition that the government organize effective monetary policies to rectify the balance of international payments promptly. There were heated debates among politicians and bureaucrats over the pursuit of expansive fiscal policy on the one hand and deflationary monetary policy on the other. The debate intensified against a background of explosive domestic inventories created by speculative investment in imports during the Suez crisis. Late in 1957 the government came up with a new monetary policy, in which orthodox manipulation of the official discount rate was supplemented by new 'window guidance' measures.[17] Through these measures the Bank of Japan directed credit restrictions between industries and enterprises, rather than depressing general economic activity by raising the official discount rate.

The new monetary policy was effective in reducing the deficit, and met the IMF requirements. Yet, however effective it was in this particular crisis in 1957, the economy could not free itself from recurring deficit crises, because the trouble lay not in the decline in exports due to excessive domestic demand, but in the growing demand for imports of raw materials and industrial machinery. During the periods of stringent monetary policy and between booms and recessions, private industry did not abandon new plant and equipment investment programmes. Through credit squeezes and administrative guidance, the government would request business to refrain from undertaking active new investment programmes, and firms were thus forced to suspend their modernization plans. But as soon as the deficit was reduced and the restrictions eased they promptly resumed their temporarily shelved expansion schemes. The rate of growth and the entrepreneurial enthusiasm propelled each other. Economic planners were inept, and offered only repetitive 'stop–go' approaches, under which they tried to maximize economic growth not so much under a balance of payments ceiling as on an up-and-down roller-coaster of trade surplus and deficit.

Uchino regards the incompetence of economic planners in this period as being reflected in the instability of the political system and the frequent turnover of government from Hatoyama to Ishibashi to Ikeda cabinets, although all were from the Liberal and Democratic parties (LDP).[18] The period was one of the most unstable in the history of Japan, and witnessed political strife in the form of the anti-Anpo (the US–Japan Security Treaty) movements of 1959 and 1960, and large-scale labour disputes and industrial strikes at the Miike coal mine from 1957 to 1961.

The anti-Anpo movement consisted of a coalition of students, labour and opposition party politicians. The scale and intensity of the movement is reported to have exceeded even the expectations of the leaders, and one of their many riots resulted the death of a female student.[19] The Kishi Cabinet was forced to resign in 1960, and the new Ikeda Cabinet was formed to rebuild the LDP and restore public confidence in the political system, which had been severely shaken by the political and industrial conflicts.

The first task which the Ikeda Cabinet took upon itself was the reconciliation of the Miike dispute.[20] Both the anti-Anpo and the Miike troubles came to an end promptly, and somewhat unexpectedly, with the announcement of Ikeda's new economic plan in December 1960. Did the strong economic performance in 1955–60 contribute to the stabilization of the political structure? Economic growth was bringing considerable benefits to the population. By 1960 the workers already in town were enjoying full employment. (Some concealed reserves of labour still existed in villages using more farm workers than they strictly needed.) The annual wage increase rose beyond the 10 per cent per annum mark, to record a continuous improvement that culminated in a rise of 24 per cent in the 1960–2 period. The economy was beginning to experience a general labour shortage, which led to such new phenomena as a considerable increase in worker mobility between enterprises. It was this that later hastened the break-down of the dual structure of the economy. The population was beginning to develop a taste for fast economic growth. The humiliating label of 'semi-industrialized' nation and the shock of defeat in war seemed to recede quickly from the people's memory. This was the moment when the government, under the new leadership of Prime Minister Ikeda Hayato, marked the beginning of a new period of economic expansion.

The National Income-doubling Plan of 1960[21]

At this time, government policy was built on two main principles: the first was aimed at high-speed economic growth and the second at freer trade. It was with these two economic policies – domestic and foreign – that the Ikeda government decided to overcome the political problems confronting it. The result was the successful stabilization of the nation's political situation, not only in the immediate anti-Anpo and Miike crisis period, but also by the eventual dominance of the Conservative party in the following years. Public support turned strongly towards a commitment to rapid economic development and participation in the free trade system

The origin of the Income-doubling Plan goes back to 1958, when academics, bureaucrats and other interested parties joined the discussion on the plausibility of salary-doubling plans. The nation's economy had been expanding continuously for some time, and despite short-term cyclical fluctuations, the Japanese people had begun to have, consciously or not, some premonition that they were about to set the pace of economic progress. As a shrewd politician, Ikeda felt that it was time to launch bold new domestic and foreign policies to uplift the image of the nation and enable it to join the ranks of the advanced nations, a goal it had long pursued. In 1959 a strategy for the development of a welfare state was proposed. This strategy was almost entirely based on economic policy developed by Professor Nakayama Ichiro, a labour economist of Marxian orientation and Chairman of the Central Labour Commission. True to Japanese understanding of 'welfare', its aim was to double the income of the population as a whole.

Ikeda, then Minister of MITI, immediately supported the proposal. He argued that it would be by no means impossible to double or even triple the salaries and wages and other forms of income of the people in Japan within the next five or ten years, as long as government economic policies could ensure the maximum utilization of the labour force. This was to be achieved by making better use of labour that was at present unemployed or under-utilized in pre-modern small-scale enterprises in the poor half of the dual economic structure. In addition, Ikeda suggested that careful monitoring of economic performance by planning and budgeting authorities might be necessary. He believed that the previous economic plans were unsatisfactory for a number of reasons. First, they had not anticipated the full growth capacity of the economy and consequently had under-estimated the annual growth of tax revenue which would come about without any increase in tax rates. Second, therefore, they had imposed low limits on the growth of government spending for fear of creating inflationary pressure and trade deficits. Third, and most importantly, they had invested too little in necessary public works, which increasingly lagged behind the expansion of the private sector and thus created infrastructure bottlenecks for economic growth.

In the 45 postwar years, a total of ten comprehensive national economic plans have been issued (see appendix table A.7). Public response to the plans has varied considerably but, by all accounts, the National Income-doubling Plan was the most important of them all. It made the strongest impression on the population as a whole by capturing and representing, as noted above, the sentiment of the people at the time, and it marked the return of government to effective economic leadership after some irresolute years.

After two years of widely publicized discussions on the theories of salary-doubling, the National Income-doubling Plan was enacted in November 1960. It called for an average annual growth of real GNP of 9 per cent for the first three years of the plan. It set the stage and created an atmosphere of high expectations for the future. The economy changed its structural features internally as well as externally in the course of the plan.

Three activities were particularly emphasized, since they represented the important contribution that was expected from the public sector:

1   The government would take responsibility for a substantial increase in social overhead capital facilities and for providing social security services. The government acknowledged shortages of port and harbour facilities, rail transportation, public highways and industrial water supply, which hindered further economic expansion. [22]
2   The government emphasized that an increase in education, training and research facilities was one of the most important conditions for economic development. It would provide financial and other assistance to research and development expenditure in science and technology.
3   The elimination of the dual structure of the economy was incorporated into the plan as basic economic policy. Various specific proposals were established in order to eliminate income and wage differences between large and small enterprises, agricultural and manufacturing sectors and regions. In order to achieve this, there was a plan to mobilize the workforce in the farming sector into expanding industrial sectors. For the first time in the country's long history of planning for industrial development, a comprehensive programme for regional economic development was incorporated into the plan. It discussed the problems of regional disparity in industrial development and income in particular, and invited regional and local governments to act to reduce the

disparities. The invitation led to fierce competition between regions, as each tried to entice private enterprises looking for new industrial locations with investment plans for technological modernization.

The Economic Deliberation Council was established and a new industrial location policy called the 'Pacific Belt Region Concept' was proposed. It aimed further to limit industrial development in the four major industrialized regions of Tokyo–Yokohama, Osaka–Kobe, Nagoya and Northern Kyushu, while channelling public investment into new industrial facilities in other areas in the Pacific Belt. However, this proposal met with opposition and complaints from those outside the favoured locations. Forced to modify the policy, the government established the new Comprehensive National Development Plan in October 1962. After petitions and other political feedback, 13 new industrial cities and six special areas were designated to receive large-scale long-term government industrial infrastructure investment.[23]

Industrial Policy for Trade and Capital Liberalization

The policy measures of the National Income-doubling Plan were basically macroeconomic and its terms of reference were as a domestic economic plan. In contrast, the import liberalization policies from 1960 to 1965, which were the second pillar of Ikeda's economic plan, were microeconomic and addressed specific industries in terms of foreign trade policy.[24]

In the discussion above, we noted that policy-makers saw the recurring trade deficits as the main restriction on economic growth. Besides financial and monetary policies for balancing foreign trade accounts, the government had been rationing imports through the direct foreign currency allocation system. Despite rapid implementation of import liberalization, which had taken place since 1955, there were still long lists of importable goods that were excluded or deterred by tariffs. Pressures for liberalization began to come from abroad: the demand from the USA became particularly strong in 1959 when, for the first time, its imports from Japan exceeded its exports to Japan. Since 1955 Japan had been included in the advanced nations of GATT and, with the European nations already having made the shift to Article 8 status by 1959, Japan was left as the only advanced industrial country still practising any of the prohibited range of import restrictions.

It was perhaps first and foremost such pressures from abroad that led the Ikeda government to consider policies for the opening of the domestic market to international competition. However, by the time the National Income-doubling Plan was structured into its final form, its planners also wanted freer international trade for domestic reasons, as a condition of very fast growth. They wanted to achieve both fast growth and a favourable trade balance by stimulating exports, and they knew that increasing industrial exports would unavoidably increase imports of raw materials, energy sources and other necessary items. They also expected that the international division of labour, as a result of worldwide trade liberalization, would help to bring a modern cosmopolitan lifestyle to the population of Japan.[25]

Another reason for shifting the balance-of-trade strategy from restraining imports to expanding exports was that the continuous restrictions on imports had created a number of distortions in the domestic economy. For example, under MITI's strict control of the allocation of foreign currency to key industries, the right to import had become an interest vested in key industries and companies, which often resulted in the phenomenon of 'import premiums'. Moreover, since foreign currency allocation was based on the reserve production capacity of each enterprise, companies were encouraged to compete for automatic currency allocations for raw material imports by over-investing to create excess capacity. Overproduction and excessive investment in plant and equipment in the key industries became an increasingly serious problem.

As was to be expected, the change of policy met with strong criticism and opposition from the business community, who regarded it as recklessly ambitious. The fear it created, even before its official adoption, was that it would invite a flood of foreign imports and capital: the former would produce large deficits in the balance of payments, and the latter would overwhelm domestic enterprise. The government nevertheless believed that liberalization was essential and an official document, the General Outline of a Plan for Liberalization of Trade Transactions, was published in June 1960, aiming to free 80 per cent of imports from restrictions within three years. This plan was linked closely with the policies of high-speed growth and full employment incorporated in the National Income-doubling Plan.

Since the actual policy procedures and the extent of import growth are well documented elsewhere,[26] we will concentrate on government efforts to nurture domestic industry to the stage of becoming internationally competitive.

Let us recapitulate the logic of the trade liberalization policy. First, the aim was to free the growth of the national economy from balance-of-payment restraints. Therefore, the speed and the extent of trade liberalization were programmed to be linked with the policies of high-speed growth and full employment in the National Income-doubling Plan. Second, policy-makers responsible for the specific industrial measures selected the export-oriented industries which would be given special assistance to expand. The sectors targeted were the heavy and chemical industries with capital-intensive production methods which were dependent on modern technology. Free trade was expected to lead corporations, industries and the overall industrial structure to become internationally cost competitive, both at home and in export markets. Third, it was also envisaged that such rationalization of industry would be most beneficial when the economy made the transition to the forthcoming capital liberalization from 1970 onwards.

The selection of the designated 'key industries' was not a new task for MITI. From the days of the *keisha–seisan* policy for coal and steel, it had accumulated the information and administrative skills necessary to identify and promote strategic industries and enterprises for industrial growth. The selection of these government proteges altered from period to period as the stage of industrial development progressed *pari passu* with the changes in conditions in export markets. During this period the target sectors were capital- and technology-intensive industries such as iron and steel manufacturing, petroleum refining, petrochemicals, automobiles, industrial machinery, electrics and electrical machinery. In the 1950s, when Japan was short of capital and industrial technology, the choice of such industries seemed to many observers to be inappropriate. But the basis of the choice was a theory of dynamic comparative advantage, in a double sense. Comparative advantage should be created rather than merely 'identified'; and the targeted industries were chosen with detailed attention to the effects that their growth would generate in other sectors of the economy. The advantages of specialization in the production of selected products in the key industries were carefully examined in view of the expansion of Japan's domestic market. It was calculated that the expansion of the domestic market would provide the basis for mass production and economies of scale for cost-competitive exports, along with rapid economic development and improvement of the standard of living of the Japanese.

The logic and *raison d'être* of the choice of the 'key' industries was as follows:[27]

1   Japan lacked land and raw material resources, but she possessed a large homogeneous population and a well-educated, vigorous labour force with a strong work ethic.
2   However, Japan was extremely short of both capital and modern industrial technology, without which her skilled and well-educated labour force could not be fully utilized.
3   The lack of land and natural resources forced Japan to export processed goods in order to finance imports of raw materials. Thus, as far as protection and promotion of infant industries were concerned, 'export promotion' had to take priority over 'import replacement' policies: that is, under the economic conditions where the trade ceiling is the crucial determining factor in the growth rate of the economy, Japan had to restrict imports of certain foreign goods and, at the same time, the key industries had to be encouraged to grow to become competitive export and export-supporting industries on the world market. Growth to meet rising domestic demand should as far as possible be in products which could also be exported.
4   In the 1950s, the negative aspect of having a large workforce was the potential for high unemployment. However, its positive aspect lay in the fact that it constituted a significant potential for economic development.

Rapid accumulation of capital was envisaged on the basis of the forecast of rapid expansion of domestic markets for the key industries.

5 The scale of the domestic market and the prospects that it offered to key industries suggested that for most purposes the market economy would be a more appropriate distributive mechanism than central planning. However, the government saw it as essential to employ some sort of control over the allocation and efficient utilization of certain productive factors which were scarce.

An extensive and systematic policy formula was elaborated by MITI officials for the protection and assistance of 'infant industries', and the maintenance of an 'efficient market structure' in the manufacturing industry. The former was achieved by a variety of measures, including tax concessions, subsidies, supply of government finance, and the relaxation of anti-monopoly laws to allow various kinds of control agreements. To achieve the latter, MITI encouraged mergers and other types of 'collusive conduct' by firms. MITI possessed the authority to grant import licences. This authority was used to control and restrict investment and new entries into the target industries. It also manipulated licences for the import of foreign technology and raw materials.

Despite many attempts, researchers have been unable to agree on the degree of effectiveness of the industrial policy.[28] Our contribution will be to make two observations about these policies. First, the trade 'liberalization' policy in this period was promoted with ever tightening import restrictions. From 1955 until as late as the mid-1960s, there was virtually no restriction on MITI officials improvising and enforcing any policy measures they thought would help to protect and nurture their selected industries. They were implementing the very essence of 'infant industry' policy. Our second observation is that the industrial policy violated the basic competitive and market principles of capitalist society. However, as to the wisdom or otherwise of that, we will suspend our judgement until later, when we will be in a position to review the role and function of the government throughout Japan's history of industrialization.

3 Evaluation of the Period

In economic terms the National Income-doubling Plan delivered what people expected. Between 1955 and 1967 the size of GNP grew by a factor of five in nominal terms and by a factor of three in real terms. The volume of international trade (imports and exports) grew by a factor of five, with an accumulating trade surplus. The specific tasks which were allocated to the public sector for the successful achievement of the plan ((1) to (3) on pages 147–8 above) achieved the desired results.[29] Japan was successfully transformed to a full employment society, with various welfare measures such as the National Health Scheme and National Superannuation Programmes.

What did the transformation actually owe to government policy?[30] The contribution of the plan and the trade liberalization policy – the government's main contributions – in bringing an improvement in the welfare of the population should be assessed most carefully. The difficulty lies basically in three areas:

1   The plan may have represented a mere political gesture, helping Ikeda and his Cabinet and party to take credit for the enthusiasm and strong investment that were already emerging most aggressively in industry shortly before the implementation of the plan. At the same time, the corporate sector was slow in introducing welfare measures, even though the major cost was carried by the government, particularly in the case of smaller enterprises.

2   An outstanding shortcoming of the plan was its utter failure to implement any measures to deal with environmental degradation and urban overcrowding.

3   The evaluation of trade liberalization policies was easier, since industries outside the key groups (such as sewing machines, cameras, bicycles, pianos, zippers, transistor radios and other audiovisual equipment, tooling machines and so on[31]) grew without government assistance. At the same time, there were industries such as coal mining which failed to grow despite considerable assistance from MITI and the Ministry of Finance.[32] As for the MITI's criteria for industrial encouragement, many industries appear to have obtained designated status without actually satisfying any of the conditions officially noted in policy guidelines. The list became so long as time went by that there seemed to be no consistent basis for selection: we are left with an impression that MITI added industries to the list as soon as they had demonstrated good performance on the international market. In short, public policy followed rather than led private performance.[33]

With regard to the actual administration of policy measures, a group of economists – T. Tsuruta and others – judge that there was grave mismanagement by MITI in that many key industries attracted excessive investment. This was because their privileged status attracted the necessary capital and there was a tacit expectation that some rescue measures would certainly be forthcoming should difficulties of over-capacity or over-production arise.[34] In addition, individual firms were motivated to invest continuously to increase their production capacity, because the allocation of import licences by MITI was based mainly on the actual size of their production capacity at a given time. The mood of the time was one of confident expansion and diversification, so firms had every incentive to secure import licences for any necessary new technology and materials. Individual firms competed to expand their production capacities ahead of others, correctly assuming that the future allocation of import quotas for their essential raw materials, resources and technology would be based on their recorded share of total production capacity. Furthermore, in times of recession cartels of one sort or another had been organized and accepted by MITI, and when production was curtailed, those quotas also were based on recorded production capacity. In a market-oriented economy a checking mechanism is expected to come into play against excessive investment, but in Japan at this time the cartel arrangements frequently legalized by MITI positively encouraged firms to go overboard in investing to increase capacity: in other words, anti-recession cartels were themselves a cause of excessive capacity during recessions, and of the general competition to invest.[35]

The MITI policy-makers are thus accused of making a serious error of judgement in putting the cart before the horse. Nevertheless, it is possible that over-investment had an indirect effect of a more helpful (perhaps unintended) kind. It is when firms have surplus capacity that they tend to think hardest about new products, new markets and new marketing methods in order to find work for their surplus capacity: therefore over-capacity may have contributed to the high rate and ingenuity of innovation through this period.

In January 1965, with the change in government to the Sato Cabinet, Ikeda's National Income-doubling Plan was replaced by the Medium-term Economic Plan.[36] It was agreed that the former had served its purpose and, in fact, had created new problems which growth policy alone could not solve. The latter was quickly revised in 1967, and again in 1970, under the same government. Its overall emphasis still lay in the task of correcting and improving the problems arising from the imbalance of growth between industries and regions (see appendix table A.7). Many people felt that these problems were inherited from the National Income-doubling Plan itself and its emphasis on growth. The period from 1955 to 1972 was the era during which the national effort was most exclusively dedicated to the achievement of rapid economic growth. Despite this, in 1965 there was a very important turning point in the Japanese economy, which affected the basis upon which public economic policy needed to be built. At the time this turning point appears to have been fully understood by scarcely anyone, least of all by the government policy-makers. Public planning of the economy continued as before, on the same assumptions as before. Adjustments to monetary, fiscal and sectoral measures in the Medium-term Economic Plan and its subsequent revisions were superficial.

What exactly was the direction that the Japanese economy took in the mid-1960s? We must first ask: At what precise point in her economic development did Japan stand in 1965? We would venture boldly to summarize the nature and significance of the transformation by saying that the economic efforts of the nation since the beginnings of industrialization in the Meiji period had at last brought to the economy a relative abundance of capital, natural resources, energy and other factors of production as compared with labour. The long-term efforts by both the public and private sectors to accumulate capital, the availability of technical changes and innovation, the changes in international markets which made for a more readily available and cheap supply of foodstuffs, raw materials and energy sources turned the equation of the availability of resources (R), capital (C) and labour (L) by 180 degrees, from $R < C < L$ to $R > C > L$.

We can be more specific with the help of table 7.4. In the labour market the transformation took place through a rapid and considerable reduction in unemployment, so that the economy became one with full employment, without the major problems of a traditionally under-employed work-force. The ratio of job offers to applicants increased from 0.35 in 1956 to exceed 1.05 in 1967 (row C in table 7.4). The effective disappearance of a reserve army in the work force – not so much a reserve army of urban unemployed, as in the Marxist model, but a reserve army of under-employed peasants ready to move to town when jobs beckoned – resulted in a dramatic decline in the differentials of wages and other working conditions between the agricultural and industrial sectors, as well as between enterprises of varying sizes and regions (row E in table 7.4). It was a period during which domestic help, such as housemaids, disappeared. A salient feature of the dual structure had been that only male workers in large enterprises received offers of permanent lifetime employment and its associated benefits. The rest of the workforce was left to accept temporary, seasonal or otherwise insecure status, with lower pay and poorer working conditions. The shortage of labour and the increase in worker mobility between enterprises initiated a rapid transformation of this element of the traditional employment system. Together with wage and salary increases, it also pushed many inefficient small enterprises out of business, while forcing others to revolutionize their methods. Many of them eventually developed to become highly efficient specialized producers, with the techniques and marketing methods to undertake advanced, high-value-added work.[37] They were quite a new breed of enterprise, distinctly different from those which had previously relied on cheap labour and poor working conditions for survival.

Labour shortages were felt first and foremost among school graduates. This forced large enterprises to hunt for and hire lifetime employees from those already employed in smaller enterprises, as well as to upgrade their temporary workers to the status of lifetime employees.[38] Competition in recruiting both trained employees and recent graduates intensified between firms, small and large, and starting salaries of employees rose, narrowing the wage differentials between senior and junior employees – the seniority wage curve began to flatten.

Labour relations altered to reflect these changes. There was a dramatic strengthening of the bargaining position of labour *vis-à-vis* management. It was during the Iwato boom in 1960–1 that the 'spring wage offensive' established its role in the annual bargaining strategy of the national labour movement. Annual wage increases across industry were established as a matter of course, and regular increments in proportion to the increase in productivity and general living costs were incorporated into the payment system, with public consensus being taken for granted.[39]

On the agricultural scene, the large exodus of workers took place at an accelerated speed. Farmers and peasants became urban workers in the secondary and tertiary industries, winning higher and more equal payment. In general, incomes became more equal across society, and increased rapidly. This in turn created a larger domestic consumer market, which further stimulated output and lifted the standard of living of the population. New lifestyles oriented towards the Western mode were noted in the majority of the population. The number of people with middle incomes increased considerably. People were enjoying their freedom as individuals, and claiming their share of the fruits of economic progress. There was a huge increase in personal consumption expenditure, in electric appliances (televisions, radios, washing machines, and so on), Western-style clothing (in place of traditional kimonos), and leisure activities (such as skiing).[40] *Showa Genroku* 'The Age of Peace and Prosperity' was the phrase coined by Fukuda Takeo – who later became Prime Minister – to describe the ebullience and the spread of new urban lifestyles and popular mass media.[41]

Economists often observe that Ikeda's National Income-doubling Plan failed to meet the new challenges created by the 'economic miracle' after 1965. The free-market system and public control measures such as administrative guidance needed substantial revision in the Age of Prosperity, with its problems of over crowding, environmental degradation and other threats to the quality of life. The single-minded pursuit of a large annual increase in GNP no longer had the same magical attraction to the population at large. It was no longer important to maximize growth.

Is this a true assessment of the period? The cry of 'Damn GNP' was first heard in 1971. Was the government's main failure its inability to shift target from 'growth regardless' to environmental care and quality of life? We do not find that interpretation satisfactory. Despite these cries, the people were by no means surfeited with growth. There was no difficulty at all in selling the economy's increasing output, and it was far from true that all Japanese households had all the material equipment, income and public services that they wanted. The trouble was not that government 'failed to stop growth'. It was a double failure: a failure to grasp that the time had come to pursue growth (i) through environmentally prudent methods, and (ii) in the new and (in Japan) unprecedented condition of a permanent shortage of labour.

This criticism is all the more apt because of the Japanese tradition of perceiving social problems as economic problems, and then attacking them using economic strategies rather than with separate social or welfare policies. Labour had become the limiting factor of production. It was no longer rational to administer 'designated industry' policies which aimed above all to economize on capital by allocating it to its most productive uses. The critical task was now to see that labour found its most productive uses. Since that would both increase workers' earnings and tend to equalize them, it suggested a characteristic Japanese solution: one that would both help GNP to grow, subject to relevant environmental and other constraints, and do the most to resolve the 'dual economy' problems of equity, and conflicts about wage shares, which were troubling Japanese society. That would in turn reduce the need for separate, publicly financed welfare services; but, to the extent that some of these would still be needed, their provision also required some economic growth. To summarize, a higher level of production was needed to give higher incomes to the workforce, whether in the form of pay or welfare provisions.

Thus, in the labour-starved economy, the focus of economic planning and the role of government had to be directed at the workers – the fundamental discipline of economics had not changed. Growth now had to be sought in environmentally acceptable ways. However, subject to that and other constraints, the maximum use of the available resources to increase the material welfare of the population was still the iron rule of economic management, and the government too had to submit to this rule. It is wrong to interpret the great surge of awareness about pollution and other quality of life issues in the 1960s in Japan as indicating a naive acceptance of the 'Damn GNP' sentiment.

To distil our argument, the National Income-doubling Plan did not die a natural death in 1965 because the population lost interest in a further expansion in economic activity. The income elasticity of the majority of goods and services in Japan continued to be positive, although it may have declined below unity. But public policy in the 1965–72 period failed to grasp the strategic implications of full employment and labour shortage in an economy which still had large technologically backward sectors; therefore it continued, with growing irrelevance, to focus on technical problems of capital allocation, and efforts to smooth out the cyclical fluctuations of economic activity.

Let us restate our observations about the period of high-speed growth in the following few words. It may be argued that the postwar reforms introduced by the US authorities, which democratized Japan's political system, the rights of labour and the ownership of farmland, were sufficient to 'legitimize' the economic growth of 1945–60; in other words, to maintain its popularity and acceptability despite the elements of hardship, inequality and capitalist exploitation. Japanese governments did not have to give much attention to the accompanying social conditions and effects of growth; that is, they did not need to take any special additional action to legitimize the economic system.

However, by 1960 those postwar benefits had become normal facts of life rather than welcome novelties, and their legitimizing force was spent. It was then that Ikeda's government shrewdly recognized a need for new incentives, new means of legitimizing the system. The promise of full employment and income-doubling was well timed for the purpose. Moreover, it was offered explicitly (although perhaps not in the Marxist meaning of legitimation) as a legitimizing measure. Full employment and doubled income were not included in the 1960 plan (as had most elements of previous plans) as a means to economic growth. They were presented as rewards of growth, rewards to workers for their contribution to growth. By 1965, with the achievement of full employment, government knew that its policies must meet labour's demands, even though its economists had not yet grasped the implications of full employment for future policies of economic growth.

The above observations suggest that Japan's experience in promoting growth before 1965 may be of little direct use to the West.[42] This is because Japan's policy in the period before 1965 was developed when labour was in plentiful supply; in other words, when there was surplus labour in boom and slump alike, even when available land and capital were fully employed – a situation distinctly different from that of the modern Western economies.

8 A Decelerated Economy, 1973–1990

To put the finishing touch to the spectacular records achieved in the period of high-speed economic growth, there came the Izanagi boom, in the second half of the 1960s. This boom came at the end of the 'long swing of economic growth' which characterized the three decades of the postwar economy from 1945 to 1973.[1] There had been the Korean War boom of 1950–2; the volume boom of 1954–5; the Jimmu boom of 1955–6; the Iwato boom of 1959–61; and this Izanagi boom came in November 1965 to set a new record of economic growth.[2] It lasted for a record 57 months until July 1970. It was the biggest boom in the history of the Japanese economy, as suggested by its nickname, which likened it to the creation of the island of Japan by Izanagi, progenitor of the Sun Goddess.

The rate of growth continued to accelerate until 1970, to achieve the highest recorded level in Japan's long history of national effort for growth and industrialization. Other indices of economic performance presented supporting evidence, in terms of full employment and stable prices, which further consolidated the high level of economic achievement as of 1970.[3]

Yet beneath such success and prosperity lay the shadow of some long-accumulated economic and social problems, which soon emerged to burst upon the national consciousness. There was growing dissatisfaction with many of the effects of very high-speed economic growth. The industrial development programmes of local governments began to be criticized from the point of view of environmental conservation. Factory workers on large-scale assembly lines became conscious of 'alienation' and began to complain about the way in which work was organized. The cry 'Damn GNP' was heard. Doubts about the magical attraction of a large GNP itself led to further questions about the government policies which had engineered the growth. As if to respond to the new anxieties, the economy slipped into a prolonged recession, which was said to have been triggered, ironically, by Japan's balance of payments surplus. The surplus, that long-sought after target of economic policy-makers in pursuit of a high rate of economic growth, became one of the biggest headaches for the same policy-makers in the years that followed. Thus the year 1971 became a crucial year in the postwar history of the economy, marking the beginning of a new era for the policy-makers.

This chapter consists of three sections. In section 1 we will review Government economic policy before the first oil crisis in 1973. In section 2 a similar review will be conducted for the 1980s. In these two sections we will attempt to follow chronologically the efforts made by policy-makers to respond to the emerging economic problems and, in so doing, to search for a new role for government. In section 3 we will discuss the reasons why the government was unable quickly to formulate effective policies for the new economic conditions.

1 Challenges to the Policies of Economic Growth

The policies of growth had enjoyed wide approval throughout the 1950s and 1960s. To recapitulate, the basic principle of the policy was that the Japanese economy could grow continuously at a high rate if the balance of trade ceiling was shifted upwards. This became possible as many industries and enterprises grew into internationally competitive exporters (see table 8.1). Groups of industries and corporations were designated by the

Table 8.1 *Productivity (value of production/employment) in Japan, the USA and West Germany in various industries (Japan = 100 in 1976[a])*

Industry	Japan (1976)	USA (1974)	West Germany (1970)
Iron and steel	100	35	18
Chemicals	100	64	57
Cars	100	83	63
Non-ferrous metals and metal products	100	83	126
Paper and pulp	100	83	130
Electrical machinery	100	97	35
Precision machinery	100	84	63
Metal products	100	104	40
Petroleum products	100	25	36

[a] Figures are not exactly comparable between the three countries. US figures are for 1974 and West German figures are for 1970. Both are compared with 1976 Japanese figures, which are shown as 100.
Source: EPA, *Economic White Paper*, 1978, Diagram 4-1-3.

government to receive various benefits, which helped them to cut costs and grow in size so that they became comparable with, if not larger than, their international competitors. The government considered 'large-scale operations' as the main source of cost competitiveness in manufacturing.[4] This was the basic logic of postwar public policy until 1971. It was appropriate logic for a small developing economy, which was short of natural resources but eager to grow.

The situation changed in 1968 when Japan's GNP surpassed that of West Germany, and the Japanese economy became the second largest in the world outside the communist bloc. The steady increase in the annual balance of payments surplus had already begun before Japan joined the large oligopolistic economies of the world. As a consequence the yen's position strengthened on international markets. Policy-makers were asked to respond promptly to the new situation. It was clear that the previous aim of 'raising the balance of payments ceiling' had become redundant. At the same time a series of new problems emerged. Problems associated with oligopolistic market systems, environmental pollution and shortages of social overhead capital emerged, and became critical issues in Japanese society. The general public felt strongly that these problems had accumulated in the process of economic growth, and therefore that public policy for growth was responsible for them.

With regard to market systems, throughout the period of high-speed economic growth the policy, particularly that advocated by MITI, had been aimed at weakening the anti-monopoly regulations which were originally introduced by the US occupation authority. As noted, industrial policy specifically encouraged individual firms to achieve large-scale operations. For a time this policy stimulated competition in investment and reduction in costs (and often prices) as firms competed to enlarge their scale of operation and their market share. Workable competition prevailed up to about 1965, particularly in many sections of heavy industrial and chemical manufacturing, despite the concentrated market structure. But as high concentration was achieved and the Izanagi boom conditions made life easier, big business in those two industries began to take joint action to determine prices, the volume of production and capacity expansion. As the recession took hold of the economy in the 1970s, this tendency spread to other industries. Control agreements and other collusive, non-competitive business dealings were practised widely across the economy. Prices of major products such as steel, chemical fertilisers and synthetic fibre remained high throughout the depressed market conditions of the 1970s.

Ironically, it was as a result of initiatives by MITI and other government agencies that numerous business associations and interest groups were formed, originally as communication devices between government and industry. By 1974, more than 20 000 business associations had been formed, covering virtually every industry in the economy. During the period of growth and expansion of the 1960s, those industrial associations and interest groups were successful in facilitating the close communication between government and business which was necessary for the effective formation and execution of industrial policies. However, as the economy moved into a decelerated stage in the 1970s they became, contrary to their planned purpose, a breeding ground for collusion; and the communications between industry and government took on more of the character which they tend to have in the West, as organizations such as the Japan Iron and Steel Federation and the Japan Automobile Manufacturers' Association, and hundreds of similar associations, were organized to liaise with government departments and to lobby for industrial policies favourable to their interests.[5]

Environmental pollution and a shortage of public goods were seen to be degrading the quality of life in the Japanese community. Private enterprise was not encouraged to invest in alleviating these problems: Japan's industrial policy in the 1950s and 1960s had been one which crudely sought productivity and profitability alone. In particular, in the target industry sectors, MITI's industrial policy encouraged industry to establish large-scale plant, while paying little attention to the effect this might have on Japan's overcrowded urban and natural environment. The government allocated most of its public expenditure to help the private sector, and to help it by raising its productivity rather than by protecting the community from its harmful effects or 'externalities'. Consequently, the problems of environmental degradation accumulated rapidly, to the point at which the crowded Japanese community began to pay high social costs. In 1971, despite the severe economic downturn, the government had to introduce full-scale anti-pollution laws.[6]

Amidst all this, late in 1973 the first oil crisis shook the very roots of the economy. Of all the oil-consuming nations, Japan felt the greatest shock. The realization that the supply of Japan's basic energy source could suddenly be cut aroused hysteria among consumers, resulting in panic buying of a wide range of goods. This soon led to real shortages in food and other household necessities. As a result, in the four months from November 1973 to February 1974 the wholesale price index rose by 30.7 per cent and the consumer price index rose by 21.2 per cent.[7] A number of businessmen took advantage of shortages and consumer confusion to engineer price rises by withholding goods from the market.[8]

To deal with these problems, MITI made extensive use of its powers of 'administrative guidance' to persuade business to behave in an orderly manner, and to reduce the speculation and panic of the 'me first' attitude. Cabinet passed two comprehensive laws, the Petroleum Supply and Demand Normalization Law and the Emergency Measures Law, late in 1973. These laws aimed to deal promptly with the hyper-inflation and deterioration in the balance of payments which followed the large increase in oil prices. It was not until mid-1978 that price levels and the rate of economic growth returned to normal.

In April 1979 the economy was hit by the second oil crisis. This time the rates of inflation and economic growth were not as adversely affected as they had been in the previous case. With the benefit of hindsight, government and business responded to the problems with relative calm and some degree of creativity. Through these two crises the economy was restructured to deal with the new international environment. Economical energy use and an overall increase in productivity were achieved. The structure of the Japanese economy underwent substantial changes, which put an end to the four decades of continuous growth.[9]

In 1974 output actually shrank. This was a shock to the Japanese, who had grown accustomed to high levels of economic growth even during periods of recession. The policy-makers showed signs of confusion and uncertainty during the two oil crises. The national economic plans for 1976–80, published in May 1976, continued to project a high rate of economic growth (see appendix table A.7) and proposed fiscal and monetary measures to achieve it smoothly. Their basic intent was to maintain economic growth while keeping an eye on both inflation and the business cycle.

No economic growth took place in 1974–5. Production in mining and manufacturing, and the productivity of factories in the industrial sector, fell below their pre-crisis levels of 1973. Until the end of the third quarter of 1974, private enterprise continued to enjoy the inflationary profits that had been produced by general shortages of goods and services. But once temporary demand subsided towards the end of 1974, private industry found itself in the midst of declining prices and accumulating stocks. Production had to be reduced. The number of bankruptcies rose to a record postwar level in 1975. The industries which suffered most from the massive increase in the cost of petroleum and electrical power were industrial materials industries such as steel, non-ferrous metals and petrochemicals – designated industries which had received much government patronage.

In February, March and again in June 1975 the government announced a fiscal spending policy together with a supplementary monetary policy to stimulate general economic activity, the public measures which came to be referred to as 'the first, second and third rounds of Measures for Economic Stimulation'.[10] These public measures did not lead to a sufficient recovery; the recession was caused by economic and social problems which the economy was experiencing in the process of its transformation from a high growth economy to one with a much more modest growth rate, but macro-economic policy-makers persisted in believing that the economy could resume high-speed growth. Many private enterprises responded by continuously expanding capital investment.

Ironically, it was O. Shimomura, a government economist who in 1960 provided the economic formula for the National Income-doubling Plan, who now in 1973 proposed his 'zero-growth theory'. It attracted only minority support. The opposite view, that the economy was in a 'transitory recession', fared a little better.[11] Government economists suggested heavier spending on public works, and drastic reductions in official discount rates.[12] At the same time, however, attempts were also made to formulate new macro and industrial policies. The policy guidance published by MITI in May 1971 ('International Trade and Industry Policy in the 1970s'[13]) had become inadequate for the new tasks that it faced. Thus the 1970s was a period of confusion, and of *ad hoc* measures by public policy-makers.

2 Transition to the Decelerated Economy

'Visions' and Administrative Guidance

Although the government's macroeconomic policies tended in practice to stick to past principles, there were new thoughts about the industrial structure of the economy, and the government's role in it. At the beginning of the 'Vision for the 1970s' published in 1974, the policy-makers of MITI observed that the economy had undergone a transformation from being a high-growth economy to a decelerated economy.[14] Consequently, it announced that the purposes and the very *raison d'être* of the existing industrial policy were to be placed under close scrutiny. In reviewing the policy, MITI identified the following three issues as being the most important for government policy.

First, policy-makers should steer the national economy swiftly away from being an exclusively growth-oriented economy to one which put greater importance on (i) improving the working conditions and living environment of the general population of the country, (ii) improving and increasing social overhead capital, (iii) improving the education system and making education more widely available to the people, (iv) developing research activities, and (v) increasing both the governmental budget and business expenditure on international co-operation and associated activities. In essence, MITI proposed that the economy should be directed to improve the quality of life and the welfare of the people through stable growth.

Second, emphasis should be shifted away from the pollution-prone, capital-intensive chemical and heavy industries to assist knowledge-intensive industries to develop the economy. Very different industries should be targeted in the era of stable economic growth compared with those selected before the first oil crisis.

Third, industrial policy was altered to restrict most policy intervention to areas where market failure was expected to cause serious economic inefficiency or damage to community welfare. This meant that the allocation of resources in general was left to the wisdom of the market. The areas noted in (i)–(v) above were seen as areas in which the problems of market failure were expected to be concentrated, thus requiring the guidance of industrial policy.

To develop industrial policies under the new conditions, MITI underwent a reorganization of its own bureaucratic structure. The number (and the relative importance) of *genkyoku* (ministries and departments), which were set up to supervise specific industries, was reduced from eight to three; the Bureaux of Basic Industries (to supervise all the target industries), of Electronic and Electric information systems and of Consumer and Household. New 'horizontal' bureaux were created to deal with inter-industry matters rather than specific industries. In 1979 six such horizontal bureaux were newly structured to formulate policies for international trade administration, industrial location and environmental protection, industrial safety and a general strategy for efficiency and the development of industrial activity in the national economy as a whole.

Along with the proposed changes in the priority of policy objectives and the organizational structure of MITI itself, the nature and form of policy measures were also greatly revised. Administrative guidance, most extensively used by MITI officials through the 1960s, was now replaced by more indirect methods. Especially for big business, planning through public administrative guidance had lost its relevance and popularity by the 1960s, when many in the business community came to show a strong dislike of government intervention in any form.[15] The move towards strengthening the Anti-monopoly Law in 1977 and the eventual decision of the Tokyo Supreme Court in 1980 to make collusion in business and trading illegal (even under MITI's procedures) effectively put an end to administrative guidance and other forms of direct government intervention.

In their place, the official publication of 'visions', such as the 'Vision for the 1970s', became MITI's major policy measure.[16] In MITI's publicity material, the word 'vision' has acquired a special Japanese connotation, indicating an 'ideal form and structure'. MITI's 'Vision' was as much an official publication as the Economic White Paper and other policy documents from other ministries. In its 'Vision' MITI projected the changing trends and future prospects for industry and the economy. It was neither a mere forecast nor mere daydreaming, but contained marked elements of planning. It depicted specific features of industry which the policy-makers wished the business community and the population to use as a guide. It also presented an ideal image of the society of the future, so that the business community and individual enterprises could direct their investment and other economic activities accordingly. In return, they would assist the planners to build an 'ideal' form of the economy. With this in mind, policies in the 'Vision for the 1970s' were revised to formulate the '1975 Vision'[17] and the 'Vision for the 1980s'.[18]

In those 'Visions' the focus of industry policy shifted from heavy and chemical industries to a group of knowledge-intensive industries, such as machine tools of various kinds (electrical, transport and precision machinery), high-tech industries (integrated circuit computing, robotics, fine ceramics and new metals), vertically integrated assembling industries, fashion industries and information-related industries. The development of these industries was viewed as desirable and suited to Japan's economic environment, and they received subsidies of various kinds and tax and financial assistance to develop research and technology. Small and medium-sized enterprises continued to receive administrative guidance from MITI to assist in the development of new products, new technology, technical know-how and managerial skills.

The logical basis of the policy support for the knowledge-intensive industries was fourfold. The first two reasons are the same as those ones given in the 1960s for heavy and chemical industries; in other words, (1) the income elasticity for the products of knowledge-intensive industries would be high, and (2) their rate of growth of productivity would also be very high, which would bring comparative cost advantages in the export market. The new reasons for policy support are stated as follows: (3) the development of the proposed industries would not create further environmental problems; and (4) they would provide better working conditions than the heavy and chemical industries. Individual industries were examined on a case-by-case basis to determine whether they were knowledge-intensive. An industry was deemed knowledge-intensive if the proportion of total cost taken up by the wage and salary cost of employing technical and professional staff was high, and the proportion of total cost taken up by capital and energy costs was low.[19]

Knowledge-intensive industries grew rapidly through the 1970s at the cost of many basic materials industries which were in decline, and which had a considerable amount of excess capacity, such as steel and other metals, cement, textiles and chemical fertilisers. Some industries, such as aluminium refining, had to be completely phased out from Japan due to the sharp increase in the price of electricity after the oil crisis. Other industries, such as textiles and chemical fertilisers, were unable to compete with imports from newly developing nations. The government introduced a Special Provisional Law for the Stabilization of Designated Declining Industries in 1978, to assist designated industries to rationalize their production structure and the re-allocation of their resources to other developing areas.[20] These industries included aluminium refining, synthetic fibre manufacture, ship-building, chemical fertilisers, cotton and synthetic fibres, and textiles.

The 1970s thus saw an abrupt change in the direction of industrial policy, away from government assistance directed at a limited number of target industries. This new direction was characterized by:

1 directing assistance more towards declining industries than expanding industries, and keeping the number of target industries to the minimum; and
2 formulating policy in more global terms to solve problems of environmental damage, energy supply, and friction in international markets.

This change is reflected in MITI's establishment of many new 'horizontal' bureaux to deal with inter-industry matters.[21]

The recession following the first oil crisis was the most severe of the postwar period, and recovery from it was sluggish. It took a full five years before the production index for mining and manufacturing industries finally recovered to the level of October 1973. The economy responded more effectively to the problems caused by the second oil crisis in 1979. By the end of the decade the average annual growth rate had declined to 5 per cent – a half of the preceding long-term performance. Until 1973, private enterprise had continued to base investment plans on the expectation that domestic demand would expand by about 10 per cent annually. The changes wrought in the domestic as well as the world economies by the oil crisis forced the managers of private enterprise to redesign their investment plans to reduce plant and equipment capacity swiftly enough to avoid a wide supply–demand gap. Many companies sought measures to reduce their workforces. The rate of increase of real wages declined drastically, leading to a fall in the real income of individuals and households, and to a reduction in the rate of growth of consumer demand to levels less than half of those enjoyed during the period of high-speed growth.[22]

Having adjusted to the new mode of economic activity, private capital was invested to transform the industrial structure in new technology-based and energy-saving directions, in accord with the government vision. At the end of the 1970s domestic demand began to revive steadily, while the general level of prices remained remarkably stable. The rise in the value of the yen helped, at least for the time being, to eliminate a source of international friction.[23] The economy appeared to be adapting to a 5 per cent annual growth rate in a successful transition to a stable decelerated economic condition.

It remains difficult to understand why the policy-makers were so slow to recognize the nature, extent and direction of the economic change, and what it required of government. Kosai observes that 'once the initial objective of overcoming poverty had been achieved, economic growth was made automatic, began to seem commonsensical, and was systematized... As systematized economic growth gains its own momentum, its original goals are lost sight of.'[24] The Japanese economy spent a whole decade in departing from the rapid growth path, adjusting to the new condition of a slower growth path, and eventually taking the first steps towards new development in the 1980s.

In Search of a New National Goal

In 1980 industry policy-makers articulated their understanding of the conditions of the government, the economy and society in general in MITI's 'Vision of the 1980s'.[25] The overview of their 'Vision' is presented in figure 8.1.

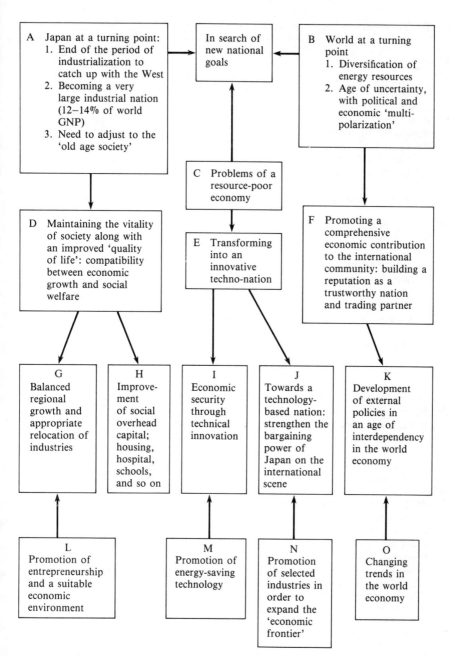

Figure 8.1   *MITI's 'vision' for Japan in the 1980s*
Source: MITI (1980).

Table 8.2   *Achievements of the postwar economy*

	1980 compared to 1946, factor of	1980 compared to prewar (average for 1934–6), factor of
Real GNP	15.1	9.1
Real GNP per capita	9.8	6.7
Real personal consumption	13.3	8.3
Real private fixed capital formation	28.0	25.7
Real government fixed capital formation	25.2	48.3
Mining and manufacturing production	52.1	17.9
Consumer durables	721.5	192.4
Consumer non-durables	23.4	6.4
Capital goods	128.8	59.8
Steel	138.5	30.1
Cars	703.8	n.a.
Houses	2.6	n.a.
Food products	n.a.	3.5[d]
Rice	1.2	1.1
Fish	n.a.	3.4[d]
Total volume of exports	217.1[a]	16.0
Total volume of imports	48.8[a]	9.8
Volume of crude oil imports	649.1	64.8
Total population	1.6	1.7
Total employment	3.3[b]	2.9[c]
Real wages in manufacturing industry	2.5[e]	3.9[e]
Labour productivity	12.1	n.a.
Consumer prices	26.9	1359.7
Wholesale prices	50.6	825.1

[a] Comparison with 1948.
[b] Comparison with 1947.
[c] Comparison with 1950.
[d] Comparison with 1978.
[e] Comparison with 1979.
n.a. indicates not available.
Sources: Bank of Japan, *Keizai Tokei Nenpo* (1966) and Ministry of Labour (1980). Reprinted by permission from Uchino *Japan's Postwar Economy*, published by Kodansha International Ltd. © 1983. All rights reserved.

In order to understand the subject matter of the figure better, the achievements of the postwar economy and the economic situation in 1980 are depicted in broad statistical terms in table 8.2. A comparison of 1946 and 1980 presents the following picture. Real GNP has increased by a factor of 15, real per capita personal consumption has risen by a factor of 13, mining and manufacturing production has increased by a factor of 52 and the volume of exports has risen by a factor of 220. Because 1946 represents the lowest point in Japan's economic activity, the comparison between 1980 and 1934–6, the prewar peak period of economic activity, is also given in the table (column 2).

In addition to the 'Vision of the 1980s', in August 1983 the Economic Council, an advisory body to the Prime Minister, published a new (macro)economic plan entitled 'Outlook and Guidelines of the Economy and Society in the 1980s'.[26] The plan had two striking features which distinguished it from preceeding government plans. First, it provided no programme of public finance; in other words, no projections of the scale of public investment or taxation and social welfare contributions for the plan's eight-year period from 1983 to 1990. Second, it proved to be a revolving plan which would be reviewed and revised each year, and the nature of each revision would depend to a large extent on the trends in public finance.

The very vague nature of the plan may be taken as an indication of the current uncertainty of economic agents about the Japanese economy. It seems that everyone in Japan agrees that the economy has reached some sort of 'turning point' or 'evaluation point', but no national consensus has yet formed on which direction(s) the economy should take next. Nevertheless, there may be some consensus, however vague, about the order of importance of the problems which now confront Japan.

Let us follow figure 8.1 and review the public view of the future direction of the Japanese economy. The central column in the figure indicates that Japan is, for the first time in its history of industrial development, in search of new national objectives. The task of finding national goals is imposed by changes occurring at home and abroad at the end of the growth era. At home, the Japanese economy is experiencing three distinct changes (A1, A2 and A3). People feel that the 100 years' continuous march towards industrialization and modernization since the Meiji Restoration in 1868 has finally led to a crossroads, at which Japan must evaluate her past achievements (A1) and choose a new direction from among the alternatives. Taking the West as a model for industrialization in the preceding years, Japan built her economic system and social structure on the basis of imported technical know-how and managerial and social skills, so as to increase her material welfare. In 1980 the standard of living of Japan's population surpassed that of most Western nations. The factors that were influential in creating among the Japanese a view of Japan's economic strength were not only actual economic achievements but also increasing numbers of reports by foreign observers such as McRae, Kahn and Vogel, who praised Japan's high-speed growth.[27] Foreign criticism of low growth rates in the British and other European economies, and the problems which have beset the US economy since the first oil crisis, provided more support for the view of Japan's experience as a success story. All of these factors helped the Japanese to build their confidence and to look for new ways 'to promote and develop their own culture and economic system and, by doing so, help increase the welfare of the world as a whole' (F in figure 8.1). This last aim tended to be encouraged by the fact that Japan had come to produce over 10 per cent of world GNP. Through its sheer size, her economy had considerable influence on the world economy. This in turn meant that Japan was obliged to be responsible in her economic conduct, lest it lead to undesirable consequences for the world economy (A2).

Another factor which calls for new policies is the ageing of the population. In 1980 it was estimated that Japan's workforce would increase by 8.6 million between 1978 and 2000. Of this 6.4 million (two-thirds) are expected to be over 55 years old, creating an age structure of the workforce in the year 2000 with 23.5 per cent over 55 and only 23 per cent under 30. The comparable figures in 1978 were estimated to be 15.5 per cent and 26.5 per cent respectively. As the average years of education increase, both categories of dependents – those not yet working, and those over 65 years old – will grow in numbers and proportion, to be supported by a diminishing proportion of people of working age.[28]

This problem is compounded by yet another, in the structure of the workforce. With the rapid expansion of the service sectors in the economy, it was estimated that the participation of women in the workforce, in particular in the age range 40–54, would rise considerably from the 1978 level (34 per cent). It was also expected that an increasing number of female workers would prefer to work on a part-time basis. An increase in university graduates was also expected and with the slowing-down of economic growth those with higher training and qualifications would compete for a limited number of career openings in government ministries and the private sector. In summary, all of these changes seemed likely to lead to considerable revision in the traditional employment system, based on a lifetime with one employer and promotion by seniority.

Externally, two aspects (B1 and B2) demand careful consideration. The first concern was with the possible diversification of energy sources away from oil to solar, water, wind, liquid gas and atomic energy. To minimize the consumption of energy, a gradual reduction in high-energy industries such as heavy and chemical industries should be planned. The second concern was with the world political and economic scene, on which a 'multi-polarization' of world power is developing. In 1960, the USA was the world leader, with its GNP representing almost 30 per cent of that of the world as a whole. In 1980 the figure was just above 20 per cent; the USA was still the largest economic and political power, but its relative importance was declining.[29] Further diversification of international interests and conflicts are expected to emerge in the future. The role of Japan on the international scene should be considered with items A2 and B2 in mind; that is, as the role of a major economic power in a changing world system.

To maintain the necessary economic strength and adaptability, industrial policy should be directed at enhancing the vitality of the private business sector so as to sustain continuing economic growth. The planned rate of growth should be evaluated from time to time, taking into consideration the achieved adjustment of the economy to the changes in A and B, roughly estimated to be 5–7 per cent per annum. In June 1984, Keizai Kikakucho (EPA) announced the somewhat ambitious figure of 7.4 per cent growth, which was supported by other ministries including MITI.[30] Meanwhile, the MITI policy-makers had suggested nine important areas (G to O in figure 8.1) towards which industrial policy should be directed in order to achieve the new national goals (D, E and F). The general concept of those ten policy-directed areas is self-explanatory in the figure. The overall message conveyed in the figure appears to have won general support from the Japanese population, one reason for this being that it called for considerable growth and change in the government's approach to the people's welfare.

3   Growth and Welfare Issues and the Role of Government

New Challenges

In 1987 and 1988 Sogo Kenkyu Kaihatsu Kikō (the National Institute of Research Advancement – NIRA) a Government-established research organization, published two research reports on the welfare and living standards of the Japanese people.[31] The first compares present-day Japan with developed societies in the West. The second is a historical study of the process of economic development over the past 100 years.[32] According to the 1987 report, the living standards and general welfare conditions of the Japanese people (leaving aside the difficulties of defining and measuring welfare) appear to have reached a comparable, if not higher, level than those of any of the advanced economies in the West. Most of that was achieved between 1946 and 1980: during those 35 years real per capita income increased by a factor of ten.

The dates are significant. Roughly speaking, the people who were born between 1910 and 1935 make up the generation who brought about Japan's rapid growth. They share the experience of the war, of wartime and postwar deprivation, and of Western stereotyping of their country as cheapjack exploiters of cheap labour and unfair trading practices. For them economic growth was more than a rational response to poverty. Through the early postwar decades it was the only mode of national recovery, endeavour and pride open to them. And the recovery of economy and nation alike seemed to be achievable only through continuous hard work. That was the basic ethos of that generation, leading them to throw all their energy into their work without paying much attention to leisure pursuits. They had normal individual ambitions. As labour union members they may have sought wage increases, shorter working hours and various improvements in the work environment. Some voted for reformist parties at election time. But they did not question the work ethos, and within a single working lifetime[33] it brought them and their children a tenfold increase in real income, and the rise of their country on the international scene to the status of 'economic superpower'. As 'workaholics in rabbit hutches' their dedication to work and economic growth may have been 'obsessive'; but, if so, it proved to be one of the most productive and well-rewarded obsessions in recorded history.

By 1971, when the slogan 'Damn GNP' was first hoisted in Japan, the growth-oriented generation was being gradually displaced, and little by little people's values and national consciousness began to change. Younger people with no memory of the war or the postwar hardships began to take an active part in society by expressing opposition to their elders. Ironically, because this generation grew up in affluence it saw no particular value in growth and affluence. The confusion and inconsistent behaviour that we observed above among policy-makers and government departments in the 1970s manifests the conflict between these two generations. In search of a change in values, the younger generation looked to the re-harmonization of an affluent society dominated by materialism as its most important task. They gladly turned away from the excessively organized and administered way of life to concern themselves with questions of welfare and equity under the slogan of 'the end of the rapid growth era'. The older generation, on the other hand, continued to be strongly attached to rapid growth, but came to see it as a means of promoting the new objectives of the younger generation. The issue of growth versus welfare emerged – only to prompt new questions. Had growth itself become undesirable; or only the ways of pursuing it, or its side-effects, or the unequal distribution of its benefits? And how should the answers to those questions shape new aims, objectives, instruments and measures for the governments which must give direction to Japan's future?

The Plan for Restructuring Society

The serious Japanese study of 'welfare' appeared quite suddenly at the beginning of the 1970s, both in Japanese publications and in works translated into Japanese. Before then, readings on welfare economics and writing about concepts of welfare had remained outside mainstream economic studies. The National Institute of Research Advancement (NIRA) mentioned above was established in March 1974 to provide the government with information and policy-making advice on various social problems which had emerged as important policy concerns at the time. The range of 'social problems' was taken to include problems concerning energy use, urban living conditions, public social services, and disparity of regional development – problems which had arisen as side-effects of rapid economic growth. NIRA was active in funding numerous research projects, commissioning enquiries and organizing workshops and seminars, so that in its first five years to 1979 more than 200 study results were published. A large number of these addressed, directly and indirectly, living standards and the general well-being of the population. 'Welfare' became a hotly debated issue among policy-makers in their effort to reappraise economic policy for growth in the past and for the future.

Among these publications, the work of Kumagai and others, summarized in figure 8.2,[34] is helpful in giving a general view of welfare and economic growth in Japan at this time.

The figure has been compiled using Kumagai's analysis, with additional items (marked by asterisks) to indicate the development of the concept of welfare as it has been conceived since the 1970s. The nature and constituents of welfare – both economic and social – change and expand over time as the nations' economic activity expands. Until the debate in the 1970s, 'welfare' had been pursued in Japan mostly through efforts to promote economic equity, primarily by means of equal pay and employment opportunities. More equal distribution of income and wealth appeared to be the most effective way of creating a 'fair' and 'just' society. On this basis,

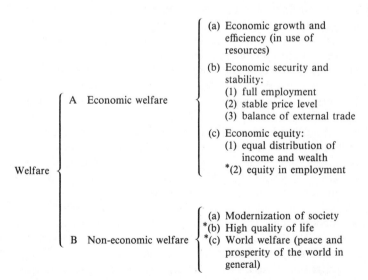

Figure 8.2 *Economic growth and welfare for policy implementation*

as we discussed earlier in chapter 4, the national effort was directed at promoting education and training in the general population at a level consistent with the resources available within the national economy. Once people were provided with equal access to education and training, individuals were expected to make the most of their opportunities and maximize their earnings in the workplace. This philosophy made little allowance for anyone who for any reason was unable to take advantage of the publicly provided opportunities. In the 1990s the legacy of this way of thinking remains: the best welfare policy is one which equips people to provide for their own welfare. But the definition of 'welfare' has continuously expanded and now involves a wider range of elements of well-being; and some of the ways of providing these elements have changed.

With the above observation in mind, let us study how policy-makers have understood the relation between 'economic growth' and the 'welfare' of the population. The following four beliefs about the policy mix conveniently capture how the relation has been perceived by different thinkers and at different times through the postwar years:

- Policy mix A: economic growth and the welfare of the population are seen as aims which can be maximized simultaneously.
- Policy mix B: welfare is seen as a means of increasing growth.
- Policy mix C: growth and welfare are seen to be conflicting objectives, whatever policy measures are adopted. The relation between the two is a trade-off or a 'zero sum', in which the one can only increase at the expense of the other.
- Policy mix D: growth is seen as a means of increasing welfare, and should be pursued only as necessary to maximize welfare.

Next, basing our study on the reading of the annual Economic White Paper,[35] let us see how the emphasis of policy has shifted from its first publication in 1947 to its most recent publication in 1989. In appendix table A.6 we show the title of each Economic White Paper, along with the major policy control, in order to indicate the trend of policy direction. We make the following observations.

First, up to 1958, that is before the National Income-doubling Plan, economic policy was directed towards economic growth in a most single-minded manner. Whether it was expressed in terms of economic recovery to the prewar level or economic independence from US procurement assistance, the aim of economic policy was expansion of production, and it was believed that achievement of this aim would bring welfare to the nation and its people. The 1951 Economic White Paper discussed the importance of the level of accumulation of wealth (assets) in addition to the level of production and consumption when evaluating the actual living standards of the population. It acknowledged that a great gap existed between the two because of the damage to productive capacity during the war. Such concern lead to a public survey of national wealth in 1955. The 1956 Economic White Paper stressed the need to modernize the economy with a view to the future. Growth in terms of sheer increase in the size of GNP should not be the sole objective of public policy; society must be transformed into a 'modern' society with advanced methods of production and new technology on a par with the West. Modernization of society, however, was still understood within the basic framework of the national need to achieve sustained economic growth and not in terms of the welfare of the population.

In the 1950s the concept of 'welfare' was understood to cover only 'economic growth' and 'economic security' (A.a. + A.b. in figure 8.2). Policy in this period falls into category A: growth and welfare come together, as aspects of the same achievement.

Second, the National Income-doubling Plan, a plan to maximize growth, widened the concept of growth for the first time so as to include equity issues. We noticed that policies to improve working conditions between sectors and within industries were proposed for the first time. They had a familiar form: maximizing economic growth was the basic way in which to reduce the differentials in wages and working conditions between sectors and regions and within industries, so that disputes about the living standards of the population would be reduced. The element of the plan which addressed the issues of regional economic development, particularly disparities in industrial development and income, failed to bring about results and had to be addressed again later in the form of a plan for rebuilding the Japanese Archipelago, in the Basic Economic and Social Plan of 1973.[36] In this plan, the government set out to solve all of the economic and social problems and quality of life issues that were caused by environmental degradation and urban congestion due to economic growth created by large-scale public spending. Despite the growth of the popular view that welfare and growth could not be pursued simultaneously, and that welfare had more constituents than the government had yet acknowledged, economic policy remained stubbornly in the confines of category B: direct attention to welfare was justified where (as in regional equalization) it would help growth.

Third, the need to build a 'welfare state' was first mentioned officially in the Economic White Paper of 1969, but at this stage the concept of 'welfare state' was not clear. It was referred to generally in the context of public awareness of the 'negative side' of economic growth in such areas as environmental degradation, shortage of housing and public facilities, and urban congestion. Central government attention to the modernization of social security systems and national health schemes took place in this period. The Department of the Environment was established in 1971.

Statistical and other information was most eagerly gathered and published in Economic White Papers between 1969 and 1979. The government sought to compare the economic standards of Japanese society with those of advanced economies in Europe and the USA in the areas of social over-head capital (transport facilities, recreation and other facilities for the well-being of people and community as a whole, such as parks, libraries, the water supply, and so on). This exercise resulted in the government dis-covering the major areas of the welfare system that lagged far behind those of the advanced nations despite Japan's high-speed economic growth. In the effort to assess the actual benefit of economic growth in providing the people with a higher real income and standard of living, the Net National Welfare (NNW) index was devised in 1974.[37] This period saw active debates and efforts to bring economic growth in line with an improvement in the standard of living of the population. It was not possible to estimate the standard of living accurately and quantitatively in the same way as GNP. Public economic policy found its direction first in category C (with growth and welfare as rivals for resources) but gradually shifted back to category B (with welfare helping growth). The approach adopted in the late 1970s was summarized in the public slogan 'welfare progress through economic growth', which at least hints at category D, although it falls short of valuing growth only for its output of welfare.

Fourth, during the 1980s the Japanese economy embarked upon a moderate growth path and, as we saw earlier, it took steps towards new developments in economic management both at home and in the inter-national arena. How did this transformation to moderate growth affect the formation of the official attitude to the relationship between growth and welfare? Will it continue to stay in the category B formula, or is it heading towards the possible new alternative listed in category D? Through a careful reading of study reports by various government departments and economic councils published in 1987–9,[38] we understand the government's present view of its role in economic activity to be as follows.

It is not clear whether, in the structure of government policy and the actual administration of policy measures, economic growth will become a less important objective than improving the welfare of the population. However, there is no doubt about the intended presence of government in the nation's economic management and activity. 'Large' government is envisaged in the sense that government will have a new and wider range of social and international considerations in mind as it attends to the direction and speed of economic growth. It may not be 'big government' in the Western sense of running a big budget or owning many public corporations, but the Japanese government expects to be bigger than before in the sense that its role and function in the national economy will increase. Market mechanisms in directing investment into particular growth areas will be replaced more and more by public guidance and administrative influence. Government rules and regulations will be taking a more active role in coor-dinating decisions about the general directions of growth, and in resolving conflicts of interest and opinion between individuals, groups and society as a whole.

We have discussed earlier how active public investment has encouraged and directed national economic growth. Another NIRA study discusses the recent trend of public investment after its decline in the 1970s.[39] It suggests that the decline should be viewed as a temporary one-off phenomenon that occurred in the process of a transition from high-speed growth to moderate growth. The 'traditional' approach of public intervention met its challenge in the adjustment of the economy's industry structure, as well as in the reduction of public revenue in the slower-growing economy. The government is now investing more in infrastructure facilities for welfare rather than for industrial development purposes, and may be expected to increase public spending through transfer payments to households (social security payments, health programmes and others) and to industry (subsidies to ease the decline of ailing industries and areas).

When the economy emerged from the period of confusion created by the two oil crises and shifted to a path of moderate growth, the government had to find a new direction and a new formula for public intervention. It has chosen to maintain the 'traditional' approach by continuing to exercise public leadership in directing the form of economic development and the pattern of industrial structure through public investment. This time the desirable areas and industries for development will be selected on the basis of their direct contribution to the welfare and standard of living of the population and not on the basis of economic growth for its own sake, as was the case with designated key industries in the period of high-speed growth in the 1950s and 1960s. The selected industries will continue to obtain government patronage through the provision of infrastructure support. The concept of 'developing the country' appears to remain the core strategy for economic growth. The government's role will continue to be supportive, and it will continue to induce private interest to accord with public purposes. With continued 'large government' the Japanese are going to build a welfare state of their own choice by their own traditional methods, in which public capital formation is expected to play an even larger role than it did during the preceding period of industrialization.

What is not yet so clear is the particular kind of welfare society that the authorities will attempt to create, and the particular policy instruments and measures that they will use for the purpose. Both will depend on the sort of people 'they' prove to be; that is, on the mind-set of the politicians and bureaucrats who devise the policies. That in turn must, of course, depend on their democratic political situation, on which parties win government in national elections, and so on. But 'they' – the authors of the public policies which have led Japan from feudalism to modern industrial affluence – have survived diverse regimes in the past, and are likely to gain rather than lose influence from the only likely change of government in the near future.[40] 'They' have been shadowy figures in this book up to now. Two tasks remain: to explore the mind and instruments of government – its particular ways of thinking and acting – through the century and a half of modernization; and then to discuss what particular kind of mature welfare society the Japanese people, with their distinctive kind of leadership, might best attempt to construct.

9 Explanations: the Nature and Government of Japanese Capitalism, 1868–1990

Our quest for better understanding of the role of the state in industrial and economic development in Japan is approaching its end. A century-long national effort has led Japan from its humble status as a small underdeveloped economy, whose population struggled to make a meagre living from the toils of the rice paddy, to what Japan is today. How have the Japanese achieved this? This question has inspired many researchers to generate various hypotheses, and a wealth of research based on the hypotheses. Writing only of those which discuss postwar economic development, Murakami divides them into two groups, those that emphasize economic factors and those that emphasize cultural factors. The former stress a set of factors in the 'objective environment', such as the labour supply, diffusion of technology, and expansion of the world market. The latter focus on factors in the 'subjective environment', including various aspects of traditional Japanese culture such as group orientation.[1] For argument's sake we could match those economic and cultural explanations by concocting a third – a political one – as follows. An old-established ruling class decided that it must modernize to secure its own and Japan's strength and independence. For that purpose it created a strong, undemocratic national government which used force where necessary to impose hard work, low pay and miserable living conditions on the mass of peasants and workers for long enough to achieve high rates of profit, capital accumulation and self-sustaining economic growth; after which, as living standards improved, it became possible to continue the growth with democratic support.

Our study does not fit in any of those pigeonholes. In part, we see the economic conditions and the culture as resources which government was able to enlist and use for economic purposes; to a certain extent, government did not simply 'find' those resources – it helped to develop them. At the same time it did depend on employing such resources; Japan's success is not simply a product of dictatorial government; the world has many backward countries whose culture and economic conditions would resist economic development even by the best of Japanese bureaucrats and entrepreneurs.

The causal analysis of complex social processes must always have a problematic element. When an effect depends on a number of necessary conditions there may be no objective way in which to compare their importance: each of them has some absolute importance. Obviously, for example, the industrialization of Japan required at least these three contributing factors: (i) a framework of government, public education and physical and institutional infrastructure; (ii) energetic private entrepreneurs; and (iii) hardworking, co-operative workers. Any of the three is entitled to say 'Without us, it could not have happened'. But that does not entitle any of the three to claim that 'We did it alone'. (We will cite such a false claim for private enterprise alone, and indicate what is wrong with it, later in this chapter.) It is not our aim to make the same mistaken claim for government. Government no more developed the Japanese economy single-handed than a driver can speed along a road without a motor car. Moreover, good cars can have good, bad or indifferent drivers. We do not argue *either* that government's contribution to modernization was more important than the contributions of business or labour, *or* that government's role in the process was always wise or competent. What we do argue is that the role of government in Japan's economic development has been unusual by Western standards, and that it gives Japan an unusual capacity to think strategically, and at times to make deliberate changes of direction, as a national society.[2] The capacity has sometimes operated illiberally. It has been misused for fascist purposes. But it has also taken a poor and backward society to wealth and independence, and may yet be used to civilize it further, perhaps inventively. It is this unusual capacity, and its difference from most Western models, that we set out to explore.

In this chapter we do what we can to understand the components of Japan's unusual capacity for effective national action. From the history as a whole we summarize information about the organization and size of the public sector; the cycles of policy through the nine periods of our study; an impression of the mentality of the generations of bureaucrats who have been the main authors of the government's economic policies; and a conclusion about the basic political economy of Japanese capitalism.

1   The Public Sector

Japan has had a strong and active government throughout. Its influence pervades much of the economic and social life of the country, using a wide range of devices, many of them unique to Japan, for the pursuit of perceived public aims. The public sector as measured in institutional and budgetary terms does not sufficiently measure the force or extent of the influence; but our analysis can begin with an outline of the sector.

The structure and spending patterns of the sector have changed over time with changing conditions and stages of economic growth. As elsewhere in the developed world, the public role has expanded through the twentieth century, but in Japan more than elsewhere the trend masks many internal changes. Public ownership or activity expands in some areas while contracting, or becoming redundant and closing down altogether, in others. It is therefore not much use arguing whether some specific public activity has been particularly large or small by international standards. It is more useful to ask whether the public sector was effectively structured, and its market influence adequate for its purposes, at particular times. If a public activity is declining, it has not so far been safe to conclude that the force or importance of government as a whole, or of government's economic role, is declining. The policy-makers may merely be replacing some objectives or instruments by others.

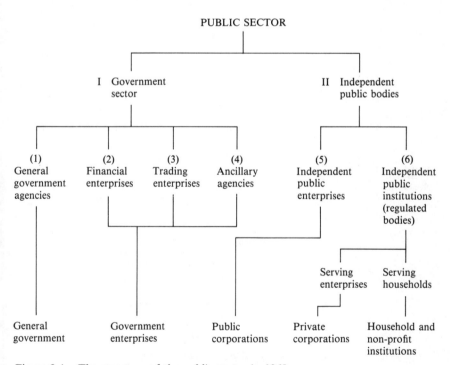

Figure 9.1 *The structure of the public sector in 1965*
Source: Emi (1966, p. 118).

Organization of the Sector

The structure and characteristics of the public sector in Japan are complex. Figures 9.1 and 9.2, should therefore be taken as simplified diagrams, revealing the basic 'bone structure' of public-sector organization. The structure of the organization of the government network is indicated in figure 9.1, while the structure of public finance is outlined in figure 9.2.

The structure and relative size of the public sector have changed over time. Tables 9.1 and 9.2 cover the century to 1983, prior to the large-scale privatization of public corporations since 1985.

In figure 9.1, the first major division is between the government sector (I) and independent public bodies (II). In figure 9.2 they are divided into general government (A) and public corporations (B). The activities of the government in figures 9.1 and 9.2 obtain their annual budget under the headings of 'The general account budget' and 'The special account budget'. When one refers to 'government activities', this generally means those

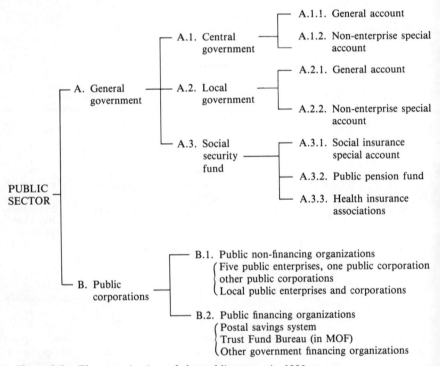

Figure 9.2   *The organization of the public sector in 1980*
Source: EPA, *Keizai Hakusho* (Economic White Paper) (1983, p. 212). The figure is presented in M. Takahashi (1986, p. 30).

Table 9.1   *GNP and fiscal sizes, 1885–1989 (1885–1940, ¥1 million; 1947– , ¥100 million)*

		Government expenditure (B)			
Year	GNP (A)	*(1)* Central government general account expenditure	*(2)* Local government expenditure	*(3)* Central and local government net expenditure	*(4)* $\frac{(B3)}{(A)} \times 100$ (%)
1885	806	61	30	89	11.0
1890	1 056	82	40	119	11.3
1895	1 552	85	55	136	8.8
1900	2 414	292	128	412	17.1
1905	3 084	420	131	543	17.6
1910	3 925	569	280	837	21.7
1915	4 991	583	295	862	17.3
1920	15 896	1 357	879	2 170	13.7
1925	16 265	1 524	1 300	2 694	16.6
1930	13 850	1 557	1 647	3 033	21.9
1935	16 734	2 206	2 118	4 057	24.2
1940	39 396	5 860	2 788	7 823	19.9
		(SECOND WORLD WAR)			
1947	13 090	2 058	905	2 473	18.9
1950	39 460	6 332	5 099	9 185	23.3
1955	88 646	10 407	11 369	16 957	19.1
1960	162 070	17 431	19 249	28 631	17.1
1965	336 425	37 230	43 651	63 011	18.7
1970	752 382	81 876	98 149	1 431 541	19.0
1975	1 519 491	208 608	256 545	375 446	24.7
1980	2 393 414	436 814	457 808	672 379	28.1
1985	3 212 903	530 045	562 935	889 058	27.7
1989	3 965 000	604 142	627 727	984 390	24.8

Note: Net expenditure for central and local government is less than the combined total of central government and local government expenditures because part of the former is allocated to the latter. It has been observed that the fiscal size of Japan as a percentage of GNP has remained relatively small (under 20 per cent) for some time throughout its history. But the situation began to change drastically after the first oil crisis, raising the ratio approaching the comparative figures observed in the West (see Shibata, 1986, pp. 28–30).
Sources: Takahashi, (1986, p. 25), Takeda (1987, p. 52) and Bank of Japan, *Keizai Tokei Nenpo*, March 1988.

Table 9.2   *Relative proportion of public sector in total national economy, 1870–1986*

	(1) Total public expenditure (1934–6 prices)	(2) Breakdown of (1) into: a Purchase of government service (%)	b Military purposes (%)	c Transfer payments (%)	d GDCF (%)	(3)	(4) e (1) GNP (%)
1870	n.a.	53.1	(26.6)	29.5	17.4		n.a.
1880	276	67.5	(20.4)	21.8	10.7		10.9
1890	410	66.0	(21.5)	18.0	16.0		21.1
1900	1 015	65.9	(33.7)	11.5	22.6		21.5
1910	2 667	59.9	(28.7)	14.7	25.4		46.9
1920	2 705	65.4	(39.2)	7.7	26.9		30.1
1930	5 539	69.2	(20.2)	9.0	21.8		40.3
1935	7 913	n.a.	n.a.	n.a.	n.a.		47.1
1940	9 296	82.9	(80.2)	5.7	11.4		45.5
1950	9 069	50.8	n.a.	9.7	39.5		55.5
1960	13 879	41.9	(5.1)	20.2	37.9		35.0
1970	22 602	36.3	(3.3)	24.9	38.8		44.0
1976	78 673	37.1	(6.7)	32.6	30.3		39.6
1980	91 099	34.9	(5.4)	31.2	33.9		46.2
1986	95 280	30.9	(6.2)	48.1	21.0		48.7

n.a. indicates 'not available'.
Sources: For 1870–1960, Emi and Shionoya (1966); and for 1970–86, Yanokota Kinenkai (ed.), relevant years.

included in 'General government' activities and services (I) in figure 9.1 or (A) in figure 9.2.

They comprise 'collective goods and services' such as law and order, diplomatic activities, defence and the prevention of epidemic diseases and part of compulsory education, social security services and some of the so-called 'built-in stabilizer' measures. Public enterprises belong to various ministries and departments of the central and local prefectural governments obtaining the special accounts budget, but they are conducted principally on the basis of an autonomous accounting system. As one would expect, the public enterprises of the central government offer goods and services which are required to meet specific regional needs such as public works, education and social services. Public corporations (II.5 in figure 9.1, and (B) in figure 9.2) are 'off-budget' government programmes. They are owned by the government, but their management is independent of government ministries and departments, and their 'self-supporting' financial structure is stressed more than that of ministerial or departmental enterprises. Public corporations can be divided into two categories, non-financing organizations (B.1 in figure 9.2) and financing organizations (B.2 in figure 9.2). Non-financing organizations are funded and supervised by central and local government.

The public financing organizations represent a significant feature of the public sector in Japan. They include two government banks, the Japan Import–Export Bank (JIEB) and the Japan Development Bank (JDB), and public finance corporations such as the Small Business Finance Corporation (SBFC), the Housing Loan Corporation (HLC), the Agriculture, Forestry and Fisheries Financing Corporation (AFFFC) and others such as post offices (PO) and the Overseas Economic Co-operation Fund (OECF).

One of the backbones of the public financial institutions was a unique credit programme which has developed into the Fiscal Investment and Loan Programme (FILP) in the postwar years. This provides a comprehensive system of government investment and credit for public enterprises and corporations, as well as for private businesses regarded as having special importance in terms of development and social policy, or for projects unable to find adequate financing through the market system. The main sources of the fund have been post office savings, public pension funds and insurance funds. As much as 30 per cent of total personal savings are reported to have been deposited in the postal savings network throughout most of the postwar years.

Over time, considerable changes have taken place in public-sector organizations and in the relative sizes and functions of central and local government: we observe changes in the 'Government sector' and 'Independent public bodies' (I and II in figure 9.1 and A and B in figure 9.2 respectively), in the allocation of capital funds through 'general' and 'special' accounts; subsidies and various financial devices of the government; and the establishment of banking organizations and networks. When the economy came out of the devastating effects of the Second World War, various drastic postwar reforms were forced upon Japan's economic managers. A completely new political and economic course was set in almost every area of national life. The government sector was significantly reformed, resulting in a considerable discontinuity in government policy in the financial and banking areas between the periods before, during and after the war. In addition, statistics both in the early period of industrialization and during the period immediately preceding the war are not completely reliable. An accurate historical understanding of the relationship between Japan's public sector and the national economy is hindered by this problem.

The Size of the Public Sector

Measures of public expenditure as a proportion of GNP, and in comparison with other nations, are useful as long as we do not accept them as indicating the full extent of the government's economic role. Table 9.1 provides such measures and shows the government sector increasing over time from 1885 to date, omitting the abnormal period of the war years. According to the table, the nominal GNP increased by a factor of 49 (on average by 3 per cent per annum) over the 55 years from 1885 to 1940. During this period, the fiscal size of government (column 3 of table 9.1) expanded by a factor of almost 88, indicating the proportional increase in the size of the public sector in the national economy. However, such an expansion of fiscal size did not take place at a steady rate. It began when the economy 'took off' around the turn of the century. Prior to 1900 the percentage of net public expenditure to GNP was slightly over 11 per cent, which increased to 13.7 per cent in 1920 and further to 24.2 per cent in 1935.

The periods of greatest expansion in government expenditure are periods of war, as shown in figure 9.3. In those periods, simple expansion of the

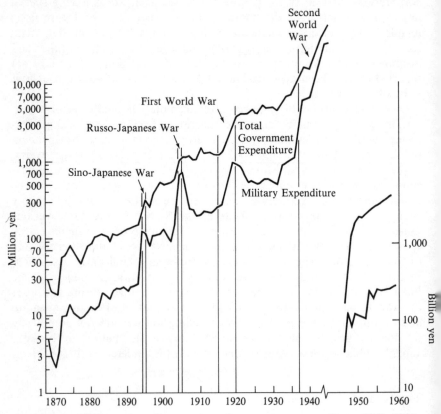

Figure 9.3   *Military expenditure and total government expenditure, 1868–1960 (at current prices).*
Source: Emi (1963, p. 26).

general government account was not enough. To meet the demands of the defence ministries, the government was forced to set up separate 'extra-ordinary military special accounts' in the Sino-Japanese War (1894–5), the Russo-Japanese War (1904–5), the First World War (1914–18), the Siberian Expedition (1919–20) and the Second World War (1937–45, counting from the outbreak of the China War in 1937). For military 'incidents' short of general war, the related expenses were disposed of as extra items of the general account. Military expenses in the narrowest sense include only the total expenses of the Ministries of the Army and Navy, and the war expenses of each government department. But to see the whole extent of government participation in the economy we must expand the concept of 'military' expenses to include public moneys spent for peacetime defence purposes and further expenses such as annuities, pensions and other forms of assistance to ex-soldiers or their survivors, and interest payments on government bonds and other borrowings made for military purposes. These are difficult items to measures accurately. The official estimates of these expenses are included in figure 9.3 in relation to total government expenditure. They fluctuate strikingly, moving sharply upwards in time of war and falling into deep troughs during peace time. Despite the military 'troughs', it is clear that total government expenditure expanded throughout the period.

How do these Japanese figures compare with those of other countries? In table 9.3 efforts are made to compare Japan with leading industrial countries. Although the figures in column 1 are for the central government only, and do not necessarily represent all public activities, they support two speculative observations. First, public expenditure, in relation to total national expenses, remained relatively large throughout the prewar years. Japan's fiscal size (general account) relative to GNE was much higher than those of the USA, the UK and Germany in the years before the First World War. In the following years the UK and France overtook Japan, but the Japanese ratio still remained higher than those of the USA and Germany. Second, we do not see the sudden increases in the size of the public sector which others experienced. In many developed countries the World Depression of the 1930s and the Second World War triggered a 'displacement' effect in which public sectors expanded sharply to substitute for private activity. In contrast, Japan's central government spending increased gradually, as the economic structure shifted slowly but continuously towards a greater participation by government.

Many researchers have tried to understand the nature and extent of the government's role in the national economy through statistics of the kind we have presented, which directly compare government activities to those of private enterprises.[3] We have already expressed our reasons for thinking otherwise. The off-budget expenses of semi-government bodies (independent public bodies – II in figure 9.1) and the financial resources raised through various public financial institutions and their networks are not

Table 9.3 Government expenditure as percentage of GNE: Japan and selected countries, 1885–1980

	Central government					Central and local government				
	Japan	UK	USA	West Germany	France	Japan	UK	USA	West Germany	France
1885	n.a.	n.a.	n.a.	n.a.	n.a.	14.6	n.a.	n.a.	n.a.	n.a.
1888	n.a.	n.a.	n.a.	n.a.	n.a.	12.1	n.a.	n.a.	n.a.	n.a.
1891	7.1	7.2	3.1	5.6	11.3	10.1[a]	n.a.	n.a.	n.a.	n.a.
1905	13.0	8.2	2.0	6.1	12.7	17.4[b]	n.a.	n.a.	n.a.	n.a.
1931–5	14.1	20.6	9.0	12.1	23.3	16.3[c]	n.a.	n.a.	n.a.	n.a.
1950	18.7	31.9	14.9	19.4	34.6	19.4[d]	n.a.	n.a.	n.a.	n.a.
1970	13.8	n.a.	26.4	16.5	25.9	20.6[e]	39.0[e]	31.4[e]	40.0[e]	40.9[e]
1975	13.9	20.8[f]	23.9	15.2	23.1	26.6	44.5	35.1	44.0	41.6
1980	n.a.	n.a.	n.a.	n.a.	n.a.	32.9	44.3	32.7	45.0	45.7
1988	15.3	27.3	22.3	13.0	25.0[g]	n.a.	n.a.	n.a.	n.a.	n.a.

[a] For 1900; [b] for 1910; [c] average of 1930–8; [d] for 1955; [e] for 1967; [f] for 1977; [g] for 1985; n.a. indicates 'not available'.
Sources: Harada and Kosai (1984, pp. 48–9), Noguchi (1987, p. 188), Minami (1986, ch. X) and Keizai Koho Center (1987; 1989; 1990, table 10-6).

included in general government expenditure. To estimate the real size of the public sector in the national economy correctly, we first need to study the creation of the public-sector structure and the workings of its network. This necessitates a study of the functions of all of the public institutions and organizations shown in figures 9.1 and 9.2, including (for example) the financing of private enterprises both by public banks and by private financial institutions acting under public administrative instructions and guidelines. But above and beyond those direct interventions, we argue for the importance of the government's ability – through education, information services, indicative planning and national leadership – to influence the private decision-making of enterprises and households in areas of investment, consumption and savings. In Japan, government has exercised a major influence on private activities between different sectors and industries, different markets and regional areas, and has encouraged the development of different products for different purposes to shape the functions and the overall industrial development of the national economy. These activities are not effectively reflected simply by analysing government spending. We need to follow the changing objectives of public policy as a whole, of which the budget activity is only a part.

2 Policy Cycles

How should we explain the policy cycles, generally of 12–20 years' duration, which we have observed through our nine historical periods, and what is their relationship to the dynamism of Japan's capitalism?[4] It is one task to explain their effects, and quite another to explain what inspired the policies themselves. Schumpeter saw the regular ups and downs of the business cycle, generated by the capitalist system, as the pump which supplied the system's dynamism by confronting entrepreneurs with continuously changing problems and opportunities. Have policy cycles performed that function for Japan?

With that question in mind we will first review the nine periods, and then analyse some characteristics of the policy choices and the people who made them.

It is convenient to anticipate one analytical device here, in order to use it in the historical review. The numerous policy measures employed from time to time can be seen as falling into two broad classes, which we will call 'policies for growth' and 'policies for efficiency'. Policies for *growth* are chosen when policy-makers identify bottlenecks: in other words, particular scarcities which limit the achievable rate of growth of the economy as a whole. Policies are then designed to improve the supply of the scarce resource – whether it be education, technology, foreign exchange, raw materials, a road or rail network or (most commonly) capital. Policies for *efficiency* aim to improve the efficiency with which available resources are being used. They may reallocate resources between firms or industries, encourage or discourage competition, alter patterns of corporate size and market strength; or they may switch some resources to welfare services or income transfers. Many of the cyclic changes come about as the bureaucrats switch from the one approach to the other, or look for the right mix of the two. (Some Western analysts would assign redistributive and welfare policies to a third category of 'policies for welfare'. But as we have argued, separate policies of those kinds were comparatively rare until recent decades, and were regarded as policies of efficiency in that they were designed to improve the working of the productive system by reducing conflict and improving co-operation; while the policy-makers continued to think of the productive system itself as the main source of the people's welfare.)

We now briefly recapitulate the stages of development, and changes of direction, which were traced in the preceding chapters.

I.   1868–1880

The early Meiji modernizers aimed to give Japan the roads and bridges, postal services, government offices and educated population which would identify her as an independent modern society, and equip her people to supply and serve in modern armed forces. The effort to industrialize was mainly by means of (i) building infrastructure, (ii) intensive foreign study of the West and its technology, and (iii) the creation of government-owned industrial enterprises. All three were policies of growth, to supply the economy with the infrastructure, technical knowledge and entrepreneurs that it lacked.

II.   1881–1900

The new (1881) regime learned from the mistakes of its predecessors. Financing infrastructure and government enterprises by printing money had been inflationary; the new regime deflated the currency, and founded the Bank of Japan and a national banking system based broadly on foreign models but with public ownership of a number of the banks, and with a strong bias towards industrial rather than other uses of savings. Plenty of technology continued to come from Britain and the USA, but for economic philosophy and policy the new government turned chiefly to imperial Germany. Public industrial enterprises gave way to aids to private enterprise; infrastructure, some non-tariff protective measures, government procurement, especially of military supplies, and a financial system to generate capital and credit for private industry. The trunk lines of the government-financed Japan Railway Company attracted private investors to build local rail networks, but the main stimulus was indirect: the developing infra-structure improved the conditions for profitable private enterprise. The short-lived government enterprises had bred some entrepreneurs. Mass education improved the quality of labour available to them. Leading public and private universities equipped and encouraged their graduates to supply modernizing leadership in government, in business, in co-operation with each other, and in the national interest. The switch from public to private industrial management was a policy of efficiency; most of the others were still policies of growth.

III. 1901–1916

Military policy moved from being defensive to being expansive as Japan expanded into Korea and North China. The war of 1894–5 and the war indemnity brought about a boom, with increased military procurement, public investment and private industrial development. Together these had a number of effects. Imports increased to produce a trade deficit. The government responded by restraining public investment, and so in due course infrastructure provision lagged behind the growing demand. Urban slums spread. Labour began to resist harsh working conditions, and until 1916 employers resisted government efforts to introduce Japan's first labour law. Industrial growth was 'taking off' in a self-sustaining way, and was reaching a scale at which it began to have substantial effects on mass beliefs, lifestyles and consumption patterns. The government encouraged the trans-formation, but it led to over-exploitation of land, forestry, fishing and other natural resources, and to increasing resistance and protest by the 'losers' due to industrialization. Successful growth policies, especially the restraint of public investment and imports, were creating an increasing need for policies of efficiency, including some which promised welfare improvements.

IV. 1917–1937

The First World War brought about an economic boom. In addition to war production for herself and her allies, Japan was able to take over some Western export markets in Asia, become a major ship-builder and ocean carrier, and turn the trade deficit into a large export surplus. Late in the war, price inflation provoked urban rice riots; then postwar depression brought rural distress and – together with news of the German and Russian revolutions – industrial strife as labour unions and Left-oriented political parties developed. The government responded by suppressing Leftist opinions and organizations, but diverted some public investment to improve city and village life. This was the economic expression of the

'Taisho democracy' (the main political achievement of which was manhood suffrage for the Diet, in 1925). With the task of reconstruction after the Great Earthquake, the government once again concentrated public investment on facilities for industrial development. It created large new industrial sites. The nation's natural resources and industrial capacity were surveyed, and a system set up to monitor them. From 1932 the Takahashi government stepped up public investment in transport and urban and village infrastructure as a full employment strategy, while at the same time extending its banking control to channel public and private lending into heavy industrial development. With these policies, and increasing material supplies from Manchukuo, Japan developed considerable self-sufficiency in steel, machinery, chemicals and arms production.

There were thus three phases of policy through period IV: policies of efficiency in the period of Taisho democracy from the war boom to the earthquake; a return to policies of growth in efforts to recover from the earthquake then the depression; then the reflationary full-employment policies of Takahashi which doubled as policies of efficiency (to employ all existing resources), and as policies of growth (to improve material standards of living while also increasing national military capacity).

V.   1937–1945

In developing and managing the war economy the bureaucracy brought its prewar experience and institutional apparatus to bear, and added considerably to them. In developing the East Asian trade block, industrializing Manchuria and integrating its mines and industries into Japan's war economy, conscripting the private munitions industry managers, developing publicly franchised and directed but privately owned and managed power, coal, petroleum and transport enterprises, sponsoring and controlling private cartels, creating the *eidanren* public corporations, and exercising overall control and allocation of scarce materials, the bureaucrats extended their skills and institutional repertoire. They were also led to reflect on the working principles of capitalism, and possible non-socialist alternatives to them. Thus equipped, the younger ranks of bureaucrats survived the purges of 1945–7 to superintend the 'miracle' of 1945–70.

VI.   1946–1955

While the Americans forced the land reform, retired the older leadership of business and government and democratized the political system, Japanese bureaucrats with extensive power began long-term economic recovery by concentrating available resources on the coal and steel industries, with assistance from a new public bank created for the purpose. They conducted another census of the nation's productive resources, set up a comprehensive statistical service, and in 1947 published a first Plan and Economic White Paper, with principles which held throughout the following decades of fast growth: namely, that the recovery of the nation from defeat and subjection was centrally an economic task; that the government should unite and lead the people in that task; and that it should plan and guide the reconstruction of the economy. The principles have held, but their application changes with the stages of growth. During the first five years the government mainly rationed scarce productive resources to designated industries. During the next five it worked to circumvent the American anti-trust rules, reduce 'excessive competition', and rationalize potential export industries to produce large, strong, cost-competitive exporters. The means included resource-rationing, tax and legal concessions, and selective credit from new public or publicly sponsored banks. Thus windfall gains from the Korean War boom were channelled to selected industries and firms. The objectives were to become independent of US aid and procurement, and to raise the 'balance of trade ceiling' on economic growth.

VII.   1956–1970

The government's aim was to have the economy grow as fast as the balance of payments allowed. To achieve that, imports and the exchange to buy them were rationed, and directed as far as possible to potential export industries; and there were 'stop–go' macroeconomic efforts to restrain imports and excessive investment by damping domestic demand. Growth allowed the policy emphasis to shift from import restriction in the 1950s to freer trade and more reliance on export growth through the 1960s, with freer foreign exchange by 1970. MITI assisted designated industries and firms with information services, import licences, credit, and action to reduce 'excessive competition' by generating very large firms and/or cartel arrangements. The aids encouraged over-investment and surplus capacity which, however, may have stimulated innovation. Also, private entrepreneurial energy was so extreme that government often found itself trying to *restrain* investment, and directing foreign exchange to material imports for existing plant when investors would rather have spent it on new equipment. Meanwhile, inflation was restrained by sometimes tense combinations of fiscal expansion (for growth) with monetary deflation (for stability). For those and other reasons there is disagreement about the actual importance of the government contribution; in other words, what the likely rate and direction of growth would have been without it.

Both government and business may be criticized on two other grounds. Government did not require and business did not apply reasonable environmental care. And although achieving full employment and reducing wage differentials in the 'dual economy' were explicit aims of policy from 1960 onward for social welfare reasons, when they were achieved the leaders were slow to grasp their full economic implications and to adapt economic policy accordingly. Policies of 'growth regardless', mainly through measures to make the best use of available capital and foreign exchange, continued for some years when different strategies, for 'growth by making the best use of available labour' and 'growth with environmental care', would have been more appropriate.

VIII.　1971–1985

Pollution brought about radical environmental reforms in 1971, and the first oil shock prompted a radical review of growth policies. Although there were emergency administrative measures to cope with the oil shock, MITI acknowledged that the area of market allocation had greatly expanded and administrative guidance should henceforth be confined to areas of serious market failure. A systematic shift in a *laissez-faire* direction began in 1973. It was followed later in this period by the sale and privatization of some remaining public enterprises, including the National Railways and government monopolies in tobacco manufacturing. The liberalization was partly to reduce ever-increasing public spending and balance the national budget in face of a reduced rate of economic growth, and partly to dispense with public activities that were no longer necessary to growth, which itself was no longer as urgent as it had been. The MITI bureaucracy was slimmed and reorganized accordingly. As a less direct, less coercive mode of indicative planning, MITI began to publish 'Visions'. They proposed that future growth should be in clean, knowledge-intensive industries to improve both environmental quality and working conditions. Broadly, that has happened as recommended. Some heavy and polluting industries began to decline and some left Japan altogether. They were helped: direct public aid shifted noticeably from helping growing industries to easing the descent of declining industries. MITI's 'Vision of the 1980s' and the Economic Council's 'Outlook and Guidelines for Economy and Society', issued in 1983, departed from precedent to make no firm forward financial projections (their authors spoke of 'flexibility', and their critics of 'indecision'). There were the beginnings of a new consensus about new policy aims: it should respond to the aging of the population; search for safer supplies of energy; arrive at responsible international policies now that Japan was a major economic power; and improve the quality of life for Japanese people.

IX. 1986–present

The new aims shape new policies and terminate old ones. There is general privatization of saleable public enterprises: growth can be left to the market for the time being. Government concerns itself with international problems, and with underlying rather than immediate welfare questions: What should 'welfare' *mean* to the Japanese people, and what exactly should economic activity contribute to it? As the problems of Japan's late-developing economy with meagre capital, resources and technology recede into past history, questions of 'allocation and efficiency' reappear to claim a high priority in national planning.

When we presently explore the reasons for the periodical changes of direction, and for the coherence and effectiveness of a number of the policy cycles, we intend to draw special attention to two or three factors, including the government's role in generating the celebrated Japanese consensus, and the role of public investment in leading development in the desired directions. We might therefore be accused of monocausal explanation, of forgetting our own injunction to remember that social causation is usually complex. It has certainly been complex in Japan. As a reminder of that, and to set the consensus-building processes into context with some of their many accompanying conditions, it may help to offer a summary typology of (i) the Japanese planners' repertoire of policy devices, and (ii) the kinds of reasons they have had for selecting and switching policies through the cycles that we have surveyed. In the government's economic role as a whole we can see a few constants, and a numerous repertoire of policy components and alternatives, which change, or the uses of which change, with changing political purposes, external conditions and stages of economic growth.

Constants Throughout the history of modernization, governments have aimed at national strength and independence. With or without military activity they have sought national strength by economic development. They have worked hard to create and nurture consensual support for national aims and economic means of achieving them.

Governments have propelled economic growth by three general means: by proposing national economic strategies and creating business confidence in them; by public investment in educational, institutional and physical infrastructure; and (variously at different times) by creating public enterprises and/or guiding, regulating, assisting and rationing resources to private enterprises.

Changing components of economic policy The components have included the following:

1   Policies for growth and policies for efficiency, as defined earlier:

Policies for growth	*Policies for efficiency*
● National system of law, education, transport and communications	● Measures, including public banks and guidance to private banks, to allocate capital to its most productive uses
● A national financial system	
● Macroeconomic fiscal and financial policies	
● Indicative planning that convinces business that it is both patriotic and profitable to invest as indicated	● Aids to designated industries and firms, including administrative allocation of scarce fuel, materials, credit, foreign exchange and tax discrimination
● Action to improve the supply of whatever factors are limiting growth	● Measures to encourage or discourage competition, or to encourage rationalization, takeovers or cartelization in particular industries
● Public provision of industrial sites and services and urban infrastructure	
	● Distributional measures to influence wage and profit shares, or to provide welfare services and income transfers

2   When it has wanted to develop key industries, the government has at different times created public enterprises; privatized public enterprises; assisted private enterprises with equity and loan capital, purposely built infrastructure facilities; favoured access to scarce fuel, materials and foreign exchange; favoured tax treatment; provided assistance with mergers, takeovers and cartels; and for declining industries, provided assistance with redundancy payments, re-training and relocation.

3   When productive resources seemed adequate, their supply and allocation has generally been left to the market. When their scarcity has limited growth they have been allocated by planned administrative guidance.

How do we explain the changes which varied the policy mix from time to time? There appear to have been significant changes of direction at intervals of 12–20 years. Some came abruptly (as in 1881, 1937, 1945 and 1971), while some came step by step (as between 1895 and 1901). Sometimes the pattern was broken by external events (as by the 1923 earthquake, the World Depression and the Korean War). However, despite its irregularities, a cyclic pattern of sorts is visible. What promoted the changes of direction? To different degrees at different times, the following appear to have contributed to the government's thinking:

- *Trial and error.* Experience prompted the government to replace unsatisfactory policies (as in 1881, 1917 and 1971).
- *Changing conditions.* Policies responded to boom, depression, changing balances of trade, civil disorder, industrial strife, pollution and military demands. The changing conditions included, at times, a *stop–go cycle*: public investment stimulated private activity to the point at which an excess of imports led policy-makers to restrain imports by restraining demand by restraining public investment; infrastructure then lagged behind the industrial and social need for it until the balance of payments recovered, or the business need of infrastructure facilities became imperative, or social unrest forced new public provisions.
- *Examples of stages of growth.* By 1881 enough infrastructure and entrepreneurial activity existed for the government to switch from creating public enterprises to supporting private ones. In 1880–5, 1917–23 and 1970–3, policy-makers judged that the economy was rich enough to afford some more direct welfare benefits. By 1965–70 industry was generating enough capital and export-earned foreign exchange for government to stop rationing them and leave most of their allocation to the market.

Three other influences on the policy cycle are harder to estimate, but we guess at them from extensive reading of the policy papers, a study of the educational influences on the policy-makers, and personal acquaintance with some of them over recent decades:

- *Generational effects.* Bureaucrats commonly spend 10–15 years at the top. When a new generation – sometimes including people who have known each other since student days and think of themselves as a 'new wave' – reach the top they bring new ideas, look for new tasks, perceive new or neglected trends which need attention, and readily discard outdated institutions and policies in which they have no personal stake.
- *Action to minimize private misuse of public provisions.* Tullock and other 'public choice' theorists believe that public regulation or assistance to private enterprise tends to divert business resources away from productive use towards 'rent-seeking' efforts to profit through political patronage, protection or subsidy, with a general loss of economic efficiency. Mancur Olson believes that such freeloading accumulates over time wherever there is continuous stable government, to become the main determinant of national economic growth or stagnation.[5] Such behaviour certainly occurs in Japan, as in other economies. For example, aids and forms of protection extended to growing industries

in the 1960s were sufficiently misused during the 1970s to attract new pro-competitive and anti-monopolist reforms in the 1980s. But strong planning and watchful administration appear to reduce rather than increase rent-seeking opportunities of that kind. In Japan the central government's economic ministries have generally been served by honest bureaucrats who have avoided the corruption which sometimes links business and politicians.[6] In 1950–5, symbolically, they were eager to dispense with US aid and dependence rather than prolong the 'unearned' financial assistance; in other words, they were against *national* mendicancy. *Internally* they are aware that measures of industrial assistance can tempt firms to milk government, especially through programmes which outlast their real need. They have accordingly been alert in revising or discontinuing programmes which have served (or failed to serve) their purposes. Fairly frequent changes, which occasion fresh thought about the administrative arrangements, and fresh scrutiny of their use or misuse by industry, seem on balance to have limited 'rent-seeking' to lower levels than it assumes in some other advanced economies.[7] This may be seen as a special case of the following more general principle.

- *Change as stimulus*. Some policy-makers think that fairly frequent changes in the economic environment stimulate business dynamism. (Of course, some businessmen on the receiving end of changing policies and regulations suspect that planning wilful changes, and persuading government that they are needed, is the bureaucrats' device for persuading government that *they* are still needed.)

3 Cycles in the Speed and Direction of Social Change

Before leaving the policy cycles it is interesting to relate them to a pioneering historical study of the process of social change in Japan. In 1985 and 1988 the National Institute of Research Advancement (NIRA) published the results of a survey of the living standards of the Japanese people year by year from 1880 to 1980. The researchers compiled 368 indices of detailed conditions of health, education, income, employment, living environment, individual and family safety and security, people's mobility between levels of income and social status, and leisure time; and also life expectancies, infant mortality rates, deaths by accident, population per physician, proportions of each age group at primary and high school and university, labour force participation, crime rates and arrest rates; GNP per capita, Gini coefficients of inequality; and so on. The purpose was to estimate the extent of national improvement, over time, in the welfare of the population.[8]

Only 133 of the indices are available throughout the 100 years, and a second study was based on those indices.[9] Its particular interest for us is that it attempted a quantitative measure of the amount and direction of social change with in each year. The researchers emphasize that the study involved a good deal of rough estimation, and also judgements as to whether changes were for better, for worse, or neutral to the people's welfare. The study proceeded by estimating the percentage change in each index from year to year, and then arriving at the number and percentage of indices that changed by more than 10 per cent from each year to the next. For example, here are eight of the indices, with their changes aggregated for the years 1881–5:[10]

		Increase/reduction over time
1	Number of reported patients contacted with notifiable infectious diseases	+41.8 per cent
2	Number of sports clubs established	+30.0 per cent
3	Number of people using public libraries	+16.0 per cent
4	Number of books published	+12.8 per cent
5	Marriage ratio by age groups	−13.0 per cent
6	Number of students per academic staff member at university	−11.6 per cent
7	Divorce rates	−6.2 per cent
8	Consumer price index	−2.8 per cent

For figure 9.4, the researchers made their own judgements as to which changes were for the better and which for the worse. They judged some to be neutral; for example, they treated index 7 as neutral because a change in the divorce rate may indicate greater freedom and enlightenment for women, or alternatively a deterioration in the quality of family life.

Most of the significant changes of policy direction (in 1881, 1901, 1917, 1937, 1946 and 1956), which we identified before the arrival of the NIRA report, can be seen to coincide with significant changes in the *rate* or *direction*, or both, of social change as indexed by the NIRA researchers. It must be remembered that there are arbitrary elements both in the NIRA estimates and in our judgement of the importance of the policy changes which define our policy cycles. Detailed study would also show that some of the policy changes chiefly *responded* to the changing social conditions indicated in the diagrams (as in 1946 and 1956), while others chiefly *caused* the changes (as in 1881 or 1937), and some (as in 1917) did a good deal of both. Despite these imperfections, the degree of 'fit' between the NIRA estimates and our identification of policy cycles appears to give the two some mutual support.

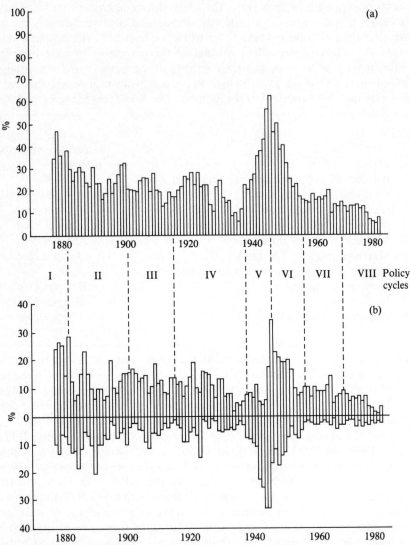

Figure 9.4   *An analysis of 133 indices of social change, 1880–1980. (a) The percentage of indices for which the value changed by more than 10 per cent in the year. (b) Improvement (above the line) and deterioration (below the line) in the indices shown in (a), for which the value changed by more than 10 per cent in the year. Indices for which there was no change in value are, of course, excluded.*
Source: NIRA (1988a, pp. 36 and 37).

4 Mentalities: Sources of Skill, Commitment and Co-operation in Business and Government

If 'policy cycles' manifest the flexible approach of the planners, it is through these tireless and steady efforts of the bureaucrats that the Japanese economy has continuously retained a powerful dynamism in order to produce the resulting industrialization. Reflecting their constant attempts to synthesize effective plans in response to changes in economic conditions, the life span of each of these specific policy measures has been, in most cases, relatively short. Yet across the policy cycles and the frequent alteration of policy aims and measures, oscillating between the two goals of growth and efficiency, there has been one element of striking continuity from beginning to end among the various and varying policy tools. The leaders of the Meiji government and their advisors – Okuma, Okubo, Fukuzawa and many other great names in that period of history – knew from the outset that it was the 'national enthusiasm' for industrial development that must lie at the very heart of economic planning. In order to animate the operation of policy measures, the ideals and messages of the state must accompany and explain the public investments if the public investments were to achieve their designed effects on private business activity. The leaders of the Meiji government wrote public programmes knowing that they would stand or fall according to the support they succeeded in attracting from the population. Without co-operative support, public plans, however carefully drafted, end up as lifeless desk bound theories in public offices. Much public effort was therefore devoted to constructing effective mechanisms for building co-operative relationships between the state, business and the people. This is a subject which has been widely discussed by researchers under the title of 'consensus-building' between government and business, and the so-called 'Japan Inc.' concept. Consensus also had to be built on a nationwide basis, across class interests – often strongly conflicting class interests. Contrary to what some scholars have suggested, the social support and base of government in Japan did not spring ready-made from tradition, nor did it bubble up spontaneously from the national culture. At no time in the history of modern economic development has the Japanese regime been fully homogeneous, cohesive or comprehensive. There have been wide divisions within and between the social groups which support the regime, and within and between the various institutions which collectively constitute the state. The same is true for industry and the population at large, both of whom included losers as well as winners from the state programmes for industrialization. The national consensus for industrial development, and for particular ways of going about it, has been, without doubt, engineering by the state, with help from some of the winners for their own purposes.

However, the long life and the full extent of the celebrated co-operation between government and business, and the effective compliance of labour and the public to produce concerted national action, cannot be sufficiently explained as self-interested domination by a capitalist class. To gain a full understanding it is necessary to understand the leaders more personally; the influences that have shaped them, and the sort of people they are. A thorough account of the mentality of the Japanese bureaucracy awaits a future study. Here, we sketch in a few pages some characteristics, first of the founding generations of business leaders, and then of the bureaucrats.

Industrial Leadership

Among the intellectual leaders of the Meiji modernization was Fukuzawa Yukichi (1835–1901).[11] He stood for the values expressed in the slogan 'civilization and enlightenment', and as a traveller to the West before the Meiji Restoration he became a main source of popular knowledge about the West when his book *Conditions in the Western World* was published in 1866.[12] It was followed by *Encouragement of Learning*[13] and *Outline of Civilization*.[14] The first opened with the famous statement that 'Heaven did not create one man above another nor below another'; and the second called for the Japanese to free themselves from constraints of tradition because once free, 'there is nothing in the world which can withstand man's courage and intellect'.

Fukuzawa founded Keio Gijuku (later to be Keio Gijuku University) in 1858, and from then until his death in 1901 he devoted his life to the creation of *jitsugyo-ka* (the industrialist) for the purpose of supplying able lieutenants for the realization of national independence. The central theme of his economic teaching can be distilled from his *Jitsugyo-Ron* (*On Business*), published in 1893.[15] He argued that something was lacking from the progress of modernization so far:

> Over forty years have passed since the opening of the country [but] the trans-
> formation of Japan into a modern society has brought results in a piecemeal
> manner, in the limited confines of the invisible arena of 'awareness of the
> advanced world outside Japan' and the 'willingness to learn more about the
> West' by the population in general. This welcome receptiveness to new ideas,
> however, has not yet generated the matching efforts to improve industrial
> technology and production which are needed to lead Japan to equality with
> the industrial powers of the West.[16]

Fukuzawa asked himself how new educational approaches might bring new life and initiative to the task of industrialization.[17] He had been training students who came from far and wide to hear his lectures at Keio in economics and modern business management, so that the college served as the main supply centre for professional managers for emerging industrial enterprises. The students had diverse means and backgrounds – former samurai, wealthy farmers, some peasants and merchants with progressive ideas. Observing that the foundations of modern enterprise had been laid by the 1890s with the launching of many merchant houses into manufacturing, Fukuzawa began to focus his teaching efforts on creating business leaders of a special kind, ex-samurai students and those who shared samurai ethics and motivation, for whom industrialization should be as much a national as a business aim. At the time, many ex-samurai still felt a traditional obligation not to engage in any profit-making activities, despite their ever-deteriorating living standard from loss of jobs and income after the Restoration. Their frustration mounted: their former education was wasted, and their ethical motivation to serve the nation stood idle. Fukuzawa wished to transform the content of the traditional 'samurai' ethic of serving the nation, to make full use of their available store of intellectual training. He coined the terms *suchonin* (managers) and *jitsugyo-ka* (industrialists) to differentiate the business activity of people for national purposes: the former engage in business activities for their own profit, while the latter enter the business world in the spirit of samurai, continuing to put national purposes before private concerns.

Many former samurai responded eagerly to Fukuzawa's teaching and went into business. With Fukuzawa's guidance, many found leading managerial positions in modern enterprises, in the service of Mitsui, Mitsubishi, Sumitomo and other future *zaibatsu* families.[18] Others started firms of their own. They all chose fields of 'modern enterprise' which were seen as the driving force of industrial activities in the West. They found satisfaction in making careers in heavy industry, chemical manufacturing and some of the traditional light industries which were seen to be developing into export industries.

Fukuzawa was not the only person who generated business efforts for national purposes. Shibusawa Eiichi, for example, promoted new industries for Japan's industrialization by directly and indirectly associating himself with the establishment of numerous companies.[19] Fukuzawa's distinct contribution lay in his methods for engineering the new 'business ethic', systematically and effectively linking private initiatives to public programmes, thereby laying the foundation of 'government–business' cooperation in the future industrial development of Japan.

The high-sounding principle of 'nation before profit', and the actual practice of linking and reconciling the two, survived through the Meiji years of industrial transition, and the Taisho years, into the 1920s. During the Pacific war production became a patriotic endeavour and condition of national survival. After 1945 came a passionate commitment to national recovery, as *all* national feeling and aspiration had to be expressed through the single enterprise of economic growth; It is vital that this history be remembered. In order correctly to appreciate the nature of the 'government–industry' co-operative relationship and the extent of its contribution towards effective public planning, we do not need to discuss (a) the dependence of business on public assistance and direct guidance (that is, 'rent-seeking' activities) or (b) cultural traits to do with the general importance of government authority in Japanese society.

We saw how business took advantage of the Sino-Japanese war in the twice-repeated *kigyo-bokko* (enterprise boom) period. Business leaders began to feel strong enough to try to flex their muscles and dispense with direct government aid.[20] This did not mean that business renounced national aims: it meant that business felt able to pursue them with less or no state help. Henceforward the initiative for maintaining strong 'government–business co-operation' came as much from business as from government, signifying the success of Fukuzawa's teaching. The linking of national and business purposes has continued, in varying forms and degrees, more strongly in some business leaders and less in others, throughout the prewar and postwar decades.

The growing confidence of business and the growing scale of its industrial operations led to conflicts with other groups, and some government attention switched from encouraging business to attending to those conflicts. We have noted the attempts to regulate labour conditions, which were frustrated by business interests in the Diet for many years before the Law of 1911 was finally implemented in 1916. (Business had its own reform programme in the development of the so-called 'Japan labour system' of secure employment and corporate welfare.) There was more immediate success for the reform measures of liberalism in the years between 1917 and 1923. But such 'welfare' concessions to some of the losers from industrialization were not as remarkable as the extent to which, at other times and through most of the century, the industrialization was able to go forward *without* much 'legitimation' of that direct welfare kind, and with a continuing faith that the industrial growth itself would be the main source of the people's welfare. Achieving that degree of support or compliance through the normal stresses of early industrial development in a society with generally low wages and poor living conditions, rather than attracting business co-operation alone, is the real measure of the government's achievement through the century to about 1965.

How was it done? This question stands at the very centre of any quest for 'lessons from Japan', whether raised by less-developed economies looking for an efficient and workable recipe for rapid industrialization, or by industrialized economies whose main concern is to apply their public resources to yield more efficient results. We seek the answer to the question in the quality of the bureaucrats themselves.

Economic Bureaucrats: their Background, Training and Functions

By the 'quality' of the bureaucrats we mean more than the expected virtues of honesty, dedication and intelligence. The meaning extends to their capacity to lead and shape public opinion, to win public trust in their leadership, and to have their plans accepted as whole strategies rather than as collections of policies, to be picked over as concessions to this or that interest, and supported or opposed piecemeal.[21]

Put differently, it is not sufficient to seek an answer to our question in the public contribution to industrialization and economic development; that is, in the cleverness or otherwise of the plans themselves, through questions such as: (a) How has the government of Japan guided investment into designated sectors of the economy? (b) What kind of trade regulations, tariff protections and export incentive schemes, tax reforms and depreciation provisions were structured? (c) How have they built different types of financial institutions, road and railway facilities, housing accommodation, hospital services and schools, libraries and parks? (d) What kind of web of planning and market relations have they synthesized? In the now vast accumulation of works by economists, economic historians and researchers of business and management activities, there are countless descriptions and estimates of the importance of public efforts in building infrastructure such as transport, communications and other facilities for production, economic institutions such as state banking, postal and saving networks, public factories and enterprises, and regulatory and administrative devices (such as MITI's 'administrative guidance' methods and the MOF's FILP system).

Those are all important pieces of the planning mechanism. But they are technical: they are merely the planning and administrative *products* of the bureaucrats. They leave the bureaucrats themselves as a 'black box', the inner nature and working – and the remarkable inventiveness – of which remain unexplained. (Also unanswered is the question of whether other societies could usefully copy Japan's institutions without also having Japan's entrepreneurs and bureaucrats.) The history and the public institutions of economic development are there to demonstrate the ingenious capacity of Japan's bureaucrats to produce effective economic planning and administration. But how are the bureaucrats themselves produced? What sort of people are they? Which of their qualities take them beyond the standard virtues of honesty, commitment and high intelligence, to enable them to see 'whole' social structures and processes, and give direction to them?

There has been little systematic study of the '*kancho* economists' (economic bureaucrats) as people: we hope to undertake such a study at a later date. Here, as a first approach, we pose three questions: (i) Where do the bureaucrats come from: what social background and educational experience qualifies them to enter the economic planning departments?[22] (ii) Once there, what further education, experience and performance enables some to get to the top as economic planners or managers in ministries, public agencies and corporations? (iii) Once on top, exactly what functions do the leaders, as a group, perform?

There are two groups. In their postwar guises, the first consists mainly of officials working in the Ministry of Finance (MOF), the Ministry of International Trade and Industry (MITI), the Economic Planning Agency (EPA) and the Bank of Japan (BOJ). These are 'career officers' who wish to be actively involved in the process of economic policy-making, and who compete for promotion on the basis of their accumulated experience and performance in policy-making units. The other group are those who are called into policy-making offices from other parts of the bureaucracy and from public-sector organizations. They contribute to particular planning tasks which the government wants to carry out at particular times. This latter form of bureaucracy is called the '*shukko*' (on-loan, or secondment) system and is widely used and popular in the Japanese bureaucracy. It meant that the size of the economic bureaux can expand or shrink from time to time, as required by the government's planning strategy. Both the whole number in any department and the proportions of permanent career officers and '*shukko*' officials change considerably between policy cycles, with the changing importance of policy for growth and policy for efficiency and allocation.[23] Such a system has a number of advantages. (1) The government can swiftly, and to any required extent, mobilize its resources of capable officials into strategic policy-making offices. (2) By lending and borrowing officials at various levels between the ministries and public agencies, good communications and co-operation are encouraged throughout the government network. (3) Perhaps most importantly, this mobility is of value in broadening the officers' on-the-job education and training, beyond the terms of reference of their own offices. For example, it has been customary for the MOF and MITI to send their officials to a large number of other government institutions, local governments, embassies and even to a few semi-governmental or semi-private organizations such as the Japan External Trade Organization (JETRO), to work temporarily as diplomats or financial attachés. At the same time, the MOF is host to officers from other ministries and government agencies, and employees from commercial and long-term credit banks.[24]

The flexible in-service approach to the development of policy-makers is also reflected in the entry qualifications for economic planning offices. To enter the policy-making offices of, for example, MOF, MITI and EPA, one does not have to hold a formal economics degree. Officers making key economic policy decisions, and economic policy administrators, have most often been graduates from the schools of law, natural sciences or engineering. They have been selected mainly on their successful demonstration of potential ability and general personality.[25] This practice should be understood in a somewhat parallel way to that observed in the selection of employees in large public companies in Japan. The government's economic affairs have thus been managed primarily by elite *generalists*, administrators whose knowledge and training in economic planning has been acquired in the process of their work experience within the economic ministries and other agencies to which they may have been seconded. As they approach and compete for high office, their experience includes developing and writing economic plans for the nation, carrying substantial administrative responsibilities, and negotiating and co-operating with their counterparts outside the economic ministries. This generally enables the government to be sure that (a) the economic plan is conceived in the broad context of the society as a whole and relates effectively to the social problems of the time, and (b) the plan is thoroughly workable through the government's network of organizations.

A selected few of those experienced in economic policy-making form the *kancho* economist groups. They occupy key posts in MOF, MITI, EPA and other economic planning offices. A most important part of their role in those eminent positions is to think strategically, and to conceive and express what are now called 'visions' of the nation's economic trends and policy directions. These visions provide the context in which formal economic plans are developed within government, are understood and attract support outside government, and are administered coherently with an eye to their broad purposes.

Thus the *kancho* economists tend to be selected and ranked by reference to their personal ability to consider the economy as a whole, in its whole social context, and to mobilize their staff resources to set and achieve their targets, rather than by their specialist capacity as economists. Our observation is that, in Japan, specialist knowledge and training of bureaucrats as economists has not been favoured as much as it has elsewhere in the world, and this stands out as one of the distinctive characteristics of Japanese economic planning. The term '*kancho* economists' is of postwar origin, but the group with such expertise and function has existed in the government network since the beginning of the Meiji bureaucracy.[26]

Academic economists, who construct and mentally inhabit the imaginary worlds of the 'neoclassical', 'post-Keynesian' and 'Marxian' economic theories, have not found many positions of influence in the planning process of the economy.[27] In recent years, however, the situation has changed somewhat. Their professional expertise seems to be appreciated, and some have been invited to contribute to policy-making as members of councils, research committees and other advisory bodies which are asked to write reports for the Prime Minister and other ministers.

In sum, our observation is that the function of economists in European governments seems to have been undertaken in Japan by teams of bureaucrats who are, above all, generalist thinkers and administrators with a specific desire to involve themselves in economic policy-making, and who perceive and consider national problems in highly economic terms, while their counterparts at similar levels of eminence in government may approach some public policy matters in jurisdictional, international, diplomatic and other terms.

These observations should not be taken as denying that economic theory and expertise have contributed in various ways to the development and administration of economic policy through the process of industrialization. However, they should be taken as suggesting strongly that the training of government economics officers, the teaching of economics and economic theory, and the practice of economic research, both in Japan and in other countries, would benefit greatly from a careful analysis of the Japanese experience in economic planning and policy-making. We will return to this theme at the end of this chapter.

5   The Logic of 'Planned Capitalism'

The study of the role of bureaucrats in the economic planning process in Japan should contribute to our understanding of: (a) where and in what ways public servants have contributed to the planning of the economy for industrial and economic development; (b) how their contribution has been organized, and with what effects on the structure of government; (c) how important are the cultural, historical and social traditions and the so-called 'situational'[28] reasons in shaping the bureaucrats' ways of thinking and operating; and (d) what economic choices Japan has made. Besides economic factors, what cultural, social and political factors lay behind such choices? Why have the Japanese chosen as they have?

We may focus on what the choices have achieved. We may naively aspire to transplant – into other economies in the West, Africa and Asia – Japan's spectacular rate of economic growth, its rising productivity of both labour and capital, its technological progress, its high level and wide diffusion of general education among the population, and other such desirable achievements of Japanese industrialization; without, that is, the motive force of militaristic ambition, environmental pollution, competitive pressure in schools and the workplace, the lack of individualism and of social freedom, and so on. Is it not possible that the brighter side of industrialization can be exported, without the inseparable pain of the darker side as experienced in Japan?

Our response to this question is, regrettably, rather negative. We do not feel that it necessarily cannot be done, but that a knowledge of the Japanese experience in itself does not reveal whether it can be done. The Japanese experience is difficult to understand except as a whole: a whole in which planning stimulates industrial and market growth which, in turn, alter the tasks and efficacy of planning; and planning and economic growth together transform the education and culture which, in turn, shape the potentialities of planning and market behaviour. We can best explain our argument by attempting to distil a very simple 'essence' of Japan's political economy.

Japan's economic system is a *capitalistic* economy, despite the fact that its modern economic growth began with a considerable initiative on the part of the state during the Restoration. The state has since continued to enlarge its function in order to carry out its committed task. 'State control' and 'capitalism', brought together by deliberate choice, have developed together over the 120 years of industrialization to build a unique system of 'government-controlled capitalism'. The public-sector structures, all of the economic institutions, the education and training organizations and the administrative networks and mechanisms, in other words the whole body of the national economy, has been developed on the basis of the coexistence of state control and capitalism.

The co-operation between state and business has been based for 120 years on mutual agreement about growth, and has been powerful enough to act as the main propellant of growth. But Japanese society is not composed of those two parties alone. Others, with interests and demands which cannot all be satisfied by the co-operative activities of state and business, emerge from time to time to challenge the system. Government responds by switching its attention to problems of efficiency, allocation and equity, coping with them as far as possible by means which are compatible with continuing growth. Meanwhile, in addition to generating social problems, growth also generates its own economic problems: at different stages of growth, different factors hinder or limit the rate of further growth. Attention then switches back from policies of efficiency to policies of growth.

However those policies of growth have changed over time, a simple pattern can be discerned:

1 The government analyses economic activity to see which factors are currently setting the limits to growth. Having identified the bottlenecks – which may be in the areas of skills, raw materials, technology and public infrastructure, but have almost always included capital – the government arrives at a strategy for economizing on the scarce resources in the short term and increasing their supply in the long term.
2 The government publishes the plan, and works hard to attract business confidence and public support for it.
3 To implement the plan, the government may use a variety of appropriate devices but, centrally, they include public investment. The investment may be in human or material capital; that is, in educational, institutional or physical infrastructure, or (where there is need) in productive enterprises. The infrastructure is designed to allow or stimulate the kinds of private investment designated in the plan. It may be accompanied by arrangements for financial institutions to channel private savings into the designated sectors.

4 Private investors, taught by experience that the government's plans are usually fulfilled, respond energetically enough to create two 'excess demands': for more private capital than currently exists; and soon for more infrastructure, in other words for more public investment.
5 Identifying capital scarcity as the factor limiting growth, the government adopts policies of efficiency to economize on it, and policies of growth to augment its supply, perhaps by measures which boost saving by directly or indirectly restraining consumption.

Note two implications of that sequence. First, public policy produces permanent scarcities, especially of capital. (Hence the paradox that capital appears to be most scarce in the national economy which saves hardest and accumulates capital fastest). Second, the scarcity is related to the projected rate of growth: the higher the planners set their sights, the greater is the scarcity. Given the urgency and ambition of the government of Japan and the energy of her entrepreneurs, there was continuous pressure through the century of industrialization (although its intensity varied from period to period) to keep growth up to the prevailing limits, and to expand the limits wherever possible.

That is not how economic theorists expect capital markets to behave. In any economy in which capital is in short supply, the shortage is expected to motivate enterprises (a) to economize on capital by capital-saving techniques and organization – so that the economy as a whole shifts in a capital-saving direction, reducing the demand for capital – while as long as the strong demand continues it (b) stimulates accumulation by bidding resources away from other uses in the economy. Thus market forces should eliminate capital shortage and restore market equilibrium. We have seen that the Japanese government acted both to accumulate capital and to ease any shortage of the goods on which investment capital is spent. Some may like to evaluate that policy as an attempt to better the market in dealing with the problem of capital scarcity. But, rightly understood, that was not the government's purpose; its plan was to direct the nation's economic activity in a way which was bound to continue the capital shortage, in other words the 'excess demand' for capital, throughout the industrialization of the economy.

That effect was achieved by a combination of means. Public policy firmly favoured industry above agriculture and both above housing, and from the 1920s heavy above light industry. To effect its policy government relied partly on controlling or influencing the investment and lending preferences of banks and other financial institutions, and (most heavily) on public investment programmes. An unusually high proportion of national income has thus been directed towards investment, leaving consumption, whether public or personal, to claim a relatively smaller part of it. The working mechanism of such public policies lies in the fact that the size (and the proportion) of income which people can allocate for consumption is determined by the quantity of goods and services produced by the economy. It is also true that people obtain their income from producing goods and services both for consumption purposes and for investment purposes. Since people can buy only consumer goods and services, they save the amount which is equal to the amount of the investment goods and services. As has been explained by Keynes, saving and investment activities are undertaken by different people, and thus there is no guarantee that the amount of savings will equal that of investment. What happens in the market is that if people's savings exceed investment, the producers of consumer goods make losses, which leads them to curtail their production activities, leaving the economy as a whole under-employed. What happened in Japan was that people were effectively constrained to consume less and save more, and their savings were channelled into investment. Government investment activities were designed to ensure that savings did not exceed investment, so that producers of consumer goods and services were discouraged, while business activities for producing investment goods and services were constantly stimulated. [29] This is seen in our earlier observation that it has been public investment (I_g) and not so much government spending (C_g) which was promoted to generate 'effective demand' during depressed times in the economy – a contrasting strategy to those customarily adopted elsewhere under Keynesian policy. [30]

If this were a book of analysis alone, it might conclude here with the following final summary.

Our study opened by asking what distinguishes the economic role of government in Japan from that of governments elsewhere. We conclude that there are four distinguishing characteristics:

1 Government thinks strategically, chooses particular directions of growth, and does much to persuade business to invest with confidence in the plan, and the population to welcome and support it.
2 Government contrives capital accumulation mainly through public investment in the infrastructure that desired industries need, and by influencing the flow of capital and other resources to those industries.
3 Most of the public planning of private activity is thus indirect, leaving individual investment and production decisions to the wisdom and spirit of the entrepreneurs and their competition with each other. That it the meaning of 'planned capitalism'.
4 However widespread the general support for economic growth, it has winners and losers. In particular, the actions of government and business hurt various sectors of society at various times and provoke opposition. Government responds, when necessary and to the extent that is necessary, by switching to policies of efficiency to improve the use of existing resources, the distribution of income or other benefits, or the working or living conditions of the people. As far as it can, the state treats social problems as economic problems that need economic

remedies rather than as separate welfare provisions. Thus in the observed policy cycles, as policies of growth and efficiency alternate or mix, we see the public efforts to synthesize accumulation and legitimation as the two economic functions of the capitalist state.

6   Does a 'Mature' Economy Need Less Government?

We face two final questions, one Marxist and one business-conservative. (1) Has Japan's celebrated government–business 'co-operation' been any more than a figleaf to conceal the capitalist domination of government? (2) With economic maturity, has the need for the relationship passed anyway, and is Japan now leaving economic activity to market forces to the extent that most Western governments do?

There is a reason for bringing these two questions together and treating them as political rather than analytical enquiries. The reason is that they will in fact be answered not by further scholarly investigation but by national decisions taken over the next decade or two. In arguing this we are not breaking with academic custom by abandoning analysis to engage in speculative prophecy. On the contrary, we are endeavouring to reason – just as Japan's political leaders and *kancho* economists must now be doing – as to the strategic choices that it would be best for Japan to make in her present situation.

We do not agree with the belief that the special economic role of government has ended.[31] What happened through the 1970s and 1980s looks much more like another policy cycle. Studying the reversals of policy about monopoly, mergers and other restrictive business practices in the transition from high-speed growth to the following period of slower growth, Ueno found a strong trend in business towards integration into a web of public regulatory measures. In his empirical study we find that the policies for high-speed growth had to be replaced when misuses of oligopoly and other sources of undesirable business behaviour and market performance accumulated to reduce the overall efficiency of the national economy, and drove government in the 1970s to switch to policies of efficiency, including much new law and regulation of corporate behaviour.[32] There has since been a further switch in the 1980s to greater concern with material living conditions and the quality of life. The government is thus as active as ever, although working on different tasks. Its fiscal share of GNP has increased by more than half since the policy switch of 1970–1.[33]

Nevertheless, some powerful people do believe that Japan's differences from the West in national economic management are coming to an end. Their arguments deserve attention not just to correct what we believe to be a mistake, but also for a more important reason. If the prophecy came to be believed widely enough it could be self-fulfilling. Some powerful interests appear to be hoping and working for that result: if enough people in government and business can be persuaded that the celebrated 'Japanese system' either has been or should be ended, it *will* be ended. It is in face of that practical possibility that the belief in the impending death of the 'Japanese system' merits attention.

The belief relies on some economic, some political and some theoretical reasoning:

Economic reasoning. First, having overtaken the West the economy is now mature, at the leading edge of world technology and productivity, generating its own growth and troubled by surpluses rather than bottlenecks, and so it no longer needs the government planning and resource-rationing which propelled its 'catch-up' growth. Second, there is currently a general internationalization of the advanced world's economy and capital markets, so it would be much more difficult than it used to be for a national government to control the use of private resources in its territory; in other words, the earlier economic role of the Japanese government might now be unworkable. Third, Japan is now the world's most efficient operator in world capital and trading markets, and so has the strongest interest in free trade. For these reasons it may seem natural to switch government *permanently* from an economic development role to a Western-style welfare role, leaving market forces to shape the productive system.

Political reasoning. It may be argued that the achievement of economic maturity at long last has brought the government–business relationship *into question*; in other words, there is now an opportunity to *decide* whether to continue it, alter it or end it by political choice. Some business interests, especially those who have been most Westernized, may believe that they would be advantaged by ending it. Since they no longer need government guidance, assistance or protection, they may feel they can do without bureaucratic interference too. The element of commitment to national purpose in the old government–business relationship may be thought to be unnecessary now that single-minded profit-seeking sufficiently maintains Japan's economic supremacy. In these new conditions it is hard to judge what has become of Fukuzawa's concept of 'business patriotism'. Some entrepreneurs may have as strong a national commitment as ever, but believe that profit-seeking is now all that they need do to serve the nation. Some may simply be selfish, as some Japanese businessmen have always been. Some may have become Westernized by a generation of relative commercial freedom, and may have come to believe that traditional Japanese government had too much authority, and that individual property rights and profit-seeking should carry no more obligations to government or nation in Japan than they typically do in the West.

Theoretical reasoning. In addition to economic and political reasons, there are also intellectual reasons. We noted that government and business have lately been paying more attention to academic economists. The non-Marxist economists tend to have an exaggerated faith in what unaided market mechanisms can achieve, and endorse the belief that a mature economy will do best under minimal government. Whether the increasing currency of such theoretical advice is primarily a cause or an effect of the more general shift of opinion is hard to tell, but whatever influence it has is mostly on the side of less government. To the extent that any Japanese business leaders feel, for any of the above reasons, that they are free of their former dependence on government and their former obligation to government, they may follow the worldwide 'swing to the Right' of the 1980s and adopt its two characteristic attitudes to government: (1) government should leave business alone – the more privatization and deregulation the better; (2) government should also minimize public investment, and public tax and welfare transfers from the property-owning and productive classes to the non-productive members of society.

These are divisive, contentious propositions. But their Japanese supporters may see in the maturity of the economy and the retreat of government from direct public ownership or control of industry a political opportunity to end the 'special relationship' altogether, and make over (a) government, (b) the concerns of business, and (c) the relations between the two to something more like the American model.

Lest this fear be thought of as unduly alarmist, we quote a sample of the opinions in question from an eminent Japanese source. Speaking at an 'International Debt Summit' in 1990, Dr Ohmae Kenichi said:

You have to give up the producer mentality, you have to become a marketer, because the value, wealth, everything else is in the marketplace... That the Japanese government picks out the winners is a myth... Cut-throat competition is the reason for strong Japanese companies. I don't know of *any* government-led industries that have become global, strong and profitable. And I don't think there is any exception in any part of the world – I'll be very surprised if you can show me some exception to this. Japan is the same way. We used to have 270 motor bike producers, now only four – but those surviving four are very strong. Automobile production is the same way. MITI retrospectively says 'We've done this, we've done this' – and therefore you have not really studied the Japanese competitors. Study them. You'll find that the winners have the same characteristics. They have the ambition and they have the will to succeed. And they have to fight against the system, the incumbents and the establishment. That's the only way, and having come this far it is easy to say that government has done the right thing. Well, they have done the right thing – they have left us alone. In most industries where they have really intervened the industry it gone. The aluminium industry, for example – see, it's really gone. Where they have intervened in terms of regional development like Hokkaido and Okinawa, those regions are crippled. There is no exception to this.

Bureaucrats are farthest away from the marketplace; they have no ability to guide, they don't have the ideas, the vehicles and concrete methods, to guide. That's why I say study the Japanese competitive scene, invest the money to learn from that market mechanism: you may be able to get something out of it.[34]

A number of things might be said about that outburst. For example, as a designated export industry, the vehicle-building industry had a decade or two of privileged access to scarce capital, credit, steel and foreign exchange, and legal and tax encouragements to merge, combine and build oligopolist strength.[35] Ingenious government created conditions in which the *industry* could recover and grow, while the fierce market competition that Ohmae describes could still determine *which firms* emerged as the oligopolists. (It was not always so. Someone who must know that the government gave Mitsubishi its first dozen ships, and Mitsui many similar benefits, should not assert that he 'does not know of any government-led industries that have become global and strong and profitable.') Even now, government does not 'leave such industries alone'. Their environmental pollution and their actual or potential misuses of their oligopolist advantages have attracted quite elaborate regulation to keep their operations physically clean and commercially competitive rather than collusive. Finally, the aluminium industry, which was helped to grow throughout the 1960s, was helped to decline in the 1980s for very good environmental and energy-saving reasons.

Those are minor details. Three more general features of the speech are relevant to our present purpose. First, the historical falsifications and misrepresentations are deployed in order to discredit any present or future government role in the economy. Second, the speaker is head of the Japan branch of an American transnational management-advice firm, with a profit-seeking interest in displacing the government as guide and adviser to Japanese business. Third, the speech implies that business should seek *only* personal and corporate enrichment; to attend to national purposes or obligations is to be 'gone' or 'crippled'.

This is a proposal for full Americanization in a double sense. Implicitly, it urges Japanese business to look to private American business advice rather than at Japanese government advice to business, and to seek profit alone rather than profit by means which also serve national purposes. Explicitly, it urges extreme deregulation; of the kind that has transformed the USA, in one decade, from being the world's largest creditor to its largest debtor, bankrupted a great many of its savings institutions, and diverted many of its banks and other financiers from financing productive investment to financing unproductive debt-based takeovers. With fully American policies, Japan could perhaps go the same American way.

A charitable view of this school of thought may see it as making the simple mistake of focusing exclusively on only one of the Japanese government's economic activities; namely, the direct support and guidance of particular industries in conditions of scarcity. When the scarcity passes and that function is rightly run down, superficial observers conclude that the government is retreating from economic leadership altogether. What has actually happened since 1970 in policy cycles VIII and IX is a shift of government attention to (1) radical environmental reform, (2) business regulation to limit the misuse of monopolist and other market strength, (3) public investment to improve the material conditions of village and city life, (4) new and expanded welfare provisions and (5) the promotion of international economic co-operation by Japanese companies.

The new role has expanded the 'size of government' as measured by its budget. It signals attention to the needs of a wider range than before of those engaged in or affected by the productive system. And it continues the government's strategic influence on the working of the economy in ways appropriate to the new 'conditions of abundance'.

Those are reasons why we do not believe that economic maturity has ended the powerful role of the government in Japan's economy. But three influences represented in the speech quoted above are converging to persuade people that the government's role *should* cease. There is the self-interest of some business sectors and individuals, who would like even less taxation and more market freedom than they currently have. There is growing public influence of the kind of academic economics that exaggerates the efficacy of market solutions to economic problems. Finally, there is the general internationalization, not only of economic markets but of media style and content and 'public culture', by which prevailing international intellectual fashions and orthodoxies tend to displace beliefs and aspirations derived from Japan's own national experience.

Is there a real danger of government, business and people at large falling for these persuasions, and giving up their traditional capacity to act together for deliberate national purposes? If that happens it will probably be regarded, rightly enough, as a victory for business. That will tend to endorse the Marxist belief that government has always been the servant of private capital, certain to lose out in any serious conflict between government and business. That was the point of coupling the 'Marxist' and 'business-conservative' questions at the beginning of this section. A victory for business over unwilling government *now* might suggest an answer to analytical questions about the relative power of business and government during their apparently willing co-operation in the past.

The analysis of this book suggests that such a weakening of the government's role neither *is* yet happening nor *ought* to happen. The present and future reasons for this conclusion are at least as strong as the historical reasons for it. One area of widespread consensus in Japan at present is the recognition of the most important economic problems which the nation now faces: (1) the political and economic problems, which arise from Japan's trading and financial imbalance with the world; (2) continuing problems of resource use and environmental protection; (3) problems of an aging population; and (4) how best to meeting rising expectations of social welfare and quality of life. None of the four is open to simple market solutions – each calls for national choices and government action. Each either is, or is likely to be, perceived by the Japanese as an *economic* problem, to be approached by deliberately improving the way in which the national economic system works. Policies for each are likely to involve plenty of scope for individual and market choice, but also some reconciliation or subordination of self-interest to national purposes. In each – and in a fifth policy area to be addressed in the following chapter – we guess that Japan is likely to do better by working out her own solutions rather than copying others. At such a time it would not be intelligent to abandon the national capacity to think ahead and act together.

10 The Neglected Producers

1 Wealth and Power in 1990

Statistically speaking, Japanese economic output has expanded to equal that of the aggregate of the European big three – Britain, France and Germany. Japan's accumulated wealth and its overseas assets, as the Japanese government estimates them, now exceed those of the USA, the nation which until recently has been richest in both.[1] Japan's rate of economic growth, although now 'decelerated', continues at well above the OECD average. Plant and equipment are running near capacity, as in the boom years of the 1960s. With labour shortages across age, skill, training and industry groups, average wages are about equal to average US wages, and wages in manufacturing industries are generally higher.

There is little wonder that so many Japanese tourists are flocking overseas, buying everything from highly priced luxury knick-knacks to hotels, office buildings, shops, houses and other properties, van Gogh's paintings and other *objets d'art*, and even historic castles in Europe and elsewhere. As wealthy as they seem to be, with all the statistics to back up the size and spending power of Japanese consumers in both domestic and overseas markets, I still hesitate to accept the reality of Japanese super-wealth. Are Japanese individuals and households – as opposed to national aggregates – really as rich, and as free of economic pressures and hardships, as their Western counterparts?[2]

This chapter is about my fellow countrymen, as individuals and families rather than as units in the national accounts. What has their productive success really won for them? What old or new directions of economic development might now do most for them?

2 Real Income

There are familiar reservations about accepting the apparent opulence of the Japanese economy and the people's lifestyle. The reservations mainly concern three aspects of contemporary Japanese life:

1 long working hours, and long hours spent in commuting to and from the workplace, especially in urban manufacturing and service sectors;
2 the inability of many workers to buy or rent adequate houses or flats at reasonable prices within reasonable reach of their workplaces; and
3 the lack of adequate social capital (called 'infrastructure facilities for livelihood' in earlier chapters) for citizens to enjoy a comfortable, interesting and sociable daily life in their homes and neighbourhoods in their housekeeping and leisure time.

The second and third items are really inexcusable. Japan is quite productive enough to make better provision for them, and the Japanese government is able and powerful enough to contrive better provisions. So far, most economic growth has been directed to furthering growth, with the traditional aim of 'equity and welfare through growth'. In addition to better environmental quality, the time has come to direct growth to providing better distribution and sharing of the now-abundant national wealth and income, and better housing and 'capital for livelihood'. These broad aims are already included in the government's published Visions, but the policy objectives and measures which have so far been adopted fall short of what is needed to fulfil such aims.

The social costs of industrial progress are not new. There have been both Western and Japanese efforts to take better account of them in reports of national income and growth. The conventional summation of goods and services produced, or value added, as Gross National Product (GNP) can be contrasted with various ways of calculating Net National Product as a better indicator of the satisfaction and happiness – the 'net national welfare' – produced by the nation's material activity. One Japanese approach to NNP sets against the gross product not only the harmful by-products of production, such as pollution, but also the hours of labour required to produce the product, and then asks what actual purchasing power the hours of labour earn. There are four reasons why a calculation of that kind suggests that Japanese people in 1990, although dramatically richer than a generation ago, are not necessarily better off than the citizens of some other countries with less GNP per head:

1 Japanese workers work longer hours for incomes which buy less of some of the necessities of life. The Japanese average from 200–500 hours (25–60 days) more work per year than some Western workforces, and

the workers then pay more – nearly twice as much in some comparisons – for necessities such as bread, rice, eggs, beef, sugar and milk.[3]

2   Many Westerners are provided with more public social facilities, in the form of parks, playing fields, golf courses, tennis courts and other sporting facilities, community centres and meeting places, than their Japanese equivalents.

3   The Japanese pay more for less housing than their Western equivalents do, and in the cities many have to accept worse locations, with longer commuting times to and from work. Instead of improving with economic growth those pressures tend to bring worse financial effects as city land prices escalate. New urban households wishing to own their housing must now expect to commit all their savings for 30 or more working years to the costs of housing land and housing finance. The new land prices are not yet fully reflected in housing rents, but some such flow-on must be expected. As owning or renting takes a rising proportion of income, the effective income of households, that is the income they can spend after housing costs, is likely to fall further below the gross income levels recorded in the national accounts, of which patriots are now so proud.

4   Western scholars estimate the material output or value added by the unpaid work done within households and neighbourhoods at between 33 and 45 per cent of the entire national output. With less home space, less community space and capital, and fewer hours at home for workers, Japanese households must be presumed to produce less material goods and services for themselves than their Western equivalents do.

3   Paper Wealth and Rising Inequality

Why have the Japanese people found themselves in such a personally disadvantageous economic position? The explanation is as follows.

The process of growth and accumulation has led the economic system to develop structures and mechanisms to which established policy measures can no longer respond adequately. Previously, it was assumed that peoples' wealth and welfare would be raised via an increase in GNP. Basically, this assumption has been accepted by the general population more or less continuously through the years, despite the heightened environmental issues of the 1960s, the economic transition after the oil crisis in the early 1970s and the sharp appreciation of the yen in the 1980s. We should briefly consider the people's responses to those disturbances.

Faced with severe and well-publicized environmental hazards, the government has reacted more or less responsibly to lead industry to allocate, under anti-pollution regulations, as much as 20 per cent of investment at the beginning of the 1970s, when the national enthusiasm for alleviation of pollution worked at peak for the purpose of pollution alleviation. People seem to have accepted the burden of such costs for 'non-productive' purposes, although it was transferred to consumers in the form of a general price rise for manufactured goods and services.

During 1973–4, the rate of growth of the economy became negative for the first time. The challenge to growth policy marked by the slogan 'Damn GNP' subsided temporarily in the next few years, reflecting, perhaps, the fact that the Japanese economy had not yet reached such an affluent stage as to tolerate negative growth for long. In the meantime, despite inflation and environmental problems, people still felt some improvement in their standard of living, though this occurred at a more moderate rate compared with previous years. Throughout the 1970s, with a pause after the oil shock, there was some reduction in working hours per annum, an increase in the labour share of income, and a reduction in salary differentials and other differential working conditions between different sized enterprises, between age groups, and between occupations with different educational and training requirements. There was thus some general increase of equality in the distribution of earned income.[4]

However, the next decade brought about an ironical combination of changes. In 1986 Japan's GNP per capita reached the world's highest level. The growth of income and accumulated wealth came partly as a result of a sudden rise in the value of the yen in relation to the US dollar and other currencies. It was also due to the continuing growth of the economy. We noted earlier that Japan's GNP had been growing at 4–5 per cent per annum, a much higher rate than that of OECD countries. But at the same time some reverse effects had begun to afflict the general population. What labour had so far gained began to be eroded gradually but steadily. Inequality began to increase, while the economy continued to enjoy buoyant growth and expansion overseas.

In order to explain such phenomena, many new terms were coined such as 'monster money', 'Japanese money', 'asset inflation' and so on, indicating the rapid accumulation of large amounts of idle money which, instead of finding productive investment uses, were drawn into speculative activities: the purchase of land and financial assets of various sorts for fast and high resale profits in *zaiteku* (fancy money-making) schemes. The period between 1970 and 1987 saw an explosive rise in the market value of financial assets. These grew at eight times the rate of growth of GNP, thereby altering the proportional ratio of national assets between (a) production (plant and machinery, factory and office buildings, forestry, housing and stockpiles), (b) land, and (c) financial assets (securities, bonds and bank deposits) from 23 : 46 : 21 to 18 : 54 : 28 respectively.[5]

The inflation of asset prices has mainly come from the surplus of idle money seeking speculative rather than productive returns. The supply of new urban land is limited, especially at advantageous locations in Tokyo and other major cities, and many owners of such land have so far been withholding it in expectation of further price increases. The supply of corporate stock to the stock exchanges is also limited in Japan by the custom and practice of so-called 'friendly shareholders'. (Much of the stock of Japanese corporations is held by affiliated firms for the maintenance of business connections, and rising share prices do not necessarily bring such holdings on to the market.) So, as with land, although to a lesser degree, an excess of demand over supply has inflated stock and share prices.

Wealth created through such asset inflation has little to do with the real wealth of the national economy. It does not reflect the capacity of the economy to produce goods and services for the increased welfare and living standards of the population. It does not provide the population with the purchasing power to acquire housing within Japan. Nevertheless, despite its 'fictitious' nature, it does transfer real purchasing power and command over resources to the owners of the inflated assets, who tend to be an already rich minority of the Japanese people.[6] So there is a general increase in the inequality of wealth. Savings are said to have increased to average more than ¥8 million (US$65 000) per household, but the majority of households fall into groups with savings between US$16 000 and $25 000. Only limited numbers of corporate and individual players are lucky enough to be able to participate in such a lucrative financial game. Wage earners have no such easy means of building up assets. In the cities it is becoming impracticable for most new households to buy their housing. As the inflated land and house prices flow through to raise rents, both home-buyers and home-renters face some decline in their effective income, after housing costs, for saving and spending. Meanwhile, the price of a number of daily necessities rose by a factor of two or three between 1970 and 1980, and more than doubled again through the 1980s, making life in Tokyo and other major cities more expensive than in New York, London and Paris.[7]

4   Reasons for Anxiety, Reasons for Hope

What all the above means is that the Japanese working population is sinking into a position of 'relative poverty' in the midst of great national prosperity: 'relative poverty' in the sense that people are not provided with comfort and well-being of the standard that could well be afforded, with no loss of capitalist growth or efficiency, if there were appropriate public direction of the land and money markets.

In addition to the financial causes of popular resentment or unease, there are others. Two decades of increasingly Westernized information and entertainment have planted new levels of 'consumerist' expectations, especially in the young. At the same time a mixture of financial pressure and personal aspiration is taking more married women, young as well as older, into the workforce, with some increase of stress from the competing pressures of work, housekeeping, and more demanding children and adolescents.

None of this should obscure the vast improvement in living standards achieved by the 'miracle'; but it means that the improvement is accompanied by unexpected levels of stress, and of resentment as the trend to greater equality is reversed. In turn, these resentments are suspected of undermining the ethic and morale of the working people, and thus weakening the driving force of Japan's capitalism – the powerful 'will to economize'.

Since the early 1980s, many reports have appeared which warn that the Japanese, particularly the young, are starting to opt out of the traditional hard-working mode.[8] Since labour surplus gave way to labour shortage as a permanent condition, enticing varieties of choice are available for life-styles outside the realm of the traditional hard-working 'corporate man'. It is reported that people are now asking 'Why work hard?' in Japan. Although some may ask that question because life has become affluent and easy, there is evidence that many people are questioning the value of hard work because of the loss of an adequate reward system for such efforts. Since the Restoration, the Japanese economy and society have been struc-tured so that people could expect that their hard work today would be rewarded with better living conditions in future.[9] But present land and housing prices and trends in spendable income and inequality cast doubt on the economic system's capacity to continue to deliver satisfying long-term rewards. The doubt is clearly shared by the government: there are many signs of official anxiety about the workers' morale, and it is a realistic anxiety about the structure of the economy and its capacity to deliver the goods, not just about its public relations. There has been a considerable 'search for national goals' and many pleas for 'maintenance of the vitality of the nation': for example, for 'Utilization of private vitality' (*White Paper on Japanese Economy*, 1980); the 'New age of growth through eco-nomic vitality' (*White Paper on Japanese Economy*, 1985); 'Maintenance of economic vitality through "globalization" and "internationalization" of business' (MITI policy report, 1989); and 'To a greater contribution for stability and prosperity of the World economy and the *kassei-ka* [vitalization] of Japanese enterprises' (Sangyo Kozo Shingikai, 1990).

To counteract those fears, there are at least three broad reasons for hope.

First, the passage from a labour-surplus to a labour-scarce economy has already brought about many beneficial effects: greater wage equality, better working conditions, and wider working choices and opportunities for a great many people.[10] It only remains to deal with the countervailing forces which flow from the great asset inflation.

Second, there has been an equally important passage from a fear-driven society to one drawn by a Utopian vision. Because the notion of 'Utopia' may attract criticism, we will first explain what we mean by it.

Behind the past economic efforts of the Japanese people there have generally been elements of fear: fear of defeat by Western aggressors, fear of colonization and dependence on Western powers, fear of humiliating identification as a backward country, a place of cheap labour and low living standards, and so on. No doubt some Japanese people dreamed up these nightmares for themselves, but they were propagated most effectively by government in its efforts to stimulate hard work and a united purpose in the nation's economic activity. They were presented as 'worst-case scenarios' which the Japanese people individually and collectively must make every effort to avoid; in other words, the people were driven to avert a 'Hell' rather than to achieve a 'Utopia' for Japan. The lurid imagination of the policy-makers has so far been much more vivid and concrete in its visions of hell than in suggesting what the alternative Utopia might be like. But the economy is now rich and secure: a descent to 'Hell' has come to seem quite unlikely. A century after the aspirations of Fukuzawa and other Meiji leaders, it is at last possible to think beyond the establishment of modern wages and working conditions to imagine a satisfactory system of welfare for everyone in Japan, without the old fears of unemployment, reduced earning capacity for workers, and loss of cost competitiveness in the nation's export industries. Moreover, to imagine positively what Japan might achieve for her people has not only become practical: it has also become necessary. Without fear to drive people, there need to be visions to draw them. To some degree at least, they need to be distinctive Japanese visions. Tolstoy may have believed that 'all happy families are alike', but the Japanese may not wish to be 'all alike' in a standardized Western Utopia: and if they did, a standard Western Utopia of leisurely self-indulgence would scarcely inspire the continuing dynamism that the present leaders hope for.

MITI was thus right to focus its 'Vision for the 1980s' on the need to identify the national goals for the 1980s and beyond.[11] But although the attempts to identify such goals and means to achieve them in the four 'Visions' published so far have been full of good sense and useful proposals, they could still be characterized as primarily backward-looking and westward-looking, in the following sense.

In Japan in modern times the usual method of arriving at a Utopian vision of good has been to select and join together aspects which appear to comprise the better parts of advanced Western society. Such exercises have been useful in understanding what other societies have achieved – to what extent and in what ways – for their own betterment. However, like the construction of a montage, the exercise helps to organize the search but it does not help us to identify the very object of the search. The improvement of the life of the Japanese people may be pursued through a reduction of working hours per week, per month, per year and per working life of employees; through an increase in job vacancies and the range and variety of employment opportunities; through an increase in the supply of goods and services for consumption; and through an ample provision of public goods and facilities. We may expand the list continuously by observing Western experience and adding item after item to the Japanese system, until Japan is so Westernized that no further additions could make it more so. This can be illustrated by reference to our earlier discussion of the NIRA historical survey of social changes and living standards. We noted with some surprise that the decades of high-speed economic growth which transformed the economy from an abundance to a scarcity of labour did not correspond with high values of change in the social indicators.[12] The period of most rapid growth appears to show a lack of dynamism (figures 9.4a and b). This is quite contrary to our expectation of a period during which national income rose rapidly to expand people's spending power, many new products and services were introduced and various new lifestyles were experimented with by many people – old as well as young, poor as well as rich – thus earning the title of the '*Showa Genroku*' period.

What can explain the apparent anomaly of stable social indicators through a period of rapid and radical economic change? A conservative explanation, in which there may be some grains of truth, might suggest that the growth of income and well-being had become so orderly and continuous – approaching but rarely exceeding 10 per cent per year in most of the aspects of well-being – that it rarely disturbed the NIRA triggers. (It will be recalled that the NIRA survey charted, for each year, the proportion of social indicators that changed upwards or downwards by 10 per cent or more, so it is possible to imagine that if income, health and welfare improved at the very high but steady annual rate of 9 per cent, these particular indicators would show no changes.)

There is some support for that explanation in the list of indicators which did change (up or down) by more than 10 per cent during the years of very fast economic growth. Most of them register standard improvements which could be expected to come with improving income education and technology. They include, for example, the number of people visiting overseas countries; the value of fire insurance contracted; numbers of organs, pianos and TV sets produced; the number of adult education courses introduced; the number of cinemas closed down; the annual reduction in the numbers of people drowned, electrocuted, or injured at their workplaces, and of cases of notifiable infectious diseases; and so on.

The 'smooth progress' explanation still seems a little too good to be true: there is too great a contradiction between the dramatic rate of economic growth and the apparent lack, or slow rate, of accompanying social change. There may be room for a different explanation. Perhaps the more radical social changes have been of kinds which escape notice by indicators that were actually designed to fit the previous century's history of social change. Perhaps the most dynamic changes, which might well escape those indicators, have been changes of mind; changes in the people's prevailing values, aspirations and ways of thinking. The economic 'miracle' itself could only have been achieved by remarkable efforts of will and commitment. Its disappointments, noted earlier, may well have brought some disillusion with the programme of 'industrialization and modernization via Westernization'.

Over the past 20 years or so, while the elements of discontent have persisted, the government has developed a reasonably popular set of national goals; 'positive contributions to the international community', 'internationalization of the people', 'conservation of the environment of Japan and the world as a whole' and further enhancement of the living standards and the individualism of the people. No-one disputes the desirability of these goals. But they are unexceptionable, like motherhood, and they are all derived from Western models, or may be thought to do so. We suspect that by themselves they are not enough – perhaps neither Japanese enough nor challenging enough – to satisfy the surging desire of the people of Japan to celebrate their great economic achievement not by sitting back and enjoying its fruits but by finding new tasks; new scope for their ingenuity and vitality and their capacity to act together with a common purpose.

We outlined three reasons for hope. The third is the subject of this book: the unusual capacity of Japanese governments and especially their economic bureaucrats to conceive national changes of direction, to cast them in economic form, to persuade the politicians and people of their wisdom, and to implement them with effective policies. We are about to propose some new national attitudes to family and household life and a radical land reform, which would be the third in Japan's modern history. In order to show why such a programme might be practicable in Japan rather, perhaps, than in any other advanced country, we will first remind readers of the particular qualities of Japanese government which could make it practicable.

5   Radical Capacities

If a radical initiative in economic policy is needed as an addition to the programme indicated in the latest 'Visions', it can expect to succeed if it fits these well-known and widely accepted qualities of Japanese society and government:

● Japan is understood to have an energetic, achieving society.
● The economic departments of the public service are generally honest and competent.
● As far as their interests allow, business and labour tend to accept and follow well-judged government leadership, and they are receptive where necessary to appeals to their long-term rather than short-term interests.
● Japanese governments are not generally inclined to adopt the Western view that government should leave the structure and direction of economic development to market forces, and then add, as separate

social policies, whatever welfare services and income transfers the people need. As far as possible, Japanese governments prefer (1) to perceive social problems as economic problems, and (2) to shape the economic system itself to deliver what people need by enabling them to provide for their own welfare.

- The preferred means of public economic influence are (1) public investment, (2) public ownership or direction of financial institutions and public influence over their types of lending, and (3) indicative planning and persuasion, with (4) direct industrial guidance only as a last resort.
- The government and the people are accustomed to making bold and timely changes of national economic direction when circumstances call for them. Such changes have included: radical reconstructions of property rights, as in the commutation of samurai pensions and the land-tax reforms which accompanied it; the protection of farmland at various periods by prohibiting its conversion to other uses; the US-inspired land reforms of 1945–6 and the effective 'repudiation by inflation' of the accompanying payments to absentee landlords; and the recent imposition of expensive environmental requirements on private industry.

The initiatives proposed later in this chapter are designed to take advantage of all those traditions and capacities.

6 Myths to be Dispelled

As a further preface to new initiatives, there is need to discard four mistaken beliefs; three which are held by many businessmen and academic economists, and one which has in the past been common in the economic ministries of government.

First, it is not true that deregulation necessarily brings about fair competition or greater efficiency in resource allocation. During the 1980s a considerable increase in corporate regulation has been necessary to maintain competition, to enforce environmental care by Japanese corporations, and to 'internalize' some of their environmental costs.

Second, the extensive privatization of the public steel-making, railways, telecommunications and other enterprises, and the more efficient performance of some of them under private management do not indicate that their public ownership was unnecessary. In most cases (as with the model plants of the first Meiji government a century earlier) the enterprises were established by public investment when no adequate private alternatives were put forward. Japanese governments have generally been quite rational in recognizing both needs for particular public enterprises, and opportunities to privatize them when conditions allow. Progress would certainly have been slower in the past, for example, without public railway-building and steel-making. The government should continue to be willing and able to supply economic necessities when private investors cannot or will not supply them.

Third, as we have argued earlier, MITI's withdrawal from direct resource-rationing and industrial guidance as shortages eased during the 1960s was a characteristic adaptation to changing needs. It did not signify a general retreat from public economic direction, as the succeeding initiatives in environmental and corporate regulation make clear.

Fourth, the Japanese government was almost certainly mistaken as well as socially ruthless over more than half of this century in believing that economic growth could be accelerated by a deliberate restraint of investment in housing. Particularly in an under-employed, labour-abundant economy, investment in housing can be a positive aid to growth. It can use otherwise-unemployed labour and materials: it can generally use them where they are, without much need to transport materials very far or move and re-house labour; it makes minimal demands on imports and foreign exchange; and people often save more, and more willingly, if saving is an effective way to own and improve their own housing. The historical evidence elsewhere[13] shows that most above-average rates of national economic growth have been accompanied by government-assisted above-average rates of investment in housing. In Japan, the sudden acceleration of house-building in the mid–1960s (to 17 units annually per 1000 of the population, when most of the developed world was building 8–10 units) did not reduce the spectacular rate of economic growth, even though it coincided with and probably hastened the transformation to a labour-scarce, high-wage economy.

7   New Directions

The remainder of this chapter recommends a further change of national direction based on new attitudes to family and household life. It may be helpful to indicate in advance what is proposed, and how it relates to the household and neighbourhood policies already in train in Japan, and to the common Western prescription for Japan of 'less work, more leisure and bigger houses'.

Current policies to improve the quality of household and communal life, mainly by public investment in local services and facilities, have been presented as social policies. They aim to give life at home and at leisure, especially for women, greater benefit from Japan's prosperity than they have so far received. In our terms, the government might be described as intending 'policies of efficiency' to reward the people for a generation of super-hard work, to reconcile them to the demanding economic system, and to legitimize it further.

We agree, but we have four things to add. First, the changes should be understood and designed as productive, not just in the sense that unpaid housework is productive of real goods and services, but as an important and timely repair of some sources of the productivity of the regular economy.

Second, the household policies should be linked to some other policies in order to make married women's entry to the workforce in Japan less stressful, and more helpful and fulfilling to all concerned, than it has sometimes been in the West.

Third, such 'home and neighbourhood' policies cannot be very effective unless they are accompanied by a radical reform of residential land pricing, and some moderate reform of the system of housing finance.

Fourth, the land reform is desirable for the equally important purpose of reversing the increase in inequality, and of social discontent and alienation, especially among the young, which arise directly and indirectly from the uncontrolled inflation of asset values.

We will now review the national aims expressed in the government's latest publications, then the reasons for our additional proposals, and then the proposals themselves.

8 Official Intentions

We have noted the broad national aims which have been expressed in MITI's 'Visions': that government and nation should work to improve the quality of individual and community life; to cope with the material problems of an ageing population; to conserve the environment in Japan and in the world as a whole; and to contribute to the economic development of the world as a whole, especially the less-developed world.

The international aims are receiving increasing emphasis. In May 1990, a statement by the Council for Industrial Structure expressed Japan's national aims in strongly international terms.[14] In addition to great wealth (it declared), Japan has now accumulated such experience and expertise in the management of industrialization and economic development that she can not only offer aid and advice to less-developed countries, but she can also contribute economic dynamism to the world economy as a whole. The Council proposes principles of action which may be summarized as more foreign aid, the promotion of free trade and 'economic growth without defence industries'. Japan already goes beyond aid and trade to become involved in active participation in the international economy: whereas a generation ago her industrialization depended on her products penetrating export markets, further growth now depends on an outward extension of Japanese ownership and enterprise. Official publications see such extension as a responsible contribution to the dynamism of the world economy – in particular in the neighbouring Asia-Pacific regions.[15] Some observers detect an echo of the Dai Toa-Kyoei-ken (Great East Asia Co-prosperity Sphere) and the doctrines of southern and northern expansion which plunged Japan into the Pacific war. But assuming that democratic government will ensure that such expansion will be peaceful and beneficent – 'economic growth without defence industries' – the Council's basic message seems to be gaining public support. Journalists have given respectability to such aspirations to international leadership as a 'Japanese dream' to take the place of the crumbling 'Pax Americana' and 'American dream'.

Whatever fearful or hopeful view is taken of these aspirations, it is clear that they cannot be achieved without effort: for example, they cannot be achieved by devoting the further growth of productivity, if any, to reducing work and increasing leisure, or to larger welfare transfers to non-earners, as some English-speaking Japan-watchers are prone to recommend. If the government's aspirations are taken seriously, they are quite demanding. From the enrichment of home and communal life and the improvement of environmental quality to the increase of foreign aid and the ambitions for international leadership, they call for continuing energy and innovation. They all require further economic growth, if not necessarily of GNP. Merely to maintain existing GNP with better working conditions, with less stressful efforts, and with cleaner but often costlier inputs and processes to reduce pollution, will require technological advances, investment and some increase in hard work or productivity or both.

The planners are well aware of this, and of a need to sustain economic performance by active public leadership, despite some shift of public opinion in favour of deregulation, freer markets and smaller government.[16] But, in pursuing the new aims and re-shaping the economy in the new labour-scarce condition, the state planners may be expected to continue the traditional strategy of promoting economic activity by encouraging the people's will to work and their 'will to economize'. That is what the planners are accustomed to, and best at, with their accumulated experience in building the supporting economic institutions, administrative networks and organisations to guide the people's economic activities in conformance with the national economizing aims. They continue to perceive most social problems as economic problems, to be solved wherever possible by adjusting the economic system. They are as anxious as ever not to sap the will to work by offering people welfare alternatives. The 1980s began as a decade of transition towards an affluent era with diversified demands for goods and services, in which leisure time – both its extent and its quality – emerged as an important item on the agenda in the 'welfare' component of the population. The bureaucrats saw in this trend a danger of the economy losing its dynamism. They foresaw a great danger to the economy, in the process of building an affluent society in Japan, of destroying the vital work incentive of the workforce, the traditional force which has driven the economic development and industrialization of Japan. Public planning appeared to be essential, and the 1980s 'Vision' was written in the belief that the Japanese must avoid the observed pitfalls in building a 'welfare economy' of the Western kind, in which the provision of public welfare packages unavoidably results in demolishing that 'vital work incentive'. The 'new capitalism' was to be nurtured by public influence on the people's states of mind, rather than by administrative guidance of their industries, but it still needed active nurture.

How should this be achieved? At the beginning of the 1990s, although there is plenty of 'vision' and persuasion, state officials are still reluctant to move very far beyond their traditional repertoire, such as 'devices to reduce national dependency on the supply of natural resources from overseas sources', 'expansion of the frontiers of national economic, social and cultural activities beyond Japan' and 'devices able to solve the problems of the ageing of society' without necessarily increasing public expenditure, pensions or other welfare payments. One general effect of these anxieties is that the government does comparatively little to improve the distribution of wealth and income, or to prevent it from deteriorating. There is some, but not too much, redistribution through the welfare system. There is no Australian-style regulation of wages, or European-style rent subsidy. Not much is being done or currently planned by those or any other means to counter the unequalizing effects which the inflation of asset values is having on people's effective saving and spending capacities: that is, on their incomes after tax and housing costs. Therefore, although some of the statements of national aims have included a mention of improving equalities, there is currently a reverse trend. It is resented, and except for some better community facilities, no action is promised to check it.

In sum, the policy-makers seem set to guide the transformation of the economy into its new labour-scarce, environmentally prudent, internationally oriented form by the use of the well-tried methods which produced the system that is now being transformed. We fear that if these methods are not augmented by some additional policies, they may prove to be less persuasive than they once were to both working men and working women; and some erosion of the existing capacity for hard work and concerted economic action may follow.

This theme may be illustrated, and our next subject introduced, by an issue on which the authorities seem content to see a lucky 'fit' between a growing problem and an independent change of market behaviour:

● Problem: Japan has an ageing population, and must expect the output of the active workforce to support an increasing proportion of retired people.
● Solution: rising proportions of women are entering employment; the workforce is thus being augmented to balance the rising demand for its output by non-workers.

For a century up to the 1960s, the rural population was a 'reserve army' from which urban industry could draw any extra labour that it needed. Now urban households fulfil this function, as more and more women seek employment. Meanwhile, public investment to improve community services and facilities – 'infrastructure for livelihood' – is expected to benefit women and make it easier for them to combine employment and housework. They are thus perceived as becoming productive at work and receiving more social support at home. Good! However, we must analyse their situation and prospects in greater depth to discover what else they contribute to Japan's economic performance, and what other supports and incentives may be needed if those other contributions are to continue.

9   Analysis: the Unnoticed Producers

Women in Employment

We may start with some basic information about the advance of women into the workforce since the economy moved into labour scarcity. [17]

1   In the female population aged between 15 and 65, participation in the workforce is rising steadily, although it is still low by Western standards. In the 1970s participation was reported to be below 30 per cent, but it has increased to 48 per cent in 1982 and 50 per cent in 1986, and is expected to have exceeded 60 per cent by the end of 1991. As a result, the female proportion of the whole workforce has risen from 31.7 per cent in 1965 to 35.9 per cent in 1985 and 40.1 per cent in 1988.

2   Two age groups are mainly responsible for the rise in the numbers of working women. The first is women in their forties: 60 per cent are employed and the proportion continues to rise. The other group consists of women aged 25–29. The increase in their participation is a recent phenomenon. In the past, women in this group have tended to withdraw from the workforce temporarily, and more often than not permanently, causing a sharp fall in the female participation rate above age 30. But the participation of this group rose from 43 per cent in 1975 to 50 per cent in 1981 and was expected to exceed 65.6 per cent by mid-1990. [18] This suggests that more and more women are electing to remain in their jobs throughout marriage and child-rearing, instead of adopting the role of full-time homemaker. [19]

3   The advance of women into the workforce has coincided with rapid urbanization, which has expanded the tertiary (service) sector of the economy, and it is in that sector – some of it developing to absorb the spending of the new women earners themselves – that women's employment has primarily expanded, in occupations such as waitressing, hairdressing, child care, nursing, teaching and saleswork of various kinds. This phenomenon is not unique to Japan; but in Japan women are

entering what amounts to permanent part-time employment to a greater extent than elsewhere. Surprising facts about recent conditions for female part-time workers are that such part-timers generally work the same number of days per month, and their total working hours are only two hours shorter than those of full time workers.[20] (Japanese critics of Western sloth may compare with Australia, where 37.5 hours is now the standard full-time working week in the majority of occupations.)

4 Most married women's part-time employment earns very low pay. In Japan part-time workers typically receive lower rates per hour than regular permanent workers; and there are still differential rates for male and female workers. Married women working part-time attract dual penalties, losing 15–25 per cent for being female and a further 30–50 per cent for working part-time. Thus, in general, they earn less than 50 per cent of male wages.

We must immediately ask if these conditions are brought upon women by market forces, or by their own preference. If the latter, what could explain such a preference within a labour-scarce economy?

Part-time employment is of course not a new phenomenon in Japan. Throughout the process of industrial development, employers have used this form of employment at great cost advantage to themselves, and at the expense of the welfare of workers who constitute a great reserve army of cheap – and, when convenient, disposable – labour.

New reasons for this old exploitative practice have arisen lately. A combination of labour scarcity, environmental reform and technological advance has been driving business to switch resources from the old heavy industries to more capital-intensive, knowledge-intensive and labour-saving activities.[21] Such changes create redundancy problems, as lifetime employees cannot be laid off. The labour scarcity compels firms to continue their commitment to the lifetime employment principle for their 'core' workforce, but they have new technological and structural reasons for wanting to increase the 'flexible' proportion of the workforce; in other words, the numbers of casual and part-time workers who can be laid off or reduced to shorter hours at will. With labour scarce, however, not many male workers are willing to accept such insecurity. Therefore most of the demand has been met by married, middle-aged and older women, who have decided to work provided that the workplace is close to home, the working hours are short, and there is none of the compulsory overtime which many regular full-time workers have to do.[22]

We have to confess that the married women workers' attitudes to these arrangements are not yet quite clear. Many research projects are under way. Preliminary indications seem to offer support for three general observations. First, of the possible motives which send women to factories and offices, family financial difficulties do not appear to play an important part. Many surveys (by interview, questionnaire and other methods of eliciting women's expressed opinions) indicate that they themselves do not regard finance as an important motivating force; so for the sake of working part-time and near to home they choose to accept lower pay than they could earn in regular employment. Second, the money is nevertheless welcome as an addition to the household budget, and especially to the household's capacity to save. Statistics of household consumption show that wives working part-time earn, on average, one-third as much as husbands in full-time regular jobs. Such two-income households find that they have 20–25 per cent more left over for saving than single-income families. The third and most important motive which draws married women into the workforce seems to be a strong and growing desire to participate in society – a society which, in their perception, is progressively opening up to them and appreciating their participation.

These trends may be expected to continue. More married women, eventually perhaps most married women, will go out and earn. Employers need them, and so will tailor jobs to fit their timetables, to interest them and to give them job satisfaction. The government will welcome (and perhaps reward through the tax system) their addition to a workforce that must support growing numbers of senior citizens. These economic changes will merge with social changes, in personal freedom and enjoyment and in attitudes to marriage, divorce, remarriage and a low birth rate. The economic system will continue to respond as it is doing already, with inventive new goods and services for working wives. Producing those goods and services will expand employment in industries traditionally staffed by women, such as cosmetics, fashion and child care. Women's education will respond, both to train women for their widening employment opportunities and to enrich their capacities for self-improvement and participation in the 'open' society.

To economic observers, including many Japanese policy-makers, these developments may seem to be wholly welcome. They look constructive to all concerned: they bring new measures of liberation and equality to women, they improve household budgets for husbands and children, and they contribute to economic growth and thus to Japan's capacity for economic leadership.

Nevertheless, before uncorking the champagne to celebrate these benign developments, we would do well to explore their possible effects on the role – commonly unnoticed and virtually unresearched – which married women have played in Japan's economic development from the beginning, and especially during the decades of 'miracle' growth.

Women at Home

We may distinguish a spectrum of possible attitudes to the domestic role of married women:

1   Apart from the child-bearing function, they may be regarded as unproductive dependants.
2   They perform useful functions of housework and child care, and support and nurture the productive workforce: they may be regarded as partners in the provision of their husbands' productive work.
3   Housework, child care, private transport and other services which household members do without payment for each other, and sometimes for their local communities – services which are mostly although not exclusively undertaken by women – can be valued at the factor costs or market prices of their commercial equivalents. As calculated for various developed Western societies, they constitute more than one-third of all output or value added. The household output is of material goods and services, as real and valuable as those which are recorded in GNP. It follows that the household capital with which it is produced is productive capital, the allocation of which is accordingly important, and should be regarded as productive investment rather than consumer spending.
4   Families are important educators and transmitters of skills, values, culture and sociability to their children. Until now, especially in Japan, most of that function has been performed by women. They are thus critical contributors to the development of productive human capital.

Can any of those perceptions of women's roles help us to understand the part played by the family and the household in the economic development of Japan?[23]

First we wish to expand the second perception – of wives as partners and service-providers to productive workers – as it has applied in Japan. In the West there has been a tendency for people to see work as necessary toil endured to earn income for the home and for leisure, with most of the joy and meaning of life to be found away from work in the family and social life, and in the hobbies and recreation which occupy the worker's leisure time. In contrast to that we believe that, to an important degree, Japanese men have tended to seek their main fulfilment and 'meaning of life' in their work and working relations, with home as a base, a place of rest and recuperation where working strength can be restored, rather than a place for very much active self-expression and fulfilment. Such an attitude rests on the assumption that, in Japan, a woman stays at home to assist and support her husband. That enables him to spend the long day as a dedicated and effective worker, bringing high labour productivity to the economy. As a partner in that personal and national achievement, a woman can – to some extent – share in its benefits.

However, times are changing, and that assumption is being challenged. More women are joining the workforce every year. Even if part-time, more are doing so in a regular, permanent and ambitious way. Not surprisingly, many are seeking personal fulfilment at the workplace in much the same manner as their spouses. This may be especially true of those without children or those whose children have grown up, but the workforce participation of young married women with children is also increasing. As a result, male workers may expect less than they used to enjoy of the service, support and encouragement at home which enabled them to dedicate themselves so entirely to their factories and offices, to high productivity and to national economic growth. Both management and, to some extent, the government are aware of this trend, and have begun to introduce measures and devices to try to counter it and maintain employees' motivation.

A more important problem for sustained economic growth in Japan, however, lies elsewhere. Another function of the family and the home in Japanese society has been largely ignored; that is the fourth role listed above, the family's role in educating and training children, and implanting in them the capacities for hard work, 'competitive co-operation', respect for national leadership and pride in national purposes and progress, which have been a primary motive force of Japan's economic success.

Ludz, an American psychoanalyst, identifies four family functions in the development and socialization of children: parental nurturant functions; the integration of the personality of children; the demonstrative lesson of the family as an example of a social system; and the transmission of the prevailing culture.[24] The last of these may have been especially important in Japan. The family implants in its offspring the system of meanings and logic not only of their language but also of their society, so that (if the transmission is effective) the children understand and absorb the society's values, or one of its contending sets of values, and however often they may transgress rules based on those values they learn not to act irrevocably against them. Ludz does not believe that formal schooling can perform these functions adequately: they are prerequisites for effective learning at school, rather than products of it, although schooling may reinforce them. (Evidence for the importance of the family contribution can be found in parts of the Third World, and in studies of children raised entirely in institutions in developed societies: formal schooling tends to be less effective in the absence of a helpful culture, and of families to transmit it.)

Japanese families may be seen simultaneously to have played a conservative and dynamic role in Japan's modernization and economic transformation. Japan's culture has been more homogeneous than most. Japanese families have continued to transmit its essentials: a certain puritanism; effective self-control; capacities for forbearance and co-operation; submission to authority and receptiveness to leadership; pride in the national culture and a sense of its difference from others; the 'will to economize' and to work hard; and seriousness of individual and collective purpose. As we discussed in earlier chapters, government planners and private firms have been able to make extremely productive use of those qualities, reliably transmitted to most of the population. Nevertheless, although it has perpetuated those traditional qualities, the role of the family has not been wholly conservative. In the history of Japan's economic policies we have observed significant changes of direction. They have come at 12-, 15- and 20-year intervals: two or three times in each working lifetime. Some of their elements could be implemented by redirecting public investment or other aspects under direct government control, but most of them also required elements of persuasion – of business leaders, workers and the general population. Some required significant changes of values and mass behaviour: as in persuading samurai to become businessmen; peasant families to send all their children to school – girls as well as boys; peasants to become factory workers; country dwellers to move to cities; exploited workers to accept 'paternal' rather than adversary industrial relations; all classes to change their lifestyles and consumption patterns; national aspirations to switch from economic growth to military expansion then back again; married women to join the workforce; people and businesses to 'internationalize' themselves; and so on.

Some of those changes required changes in families' lifestyles, internal divisions of labour, religious and social beliefs, forms of recreations, the educational curriculum, and in the balance between competitive and co-operative impulses (or the capacity for 'competitive teamwork') in children's aspirations.[25] The task of accepting, implementing and transmitting many elements of these changes has fallen to women, who appear generally to have responded positively, thus acting as agents of change as well as of social conservation. For the first century of modernization the main voices interpreting the world and the nation's needs to Japan's families were those of government, and a Press that was generally sympathetic to government. Just as the government's direct economic controls were supplemented by its persuasive influence over private business aims and decisions, so the effects of legal and educational changes were supplemented by the government's diffuse influence over family beliefs and values. Commercial radio and television and a diversified Press has changed all that for the present generation. So has the new propensity of business leaders (including some media owners) to belittle and oppose the role of government. But until recently there has been considerable integration between state and family, to preserve the qualities of citizenship that the government believed to be important and to change those which it believed should change.[26]

The Decline of State and Parental Influence

The transmission of values and attitudes that we have just described has come under stress in recent times from a succession of economic changes, which may be summed up as: (i) the withdrawal of men from much of family life, from the 1950s onwards; (ii) some withdrawal of women (also into the workforce) from the 1970s onwards; (iii) rising prices of urban housing and declining opportunities for its occupants to own it, from the 1980s onwards; and (iv) throughout the period, some growing displacement of traditional and government influences on family values by the increasingly intensive international commercial media.

The absence of men from family life follows from the hours they spend at work and commuting. Although much is made of Japanese commuting time, the hours of work are much more important in differentiating Japanese from Western experience. At the 1985 census, male workers in Tokyo averaged about an hour and a half a day – 45 minutes each way – between home and work; male workers in Sydney averaged only about 8 minutes less each way. However, male workers in Tokyo between 25 and 59 years of age averaged 52.3 hours of work each week, while their Sydney equivalents averaged 36.4. The difference each day, and for most the difference between 5 and 6 days at work each week, makes a critical difference to the presence of fathers during the waking hours of pre-school and primary school children. Sydney males averaged six times as much time at housework, including child care, as did Tokyo males.[27] One condition of the 'economic miracle' has been the shaping, almost entirely by their mothers, of Japanese children's identity, self-discipline, values and first perceptions of society and nation. There is a need to amend the second of the attitudes to the domestic role of married women which we listed on p. 234, the distinctive Japanese perception of wives as supportive partners, sharing some of the credit for their husbands' productive work. It may well be through their children's productive work, through 30–40 adult years as willing 'workaholics', that Japanese housewives contribute most to the nation's economic performance.

However, many are now giving less time to that function. We noted earlier the motives which seem to be drawing women, including young married women, to go out to work. Despite the preference of some for part-time work, 77 per cent of Tokyo's women workers were full-time workers in 1985. All Tokyo women over 15 years of age – full- and part-time workers and non-workers – averaged about 45 hours per week altogether of housework, commuting and paid work (about 5 hours, or 12 per cent, more than Sydney women averaged).[28] The averages, which include widowed and invalid and retired women as well as fit women of working age, are not very illuminating; it matters more that almost 60 per cent of Japanese women in the child-rearing years from age 25 onwards now go out to work.

In addition to some withdrawal of time from parenting, other influences may be affecting the quality and purpose of the parenting. The progress of New Left, Feminist and Women's Liberation movements during the 1970s, the campaigns for equal pay and opportunity, and the efforts to eliminate gender-linked roles and occupations all arose from shifts in women's aspirations, and helped the shifts along. 'Liberation' has its darker side in the stress associated with the rising number of already fatherless families, now increasingly motherless as well. We do not suggest that 'liberated' women or working women make worse mothers: many may derive confidence and broader vision from their social and working life away from home. But, for that very reason, their transmission of national and paternal aims and dutiful values to their children may be less single-minded and unquestioning than it used to be. That we cannot measure such changes does not mean that none are occurring. It would be ironical if this further increase in Japan's productivity, achieved by attracting married women into the workforce, were to disable a main part of the mechanism which generates the national 'will to economize'.

The stresses of working mothers have come at a time when many children are also under increasing pressure. Working mothers with less time and nervous energy left for their children still feel a duty to drive the children to compete hard for entry to the more prestigious schools, universities and 'life-employment' companies; or if the children lack the talent or status to enter those exalted competitions, to compete just as hard in the rougher world of trade training and insecure employment outside the 'lifetime employment' system. During the 1960s and 1970s these pressures brought about sharp increases in youth crime, suicide and apathetic, defeated attitudes to study and work. The 1980s have added an increase in domestic violence, often against parents, as adolescents rebel and challenge the judgement and authority of their elders.

Finally, as young workers come to form households of their own they encounter the uncontrolled inflation of urban land and housing prices. The rate at which the inflation is proceeding makes it pointless to give a quantitative account of it here: the rapidly changing information belongs in newspapers, not in a book with some years of shelf life. In 1990 there are various estimates that 30 years' saving from one income, or perhaps now from two, may still suffice to buy an apartment in a major Japanese city – but for how much longer can not be predicted. In practice, what is needed to buy a house in a city is not earned income but accumulated or inherited capital. Young adults are abandoning hope of owning their accommodation, or expanding it very much as their households grow, or bequeathing the means of ownership to their children. The new prices cannot bring about a fully proportionate flow-on to rent levels, because most Japanese incomes could not yield such rents; but some flow-on seems inevitable, leaving tenants less income to spend or save after tax and housing costs. If the land and housing business continues to be left to 'market forces', some second-round effects are likely. With super-inflated land prices but with rents limited by the incomes of most of the population, investors will be reluctant to build new low- or medium-priced rental housing in the cities. Nevertheless, the demand for it must increase as the inflated purchase prices exclude more households from ownership. Therefore, a further, increase in rents, caused by shortage, is likely. All these frustrations, with their unfair effects on the distribution of housing and wealth and income, converge most acutely on young parents through the early household years when they are introducing their children to the nature of their society, the benefits that it confers on them, and the principles of good behaviour within that society.

It is too early to judge the effect that these trends may have on work incentives in Japan. In some English-speaking countries they would be expected to topple a government which let them continue for any length of time. Japanese voters may become equally hostile if they see the government as responsible for the ill effects of the asset inflation. There is good reason to hold the government responsible. Throughout this book we have paid tribute to the efforts of Japan's bureaucrats to plan and guide economic development consistently with business freedom and market efficiency, and without themselves becoming the creatures of any of the economy's profit-seekers or other sectional interests. It has been partly a unique achievement, differing in important ways from Western routes to affluence. But if so much of what Japan has achieved over more than a century of economic development is due to the initiatives and independent thinking of her bureaucrats, they must also accept responsibility for the current asset inflation and the increasing inequalities that are flowing from it.

If, in these various ways, some stress and uncertainty is afflicting the 'enculturation' of Japan's children (their education to understand their own cultures), and they must grow up to face frustrations and injustices in land and housing markets – that is, frustrations in household and family life – from which their Western counterparts are comparatively free, Western experience may hold some new interest for them. For a generation, cinema and television have brought increasing quantities of popular Western entertainment into Japanese households. There has been much anxiety and many complaints about the amount of violence and other bad behaviour depicted on screen, much of it depicted as masculine, honourable, patriotic, and so on; and about the advertising which comes with it, full of consumerist inducements to borrow and spend rather than work and save. At the same time, Western comedies and TV 'soaps' depict family life in capacious houses and gardens, owned by their occupants and apparently available to households of all classes. Thoughtful viewers will notice that the happy and eventful family life is based on an alluring mix of home ownership, short working hours and leisure time as the locus of much, perhaps most, of the people's joy and fulfilment in life. It may be from these imported visions, at least as much as from business campaigns for deregulation, small government and 'letting the market rule', that the traditional motive force of Japanese productivity and growth is in danger.

This catalogue of troubles has not been drawn up to exaggerate Japan's social and educational ills. Its purpose is only to suggest that some traditional and still important generators of Japan's human capital and 'will to economize' are being eroded, and not yet adequately repaired or replaced.

10 Programme

A Western Strategy

Before proposing radical additions to the government's vision of Japan's development, we should consider with a genuinely open mind a more Western or 'market-driven' alternative. An argument in favour of it might run like this: Japan has now equalled or surpassed the best Western performance at work, and is accordingly taking up the responsible role of a leader in the international economy. Japan is well on the way to the highest standards in science, and in the arts it is achieving excellence in an appropriate mix of Western and traditional Japanese arts. Where Japan lags behind is in provisions for life away from work. It does not yet provide the mass of its population with the amount of leisure, the capacious housing or the diversity of local communal facilities which the most advanced Western societies offer to all but the poorest of their people. If the direction of future development is left entirely to market forces, especially to market forces shaped by commercial marketing strategies and advertising, Japanese households seem likely to exercise their consumer sovereignty by distributing their spending in much the same way as do American households, whose tastes are shaped by watching much the same television. As a reward for generations of very hard work they may well want the only substantial fruits of affluence they have not yet obtained; Western standards of household space, equipment and recreational apparatus, and time to allow them to enjoy them properly – Western hours of work and leisure.

Such a strategy would require that the government continue to provide basic infrastructure, regulate environmental quality and enforce honest corporate behaviour, as Western governments do. Beyond that it might hope to leave most economic decision-making to the spending choices of the consumers, as many Japanese business voices are now urging it to do. Even if deregulation allows some unpopular increase in inequality, that may be healthy: when the government gives up trying to motivate work by thought control, in other words by frightening people into working hard to save the nation, work will need all the more to be motivated by the normal sticks and carrots of differential pay, and welfare policies which do not offer comfortable alternatives to work.

We should acknowledge that such a strategy, or deliberate abstention from strategy, has much to commend it. Subject to some hazards noted below, it is workable. It is the easiest course for government to take: it is in accord with the trend to smaller government and does not require any unpopular action or radical change of direction. To the extent that North American or Western European lifestyles and satisfactions are achieved, we know from experience that people can be happy and satisfied by those means.

Nevertheless, there would be hazards of two kinds. First there are well-known shortcomings of Western societies, which Japan might be better without. Besides adversary relations between business and labour and business and government, and an incapacity for concerted national action or deliberate changes of direction, there are also neglected and latch-key children, unpleasant rates of crime and drug abuse. Some of those are effects of the Western liberal obsession with the freedoms of fully formed adults, without care for the processes which determine the character of the adults that society is bringing up.

Second, there are practical hindrances to implementing a Western strategy in Japanese conditions. We personally think the first objection is the more important of the two: we would prefer a distinctly Japanese strategy, and the greater diversity between national cultures that the world would thus retain. But for those who would prefer a Western strategy, there would be practical difficulties. Japan does not have the natural resources to produce output and income as easily as most of the leading Western economies do. (In the figures cited earlier, for example, Japanese hours of work exceed Australian hours of work by more than Japanese GNP per head exceeds Australian; there is reason to believe that with equal work and equal leisure Japanese output would once again lag behind that of more richly endowed countries.[29]) Japan does not have enough usable land to offer British, North American or Australian quantities of private housing and garden space to more than a small minority of its urban population. The more comparable Western societies would be the Netherlands and Germany, whose population densities lead them to house many city-dwellers in apartment buildings rather than separate houses, as Japan does. But their urbanization is in many small cities, with well-developed social and recreational facilities. Their city residents can live closer to their work, to their urban recreations and to the countryside than can many residents of Tokyo, Osaka, Nagoya and even the 'smaller' Japanese cities with populations of two or three million. Moreover, because they share some of the problems of scarce land and dense population, German attitudes to work and to their polluted environment are not so different from those of the Japanese. A German model would not offer a great deal of the spacious, leisurely lifestyle to be observed in American TV soap operas of suburban and provincial life. Finally, in both the extensive suburban fabric of the English-speaking cities and the denser cities of northwestern Europe, a variety of government programmes have long ensured that acceptable housing, whether owned or rented, is available to most households on reasonable financial terms. If Japan were to seek full Americanization at work and at home, it could not be achieved by leaving the process 'to the market'. The radical land and housing reforms discussed below as part of a 'Japanese strategy' would be just as necessary to make a Western strategy work and keep it popular.

A Japanese Strategy

What we mean by a Japanese strategy is conditioned by a number of facts of Japanese life and environment, as follows.

Japan's geography and natural resources require that, in order to stay in front, the Japanese may well have to work longer hours than most, at least in the foreseeable future. It is undesirable that this be at the expense of children's education, or that it impose double stress on women. Women's equality, and entry into full membership of society, should be achieved by means compatible with good child care and development. The land shortage requires that city people live quite densely, without extensive private space for games and recreation, workshop hobbies and so on. An underrated advantage of 'late developers' at industrialization should be the opportunity to observe the dark side of Western affluence, and avoid as much of it as possible. In all these circumstances there is much to be said for Japan building on, rather than trying to discard, her particular advantages. We have noted that Japanese people are accustomed to seeking much of their fulfilment and enjoyment of life, directly or vicariously, away from home: in national achievements, at work and in sociable community life. They have the capacity to generate effective economic leadership and to co-operate with it. There is nothing necessarily fascist or sheep-like in this enviable capacity for concerted action, which has flourished better than ever before during 40 years of democracy. The democratic success owes much to the presence of an honest, intelligent and creative bureaucracy. It owes even more to the propensities built into the people by their upbringing, especially we believe their parental upbringing. Therefore, if Japanese people wish to retain and improve a distinctive Japanese way of life, they may have good reason to continue:

- to co-operate and compete energetically as members of an 'achieving society';
- to endow their children with hard-working, self-reliant, sociable natures and shared ideals; and
- to reconcile themselves to their shortage of private space by continuing to look for much of the joy and meaning of life away from home; in their work, their communal social life, and their pride as participants in Japan's peaceful national and international example and achievements.

However, to keep such a strategy workable and popular, Japan also needs:

- to check the trend towards greater inequality, and
- to adopt divisions of labour which allow women a fairer share of the work, social life and leadership of such a society.

Both those aims require, among other things:

● a radical correction of the current excessive inflation of land and housing values.

To detail such a strategy we may use the format used in table 2.1 (p. 46), to set out national aims, then economic objectives, instruments and measures for achieving them:

1 *National aims.* Maintain an achieving society, with its continuing prosperity contributing to the welfare of the world.
2 *Economic objectives.* Continuing the growth of economic productivity. Using it not necessarily to expand GNP, but to improve international aid and co-operation, to protect environmental quality in Japan and the world, and to improve individual living and working conditions, paying special attention to the conditions of household, school and community life for young parents and their children.
3 *Economic instruments.* Public investment. Regulation of private financial institutions. Intervention in urban land and housing markets by regulation and public dealing. Public influence on educational and training institutions.
4 *Economic measures*:
   ● Public investment in 'infrastructure for livelihood'.
   ● Segregation of a flow of housing finance at regulated interest rates.
   ● Segregation of residential from business land markets, with measures to restrain residential prices and rents.
   ● Where necessary, related measures of rent control and public housing supply in rental housing markets.

Let us explain these items in more detail.

Aims Above all, 'Maintaining an achieving society' should mean maintaining methods of parental and school upbringing which will continue to produce (as far as possible, with all due allowance for infinite individual variation and human error) hard-working, self-reliant, sociable people with a serious sense of purpose and shared ideals.

Objectives 'Continuing economic growth, but not necessarily of GNP' expresses the need for continuing economic improvements, of which some will, but many will not, add to GNP as conventionally measured. For example, some production costs must rise as environmental policies require better energy economy, more recycling, cleaner manufacturing processes, more waste-processing, and so on. To maintain present material standards of living by such more costly means requires some growth in productivity, by technical improvement or harder work or both, much of which will not expand GNP.

The same is true of some physical and other improvements to working conditions. Even in an achieving society, some reduction of working hours and increase of leisure is desirable in Japan, and if real incomes are not to fall, that also must be achieved by technical progress: in other words, by economic growth which is taken in the form of more leisure rather than more GNP. Effective international aid usually has costs, even when it takes the desirable form of raising the indigenous productivity of the areas concerned; it may appear in Japan's GNP, but if it is not matched by growth it must reduce Japanese household income. Capital investment in community facilities figures in GNP in the year of investment, but much of its ensuing product, in other words its use by the citizens over the years, does not. Nor does it help GNP in the short run to reserve a substantial share of young women's working time for stress-free parenting. (Compare the human costs, and in the long run perhaps economic costs, of the higher GNP which can be produced by a pattern of full-time employment by parents with full-time institutional day-care for their children; in the few morning and evening hours which mothers can spend with their young children, children and housework must compete for (often somewhat tired) attention.)

There is also a need for some growth to improve Japan's housing. If North American standards of indoor and outdoor space are not to be achieved, it should at least be possible to offer the equivalent of Dutch or German family apartments, to allow (for example) study/bedrooms with reasonable storage space for growing children; some workroom or hobby space; comfortable space to entertain friends; and space and insulation to allow the use of keyboards and other musical instruments. Even if much fulfilment is to be sought away from the home, there is still a need to reduce the present over-crowding of much of Japan's housing. Although that range of improvements may not do much to expand GNP, it all requires some continuing growth in productivity, which will not be achieved by sitting back to relax and enjoy the affluence that has already been achieved. There is a continuing need for a good deal of the energy and ingenuity which worked the 'miracle' a generation ago.

Instruments Two of the necessary instruments are traditional ones; public investment, and public ownership or regulation and guidance of financial institutions. Means also exist to influence the types of education and training offered by public institutions; and may need to be created to intervene in urban land and housing markets through regulation or public dealing.

Measures We need not detail measures to implement the widely accepted aims expressed in the current publications of MITI, EPA, the Council for Industrial Structure and others; in other words, measures related to the government's international, environmental and communal aims. We merely add three general considerations about the choice of projects for public investment in 'infrastructure for livelihood':

1   It may be worthwhile developing existing local government institutions to allow consultation with citizens on a very local basis about the facilities that they most want to have. Although bureaucrats may find such consultation time-wasting and inexpert, it can economize on investment by ensuring that the facilities provided are genuinely wanted and likely to be fully used.
2   Such provisions should obviously be biased towards facilities which do not use too much land, and can be built on a small scale at many locations, so as to be accessible to as many residents as possible: not land-hungry baseball fields and golf courses, but swimming pools, squash and tennis courts, centres for adult education, for learning and practising arts and crafts, for amateur music and drama; meeting places for young people; community centres as meeting places and venues for chess and card-playing clubs, *ikebana* and *haiku* classes, Zen practice and *judo* training.
3   In community and school facilities there should be an emphasis on inviting children and young people to participate in active forms of recreation, especially those which develop physical or intellectual skills. It does not matter whether the skills are saleable for employment purposes. What matters is to encourage the taste for action, for the development and use of skills, and for co-operative and competitive activity with others, as preferred alternatives to the passive reception of recorded and broadcast entertainment in restricted housing space.

These considerations follow from the official intention to improve community 'infrastructure for livelihood'. They are also relevant to the objectives which we seek; to add to the national programme. Those additional objectives are (i) to give parenting, especially by women, the importance and support which it deserves for reasons of both social justice and national productivity; (ii) to check the trend towards greater inequality of wealth and income; and (iii) to assist both of those purposes through a radical land reform. Measures for those purposes might include the following.

Women's employment   The entry and rapid advance of women in the labour force is the most important single effect of the transformation from a labour-abundant to a labour-scarce economy. It increases output, and it offers women new social, economic and intellectual opportunities of the highest importance. But if the change is to do more good than harm, both to women and in the long run to the nation's economic performance, Japan must not proceed to impose intolerable burdens on its female members. There is a danger of that if an attempt is made to combine Western visions with Japanese economics. Many Western concepts of gender equality aim to equalize men's and women's tasks both at work and at home, confining children to school or all-day child-care centres during the working day. In our opinion that arrangement is not necessarily best for children even when it works as planned, and it rarely works as planned: with two paid jobs to do, and a third at home in the form of the day's housework and morning and evening attention to children, the men tend to do one and an eighth jobs and the women one and seven eighths.[30] Except for a few chief executives, those women are the most stressed and hardest worked members of their societies, and their marriages and relationships with their children often suffer from the stress. In Japanese conditions, with longer hours and more days of work and commuting, and an even greater reluctance of male workers to do much housework, the attempt to combine parenthood with two full-time jobs must usually expose women, and their services to their children, to extreme toil and stress.

Is this therefore a conservative plea for women to content themselves with their traditional, subservient role as housewives? Certainly not. It is a plea for government support and encouragement for further improvement and wider provision of what is already available to the more fortunately placed female parents in Japan. It should be possible for women to establish themselves in occupations before having children; to 'keep their hand in' with part-time or occasional or home-based work during their years with young children; to enjoy genuine public assistance in their parenting role; and then to return, if they wish, not only to full-time work but to genuinely equal opportunities at work. Japan does not merely need the services of its women to operate sewing machines or gut chickens: they are also a reservoir of professional, managerial and leadership dynamism that is only just beginning to be tapped. What is required, in as many industries and services as possible, is to end the conflict between parenthood and occupational ambition. In more than half of all occupations, a woman's actual functional capacity for skilled or managerial work in middle life need not be impaired by having spent some earlier years bringing up children. Measures to reconcile the two might include, first, the articulation of a national determination to reconcile them; then national study and recognition of the range of industries and occupations in which, with appropriate retraining where necessary, it is practicable for people to resume careers after periods of absence or part-time work; extensive public and corporate provision for such retraining; and, wherever the relevant skills and retraining arrangements make it functionally possible, a rule that for purposes of lifetime employment, seniority and promotion, years raising children count equally with years in employment. Such practices should be made acceptable through education, on the basis of an emphatic national recognition of the parental contribution to Japan's human capital and productivity.

Land and housing   The excessive inflation of Japan's urban land prices has not yet prompted effective collective measures. To avoid outright confiscation or (when debts are secured on inflated values) forced insolvencies. the following may be considered.

First, it needs to be recognized that these are markets in which it is right to intervene. There is no reason at all to expect that open market competition for urban land or for the finance to buy it will produce efficient allocation of land between business and household users.[31] This is not simply because of the unequal market strength of individual households on the one hand and wealthy investors, speculators and corporations on the other, with large amounts of asset backing, credit and tax advantages. Even if their bargaining strengths were equal, competition between them would still not be economically rational. Corporations can finance land purchases from profits from the use of the land. Households cannot do that, although their use of housing to generate human capital and labour power may well be as productive as business uses of the land would be. If business competition is allowed to raise residential land prices too, much unnecessary harm may be done both to the efficient allocation of housing and to the distribution of wealth and spendable income.

Therefore, there need be nothing economically inefficient in well-designed public intervention in the markets for residential land and finance. Japan has regularly segregated and protected agricultural land, and has had two major land reforms in modern times. An urban land reform might be designed on the following principles:

- Residential land should be reserved from conversion to other uses. When urban growth or public needs require its conversion, that should be effected by public dealers buying at residential prices and selling at business prices. As cities grow, their new land should be dealt in by such public dealers, or zoned in advance for residential, public and business uses.

- Residential prices and rents should reflect construction costs plus as much land price as is necessary to clear the market between household bidders for the available housing or land.

- The measures which already provide home buyers with housing finance at restrained interest rates should be further developed. Such privileged finance may be rationed if necessary (to buyers with an income limit, houses within a price limit, first-time buyers, and so on).

- Such privileged finance might be extended to investors building low-priced rental housing who are willing to accept contractual rent controls.

- Wherever separate title to rental housing units is available, landlords might be required to sell, at rent-related prices (for example, at 10, 12 or 15 times the annual rent) to tenants wishing to buy and able to pay.

Supporting measures, and transitional measures to avoid ruining existing indebted owners, might include the following:

- Effective decentralist policies to direct new job-creating investment to small cities or to district centres within the large metropolitan areas.
- Measures to encourage land-intensive imports. With Japan's export and exchange surpluses she can afford to import more food in order to release agricultural land for urban and residential use.
- If all else fails, rent controls. They do not necessarily have ill effects if public investors supply enough new rental housing to offset any shortfall in private supply which the rent controls may cause. Rent controls may also be coupled with tenant rights to purchase, as suggested above, with the rents and purchase terms set to encourage landlords to sell.
- A publicly assisted moratorium or repayment assistance for recent investors in rental housing the value of which falls, as a result of government action, below the debt secured on it.

In making such detailed suggestions we are not presuming to teach the government its trade. Actual measures would be designed using the experience and skill of Japan's bureaucrats. The above items are merely examples of types of measure which might find a place in a programme to segregate urban residential land and housing markets, permanently restrain their price levels, restore home purchase as an incentive to work and save in Japan, expand its role as the chief diffuser of inheritable wealth among the mass of the population, and secure the basis for good parenting.

Some transitional elements of such a programme would be expensive. Subsidized or regulated interest rates for eligible housing loans would impose a small permanent charge on the government or the financial system. Our next proposal is that this reform should be perceived as productive investment.

Education   At the beginning of the Meiji period the planners made the critical decision to treat formal education as productive investment, and since then Japanese governments have not skimped on it.[32] It is for the first governments of the Heisei period now to perceive informal parental and family education in the same way, and to rescue it from some present threats. As the share of educational influence passes from government, parents and schools, and even perhaps from the more responsible newspapers and broadcasters, to be exercised by the popular media for their own and their advertisers' profit-seeking purposes, it seems prudent to strengthen, as far as can be done without provoking a reaction, the civic and moral elements in parental and school education, and perhaps to induce the commercial channels to give more time to the serious and educative kinds of children's programmes. All over the democratic world, the family and the school are expected to impart values and habits of good behaviour:

honesty, compliance with the law, care for the environment, respect for other people's interests and feelings, respect for good art and literature, and respect for cultural heritage including national and ethnic heritage. There need be nothing oppressive or undemocratic in encouraging Japanese households and schools to impart to children the best of Japanese culture, character and productive energy. At home and at school, these values should have equal priority with the skills whose uses they guide.

Apart from that general function, the public educational system should direct most of its resources to educating and training productive skills rather than to the paper-shuffling, asset-trading, speculative and predatory skills, which can well be left to user-paid private educational services.

Part-time and adult education should develop more than merely 'baby health' services to educate young parents in the educational and child-development aspects of parenting, and in the importance and long-term effects of active rather than passive recreations for their children.

There should be extensive development of the educational, training and retraining services necessary to equip women who have brought up children to resume full-time employment on equal terms and without disadvantage.

Family life   There should be full and persuasive official recognition of, and material support for, the contribution of family life to the upbringing of children and the characteristics of Japanese people. This is not meant as a little material rhetoric with which to end this book. Through their influence on children and support of spouses, women have been a critical source of Japan's human resources and drive for economic growth. Their contribution has so far had minimal official recognition or material help. It needs both now, because the conditions which sustained it in the past are changing rapidly. The labour-scarce economy is tempting, and house prices are driving women away from home to the workforce. Other changes are subjecting children and young people to conflicting influences, which may be violent, hedonistic or senseless. Many of the changes are sophisticating Japanese people desirably, and liberating Japanese women, most desirably. But action is needed to order and reconcile the conflicting demands on women. Action is needed to balance the commercial temptation of children, through more active, challenging, character-building recreation. Action is needed to arrest the increase in inequality, to sustain the 'will to economize', and to restore the housing incentives to work and save.

Japan is fortunate that its government and people have an unusual capacity to decide upon and work to achieve aims such as these. This is not the time to relinquish that capacity.

Notes

Introduction

1   Patrick and Rosovsky (1976b, p. 3). The extent of the rapid and sustained economic growth over the pre- and postwar years depends on (a) when we place the initial date of Japan's industrialization (the date of her 'take-off' in Rostow's sense) and (b) the economic conditions (measured, for example, by per capita GNP) from which the whole exercise of economic growth began. So far, the estimate of Kuznets has been widely accepted: he suggests that Japan commenced her industrial development sometime in the 1874–79 period from her initial economic level of US$74; that is her 'take-off' began roughly 100 years after that of England, with a per capita income equivalent to only a third of that of England. However, recent studies have cast some doubt on such estimates and locate the initial 'take-off' period much earlier in the last century. These estimates have revised the initial level of income upwards to reduce Japan's overall economic growth records to less spectacular dimensions. See, for example, papers included in A. Hayami (1986): chapters 2 (Yasuba) and 3 (S. B. Hanley) are particularly relevant. See also Kuznets (1971).

2   Can skills thus far devoted to industrial development be applied to 'elevating the moral standards of the men and women' of Japan? This aspiration may be less naive than it sounds. The quotation is from the autobiography of Fukuzawa Yukichi, the great business and educational philosopher and founder of Keio University. It reads in full 'I should like to put my further efforts toward elevating the moral standards of the men and women of my land to make them truly worthy of a civilised nation.' The book has been continuously in print since it appeared in 1899, and is selling more copies now than ever before. Its moral theme appeals to widespread and oft-noted feelings of disappointment and regret at what people see as a deterioration of national behaviour and spirit. The feeling takes

more focused and fashionable form in studies under such titles as 'business culture', 'eco-ethics', 'economic animals', 'culture of shame' and 'corporate capitalism' (see Fukuzawa, 1960, p. 323; Nishibe, 1990; Imamichi, 1990; S. Yamamoto, 1989).

3 Another Western alarm: Taggart Murphy, an American banker, questions Japan's capability and willingness to make such a contribution despite her command of a large share of world wealth because she lacks a global vision of the world economy (see Murphy, 1989, pp. 72–83). But what are the Japanese responses to such a criticism? See, for example, the speculation attempted elsewhere by the present author (Sheridan, 1992, ch. 7).

4 Discussion over 'welfare provisions' and 'quality of life' issues still remain little beyond the preliminary stages for policy proposals and brainstorming exercises. We will return to this important issue later, in our last chapter.

5 For a brief outline of this observation, see, for example, Hollerman (1988).

6 There are several variants of this explanation, and its elements are not always clearly articulated. For example, Y. Murakami treats the Japanese economic system as a 'political economy' in which market processes of development needed to be supplemented by political aid from outside the economic system. This was because, unlike the Western societies which built their industrialization on pre-existing physical and social infrastructure, Japan's industrialization began without such infrastructure, and government had to supply it. There is still some ambiguity in Murakami's account. It is not clear whether he means to say that the initial lack of infrastructure led government to take a permanent leadership role in the economy, or whether the role is seen as temporary until the necessary infrastructure was in place. There is also some ambiguity between competition and government planning as *complementary* principles, with government setting goals and planning the path of development, or as *conflicting* principles so that the art of running a mixed economy is to find the right proportions of the mix. The first view seems to prevail in the original and the second in the English version of the cited article, but it is not clear whether the difference is intentional or merely a matter of translation (Y. Murakami, 1987a and b, esp. p. 56).

7 The Tokugawa economy is the subject of a great deal of recent research, much of it available, as yet, only in Japanese. For new discoveries and interpretations, see chapters by Umemura and Hayami, Iwamoto, Tashiro, Saito and Shinpo, and Hasegawa in Umemura et al. (1988–90; vol. 1, 1988).

8 See also, for example, Tominaga (1990, pp. 398–9) for supporting observations.

9 Lewis (1955, pp. 376–7).

10 Minami (1986, ch. 3).

11 Ibid., in particular pp. 46–50.

Chapter 1   Feudalism and modernization

1 Our understanding derives substantially from the following: A. Hayami (1968 and 1973), A. Hayami and M. Miyamoto (1989). Yasuba (1987),

Miwa (1987), Nishikawa (1985a), Umemura et al. (1988–90, vols 2 and 3) and Wray and Conroy (1983).

2   See, for example, Saito (1988) in Umemura et al. (1988–90, vol. 1).

3   There is some evidence that population growth was not slow in the early Edo period in the seventeenth century, but little growth appears to have taken place after the middle of the century. It is estimated that the total population of Japan stayed at around 30 m for a century prior to the Restoration (Miwa, 1987, p. 11).

4   However, we must hasten to refer to Fukuzawa Yukichi's much quoted observation that Tokugawa samurai and peasants, let alone merchants and tradesmen, were already practising economic calculation in selecting the crops to be planted and in the sale of their goods and services (see, for example, Fukuzawa, 1877). For an understanding of the emerging economic production for the market in this period, see works included in Umemura et al. (1988–1990, vol. 1).

5   A. Hayami (1973, pp. 91–4).

6   For various interpretations of the Meiji Restoration, see Beasley (1972), Nagai and Urrutia (1985) and Umemura et al. (1988–90, vol. 3).

7   The Edo period extended over 264 years, from 1603 when Tokugawa Ieyasu founded the Edo *bakufu* (central government) through the unification of the country to the year of the Meiji Restoration in 1867. For a brief outline of the transition period to a feudal society and its development in the Edo period, see, for example, Sakamoto (1971).

8   *Buiku* means 'to bring up with care'. It is a unique industrial policy developed in the late Tokugawa period. For further discussion, see Nishikawa (1985a, ch. 3).

9   English readers may refer to Morris-Suzuki (1989, pp. 34–8) for a brief review of their works.

10 Maruyama (1974, pp. 345–6).

11 The eventual accommodation for the demand came in 1860 at the cost of the assassination of the shogunate great elder Ii-Naosuke in March of that year (the Sakurada-mon incident).

12 Maruyama (1974, pp. 346–8).

13 Sakamoto (1971, pp. 86–102).

14 See, for example, Goldsmith (1983, ch. 2) and Allen (1981, ch. 1).

15 Goldsmith (1983, p. 21).

16 Brief overall outlines of the policy can be found in English-language studies such as Allen (1981, see chs 1–3 in part 1); but for academic discussions of the policy, readers should consult Japanese texts such as M. Kobayashi (1980), Umemura et al. (1988–90, vols 2 and 3) and Sugiyama and Mizuta (1988).

17 See pp. 126–7 in chapter 6 above.

18 See, for example, S. Sugiyama (1990) and Uchida (1990) in Umemura et al. (1988–90), vols 3 and 4 respectively.

19 Even during the peak years of the operation in 1870–75, the budget of the Ministry of Home Affairs is reported to have comprised no more than 17 per cent of total government expenditure (M. Kobayashi, 1980, ch. 2).

20 Ibid., chapter 1.

21 A civil war between the government and a group of dissatisfied anti-government dissidents (Kobayashi, 1980, pp. 80–81).

22 Yamamoto (1976) and Kobayashi (1980).

23 Oshima et al. (1983, vol. 2).

24 For case studies describing the actual development procedure of government and business relations in the areas of gold, silver and coal mining, steel mills, ship-building and spinning industries, see M. Kobayashi (1980, part 2).

25 See Kobayashi (1980, pp. 101–114).

26 M. Kobayashi (1980), pp. 15–24.

27 Kobayashi (1980, part 2) and K. Nakagawa (1981; 1985, pp. 3–6).

28 Under commercial treaties negotiated in 1858, and later in 1866, Japan's tariffs were placed under international control and set at levels that opened her backward agrarian economy to the full impact of the advanced industrial economies. It may be said that this had considerable impact on the population as a whole – not just the samurais – and lead to support for the national slogan of *fukoku–kyohei*.

29 Kobayashi (1980, pp. 221–5).

30 The discussion concerns the relative importance of three major factors: (1) the government's need to raise funds through the sale of public plant; (2) the public assessment that industry was by then already adequately developed, therefore justifying little further assistance from the government; and (3) the sale of plant to encourage the building of a strong industrial base around monopolistic industrial capital (to be developed as *zaibatsu* groups). See, for example, Kobayashi (1980, pp. 3–24), H. Yamamoto (1976) and Oshima et al. (1983, vol. 2).

31 The areas currently envelope the Kagoshima, Yamaguchi, Kochi and Okayama prefectures in the southern part of Japan.

32 There are other views. Ishizaka, for example, sees different purposes in the establishment of the Ministry of Industrial Development and Naimu-sho (the Ministry of Home Affairs) and connects them to the different beliefs about industrial development of the two political guardians of the ministries, Okuma (for the Ministry of Industrial Development) and Okubo (for the Ministry of Home Affairs). There were related differences between supporters of English democratic and free-trading principles and supporters of protection and strong government, and between those interested in modern and traditional industries (Ishizaka, 1965).

33 Nishikawa informed me that he found volumes of records of communications between the *kobusho*, consular officials in overseas countries, and chambers of commerce in various prefectures all around Japan. What this indicates is that consular officials were working under the ministry's instruction, to collect supply price data for various products in the international market. The ministry seemed to have supplied such information to various interested businesses via the Chamber of Commerce, so as to keep individual entrepreneurs well-informed of the cost of raw materials and exports from various overseas market sources (see S. Nishikawa and Abe, 1990, pp. 36–45).

34 See Fuzukawa (1893) and Miwa (1987, ch. 5).

35 See T. Nakamura (1984, pp. 85–91).

36 For a critical evaluation of the contributory effects of government privatization policy during this period in forming the emerging *zaibatsu*
monopoly, see, for example, Kobayashi (1980), Lockwood (1965, ch. 10)
and Miyamoto and Nakagawa (1971–7).

37 Kobayashi (1980, p. 148).

38 Banno presents a thought-provoking new interpretation of the importance
of the Meiji 14th Year Incident, locating the year 1881 at the halfway point
of the 27-year period of the formation and development of the Meiji
government, counting from the Restoration in 1868 to the outbreak of the
Sino-Japanese War in 1894. See Banno (1989) in Umemura et al. (1988–90,
vol. 3).

39 Mizuta (1988, p. 14).

40 Ibid.

41 In 1873 when the Ministry of Home Affairs was created it was given control over the entire local government system. To see how the government
bureaucracy was gradually centralized in the 1880s, readers are advised to
refer to, for example, McLaren (1976).

42 Mizuta (1988, pp. 21–3).

43 See chapters by Tamaki, Omori and Sugiyama in Sugiyama and Mizuta
(1988).

44 The German imperial government, created by German unification in 1866
and 1871, was an almost exact contemporary of the Meiji regime. It had
an able, well-educated, conservatively inclined public service with a long
and successful Prussian history. The military and civil leaders agreed that
industrial capacity had become the main source of military capacity, and
that scientific and technical capacity had become a main source of industrial advantage. Therefore the German government was providing general
and technical public education; financing technical research institutions;
encouraging investment in steelmaking with very long term armament and
naval building programmes; and providing general tariff protection to
German industry. In 1885 Germany began to acquire an overseas empire
and, faced with a working-class socialist party and a strong growth of
trades unions at home, some leaders began to look at patriotism and
imperial pride as attractions that might draw the new middle classes to the
conservative regime, strengthening both in the class conflicts that were to
be expeced in industrial society.

Chapter 2   Developing Japanese capitalism

1 Rostow (1960, pp. 39–40).

2 Smith (1973).

3 In addition, Kuznets further explores his comparison of Japan with France
in 1831–40, America in 1834–43, possibly Germany in 1850–59, Australia
in 1860–70 and Canada in 1870–74. See Kuznets (1971, tables 1 and 2) and
Ohokawa and Rosovsky (1973, p. 11).

4 Ohokawa and Takamatsu (1974, p. 202) and Bank of Japan, *Hundred-
Year Statistics of the Japanese Economy*, 1966, pp. 28–9.

5 Kuznets (1971, p. 24).

6   Kuznets (1971, table 3).
7   Hanley (1986).
8   Maruyama reports an interesting argument put forward by a Japanologist at Oxford. It asserts that the specific political structure in the feudal days – the central shogunate authority and numerous *hans* – provided the Japanese with sufficient skill and experience for them to survive in the complex world of international power politics in post-Restoration years. See Maruyama (1986, vol. 3, p. 240).
9   For detailed studies of the policy and the period, see Allen (1981, ch. 3), Miwa (1987, ch. 4), Teranishi (1982, pp. 127–41) and Goldsmith (1983, pp. 27–54).
10 See A. Kobayashi et al. (1981, pp. 104–5).
11 See Kobayashi et al. (1981, pp. 112–13) and Allen (1981, ch. 3).
12 See Allen (1981, pp. 50–51).
13 The proportion of tenant farming increased from 35.9 per cent in 1883–4 to 37.5 per cent in 1888 and 40.2 per cent in 1892 (Miwa, 1987, p. 62).
14 The total assets of financial institutions (including government paper money) is reported to have been equal to only 6 per cent of national wealth in the mid-1880s (Goldsmith, 1983, p. 34).
15 This is demonstrated by the long-established tradition of appointing former high officials in the Ministry of Finance as the govenor and vice-governor of the Bank, to secure close administrative links between the ministry and the Bank.
16 It is estimated that government deposits formed one-third of its total funds (Goldsmith, 1983, p. 47).
17 For a detailed study of the financial system of the Meiji period and its selection of the industrial development strategy, see Teranishi (1982, ch. 3).
18 Annual price increases in this period were kept well below 7 per cent. Ando (1978, p. 4).
19 See NIRA (1988b, ch. 1).
20 See Yamada and Hayami (1970).
21 By the late 1880s most economies with which Japan was trading had moved to adopt the gold standard. Two considerations prompted Japan to follow suit. First, the rates of exchange between gold and silver (on which Japan was basing its trade account) were moving constantly in a most unstable manner. Second, India, one of the important trading rivals for Japan at the time, finally put its long-contemplated currency reform plan into operation in 1893, so as to strengthen her trading position in the export markets of Asia. Japan made the decision to adopt the gold standard at that time. It only remained to find the earliest favourable opportunity. The export boom of 1870–83 had helped, although it was the depreciation of silver in terms of gold and the receipt of large indemnity after the Sino-Japanese War of 1894–5, that made the adoption easy. The switch had mixed effects, but the decision was made more on the basis of 'national desire' than of economic calculation. The matter deserves further investigation in terms, among others, of the study of the mind-set of the economic policy-makers of the time. The background for such an investigation may be found in T. Nakamura (1984, ch. 2).

22 During 1885–1900 the rate of increase in wholesale prices was kept within 3–4 per cent while that of consumer prices was kept between 5 and 6 per cent. The average cost of living increased at the satisfactory rate of 2–3 per cent (Ando, 1987, p. 4; see also NIRA, 1988b, ch. 1).

23 See Ando (1978, pp. 64–5).

24 See Takizawa, quoted in Kajinishi et al. (1962, vol. 2, ch. 1, p. 17). See also Umemura et al. (1988–90, vol. 4, pp. 370–2).

25 It can be estimated that the total expenditure for the war had amounted to about ¥200 million, or about 7 per cent of the GNP of the time. The indemnity payment was ¥366 million, with the acquisition of Formosa (Taiwan) and the Pescadores (Ando, 1987, pp. 66–9).

26 Shirohara (1972) pp. 144–7.

27 See Lewis (1955, p. 23).

28 This phrase is coined to express the policy of industrial promotion.

29 For a more thorough discussion of this subject, see, for example, Dore (1965), H. Uchida (1990) and Miyamoto (1990).

30 In the first instance compulsory schooling for four years was established to provide already partly educated children with the capacity to read, write and follow basic arithmetic systems. The coverage was further extended to six years in 1907.

31 For further information on the establishment of new public institutions and the government structure in the Meiji era, see Beasley (1972), Wilson (1957) and Banno (1989).

32 See Lewis (1955, pp. 23–56).

33 See Lewis (1955), loc. cit.

34 See Kirschen et al. (1964, pp. 3–27).

35 Kirschen et al., op. cit., pp. 3–5.

36 See Lewis (1955, ch. II).

37 By orthodox economists, we refer to those economists whose research tools are limited only to neoclassical, Keynesian and Marxist orientations.

38 See, for example, Ohokawa and Rosovsky (1973, pp. 217–50) and Patrick and Rosovsky (1976a, pp. 6 and 920).

39 See Bennett and Levine (1976).

40 Some understand that it resulted in the political ability of the country to wage wars (Ohokawa and Rosovsky, 1973, p. 217).

41 See Sumiya (1969, vols 1 & 2).

42 See Johnson (1988, p. 3) for further discussion on this point.

43 See Ritschl (1958).

44 See Ohokawa and Rosovsky (1973, p. 231).

45 See Sheridan (1977) for further information.

46 See Patrick and Rosovsky (1976b, p. 43).

47 See Lewis (1955, p. 23).

Chapter 3   Capital accumulation and economic growth

1 The period is often referred to as the 'Taisho democracy'. See also footnote 41 in chapter 4.

2 Ohokawa and Takamatsu (1974) p. 200.

3   Ohokawa and Takamatsu (1974, p. 199).
4   For insight into the planners' intentions between the wars, see T. Itoh (1989) and Nakamura (1983, pp. 121–32).
5   Miwa (1987, pp. 121–3), Bank of Japan (1986) and Ohokawra and Takamatsu (1974).
6   See Sawamoto (1982, p. 29).
7   See Goldsmith (1983, p. 29).
8   Ohokawa et al. (1965–88) LTES, Vols 3, 4 and 7.
9   It averaged at about 10 per cent in 1885–1900, but rose to 16.2 per cent in 1901–20 and to exceed 20 per cent in the 1921–38 period. In addition to the LTES study, see also Minami (1986, ch. 6), for the outline of the growth trend and composition of capital formation in the long historical perspective of industrialization in Japan.
10   See Ohokawa and Rosovsky (1973, p. 30).
11   See, for example, H. Yamamoto (1976), Minami (1981, 1986) and Rosovsky (1961).
12   The annual growth rate of net capital formulation was 5.4 per cent in the prewar period of 1889–1938 and 10.8 per cent in the postwar period of 1956–80. These are much higher than economic growth for those two periods, estimated at 3.2 per cent and 7.7 per cent respectively (Minami, 1986, pp. 43 and 161).
13   See Ohokawa and Rosovsky (1973, pp. 30–4).
14   See Minami (1986), figures 6.1 and 6.2 on pp. 164 and 166.
15   See Minami (1986), figures 6.1 and 6.3 on pp. 164–78.
16   Minami estimates that more than 30 per cent of the components of effective demand were generated by gross domestic fixed capital formation in Japan before the Second World War (Minami, 1986, table 6.7, p. 177).
17   See Shinohara (1986, table VII.2) and our appendix table A.1.
18   See Ohokawa and Rosovsky (1973, p. 147).
19   See Komiya (1975a, p. 8).
20   Public investment played a comparable role in Australia from 1860 to 1890, when, like Japan, Australia had to build a modern infrastructure from next to nothing.
21   See Rosovsky (1959, pp. 350–73).
22   Excluding members of the armed forces, central and local government employees represented only 0.6 per cent of the total workforce in 1880, 2.6 per cent in 1910 and 4.8 per cent in 1930.
23   It was estimated at no lower than 12–14 per cent throughout the period before the Second World War (Ando, 1978, p. 17).
24   See Minami (1985, pp. 189–95) for further discussion on this point.
25   Ibid., pp. 193–5.
26   Ohokawa and Takamatsu (1974) and Shinohara (1972).
27   Emi (1971).
28   See Azuma (1984, pp. 119–21).
29   See Sawamoto (1982, pp. 41–66).
30   See T. Iida and Yamada (1976).
31   'Social capital' is the purest translation of the Japanese term *shakai shihon*, but it merely means 'for public use' without the common Western

meaning of service to the people's social life or welfare. We have usually therefore rendered it as 'infrastructure capital' to avoid confusion with the third category of 'capital for livelihood'.

32 T. Iida and Yamada (1976, p. 120).

33 'Social capital' in the study can be approximated by 'infrastructure and other public capital' NIRA (1987).

34 See Sawamoto (1982).

35 Following the so-called Unequal Treaties made with the Western powers during the 1850s and 1860s, Japan had been without tariff autonomy or jurisdiction over foreigners throughout the Meiji period. Government leaders saw the vital necessity of improving national status in order to free Japan from this degrading situation. Efforts to achieve this took the form of the 'Westernization' of society, by such measures as lighting the main streets of Tokyo with gas lights, and building the Rokumeikan – a government hall – for public receptions, social parties and functions, adopting modern Western style and luxuries. Nightly balls were organized, and representatives of government departments and business and other circles attended wearing Western-style dinner-jackets and evening dresses.

36 See Nakamura (1971, p. 71).

37 It is reported that most public works which were promoted in the early stages of industrial development in Japan were constructed through traditional labour-intensive methods. This helped the government to save on expenditure, but also helped the economy to manage industrialization while updating materials and technology which, in turn, saved foreign currency.

38 The survey used the term 'hidden or underground' money to refer to such idle funds (NIRA, 1987b, ch. 1).

39 Minami reports that in 1895 the private railway network expanded by 2 731 km, compared with an expansion of only 955 km in the National Railway network (Minami, 1985, p. 47).

40 See Nakamura (1984, chapter 2 in part 2).

41 Emi (1971).

42 This is reflected by the increase in the capital : output ratio (see Minami, 1986, chart 6.3 on p. 178, and pp. 142–4).

43 Gross capital stock in housing per capita is estimated at ¥196 in 1855: it subsequently increased to ¥243, but declined to ¥225 in 1930 and ¥226 in 1940 (Ohkawa and Shinohara, 1979, pp. 366–9).

44 See Sawamoto (1982, p. 74).

45 In the cotton industry, for example, the prewar growth continued in the following years. The number of spindles is reported to have risen from 2 415 000 in 1914 to 3 814 000 in 1920 and, after a setback through the destruction of some 900 000 spindles in the Great Earthquake of 1923, to 6 6500 000 spindles in 1929 (Allen, 1981, p. 123).

46 Ohokawa and Takamatsu (1974, p. 135).

47 It was in 1936 that Japan surpassed Britain and became the largest exporter of cotton piece goods. A large proportion of this increase in trade came principally from Asia, including Taiwan, Korea and Manchukuo, which were placed under Japan's strict political control. There were also increases

in exports in Europe, South America and Africa. The flood of inexpensive Japanese goods into the world market, due partly to this devaluation of the yen, provoked criticism against Japan for pursuing 'unfair competition'.

48   T. Nakamura observes that public spending which went into public works eventually went into the pockets of the farming population and resulted in income redistribution effects (T. Nakamura, 1971, p. 252).

49   It should not be forgotten that this was accompanied by more intensive and longer working hours for those farmers who stayed at home: particularly for women, those less fit men who could not go to cities for factory work, children and older family members.

50   The economic policy which Takahashi and his government promoted was by no means one of military expansion. From 1934 he attempted to control military spending in order to avoid inflationary pressure in the economy. For further discussion on the Takahashi financial policy, see Miwa (1979), and Nakamura (1971, pp. 233–44).

51   In the early period of industrialization the activities of financial institutions were dominated by the short-term banking system, but this predominance declined rapidly. By 1913 the new issue ratio of financial institutions outside the short-term banking system rose to 3 per cent of national production, from the preceding 1 per cent (the 1886–1900 average) (Goldsmith, 1983, p. 55).

52   See Goldsmith (1983, p. 56).

53   The rise and fall of the combine is well portrayed in *Nezumi* (Shiroyama, 1977).

54   As a supporting device the government promoted rapid integration of commercial banks, in the hope that the larger scale would improve their resistance to bankruptcy. The number of banks declined from 2001 in 1920 to 625 in 1932 (Teranishi, 1982, pp. 311–36).

55   Ministry of Finance, *Showa Zaisei-shi*, vol. 6, and Nakamura and Odaka (1990, pp. 26–30).

56   It fell from ¥89 in 1919 to ¥81 in 1920 and, further, to ¥80 in 1922 (Kajinishi et al., 1962, part III, ch. 1, p. 176).

57   See Kajinishi (1962, part IV, ch. 7).

58   Between 1919 and 1925 more than a third of the total government bonds were first subscribed by the Bank of Japan and then sold to the population in general through post offices (Kajinishi, 1960, part IV, ch. 1, p. 18).

59   See, for example, EPA (1988).

60   See EPA, *Annual Report on National Accounts* (1966) and Sawamoto (1982, tables 27 and 28).

61   See Takeuchi (1967, p. 19).

62   The following discussion has benefited from the argument presented by Lockwood (1968, pp. 240–2).

63   This high proportion in national wealth due to the value of land is to be expected in pre-industrial economies. However, in Japan the proportion continued to remain high throughout the period of industrial development. Comparative data of the share of land as a proportion of the total value of national wealth are as follows:

Japan	1905	37 per cent
	1910	33 per cent
	1913	43 per cent
	1917	30 per cent
	1919	38 per cent
	1924	22 per cent
	1930	37 per cent
	1935	30 per cent
USA	1870	50 per cent
	1912	37 per cent
	1928	31 per cent
	1938	30 per cent
England	1688	55–60 per cent
	1800	43 per cent
	1932–4	10 per cent
Germany	1911	23 per cent
France	1890	34 per cent
Italy	1924	36 per cent
Australia	1903	38 per cent

See Goldsmith (1950; 1983, p. 10).

64 See T. Nakamura (1985, ch. 3).
65 This is our assessment from the reading of statistical information and various general writings of the life of the people in the prewar Japan: see, for example, NIRA (1988a), particularly chapter 7.
66 Emi (1971, p. 21)
67 This figure does not include local government employees, for whom there is no recorded information available (Emi, 1963, p. 5).
68 Allen (1981, p. 173), for one, takes such a view. A brief comment on the Taisho period follows. How liberal or democratic did Japan become by the Taisho period? Did the militarism of the 1930s arise from particular features of the Taisho era and, if so, how did party government give way to military ascendancy so readily? In the modern history of Japan this period seems to be one of the least understood, by both Japanese and outside researchers. Many foreign scholars have studied the period and discovered that the nature of the Taisho 'democracy', essentially from the beginning, was less democratic than it appeared (Duus, 1968 and Kenneth, 1977). If the Taisho period was less democratic and liberal than used to be supposed, it may be easier to explain the 1930s as a logical rather than an aberrant phase in Japan's long-term history (Wray, 1983, pp. 172–4). The period is also one of the more difficult ones for Japanese economists

and economic historians. Throughout the 1920s, intellectual and social conflicts complicated each other: communists and social democrats wanted to mobilize industrial workers and tenant farmers; Marxist intellectuals wanted to understand the nature and future direction of Japanese capitalism; and governments wanted more control of the daily life and religion of ordinary people in a period of civil unrest. There are many autobiographies and personal accounts of political activity in the period (regrettably few in English) from which the real depth of conflict and unrest may be judged (Banno and Waswo, 1990, p. 129; Hibbert, 1960).

Chapter 4 Social policy in economic policy

1 The poverty and deteriorating living standards of many Meiji workers are documented carefully in Matsubara (1893) and Yokoyama (1898).
2 For the *keisei–saimin* philosophy, see Maruyama (1963, chs III–V), Najita (1987, ch. I) and Sumiya and Taira (1979, pp. 3–5).
3 See T. Nakamura (1984, pp. 11–13).
4 See Ohokawa and Takamatsu (1974, p. 77).
5 See T. Nakamura, loc. cit.
6 See Minami (1986, p. 38).
7 See Ohokawa and Rosovsky (1973, ch. 8).
8 In an effort to learn how the living conditions of the general population of Japan have improved commensurate with the industrial development in the past 100 years, a research committee was established by the government in 1970. The committee was developed into Kokumin Seikatsu Shingikai (Council for Living Conditions of the Population) in 1974. It has engaged in developing a set of social indices that are adequate for estimating the living conditions of the population. In 1986 it published 368 indices to follow the changing trends in the living conditions of the population from a long-term historical perspective (NIRA, 1984, 1988a).
9 See Minami (1986, pp. 394–7).
10 See Minami (1986, ch. 11).
11 See Goldsmith (1983, pp. 37–8).
12 See Minami (1986, ch. 11).
13 See NIRA (1988a, ch. 1).
14 Our evaluation of the prewar years suffers most severely from the limitations of relevant information and allows us to speculate only in the most general terms. In more recent postwar years, more information has become available on non-quantifiable and not strictly economic aspects of welfare.
15 See Ohokawa and Rosovsky (1973, ch. 9).
16 Ibid., pp. 231–6.
17 See Bennett and Levine (1976, p. 442).
18 See Reischauer (1954, p. 62).
19 See Gleason (1965, 1989).
20 See Y. Nakagawa (1979) and Vogel (1979).
21 See Dore (1987).
22 It originated in a 1979 European Commission report, and has since been

used to describe the poor housing conditions of businessmen living in metropolitan areas of Japan.

23 For the understanding of the approach, see, for example, Najita (1987, ch. 2) and Sugihara et al. (1990, chs 1–3 in part I).

24 See Sugihara et al (1990, chs 1 and 2 in part II), Tominaga (1990, ch. 5) and Naramoto (1982, pp. 138–45). Questions about the Japanese approach to welfare, hitherto the preserve of economists and economic historians, have begun to interest historians of political, social and economic thought. Sugihara and others propose a new concept of '*minpu*', by which they mean the individual – as opposed to the '*kokufu*' or national – accumulation of wealth. People work, earn and accumulate physical and financial means of emancipating themselves from material hardship and its associated public and domestic stresses; it is in their happier and culturally richer states of mind and feeling that a part at least of their welfare exists, without appearing in the national accounts. See Sugihara et al. (1990), especially chapter 4.

25 See Dore (1987, p. 227).

26 It is difficult to name explicit, quotable sources for this impression; it is present as the unspoken or diffusely expressed assumption of many public policy papers. Among the most important sources or confirmations of her observations, the author acknowledges Honjo (1966), Nishikawa (1979), Umemura et al. (1988–90, vols 2 and 3 and Sugihara et al. (1990).

27 See, for example, G. Ono (1922) and Goldsmith (1983, pp. 35–6).

28 What consolation for their working and living conditions did the common people gain from the wars? Economic development was stimulated by government military spending and allied demands. Perhaps people took pleasure in the nation's greater international power and prestige, and in the honour of being invited to the 1919 peace conference as one of the Great Powers. Did these and other factors legitimize Japan's aggression in the minds of the mass of Japanese people? See Ike (1968, pp. 204–5), McLaren (1973, pp. 221–5) and Banno and Waswo (1990, pp. 128–9). See also Marshall (1983), Crump (1983, ch. 7), Hirschmeier and Yui (1975, pp. 154–5) and Okayama (1979).

29 Miwa (1987, pp. 86–100).

30 See Kajinishi et al. (1962, part II, ch. 1, pp. 120–33).

31 Kajinishi et al., loc. cit.

32 Quoted in Macpherson (1987, p. 63).

33 See Kajinishi et al. (1962, part II, ch. 1, p. 140).

34 For further information, see, for example, Sumiya (1978, pp. 82–4) and Allen (1980, pp. 75–7).

35 The minimum working age could be lowered to 10 years with the permission of a local government official, and night labour was allowed in enterprises with two or more work shifts, including the great majority of textile factories (Miwa, 1987, pp. 165–6).

36 See Sumiya (1978, pp. 178–87 and 188–98) and Orchard (1976).

37 The debate between Fukuzawa and Soeda-Juichi, a leading government figure, in formulating the Act is illustrated by Nishikawa to help us understand the economic thinking of the time (Nishikawa, 1988, pp. 4–8).

38 See Smith (1988, ch. 10).

39 See Bureau of Statistics, *Statistical Yearbook*, 1930, 1950 and 1965.
40 See The Bank of Japan, *Hundred Years* (1966), tables 7 and 8.
41 The Taisho period spans 14 years, from 1912 to 1926. It falls between 44 Meiji (1873–1911) and 67 Showa (1926–88) years.
42 See Ando (1978, p. 100) and Allen (1981, pp. 116–17).
43 See NIRA (1988b, p. 8).
44 See Kajinishi et al. (1962, part II, ch. 3, pp. 515–9).
45 See Bank of Japan, *Meiji Iko* (1966), issues for 1914–26.
46 Bank of Japan, loc. cit.
47 Ohkouchi wrote his personal experience and analysis of, as academic researcher, the way in which the liberal period was terminated in 1923 (Ohkouchi, 1979, p. 7).
48 For an explanation of the Meiji Constitution of the 1882–1931 period, see Ishii (1985, pp. 112–21).
49 See Bank of Japan, *Hundred-year Statistics* (1966); and Kajinishi et al. (1962, part II, vol. 1, pp. 208–9) and S. Itoh (1990).
50 For the development of Japan's industrial relations, see, for example, Tominaga (1990, ch. 10) and Hazama (1971) and Gordon (1985, chs 1 and 2).
51 See Smith (1988, p. 270).
52 See Miwa (1987, p. 127).
53 K. Iida (1987, p. 7).
54 The association was founded following a German model of an academic study group at that time (K. Iida, loc cit.).
55 Iida (1987, p. 6).
56 See T. Nakamura and Odaka (1990, pp. 34–7).
57 The period may be called as 'the era of unbalanced growth', when the difference of productivity between the farm sector and the newly expanding industrial field began to emerge. Following the stagnation of the improvement of agricultural technology throughout the 1920s, which resulted in a considerable slow down of productivity, the farming sector as a whole, which had been developing steadily since the Restoration years, began to face various hardships – a chronic farm crisis emerged. Worldwide agricultural depression, which coincided with the emergence of such problems, aggravated the difficulties. Odaka has compiled more recent statistical information to interpret the period in a new light (see T. Nakamura, 1971, ch. 8; Odaka, 1989).
58 See Teranishi (1989, pp. 37–72).
59 The total cultivation of land is reported to have increased slowly. In the case of rice, the major product, the total area increased only by 16.5 per cent between 1888 and 1920. But the productivity (yield per area of land) increased rapidly, so that total national rice production rose by 24 per cent between 1900 and 1924. Despite this, however, the living standard in villages continued to deteriorate with the loss of real income (see Allen, 1981, pp. 256–7; Kajinishi et al., 1962, part II, vol. 3, pp. 642–9).
60 For the explanation of the phenomenon, see, for example, Ohkawa and Rosovsky (1972, p. 228). See also Umemura et al. (1988–90, vol. 6), in which the contributors present their study results from various angles and standpoints to explain how the phenomenon has been developed, as well as

the influence of government industrial policy of the period in forming such a skewed structure in the economy as a whole.

61 The specific experiences of the economic development in the years from 1900 to 1937 have attracted a great deal of research and argument inside and outside Japan, by economists and economic historians and also by political scientists, a number of whom within Japan were also political activists at the time. Many fertile ideas have been generated; but there have been differences between Japanese and foreign scholars' perceptions of the problems of the period. The surging problems that arose from the unbalanced growth of the economy have been much studied by Japanese scholars. That concern coincided with the emergence of many Marxist intellectuals in search of a correct path of development for Japan (Sumiya and Taira, 1979, pp. 5–9). In the 1920s an active debate developed about the nature and degree of capitalist development in Japan, referred to as the Debate on Japanese Capitalism (*Nihon Shihonshugi Ronso*). It divided most economists between two schools of thought, the *Koza-ha* (lecturer) faction and the *Rono-ha* (labour-farmer) faction. The former stressed the continuing semi-feudal aspects of Japan, while the latter stressed the characteristics which Japan shared with the advanced industrial economies of the West. England was taken as the model of capitalist development, and the debate concerned the extent of, and the reasons for, Japan's backwardness. From its origins in economic theory the debate was publicized with the foundation of the *Rono-ha* in 1927, and politicized in the 1930s until it was ended with the mass arrests of Marxist-trained university professors in 1938.

The debate is often regarded as having concerned Marxists only. That was not so. The debate involved all students of the economics of the time, addressing issues such as agricultural development, landlord–tenant relations, wages and employment, and the changing industrial structure. The debate should not be forgotten as an unimportant incident in the prewar history of economic thought. To a considerable extent, the postwar economic studies, which were characterized by sophisticated techniques and more abundant information, were made possible by the accumulated research and argument of this debate. T. Nakamura (1984) writes, in Japanese, an Appendix to his book to show in detail how important this debate was to the progress of research in economic history in Japan. The Appendix is omitted from the English edition (1981), presumably because of the observed lack of interest in this particular subject among English-speaking scholars.

Both Marxists and others debated how far Japan's economic growth was export-led. Exports expanded throughout the period, and some 'uniquely Japanese' institutions were born, including the General Trading Company, which typically imported raw material, sublet it for processing by many small manufacturers, and exported the finished products (Yamamura, 1976; Allen, 1981, pp. 96–9, 112–115). The competitive prices of Japanese exports generated fast export growth, and foreign accusations of 'social dumping'. Japanese scholars were equally concerned with the lag between productivity and wages. Non-marxians thought that it denied the working population a fair share of the fruits of economic growth. Marxians saw a vicious circle of low wages and high rates of exploitation and capital accumulation resulting in a limited domestic market, pressure to export, and a further increase of cheap industrial labour (Macpherson, 1987, pp. 47–52). Foreign scholars were more interested in 'the nature of Japan's imperialism', as revealed in particular devices and incidents of expansion. Recent Japanese studies of the economic history of the period search it for the origins and promotion of the movement towards 'planned capitalism'. Material has been accumulated about economic institutions, the forms and mechanisms of public administration and the training of bureaucrats, and the collection of basic economic, demographic and geological information about the home and colonial territories: (T. Itoh, 1989; T. Nakamura, 1990). In the process the government administration accumulated autonomous power and capabilities that were very different from those to be found in Western democracies. Japanese scholars thus see 'the nature of Japan's imperialism' in the context of the development of the economic capacities of government, rather than merely as the history of external expansion which has chiefly interested Western scholars.

62　See Ando (1978, p. 119) and Odaka (1989).

63　See Bank of Japan, *Hundred-year Statistics* (1966, p. 26); and Goldsmith (1988, p. 74).

64　For a discussion of 'social deprivation' problems in the so-called 'post-industrial society' in Japan, see, for example, Bennett and Levine (1976, pp. 439–92).

65　In order to avert immediate financial collapse at the time of the earthquake, the government ordered all banks to close for a month. When they re-opened, the Bank of Japan provided them with a guarantee against losses from transactions.

66　See Johnson (1982, pp. 97–100).

67　Johnson, loc. cit.

68　The percentage of workers employed in establishments with over 500 workers declined sharply between 1927 and 1931, from 11.8 per cent to 5.1 per cent in food-processing, 41.3 per cent to 33.3 per cent in textiles, and 44.7 per cent to 28.1 per cent in heavy and chemical industries (Shoko-sho, 1935).

69　See Johnson (1982, p. 97).

70　See MITI (1977), chapters on May 1934 and April 1935 periods.

71　See Smith (1988, ch. 10).

Chapter 5　Economic conduct of the Pacific War

1　How should we observe and explain the economic management of the Pacific War? How should we interpret the national effort in these periods of turmoil and aggression? Many people inside and outside Japan have written extensively, and spoken in diverse contexts and occasions, about that gigantic event in our recent history. New information is continuously discovered, hidden facts unearthed and fresh ways devised to approach and interpret the period. Among others, two questions have loomed large in writing this chapter. How should we connect the short life and sudden ending of the liberal efforts of the Taisho years with the following transition to the militarist and aggressive expansion, first into Manchuria then to open war with China? And how should we locate the experience of preparing and managing the war economy in the general history and shaping of Japanese capitalism? In wrestling with these large questions I read widely, beyond the strictly economic literature. In all that reading I acknowledge special debts, both in writing the present chapter and in making sense of my personal memories of the period, to Muruakami (1983), Livingston (1973, vol. 2), Kindainihon Kenkyu-kai (1987) and chapters by T. Nakamura, A. Hara, Miyazaki and Itoh and Mikuriya Takashi in Umemura et al. (1988–90, vol. 7).

I add some memories, on the probably spurious ground that they may alert readers to the author's likely biases. I have fragmentary infant memories of living with severe shortages of food, clothing and housing in Tokyo in the immediate postwar years. Among the returned soldiers were two temporary teachers at our primary school. One, according to gossip, was trying to build a base in our school to establish a teachers' union, under guidance from the new and expanding Japan Communist Party; while the other had escaped by half a day from having to do his national duty as a *kamikaze* pilot. Both – and others – were officially required to teach us novel things about democracy, the free market system and other wonderful things to be found in the USA. An aunt returned from Manchuria without her army husband. An uncle returned to tell us about managing the Manchurian railway. Another uncle had converted his tuna fishing boats to transporting arms and ammunition about the Pacific. A fourth uncle was said to have died leading a '*banzai*' attack.

2   Ohkawa and Rosovsky (1973) and Ando (1978), for example, fall into this category.

3   Allen (1981) includes chapters on 'prewar' and 'postwar' together in one volume, without relating one to the other. On the other hand, many economists direct their attention towards the postwar years which began in 1945, or more frequently in the 1950s, leaving the prewar analysis to economic historians.

4   See Minami (1986, p. 419).

5   The following observations owe much to Ando (1987), T. Nakamura (1983b; 1986, lectures 2 and 3), Cohen (1949) and Kindainihon Kenkyukai (1987).

6   Manchuria was taken over by the Japanese Army in September 1931, from which date to the end of the Pacific War it remained as a dependency of Japan, as the puppet state of Manchukuo. For further information, see, for example, Jansen (1975) and Schumpeter (1940, pp. 789–854).

7   See Teramura (1987, pp. 89–99).

8   The author gained considerable assistance in understanding the economic management in Manchuria from non-economic writings, including those of Natsume Soseki and Kawamura.

9   See A. Hara (1989, pp. 242–8).

10 Many of those established in Korea were handed to the Koreans after 1945 to form the basis of her industrial development (see, for example, Jones and Sakong, 1980, ch. 2).

11   See Nakamura (1986, lecture 3) and Shiozaki (1979).
12   The origin of the doctrine can go back to the *teikoku kokubo* (Imperial national defence) policy of 1907, in which the hypothetical enemy was determined to be first Russia, and then the USA, Germany and France. The policy was re-defined in 1918, and then in 1923, when it was still promoted by private citizens. In 1936 it was finally adopted as national policy.
13   See Shiozaki (1979), Kobayashi (1975), Hara (1987) and Nakumura (1989, pp. 1–37).
14   See Cohen (1949, p. 54).
15   Johnson reports Cohen's remarks that 'the war-time economic effort … was to be placed upon a further shift in resources from non-war to war uses rather than upon a lifting of the whole level of output' (Johnson, 1982, p. 158).
16   This section owes much to T. Itoh and Watanabe (1987).
17   The basic formula of the *eidanren* public corporation has survived the war in the present Teito Rapid Transit Authority, the public segment of the Tokyo subway.
18   See Shiozaki (1979), M. Miyazaki and O. Itoh (1989), Nakamura (1989, pp. 1–32), Ando (1987) and Hara (1989, pp. 85–94).
19   University of Tokyo, Shakai Kenkyu-jo (1979).
20   For the development of 'anti-market' and 'anti-capitalist' thinking in this period, see Nakamura (1989, pp. 8–10), Hoston (1986), Maruyama (1979) – especially the author's introduction to the first four chapters on Japan's ultra-nationalism and fascism – and Tominaga (1990, pp. 192–4 and 391–4).
21   Johnson (1982, chs 3–5) and Nakamura (1984, pp. 6–7 and part III, pp. 121–5) demonstrate the various institutional and administrative links between wartime and postwar periods by the observation of frequent and strong similarities in the way in which public and private industry co-operated and communicated during those two periods.
22   See Ando (1973a, ch. 6).
23   See Ando (1973a, p. 179).
24   See Teramura (1987, pp. 82–3).
25   They were often referred to under the general term *shinkanryo* ('new or reform bureaucrats'). This term was coined by journalists, and no clear definition has been found to describe exactly who they were and what functions they performed as against other civilian bureaucrats in the management of the war economy in the period concerned. Some tried to describe this group of new bureaucrats loosely using various adjectives such as 'anti-party, nationalistic, pro-military, pro-fascist and in favour of strengthening Government control'.
26   See Ando (1973a), and Komiya and Yamamoto (1981).
27   For the structure of the association, see, for example, Fletcher (1975 and 1982). What has the association attempted and actually achieved and promoted? See Mikuriya (1989, pp. 249–54), and Shibagaki (1979).
28   See Hayashi (1979, pp. 41–2).
29   The research was supervised by Ryu Shintaro, an editor of the *Asahi Shinbun* (newspaper).
30   See pp. 50–1 in chapter 2 above.

31 The observation is made by economists with varying ideological orientations: see, for example, Nakamura (1989, p. 10) and Matsushima (1973).

Chapter 6 Reconstruction

1 T. Nakamura (1980, p. 58).
2 K. Hara, 'Sekai Keizai no Henkaku to Hatten' quoted in Uchino (1983, pp. 251–2).
3 See Kodansha (1983, vol. 6, p. 224).
4 For further information concerning the war-caused damage to the nation's production capacity, national wealth and the consequent reduction in the living standard of the population, see Uchino (1983, pp. 7–13) and Ando (1978, pp. 138–9).
5 The years from 1919 to 1952 were the hardest time for the Japanese people, both collectively and individually. Their capacity and conscience were tested most severely, in their wisdom as well as in atrocious folly. Economic history reveals only a fraction of what took place in that tumultuous time: in no other period of Japanese history is it so important for readers and researchers to read widely about the people's experience as a whole before trying to understand particular details or aspects. Many Japanese sources for the period are now translated into English. They take various forms: social and political history, biography and autobiography, diaries, memoirs and other personal notes and records, official documentation, novels. Let Japanese people speak for themselves of the experience of that epoch: see Noma (1956), Ohoka (1957), Terasaki (1957), *Mainichi Daily News* (1975), Chuman (1976), H. Murakami (1982) and Hane (1987).
6 As early as 1942, the USA began to plan for their occupation of Japan. There were two distinct approaches, each strongly held by its protagonists. One, strongly anti-Japanese, focused on feudalistic and totalitarian elements in Japan, and was determined at all costs to destroy them, to uproot any inclination or capacity to wage another war. The other, more moderate, approach involved the appreciation that there had been many liberal politicians and supporters who had tried hard to prevent the war, and should be empowered to democratize Japan. The eventual plan issued on 29 August 1945 is said to have been the result of compromise between the two programmes (see Livingston et al., 1976, vol. 2, pp. 6–13; Storry, 1983, ch. 10; Johnson, 1988, ch. 4). With regard to economic reforms (of land, business and labour), some scholars in Japan see the Second World War as more than the traditional armed struggle between powers, after which the victors seek only advantages for themselves. The war was seen by the Western allies as a dispute about right and wrong, a battle between civilization and barbarism, humanity and inhumanity, justice and injustice. They consequently believed that victory entitled them to reform the domestic government and culture of the defeated countries (Kyogoku, 1987, pp. 4–5). Rural poverty was a curse of prewar Japan: its causes included surplus population, and inequalities of land ownership and land distribution among tenants. The occupation's land reform addressed those

problems by redistributing agricultural land (Dore, 1958). To destroy Japan's heavy industry and military potential, the Americans decided to dissolve the *zaibatsu* system by breaking up over 300 leading companies. The original plan was not fully implemented, and many company splinters came together again, although often in different combinations (Hadley, 1970). Who could be relied on as a main base for a democratic regime in Japan? The new political structure was designed to strengthen the working class against the business middle class and farmers. Union organization was encouraged, and legal changes were made to strengthen employees' bargaining power against employers (Levine, 1958; Morris, 1960).

7   See Uchino (1983, table 6 on p. 84).

8   See, for example, Hadley (1970), Lockwood (1965) and Livingston et al. (1976, vol. 2).

9   The oft-quoted statement which came from Washington to MacArthur, 'You are not to assume any responsibility for the reconstruction or strengthening of the Japanese economy', shows that the belief of some Japanese leftists at the time in the occupation army as 'a people's liberation army' was a romantic fantasy.

10   See Kosai (1984, p. 31).

11   Kosai notes that Arisawa may have obtained the original idea for the Keisha Seisan approach in Hayek's work: see Kosai (1984, footnote 8 on p. 32) and Hayek (1931, p. 94).

12   It was also called the Reconversion Finance Bank in GHQ documents (Uchino, 1983, p. 35).

13   It had an earlier history as one of the government-sponsored special banks which provided long-term credit to enterprises in the manufacturing sector before the war. After the war the bank switched temporarily to the status of an ordinary bank; but in 1952, following the inception of the Long-Term Credit Bank Law, it once again became a long-term credit bank. For further information, see Teranishi (1982, ch. 7), also pp. 37–8 above.

14   In May 1947, a radical reorganization leading to a considerable expansion in the size of the board was carried out. The number of bureaux and sections increased to house an increase in staff from 316 to 2000 by transferring all staff involved in economic planning matters in various ministries into the board – a centralization of the economic planning system in the Board. From the board, the present Ministry of International Trade and Industry (MITI) was subsequently formed (Uchino, 1983, pp. 37–8).

15   The economic background which led to the publication of 25 White Papers between 1945 and 1971 is outlined in Kosai (1972). See also appendix table A.6. below.

16   Economists, both neoclassical and Marxian, confronted the challenge. Their relations with Western theories and researchers drew attention to the peculiarities of the Japanese society, culture and economy. The problems and confusions among economists in Japan at the time are explained in Tsuru's (1964) introduction to the new developments of economic thought in the immediate postwar years.

17   This was the case even with the *Ronso* (Debates) in 1927–38, which were described in chapter 4 (p. 104 above).

18   See Toyota Jidosha Kogyo (1967).

19 See Uchino (1983, p. 56).
20 Kosai writes of the time of this priority production as follows: '... six *gos* of rice were rationed to coal miners and 3 *gos* to members of their families; at what is still called the 'Golden Hour' on Thursday evenings at 8:00 p.m., NHK Radio [the national broadcasting corporation] broadcast a special 'Evening Program for the Mining Community'. Public notice-boards on street corners proclaimed the rate of progress in rice deliveries to the government and in coal output the way the number of traffic fatalities and injuries is displayed today'. One *go* is equivalent to 0.18*l* (Kosai, 1986, p. 42).
21 See EPA (1972, pp. 60–4).
22 Kosai notes that the successful increase in coal and steel production in this period was not the making of the Priority Production program alone, but owed much to the occupation, which imported and released basic materials such as crude oil, coking coal and iron ore (Kosai, 1984, pp. 36 and 42–3).
23 See Uchino (1983, p. 70).
24 See Toyota Jidosha Kogyo (1967) and Yamaguchi et al. (1982, vol. 1, pp. 57–8).
25 See Uekusa (1982, ch. 2).
26 The term is ill-defined and caused debates over the assessment of the exact nature and extent of competition in Japan. For further discussion, see, for example, Ueno (1988, ch. 3) and Komiya et al. (1984, pp. 12–16).
27 See McRae (1967).
28 Quoted by Johnson (1982, p. 27).
29 See, for example, Yamaguchi (1982, pp. 128–37).

Chapter 7   High-speed economic growth

1 See EPA, *Keizai Hakusho*, 1956. See also appendix table A.6.
2 The economic performance in the 1951–5 period may be compared with that of 1946–51 and 1965–70 as follows:

	Average annual growth rate		
	1946–51	*1951–5*	*1965–70*
GNP (real)	9.5	8.6	12.1
Investment (nominal)	8.3	10.8	18.0
Personal saving (nominal)	4.7	10.7	18.5

Source: compiled from EPA, *Annual Report on National Accounts*, 1950, 1965 and 1973.

3 See McRae (1967).
4 See Kahn (1970), Vogel (1979) and Johnson (1982).
5 How did the Japanese people experience the period of high-speed growth, and what did it bring to the Japanese economy and society? Twenty years after that phase effectively ended, many researchers in Japan are now

searching its history for the roots of the 'miracle'. Among very many publications, many of the most interesting are personal accounts of their experience by policy-makers and their professional and academic advisers, and by business and trade union leaders. Unfortunately most of them are in Japanese only: those available in English are Kosai (1981), Uchino (1983), Okita (1983) and *Economist* (Tokyo) (1984).

6   See Johnson (1982, p. 3).
7   See United Nations, *Statistical Yearbook*, 1981.
8   See Nakagawa (1979).
9   See Yasuba and Inoki (1989, pp. 16–31).
10 For further information on trade and capital liberalization, see for example, Uchino (1983, pp. 116–20), Johnson (1982, ch. 8) and Hollerman (1988).
11 See Johnson and Hollerman, loc. cit., and M. Itoh et al. (1991, p. 22).
12 See Odaka (1989, pp. 153–60).
13 See Kosai (1989, pp. 210–17).
14 Ibid., pp. 213–17 and T. Nakamura (1984, p. 177).
15 See T. Nakamura (1984, pp. 174–9).
16 Following the fluctuating waves in the balance of international payments from 1955 until 1965, we count deficits in 1955 (first quarter), 1956 (third quarter)–1957 (third quarter), 1961 (second quarter–last quarter), 1964 (second quarter) and 1965 (first quarter) (EPA, *National Accounts*, 1955–70).
17 In parallel with MITI's administrative guidance, window guidance had no legal basis but was effective as an anti-inflationary measure given the economic conditions and system of the time.
18 See Uchino (1983, pp. 98–9). This comment is made on his working experiences at the Economic Stabilization Board, the Economic Deliberation Council and later at the Economic Planning Agency (op. cit., p. 10).
19 For further discussion on the Anpo movement, see I. Muto (1970).
20 See Martin (1973).
21 A number of studies have been published that discuss the plan and the actual performance of the economy. See for example, Tsuruta (1984), T. Nakamura (1984, ch. 6; 1986, lecture 6), Kosai (1981, 1989) and Yasuba and Inoki (1989).
22 Nearly one-third of the general account budget was allocated to public works for building infrastructure facilities. Public funds from other sources were also directed towards this field in this period, so that annual investment in transport capacity (for example, road, railway and air) was reported to have more than doubled between 1968 and 1970 (Rikuun-Kyoku, 1973).
23 See Yamaguchi et al. (1982, vol. 2, part V).
24 For specific policy measures for the purpose of trade and investment liberalization in this period, see Kosai (1989, pp. 232–54), Hollerman (1988, chs 2–4), T. Nakamura (1984, ch. 6) and Komiya and Itoh (1988).
25 See Uchino (1983, p. 118).
26 See, for example, Tsuruta (1982), Hollerman (1988), Odaka (1989) and Kosai (1989).

27 See Sheridan (1977).
28 As an attempt to fill in this gap, a large-scale study project was organized in 1982. Many conferences were reported to have taken place in the following two years, and the results of the study were published in Komiya et al. (1984), and also M. Itoh (1991).
29 See Uchino (1983, p. 124–8).
30 Only relatively few studies in English were published about the postwar economic policies of Japan before 1970. Myths about a stereotypical government–industry collaboration dominated these early works. Since then, a rush to fill the research gap has taken place, and there is now a lot of carefully prepared material available on this subject. Readers are advised to consult the bibliography in Boger (1988).
31 See Yamaguchi et al. (1982, vol. 2, part IV).
32 See Yamaguchi et al., loc. cit.
33 See Komiya et al. (1984, pp. 8–11).
34 See, for example, Tsuruta (1984), T. Nakamura (1981, ch. 6) and Komiya (1975b).
35 Tsujimura makes the very interesting observation that publicly organized control agreements in the postwar years in Japan have, in fact, created extremely strong competitive markets. This is due to the fact that control agreements save numbers of marginal producers from bankruptcies in times of depression, so that the number of producers remains large in many industries (see Tsujimura, 1984, pp. 11–31).
36 For a more detailed discussion on the national economic policies in the period after 1965, see T. Nakamura (1986, lectures 6 and 7) and Kosai (1981, part III; 1988, pp. 254–72).
37 S. Nakamura refers to these small to medium-sized enterprises as '*chuken kigyo*' (middle sized enterprises) and studies the new characteristics which seem to be contributing to their effectiveness in competing with larger counterparts (S. Nakamura, 1982).
38 It is fair to note here that changes in the demographic pattern and other changes in society contributed to the shortage of labour in the period. For example, the birth rate in the years 1938–45 was abnormally low. However, the postwar baby boom generation did not enlarge the labour supply in the 1960s, because this generation continued its education beyond junior high school level (12–15 years).
39 Labour's share of the total value-added, however, declined from, 89.5 per cent and 84.9 per cent in the 1946–51 and 1951–5 periods to 80.6 per cent in the 1965–70 period (EPA, *Keizai hakusho*, relevant years).
40 The percentage proportion of household consumption directed towards food, housing and clothing fell from 61.8 per cent in 1955 to 52.5 per cent in 1965 (Statistical Bureau, *Annual Report in Family Income and Expenditure Survey*, 1963 and 1980).
41 The Genroku era spanned the years 1688–1704. It was the time of Renaissance for Japan, with brilliant activity in literature and the arts, as represented by the work of Basho, Saikaku and Utamaro.
42 By 1980, by such criteria as living standards, levels of technology and rate of economic growth, Japan had moved into a new phase from which the 35 years of the 'postwar era' could be seen in historical perspective. What

were the changes that concluded the postwar era? From a Japanese perspective, Japan had finally caught up with the advanced industrial West.
From a Western perspective, Japan had become a major economic power
with her GNP 12–13 per cent of the world total and about two-thirds of
that of the USA. Neither Japan nor the rest of the world can any longer
act regardless of each other, and others cannot ignore Japanese competitive pressures on them. As the Japanese economy is further integrated
into the world economy, Japanese and foreign study of the Japanese
economy have an increasingly common basis. There are still differences. In
1976, Patrick and Rosovsky remarked that '... Japanese growth was not
miraculous: it can be reasonably well understood and explained by ordinary causes', and the mistaken use of stereotypes and ideal types to explain
it is almost all 'the fault of the foreign observers having been ignorant of
Japan' (Patrick and Rosovsky, 1976, p. 6). But in 1988, Okimoto and
Inoguchi (1988, p. 7) posed a list of questions about the Japanese political
economy including the following: 'Can national differences in institutional
structure and public policies be accommodated within the international
system without giving certain countries (like Japan) "unfair" advantages?'; 'How different is Japan from the political economies of the United
States, Western Europe, and other advanced industrial states?'; 'Do the
differences pose special problems for Japan's integration into the international community?'; 'Are the differences diminishing over time as
Japanese institutions and attitudes undergo the process of "internationalization"?' In short, they ask '... if Japan's political economy begins to lose
its distinctiveness as it is integrated more fully into the international
system?' Almost half of the contributors, both Japanese and American, to
the publications by the National Institute for Research Advancement
(NIRA) cast doubt on the issue, rejecting the hypothesis of 'eventual con-
vergence' (Okimoto, 1988; Katzenstein, 1988; Krasner, 1988; Pyle, 1988;
Hollerman, 1988). They are of the opinion that, despite constant and rapid
adaptation to changes in the external environment, Japan's economic
system at home is not likely in the foreseeable future to lose all the features
that distinguish it from other advanced industrial economies. There are
also important questions about the impact of Japanese institutions on the
external environment and on nations which interact with Japan. The study
of Japanese political institutions, their policy-making processes, and
the mind-set and training of bureaucrats emerge as important research
agendas.

Chapter 8   A decelerated economy

1   Following Ohokawa and Rosovsky, who observed a rising 'trend rate of
growth' throughout the pre- and postwar years, Minami tried to see if the
Japanese economy grew at an accelerated rate in the postwar years. He
estimated that on average the annual growth rate for the postwar period
was 7.7 per cent, which compared with 3.2 per cent for the prewar period,
and that the rate of economic growth of the Japanese economy had

increased by 0.368 percentage points every ten years (Minami, 1986, pp. 50–1).

2   For further information on the trends of economic growth in the period, see Uchino (1983, pp. 155–69) and Minami (1986, pp. 48–59).

3   The annual rate of inflation actually fell in this robust period of growth (Statistical Bureau, *Japan Statistical Yearbook*, 1973).

4   Many MITI officers were ambitious for all of Japan's important industries, such as steel, automobile manufacturing, chemicals, textiles, electric equipment, electronics and ship-building, to be equipped as large-scale enterprises (see Morikawa, 1977).

5   For further discussion on the changes which took place in the market conduct of major industries in the 1960s and 1970s, see Ueno (1988, ch. 3).

6   The very first public attempt to legislate and provide the general population with health protection and the conservation of the environment was manifested in Kogai Taisaku Kihon Ho (the Pollution Countermeasures Basic Law) in 1967. It prescribes anti-pollution measures for air, water, noise, vibration, ground subsidence and offensive odours. It set up the Environmental Pollution Countermeasures Council. The law aimed to pursue 'harmony between the protection of the environment and economic development'. The law was amended in 1971 and marked the beginning of pollution control and regulation in Japan. In the long national effort for industrialization, this was the first serious *reconsideration* of the single-minded pursuit of industrial growth.

7   This figure does not convey the real extent of the price increase of daily necessities. For example, Uchino lists price rises of the following items: cabbage, over 400 per cent; sweet potatoes, 300–400 per cent; spinach, onions, lettuce, carrots, turnips, cauliflower, toilet paper, 200–300 per cent; noodles, potatoes, radishes, mackerel, wall construction, 80–200 per cent; school uniforms and men's shirts, 50–75 per cent (Uchino, 1983, p. 278).

8   For a detailed analysis of the Japanese economy in the first oil crisis period (1973–6), see Yoshitomi (1977).

9   See Uekusa (1984, pp. 86–8).

10   For a general explanation of the economic conditions during the oil crisis period, see Uekusa (1984, ch. 6), Tsuruta (1982, ch. 8) and Itoh et al. (1991, pp. 25–32).

11   Uchino (1983, p. 209).

12   For a detailed explanation of government fiscal and monetary policy for economic stimulation in this period, see Kosai (1989, pp. 254–72) and Ogura and Yoshino (1984).

13   MITI, *70-nendai*, 1971.

14   MITI, *Choki Vision*, 1974.

15   For the government and business relationships in various industries in manufacturing, commerce and agricultural sectors, see *Economist, Tokyo* (1984, vols 1 and 2).

16   MITI, *Choki Vision* (1974, 1975) and *70 nendai* and *80 nendai*; see also Komiya and Yokobari (1991, pp. 11–25).

17   MITI, *Choki Vision* (1975).

18   MITI, *Choki Vision* (1975), *80-nendai* (1981) and *MITI Handbook* (1986).

19 For further discussion, see Sheridan (1984, pp. 430–41).
20 See Ukekusa (1984, pp. 84–6).
21 See Komiya (1975b).
22 See Uchino (1983, p. 219).
23 The value of the yen against the US dollar rose steadily from ¥360 to ¥296.79 in 1975, to ¥219.14 in 1979, to ¥220.53 in 1981, and further to ¥125.00 in 1989 (Keizai Koho Center, 1982, table 6–7).
24 See Kosai (1986, p. 168).
25 MITI, *80 nendai* (1980).
26 See appendix table A.7.
27 See McRae (1980), Kahn (1970) and Vogel (1979).
28 See Keizai Koho Center (1989, tables 1-2 and 1-3).
29 See Keizai Koho Center (1989), loc. cit.
30 See EPA, Economic White Paper, (1984).
31 See NIRA (1988a,b).
32 NIRA was established by the introduction of special legislation in March 1974. It receives funds from national and local governments as well as from the private sector. We will discuss the importance of NIRA later in this section.
33 The working life of the average Japanese office worker stretched from 34–36 years (for university graduates) to 37–39 years (for high school leavers).
34 See Kumagai (1972) and Kumagai et al. (1979, ch. 9).
35 See appendix table A.6, Kosai (1972) and Sawa (1984).
36 See Uchino (1983, pp. 189–92 and 275–6).
37 See Economic Council of Japan (1974) and NIRA (1988a,b).
38 See NIRA (1988b).
39 See NIRA (1984).
40 Two rounds of administrative reform in the 1980s brought many changes to the policy-making processes and administrative procedures of the government. What the whole effect will be on the structure of power and the working of the system is not yet clear, but some changes are apparent in public economic policy-making and management. In the period of high-speed growth, there was energetic competition between leading bureaucrats and their ministries for 'shares of the action', and to a considerable degree they operated the state as a progressive entrepreneur, providing funds, plans and guidance for projects in aid of national objectives (see Dore, 1987, pp. 6–8). But in a more stagnant economy in the 1980s, severe budget restrictions and growing frictions in overseas trade have curtailed entrepreneurial opportunities. Bureaucrats have retreated to more defensive roles and concerned themselves more with revenue and financial control, leaving progressive policy-making (and pork-barreling) to members of parliament. New expressions have been coined: *toko-kantei* for the predominance of political parties and decline of bureaucracy; and *zoku-giin* for members of parliament with vested interests and influence in specific policy areas. There is research interest in the changing roles and relations of bureaucrats and members of parliament in particular ministries and policy areas and in overall coordination of home and of foreign

policies, and in the effects of changing circumstances and government responses on the traditional 'administrative guidance' and 'administrative discretion' (see Tanaka and Morita, 1991, pp. 41–4; Yamamura and Yasuba, 1987; in particular George and Yamamura, 1987; Muramatsu and Krauss, 1987; Kosai 1987).

Chapter 9   Explanations

1 Murakami (1987b, p. 33).
2 In order to acknowledge clearly the distinctive nature of the Japanese economic system and its role in the development of industrialism compared with Western economies, some researchers have invented special terms for Japan's economy such as 'New Capitalism' (Lockwood), the 'Japanese Model' (Johnson) and 'Regulated Capitalism' (Dore) (see Lockwood, 1968; Johnson, 1982; Dore, 1987).
3 See, for example, Peacock and Wiseman (1960), Buchanan and Flowers (1975) and Takahashi (1986). Other researchers doubt the effectiveness and relevance of such measures as the basis for estimating the size and growth of government activities (see, for example, Butlin, 1982, pp. 6–8).
4 Studying only post-war years, Calder quite independently reports his observation of policy cycles as 'the pronounced *oscillations* in Japanese domestic policy-making' (author's emphasis). According to him, these oscillations bring about the shift 'between quietism and change [of policy], between efficiency and welfare, between creativity and markedly more rigid approaches to policy...' Such a characterization addresses different study dimensions and raises different issues for enquiry than ours do (Calder, 1988, p. 5).
5 See Tullock (1980) and Olson (1965).
6 Generally speaking, unlike many East Asian countries Japan's bureaucracy has traditionally been relatively free from corruption (see Japan Culture Institute, 1979, pp. 82–3). The absence of a system of large extended families is suggested as one aid to Japanese honesty (see Kyogoku, 1985, p. 5). Other reasons include Japan's having set up Western-style laws and precisely organized bureaucratic networks, supported by vigorous training of public servants, from the very beginning of industrialization.
7 Harada and Kosai argued that Japanese economic policies actually reduce 'rent-seeking' activities in business and thereby encourage maximum economic growth. However, their reasoning differs from ours; they seek the explanation in the small size of government expenditure (Harada and Kosai, 1987).
8 See NIRA (1985).
9 See NIRA (1988a,b).
10 See NIRA (1988a, p. 35).
11 For further information about the man, his works and the critical evaluation of his thoughts and works on the future direction of Japanese society

as well as business education, see his autobiography and other work now available in English (Fukuzawa, 1960, 1985) and works, for example, by Craig (1968) and Maruyama (1986).

12 See Fukuzawa (1866).
13 See Fukuzawa (1874).
14 See Fukuzawa (1875).
15 *Jitsugyo-Ron*, in Fukuzawa (1893, pp. 257–317).
16 See Fukuzawa (1893, pp. 259–60).
17 The following passage on Fukuzawa's teaching owes much to assistance given generously by Professor Nishikawa Shunsaku of Keio University.
18 It may be helpful to note, for the foreign reader, that many of these *jitsugyo-ka*, or former samurai, are said to have joined the service of merchants who had formerly been inferior to themselves on the social ladder, on the grounds that they wished to direct their accumulated wealth, the major source of capital accumulation available in the period, to national purposes (see Yasuoka et al., 1978).
19 See Oshima et al. (1983, vol. 3, ch. 6).
20 For example, Nakamigawa Hikojiro of Mitsui, a nephew and distinguished student of Fukuzawa at Keio, began resolutely to cut close ties with government officials, so as to keep the relationship of his company with bureaucrats strictly defensible according to economic and management criteria. He is reported to have flatly refused credit accommodation without due security to a very senior man in the economic planning authority. There are more such examples, which make Nakamigawa's behaviour the rule rather than the exception among newly emerging business leaders of that period (Yasuoka, 1978, p. 21).
21 For the examination of the role, function and relative power of economic bureaucrats in the writing of economic policy measures in contemporary Japan, see, for example, Nakano (1986). On the organizational structure, administration networks and the areas of legal and administrative authority of each ministry and government office in Japan, see Kyoiku-sha (1981).
22 Studies by Kubota (1969), Muramatsu (1981) and Koh (1989) address part of the question.
23 There are also cases in which officers in local government are seconded temporarily to central government offices. They are not called '*shukko*'.
24 For further information, see Kyoiku-sha (1981, particularly 'Ministry of Finance', ch. 11) and Komiya and Yamamoto (1981, p. 627).
25 Relating to the postwar experience, Komiya observes that these high-ranking officers become influential in the economic policy-making process *not* because of their demonstrated ability to apply advanced knowledge of economics and economic theory to the issues under consideration, but rather because they can demonstrate their wide experience as generalist administrators, and can react promptly to new problems and changing circumstances, mobilize knowledge and information, and thereby build up consensual support among those concerned through their skills of persuasion and negotiation and their accumulated personal contacts in relevant offices and places (see Komiya and Yamamoto, 1981, p. 605). For the

prewar experience, similar observations are presented in studies by Johnson (1982, p. 315).

26 Sugihara names Soeda Juichi (1886–1929) as the very first *kancho* economist. Shimomura Osamu, with his National Income-doubling Plan, can be said to be one of the most prominent examples in postwar years (Sugihara, 1984, pp. 67–70).

27 See Tsujimura (1984), chapter 7.

28 See Johnson (1982, p. 8).

29 The supply of consumer goods and services in Japan has been kept curtailed in comparison with that for investment purposes, this having continued almost throughout the period studied. This trend is indicated by the continuous rise of price levels for the former in comparison with the latter. This Japanese experience has been distinctly different from that in the West. For example, the price index for capital goods and services is reported to have risen faster in the USA, UK, Canada, Sweden and Denmark throughout the prewar years; and in the postwar years, that trend has appeared in almost all OECD economies, making the Japanese case look distinctly odd (Minami, 1981, p. 306).

30 See pp. 58–61 in chapter 3 above.

31 Hollerman refers to the move towards free trade and capital investment in Japan in terms of 'Japan Disincorporated' to distinguish from the preceding period of 'Japan Incorporated' (Hollerman, 1988).

32 Ueno (1988). See part IV in particular.

33 Keizai Koho Center (1975; 1990, table 10-6).

34 Conference held in Melbourne, 2 March 1990, organized by the Business Council of Australia.

35 See H. Muto (1984).

Chapter 10   The neglected producers

1 Keizai Koho Center (1990, tables 4-6–4-9) and EPA, *Annual Report on National Accounts* (1990, part II).

2 An attempt is made to see the comparative difference in living standards of people in major cities in Japan and those in Sydney, Australia. How comfortable and well off are the Japanese compared with the residents of Sydney? With all the difficulties associated with inter-country comparisons of this kind, the study indicates that at the beginning of the 1990s it is still the case that most Australians enjoy more comfortable lives with more and richer facilities to accommodate their daily necessities than their counterparts in Japan (Castles, 1992).

3 See, for example, JAPEC Group (1986), Shinohara (1986, ch. VI).

4 See Shinohara (1986, ch. VI), EPA (1988, p. 31) and Shimada (1990).

5 See EPA (1988, p. 53). Such an inflationary trend in asset and land values came about through several periods of marked leaps and bounds, led by speculative buying. In the case of land prices, these jumped by an amazing factor of ten in the period of only two short decades. The first rise came in the early 1970s under Tanaka's 'remodel the Japanese Archipelago' programme. Another climb came in 1980 and 1985–90, with the accumulation

of idle money. The rise in stock values is a relatively recent phenomenon which commenced in the early 1980s, but the speed at which stocks have risen since 1986 is most disturbing, as it almost exceeds the value of GNP.

6   Every home-owing household benefits notionally by the inflation of its house value; but for most, that is not a realizable asset, because to sell it would entail buying a replacement house at the same inflated price. Meanwhile, new households and other first-time buyers are increasingly excluded from the market altogether.

7   Keizai Koho Center (1990, p. 75).

8   For example, in 1983 the government published a white paper on lifestyle to 'examine the new phenomenon which had emerged to affect the very foundation of Japanese society'. It discussed matters such as the increasing number of nuclear families and single-member households; the rapid aging society; the rising rate of workforce participation among women, especially married women with young children; and decline of the large family and marriage itself as a social institution, with rising numbers of divorces and separations (Ministry of Welfare, 1983). See also Iwanami Shoten (1991), no. 14, pp. 49–61.

9   How true this observation is can only be established by multidisciplinary investigations which take account of improvements earnings, social status and mobility and education opportunities and other aspects of the living standard of the population. NIRA's study follows along these lines and their results (1988a,b) support our observation.

10   See Yasuba and Inoki (1989, pp. 282–9).

11   MITI (1980, 1984, 1986).

12   The average percentage change of the social indicators is recorded as being in 1940–5 (40.7 per cent in 1945), followed by 1895–1900 (32.4 per cent in 1900) and 1885–90 (30.5 per cent in 1890), with other prewar years (1910, 1920, 1930 and 1940) recording 20–25 per cent. In contrast, in 1970 and 1980 the figures were very low, at 10.3 per cent and 7.6 per cent respectively (NIRA, 1988b, tables 1-4 and 1-5 on pp. 40–51).

13   See Grimes (1976) and B. Ward (1978, p. 112).

14   Sangyokozo Shingikai (1990).

15   EPA (1987; 1990, part II).

16   See, for example, Hollerman (1988, ch. 4) and Pempel (1982, particularly chs 7 and 8).

17   For further information, see Sano (1989, ch. 8), Mishima (1990), Iwao (1991), Fujitake (1991) and Iwanami Shoten (1991) in particular pp. 43–4.

18   Iwao and Fujitake, op. cit.

19   *Asahi Shirbun*, 13 March 1992.

20   Shinotsuka (1982, p. 163).

21   See Sheridan (1984).

22   See Iwao (1991)

23   Projecting the view that differentiation between male and female roles is an essential part of cultural systems, Hasegawa argues that the sexual equality is a matter of mutual co-operation and support between men and women, without ranking their work in terms of superiority or inferiority. On the basis she objects to the introduction in Japan of the domestic legislation proposed by the United Nations (Hasegawa, 1984).

24 Ludz (1972, pp. 183–92).
25 How has the family, as the basic unit of society, changed with economic development, industrialization and Westernization of the society? There are questions about family organization in the prewar years, and its response to the postwar reform which introduced equal rights to inheritance; effects on working-class families of the decline of the rural social base; the decline of family size following the general acceptance of birth control; the increase in land prices and the limited housing space; various government policies relating to the family; and the role of women in the care of the elderly (see K. Fujita, 1985; Hancock et al., 1983; Hashimoto, 1985; Holden, 1983).
26 This argument is not mere supposition. From reading more than 200 autobiographies, biographies, diaries and interview reports of Japanese people from several generations, and with diverse backgrounds and careers, I have come to believe that informal education by parents at home appears to have a greater influence in forming people's personal value systems and economic attitudes than has generally been recognized. This is part of a study – which may prove to be an important one – of the relationship between the making of what may be loosely called 'an achieving society', expressed mainly through economic activity, and the nature of the education and 'socialization' that Japanese children have received at home through the process of industrialization and economic development since the Restoration. Little systematic study of this particular relationship seems to have been attempted as yet in Japan.
27 Castles (1992) p. 99.
28 Castles, loc. cit.
29 Can many industries in Japan reduce annual working hours without reducing much of their competitiveness in export markets? This and other related questions concerning the work and leisure mix of Japanese people have begun to attract study efforts, both in business and government offices. See, for example, MITI's 'Report of the likely effect of the reduction of working hours in various industries in Japan' (mimeo, supplied privately to the author, 1992).
30 See Iwao (1991).
31 Orthodox economic theory expects correctly that in the process of economic growth the productivity of land will rise faster than that of other factors of production. This is because, first, the accumulation of reproducible factors (building and machinery, and trained human labour) which can be used together with land to produce goods and services will take place rapidly so that land use becomes more intensive, leading its marginal productivity to increase at a faster rate than that of other factors. Second, urban and industrial growth and rising income expand demand for residential land. In both cases some increase in land prices is healthy, both to sort out the land between its potential users and to induce them to use it economically. Differentiated prices allow the most productive business users to beat the business competition for the land they want. Differentiated prices also serve to clear the residential land market, as richer households bid for the more desirable locations and poorer households accept the poorer locations: although the efficiency of this market is more

dubious, because the richer households who obtain the most and best housing are not necessarily the households who will use their housing most productively. But observing the utility of competition *within* each market, theorists have forgotten to ask themselves what benefits flow from competition *between* households and business. Where land is scarce, as in Japan, that competition can do multiple damage. Households may be cramped for space. Inflated housing costs make unnecessary and unproductive inroads into their spendable income. And the business freedom to buy land and thus locate employment anywhere, regardless of the congestion and commuting which the location causes, has led in Japan in overcentralized concentrations of employment, which are becoming more and more difficult to link to adequate housing for the workforce. The employees pay the price of such inefficiency in commuting time, lost from leisure and parenting.

32   Many observers suggest that the Japanese education system has been an outstanding success and has contributed to the rapid industrialization (Passin, 1965; Reischauer, 1977; Vogel, 1979; Amano, 1986). However, the report to the Prime Minister, published twice in mid- and late 1985, warned that the education system needed urgent reform to address long-accumulated problems in the training and education of the people of Japan (Ad Hoc Council on Education, 1985). Education became the subject of heated debate in the following years. The educational environment was thought to have deteriorated; there were problems in teacher–student relations; in the role of moral education in providing young people with a balanced sense of individual rights and responsibilities acceptable to the Japanese society; in the 'entrance examination hell'; and in the increase in well-educated college graduates without a matching increase in well-paid white-collar jobs with promotional opportunities (see Amano, 1986). The Ad Hoc Council (1985) proposed two aims of reform as the most important: to build a culture in which individual creativity can flourish; and to provide education that will enable people to contribute to international society while retaining a Japanese identity, based firmly in Japan's traditional culture. As a first step, employers were asked to select and promote employees without the traditional bias in favour of those from particular schools. Education is said to be one of the most conservative of social institutions: the more drastic the proposals for reform, the stronger the reaction tends to be. Nevertheless, in Japan's case two large reforms have been accomplished – one in the 1870s by the Meiji government and one in the 1940s by the Allied authority (Nagai, 1971; Kinmoth, 1981). It will be important to see what the new round of reforms will do to the bureaucrats in Japan's government offices (Spaulding, 1967; Amano, 1986; Takeuchi, 1990).

Bibliography

Note: Transliterations of Japanese words make no attempt to indicate accents or vowel length.

(1)   Government Publications

The English title is given when side-by-side translation is available.

Bank of Japan, *see* Nihon Ginko
Bureau of Statistics, *see* Naikaku Tokeikyoku
Economic Council, *see* Keizai Shingikai
Economic Stabilization Board, *see* Keizai Antei Honbu
EPA, *see* Keizai Kikaku-cho
Keizai Antei Honbu (Economic Stabilization Board)
  Taiheiyosenso niokeru Wagakuni no higai Sogohakusho, 1949.
Keizai Kikaku-cho (Economic Planning Agency – EPA)
  1970 National Wealth Survey of Japan, vol. 1, *Summary Report*.
  Shiryo Keizai Hakusho 25-nen, 1972.
  2000-Nen no Nihon, 9 vols, 1984.
  Summary Report and National Accounts, 1988, (ed.).
  Nihon no Sogokokuryoku, 1987.
  Asia Taiheiyochiiki Han'ei no Tetsugaku, 1990.
  Annual Report on National Accounts.
  Keizai Hakusho, White Paper, annual.
  Kokumin Shotoku Hakusho, annual.
  Kokumin Shotoku Tokei Nenpo, annual.
Keizai Shingikai (Economic Council of Japan)
  NNW Measurement Committee, *Measuring Net National Welfare of Japan*, 1974.
  2000 Nen no Nihon, various series.
Kosei-sho (Ministry of Health).
  Kosei Hakusho, annual.

League of Nations
  Industrialization and Foreign Trade, 1945.
Ministry of Finance (MOF), *see* Okurasho
Ministry of Health (MOH), *see* Kosei-sho
Ministry of Labour (MOL), *see* Rodo-sho
Ministry of Welfare (Koseisho) 1983: *White Paper on Lifestyle (Seikatsu Hakusho)*. Tokyo.
MITI (Ministry of International Trade and Industry), *see* Tsusan-sho
Nihon Ginko (Bank of Japan)
  Hundred-year Statistics of the Japanese Economy, 1966.
  Meijiiko Honpo Shuyo Keizai Tokei, 1966.
  Money and Banking in Japan. New York: St Martin's Press, 1973.
  Economic Analysis of Government Activity, Empirical Approach.
  Keizai Tokei Nenpo, annual.
NIRA (National Institute for Research Advancement), *see* Sogokaihatsu Kenkyu Kiko
Naikaku Tokeikyoku
  Teikoku Tokei Nenkan (Statistical Yearbook), annual.
  Annual Report on Family Income and Expenditure Survey, annual.
Norin-sho (Ministry of Agriculture)
  Abstract of Statistics on Agriculture, Forestry and Mining, 1988.
Okura-sho (Ministry of Finance)
  Showa Zaisei-shi. Tokyo: Toyokeizai Shinpo-sha, 1954–65 and 1976.
Rikuun-Kyoku
  Rikuun Tokei Yoran, annual.
Rodo-sho (Ministry of Labour)
  Yearbook of Labour Statistics, annual.
Sangyokozo Shingikai (Council for Industrial Structure)
  Interim Report, May 1990.
Shoko-sho (Department of Commerce and Industry)
  Kogyotokei-hyo (Factory Statistics), 1935.
Sogokaihatsu Kenkyu Kiko (National Institute for Research Advancement – NIRA)
  Seifukatsudo no Keizai Bunseki, 1984.
  Seikatsu Suijun-no Rekishiteki Suii, 1985.
  Gendai Nihon no Seiji Keizai. Domestic Scene, vol. 1, 1987a.
  Shinbunnimiru Shakaishihonsetsubi no Rekishiteki Hensen, 1987b (vol. 1 for Meiji and Taisho periods) and 1987c (vol. 2 for Showa period).
  Seikatsusuijunno Rekishiteki Bunseki, 1988a.
  Seikatsusuijunno Rekishiteki Kenkyu, 1988b.
  Nenpo Shinku Tanku, annual.
Sorifu Tokeikyoku (Statistical Bureau)
  Annual Report on Family Income and Expenditure Survey, annual.
  Nihon no Tokei, annual.
Tsusan-sho (Ministry of International Trade and Industry)
  Kogyotokei 50-nen shi, 1961.
  70 nendai-no Tsushosangyo Seisaku, 1971.
  Sangyokozo no Choki Vision, 1974 and 1975.
  Sangyoseisakushi Kenkyu Shiryo, 1977.

80 nendai-no Tsushosangyo Vision, 1980.
MITI Handbook, 1984 and 1986.
Kyōzonteki Kyoso eno Michi, 1989 (summary translation in English available under the title *International Trade and Industrial Policy – Toward Creating Human Values in the Global Age*, 1990).
Statistical Bureau, *see* Sorifu Tokeikyoku
United Nations
Statistical Yearbook, annual.

(2)   Books and Articles

Items listed below comprise those quoted in this book as well as those from which the author gained considerable benefit.

Abbegglen, J. C. 1958: *The Japanese Factory: Aspects of its Social Organization*. Glencoe, Ill.: Free Press.
Abe, Y. 1968: *Nihon no Kokufu*. Tokyo: Shiseido.
Ad Hoc Council on Education 1985: *Report to Prime Minister*, June and October.
Agarwala, A. N. and Singh, S. P. (eds) 1958: *The Economics of Underdevelopment*. Bombay and London: Oxford University Press.
Aida, Y. 1966: *Prisoner of the British*. London: Cresset Press.
Akita G. 1967: *Foundations of Constitutional Government in Modern Japan, 1868–1900*. Cambridge, Mass: Harvard University Press.
Allen, G. C. 1965: *Japan's Economic Expansion*. London: Oxford University Press.
—— 1980: *Japan's Economic Policy*. London: Macmillan.
—— 1981: *A Short Economic History of Modern Japan* (4th edn). London: Macmillan.
Amano, I. 1986: The dilemma of Japanese education today. *Japan Foundation Newsletter*, XIII (5), 1–10.
Ando, Y. 1973a: Nihon senji keizai to 'shinkanryo'. In Y. Takahashi (ed.) (1973).
—— (ed.) 1973b: *Ryotaisenkan no Nihonshihonshugi*. Tokyo: University of Tokyo Press.
—— (ed.) 1976: *Nihonkeizai Seisaku-shi Ron*. Tokyo: University of Tokyo Press.
—— 1978: *Kindai Nihon Keizaishi Yoran*, (2nd edn). Tokyo: University of Tokyo.
—— 1987: *Taiheiyo senso no Keizaishiteki Kenkyu*. Tokyo: Tokyo University Press.
—— 1988: *Comparative International Statistics*.
Arisawa, H. and Ando, Y. (eds) 1980: *Showa Keizai-shi*: Tokyo: Nihonkeizai Shinbun-sha, 2 vols.
Asahi Shinbun, 15 March 1992, pp. 9–18.
Azuma, M. 1984: *Wagakuniniokeru Shakaishihon Keisei*. In NIRA (1984), pp. 97–137.
Baba, N. 1969: 1930-nendainiokeru Nihon chishikijin no doko. *Shakai Kagaku Kiyo*, 41.
—— 1972: *Manshujihen-eno Michi*. Tokyo: Chuokoron-sha.

Banno, J. 1989: Meiji kokka no seiritsu. In Umemura et al. (1988–90), vol. 3, ch. 3.

—— and Waswo, A. 1990: Modern and contemporary history. In Toho Gakkai (1990).

Barnhart, M. A. 1987: *Japan Prepares for Total War: the Search for Economic Security, 1919–1941*. Ithaca, NY: Cornell University Press.

Beasley, W. G. 1972: *The Meiji Restoration*. Stanford, California: Stanford University Press.

—— 1985: *The Modern History of Japan*, (3rd edn). London: Weidenfeld & Nicolson.

Bennett, J. W. 1967: *Japanese Economic Growth: Background for Social Change*. In Dore (1987), chapter XIII.

Bennett, J. W. and Levine, S. B. (eds) 1976: Industrialisation and social deprivation: welfare, environment and the post-Industrial society in Japan. In Patrick (ed.) (1976).

Berg, I. (ed.) 1972: *Human Resource and Economic Welfare: Essays in Honor of Eli Ginzberg*. Cambridge: Cambridge University Press.

Bieda, K. 1979: *The Structure and Operation of the Japanese Economy*. Sydney: John Wiley.

Block, F. 1977: The ruling class does not rule. *Socialist Revolution*, 33, 6–28.

Blumenthal, T. 1970: *Saving in Postwar Japan*. Cambridge, Mass.: Harvard University Press.

—— 1972: *Nihonkeizai no Seicho Yoin*. Tokyo: Nihonkeizai Shinbun-sha.

Boger, K. 1988: *Postwar Industrial Policy in Japan: an Annotated Bibliography*, Metuchen, NJ, and London: The Scarecrow Press.

Bornstein, M. (ed.) 1975: *Economic Planning, East and West*, Cambridge, Mass: Ballinger.

Borton, H. 1940: *Japan Since 1931: its Political and Social Developments*. New York: Institute of Pacific Relations.

Bronfenbrenner, M. 1961: Some lessons of Japan's economic development, 1853–1938. *Pacific Affairs*, 34 (1), 7–27.

—— 1983: Western Economics Transplanted to Japan. Presidential Address, History of Economic Society, Annual Meeting, pp. 5–18.

Buchanan, J. M. and Flowers, M. R. 1975: *The Public Finance: an Introductory Textbook* (4th edn). Homewood, Ill.: Irwin.

Butlin, N. G. 1962: *Australian Domestic Product, Investment and Foreign Borrowing 1861–1938/39*. London: Cambridge University Press.

—— 1964: *Investment in Australian Economic Development 1861–1900*. London: Cambridge University Press.

—— et al. 1982: *Government and Capitalism*. Sydney: George Allen & Unwin.

Byas, H. 1942: *Government by Assassination*. New York: Alfred A. Knopf.

Calder, K. E. 1988: *Crisis and Compensation: Public Policy and Political Stability in Japan, 1949–1986*, Princeton, NJ: Princeton University Press.

Cameron, R. (ed.) 1967: *Banking and Economic Development: Some Lessons of History*. London: Oxford University Press.

Castles, I. 1992: Living Standards in Sydney and Japanese cities: a comparison. In Sheridan (1992), chapter 6.

Caves, R. E. and Uekusa, M. 1976a. *Industrial Organization in Japan*. Washington, DC: The Brookings Institution.

—— 1976b. Industrial organization. In Patrick and Rosovsky (1976a), pp. 459–523.

Choki Keizai Tokei (Estimates of Long-term Economic Statistics of Japan since 1866 – hereafter LTES), K. Ohokawa, M. Shinohara and M. Umemura (eds). Tokyo: Toyo Keizai Shinpo-sha.

Vol. 1, Ohkawa, K. and Takamatsu, N. 1974: *Kokumin Shotoku* (National Income).

Vol. 2, Umemura, M. and Akasaka, K. 1988: *Jinko to Rodoryoku* (Population and Labor Force).

Vol. 3, Ohkawa, K. et al. 1965: *Shihon Stokku* (Capital Stock).

Vol. 4, Emi, K. 1971: *Shihon Keisei* (Capital Formation).

Vol. 5, Emi, K. and Itoh, S. 1963: *Chochiku to Tsuka* (Savings and Currency).

Vol. 6, Shinohara, M. 1967: *Kojin Shohi Shishitsu* (Personal Consumption Expenditures).

Vol. 7, Emi, K. and Shinohara, M. 1966: *Zaisei Shishitsu* (Public Expenditures).

Vol. 8, Ohkawa, K. et al. 1965: *Bukka* (Prices).

Vol. 9, Umemura, M. et al. 1966: *Noringyo* (Agriculture and Forestry).

Vol. 10, Shinohara, M. 1972: *Kokogyo* (Mining and Manufacturing).

Vol. 11, Fujino, Seizaburo, Fujino, Shiro and Ono, A. 1954: *Seni Kogyo*, (Textile Manufacturing).

Vol. 12, Minami, R. 1965: *Tetsudo to Denryoku* (Railways and Electric Power).

Vol. 13, Shinohara, M. and Umemuna, M. 1958: *Fuken Keizai Tokei* (Local Government Statistics).

Vol. 14, Yamazawa, I. and Yamamoto Y. 1954: *Boeki to Kokusai Shushi* (Trade and Trade Balance).

Chuman, F. K. 1976: *The Bamboo People: the Law and Japanese–Americans*. Calif.: Del Mar.

Chuokoron-sha 1979: *Nihon no Rekishi*. Tokyo: Chuokoron-sha.

Clark, C. 1951: *The Conditions of Economic Progress*, 2nd edn. London: Macmillan.

Cohen, J. B. 1949: *Japan's Economy: War and Reconstruction*. Minneapolis: University of Minnesota Press/London: Oxford University Press.

Craig, A. M. 1968: Fukuzawa Yukichi: the philosophical foundations of Meiji nationalism. In Ward (1968), chapter IV.

Crawcour, E. S. 1965: The Tokugawa heritage. In Lockwood (1965), pp. 17–44.

Crump, J. 1983: *The Origin of Socialist Thought in Japan*. London and Canberra: Croom Helm/New York: St. Martin's Press.

Deane, P. 1965: *The First Industrial Revolution*. London: Cambridge University Press.

—— and Cole, W. A. 1962: *British Economic Growth 1688–1959: Trends and Structure*. London: Cambridge University Press.

Denison, E. F. 1967: *Why Growth Rates Differ: Postwar Experience in Nine Western Countries*. Washington, DC: The Brookings Institution.

—— and Chung, W. K. 1976: Economic growth and its sources. In Patrick and Rosovsky (1976a), pp. 63–151.

Dore, R. P. 1958: *Land Reform in Japan*. Oxford University Press.
—— 1965: *Education in Tokugawa Japan*. London: Routledge & Kegan Paul.
—— (ed.) 1967: *Aspects of Social Change in Modern Japan*. Princeton, NJ: Princeton University Press.
—— 1973: *British Factory – Japanese Factory: the Origins of National Diversity in Industrial Relations*. London: Allen & Unwin.
—— 1986: *Structural Adjustment in Japan 1970–82* (with a contribution by K. Taira). Geneva: International Labour Office.
—— 1987: *Taking Japan Seriously: a Confucian Perspective on Leading Economic Issues*. London: The Athlone Press.
Dorfman, J. 1959: *The Economic Mind in American Civilization*. New York: The Viking Press, 5 vols.
Dower, J. W. 1975: *Origins of the Modern Japanese State: Selected Writings of E. H. Norman*. New York: Random House.
—— 1979: *Empire and Aftermath: Yoshida Shigeru and the Japanese Experience, 1879–1954*. Cambridge, Mass.: Harvard University Press.
Dunlop, J. T. and Galenson, W. (eds) 1979: *Labor in the Twentieth Century*. New York: Academic Press.
Duus, P. 1968: *Party Rivalry and Political Change in Taisho Japan*, Cambridge, Mass: Harvard University Press.
—— 1983: The take-off point of Japanese Imperialism. In Wray and Conroy (1983), pp. 151–62.
Economic Stabilization Board, *see* Keizai Antei Honbu in (1) above.
Economist (Tokyo) (ed.) 1977–79: *Sengo Sangyoshi eno Shogen*. Tokyo: Mainichi Shinbun-sha, 5 vols.
—— 1984: *Shogen: Kodoseicho-ki no Nihon*. Tokyo: Mainichi Shinbun-sha, 2 vols.
Eichen, C. and Witt, L. (eds) 1964: *Agriculture in Economic Development*. New York: McGraw-Hill.
Emi, K. 1963: *Government Fiscal Activity and Economic Growth in Japan 1868–1960*. Tokyo: Kinokuniya.
—— 1966: *Zaisei Shishitsu*, LTES, vol. 7.
—— 1971: *Shihon Keisei*, LTES, vol. 4.
—— and Ishii, H. 1979: Government accounts: expenditure and revenue. In Ohkawa and Shinohara (1979), pp. 195–202.
—— and Ishiwata, S. 1979: Capital formation and capital stock. In Ohkawa and Shinohara (1979), pp. 177–94.
—— and Mizoguchi, T. 1968: *Kojin Chochiku Kodo no Kokusai Hikaku*. Tokyo: Iwanami.
—— and Shionoya, Y. 1966. *Zaisei Shishitsu*, LTES, vol. 7.
Encyclopaedia Britannica, Inc. 1974: *The New Encyclopaedia Britannica* (15th edn), *Macropaedia*, vol. 10. Chicago, pp. 34–57.
Fei, J. C. H. and Ranis, G. 1964: *Development of the Labor Surplus Economy: Theory and Policy*. Homewood, Ill.: Irwin.
—— 1975: A model of growth and employment in the open dualistic economy: the case of Korea and Taiwan. *Journal of Development Studies*, 11 (2), 32–63.
Firestone, O. J. 1958: *Canada's Economic Development 1867–1953: with Special Reference to Changes in the Country's National Product and National Wealth*. London: Bowes & Bowes.

Fisher, J. K. 1987: The Meirokusha and the building of a strong and prosperous nation. In Wray and Conroy (1983), pp. 83–9.

Fitzgerald, T. 1990: *Between Life and Economics*. ABC Enterprises/Boyer Lecturer: Crows Nest, NSW, chapter 3.

Fletcher, W. M. 1975: Ideologies of political and economic reform and fascism in pre-war Japan. Ph.D. dissertation, (available in mimeo form). Yale University.

—— 1982: *The Search for a New Order*. Chapel Hill: The University of North Carolina Press.

Fujino, S. 1965: *Nihon no Keiki Junkan: Junkanteki Hattenkatei no Rironteki, Tokeiteki, Rekishiteki Bunseki*. Tokyo: Keisoshobo.

—— 1966: Business cycles in Japan, 1868–1962. *Hitotsubashi Journal of Economics*, 7 (1), 56–79.

—— 1968: Construction cycles and their monetary–financial characteristics. In Klein and Ohkawa (1968), pp. 35–68.

—— 1977: Inflation to shitsugyo. In Ohkita and Uchida (1977), pp. 17–48.

—— and Igarashi, F. 1973: *Keiki Shisu 1880–1940*. Tokyo: Institute of Economic Research, Hitotsubashi University.

—— and Teranishi, J. 1975: Shikin junkan no choki dotai: yobiteki bunseki. *Keizai Kenkyu*, 26 (4) 334–58.

——, Fujino, S. and Ono, A. 1979: *Sen-i Kogyo*, LTES, vol. 11.

Fujita, K. 1985: Bibliographical syllabus of the political economy of women in Japan. *Japan Foundation Newsletter*, XIII (1), 11–17.

Fujita, S. 1966: Tax policy. In Komiya (1966a), pp. 32–59.

—— 1975–6: Fiscal policy in postwar Japan. *Japanese Economic Studies*, 4 (2), 27–58.

Fujitake, A. 1991: Women at work. In *Japan Update*, December, p. 25.

Fukuzawa, Yukichi 1866: Seiyo jijo. in *Fukuzawa Yukichi Senshu* (hereafter, *Senshu*) (abridged 1st edn), vol. 1. Tokyo: Iwanami.

—— 1874: Gakumon no Susume. In *Senshu*, vol. 3.

—— 1875: Bunmeiron no Gairyaku. In *Senshu*, vol. 4.

—— 1877: Kyuhanjo. In *Senshu*, vol. 12.

—— 1893: Jitsugyo Ron. In *Senshu*, vol. 8.

—— 1899: Fuku-oh Jiden. In *Senshu*, vol. 10.

—— 1960: *The Autobiography of Fukuzawa Yukichi* (original text 1899; new translation by E. Kiyo'oka). Tokyo: The Hokusei-do Press.

—— 1970: *An Outline of a Theory of Civilization* (translated by D. A. Dilworth and G. C. Hurst) Tokyo: Sophia University Press. (Original text 1875.)

—— 1985: *Fukuzawa Yukichi on Education* (translated by E. Kiyo'oka). Tokyo: University of Tokyo Press.

Fuse, A. 1984: The Japanese family in transition. *Japan Foundation Newsletter, Parts I and II*, XII (3 & 4), 1–24 and 1–10 respectively.

George, C. and Yamamura, K. 1987: The future of industrial policy. in Yamamura and Yasaba (1987). pp. 423–68.

Gerschenkron, A. 1962: *Economic Backwardness in Historical Perspective: a Book of Essays*. Cambridge, Mass.: Harvard University Press, The Belknap Press.

Gleason, A. H. 1965: Economic growth and consumption in Japan. In Lockwood (1965), pp. 391–444.

—— 1989: The level of living in Japan and the United States: a long-term international comparison. *Economic Development and Cultural Change*, 37 (2) 261–84.

Goldsmith, R. W. 1983: *The Financial Development of Japan, 1868–1971*. New Haven and London: Yale University Press.

—— and Saunders, C. (eds) 1959: *The Measurement of National Wealth*. London: Bowes & Bowes.

Gordon, A. 1985: *The Evolution of Labor Relations in Japan, Heavy Industry, 1853–1955*. Cambridge, Mass.: Harvard University Press.

Goto, A. 1982: Business groups in a market economy. *European Economic Review*, 19 (1) 53–70.

Grimes, O. F. 1976: *Housing for Low Income Urban Families: Economics and Policies in the Developing World*. Baltimore: Published for World Bank by Johns Hopkins University Press.

Hadley, E. M. 1970: *Antitrust in Japan*. Princeton, N.J.: Princeton University Press.

Haitani, K. 1986: *Comparative Economic Systems: Organizational and Managerial Perspectives*. Englewood Cliffs, NJ: Prentice-Hall.

Hamada, F. 1971: *Setsubi Toshikodo no Keiryo Bunseki: Shihon Stock no Seicho to Toshikodo*. Tokyo: Toyo Keizai Shinpo-sha.

Hancock, K. et al. 1983: *Japanese and Australian Labour Market: A Comparative Study*. Canberra: Australia–Japan Research Centre. (mimeo).

Hane, M. 1987: *Emperor Hirohito and his Chief Aide-De-Camp: the Honjo Diary 1933–36*. Tokyo: University of Tokyo Press.

Hanley, S. B. 1986: The standard of living, population patterns, and the level of physical well-being: the legacies for Japan's industrialization. In Hayami (1986), ch. 3.

—— and Yamamura Kozo 1977: *Economic and Demographic Change in Preindustrial Japan 1600–1868*. Princeton, NJ: Princeton University Press.

Hara, A. 1987: *Taiheiyosenso-ki no seisanzokyo seisaku*. In Kindainihon Kenkyukai (ed.) (1987), pp. 231–59.

—— 1989: Senji tosei. In Umemura et al. (1988–90), vol. 7, ch. 2.

Hara, K. 1978: *Syakai Keizai no Henkaku to Hatten*. Tokyo: Shinhyoron-sha.

Harada, Y. and Kosai, Y. 1984: Economic development in Japan: a reconstruction. In Scalopino et al. (1984), pp. 43–62.

—— 1987: *Nihonkeizai Hatten-no Big Game, Rent-seeking Katsudo-o Koete*. Tokyo: Toyo Keizai Shinpo-sha.

Hasegawa, M. 1984: Equality of the sexes threatens cultural ecology. *Economic Eye*, June 1984, pp. 23–61.

Hashimoto, H. 1985: Women's studies programme in Japan. Paper presented at the Michigan Women's Studies Association Conference (April).

Hashimoto, T. 1984: *Daikyōkōki no Nihonshihonshugi*. Tokyo: University of Tokyo Press.

Havens, T. R. H. 1974: *Farm and Nation in Modern Japan – Agrarian Nationalism 1870–1940*. Princeton, NJ: Princeton University Press.

Hayami, A. 1968: *Nihonkeizaishi eno Shikaku*. Tokyo: Toyo Keizai Shinpo-sha.

—— 1973: *Nihonniokeru Keizaishakai no Tenkan*. Tokyo: Keio Tsushin.
—— 1975: Jinko to keizai. In Shinbo et al. (1975), pp. 21–118.
—— (organizer) 1986: Pre-conditions to Industrialisation in Japan, Ninth International Economic History Congress, Bern.
—— and Miyamoto, M. (eds) 1989: *Keizaishakai no Seiritsu, 17–18 Seiki*, Tokyo: Iwanami.
Hayami, Y. 1973: *Nihon Nogyo no Seicho Kadai*. Tokyo: Sobun-sha.
—— 1975: *A Century of Agricultural Growth in Japan: its Relevance to Asian Development*. Tokyo: University of Tokyo Press.
—— (ed.) 1983: *Rekishinonaka-no Edo Jidai*. Tokyo: Toyo Keizai Shinpo-sha, Tokei Sensho.
—— and Yamada, S. 1969: Agricultural productivity at the beginning of industrialization. In Ohkawa et al. (1969), pp. 105–35.
—— and Ruttan, V. W. 1971: *Agricultural Development: an International Perspective*. Baltimore: Johns Hopkins Press.
Hayashi, S. 1979: Taiheiyo senso. In Chuokoron-sha (1979).
Hayek, F. A. 1931: *Price and Production*. London: Routledge and Kegan Paul.
Hazama, H. 1971: *Nihonteki Keiei*. Tokyo: Nihonkeizai Shinbun-sha.
Heilbroner, R. L. 1970: *Between Capitalism and Socialism*. New York: Random House.
Hellmann, D. C. 1988: Japanese politics and foreign policy: Elitist democracy within American greenhouse. In Inoguchi and Okimoto (1988) pp. 345–78.
Henmi, K. 1969: Primary product exports and economic development: the case of silk. In Ohkawa et al. (1969), pp. 303–23.
Hibbert, H. 1960: *The Floating World of Japanese Fiction*. New York: Grove Press.
Hirota, M. 1980: *Fukuzawa Yukichi Kenkyu*. (2nd edn), Tokyo: University of Tokyo Press.
Hirschman, A. O. 1958: *The Strategy of Economic Development*. New Haven, Conn.: Yale University Press.
Hirschmeier, J. 1964: *The Origins of Entrepreneurship in Meiji Japan*. Cambridge, Mass.: Harvard University Press.
—— and Yui, T. 1975: *The Development of Japanese Business 1600–1973*. London: George Allen & Unwin.
Holden, K. C. 1983: Changing employment patterns of women. In D. W. Plath (ed.), *Work and Lifecourse in Japan*. Albany: State University of New York, pp. 34–45.
Hollerman, L. 1988: *Japan, Disincorporated, the Economic Liberalization Process*. Stanford: Hoover Institute Press.
Honjo, E. 1966. *Nihon Keizai Shiso-shi Kenkyu*. Tokyo: Nihon Hyoron-sha, vols 1 and 2.
Horie, Y. 1965: Modern entrepreneurship in Meiji Japan. In Lockwood (1965), pp. 183–208.
Hyodo, T. 1971: *Nihon ni okeru Roshikankei no Tenkai*. Tokyo: University of Tokyo Press.
Hoston, G. A. 1963: Japanese imperialism and agression: reconsiderations – I. *Journal of Asian Studies*, 22 (4), 469–72.
—— 1986: *Marxism and the Crisis of Development in Prewar Japan*. Princeton University Press.

Hozelitz, B. F. (ed.) 1968: *The Role of Small Industry in the Process of Economic Growth*. Paris and The Hague: Mouton.

Ichino, S. 1980: The structure of the labor force and patterns of mobility: 1950–1965. In Nishikawa (1980), pp. 41–66.

Ienage, S. 1979: *Japan's Last War*. (translated from Japanese original text, *Taiheiyo Senso*, Tokyo: Iwanami, 1968). Canberra: Australian National University Press.

Iida, K. 1987: *Shakai Seisaku no Kihon Mondai*. Tokyo: Aki Shobo.

Iida, T. and Yamada, H. 1975: *Shakaishihon no Keizaigaku*. Tokyo: Yuhikaku, in Iida and Yamada (eds) (1975), vol. 3.

—— (eds) 1975: *Nyumon Keizaigaku*. Tokyo: Yuhikaku.

Ike, N. 1968: War and modernisation. In Ward (1968), chapter VI.

—— 1969: *Beginning of Political Democracy in Japan*. New York: Greenwood.

Ikema, M. (ed.) 1986. Australia Keizai eno Shiten. Tokyo: Nichigo Chosa Iinkai (mimeo).

Imamichi, T. 1990: *Eco-Ethica*. Tokyo: Kodansha.

Inoguchi, T. and Okimoto, D. I. (eds) 1988: *The Political Economy of Japan: the Changing International Context, volume 2*. Stanford, California: Stanford University Press.

Ishi, H. 1974: Long-term changes of the government saving rate in Japan. *Economic Development and Cultural Change*, 22 (4), 615–33.

—— 1976: *Zaisei Kozo no Anteikoka: Builtin Stabilizer no Bunseki*. Tokyo: Toyo Keizai Shinpo-sha.

—— 1979: *Sozei Seisaku no Koka: Suryoteki Sekkin*. Tokyo: Toyo Keizai Shinpo-sha.

Ishii, R. 1980: *Nihon'no Seijisoshiki*. Tokyo: University of Tokyo.

—— 1985: *Meiji Tasho-ki no Keizai*. Tokyo: University of Tokyo Press.

Ishikawa, K. 1974: Meijiki ni okeru kigyosha katsudo no tokeiteki kansatsu. *Osaka Daigaku Keizaigaku*, 23 (4), 85–118.

Ishikawa, S. 1967. *Economic Development in Asian Perspective*. Tokyo: Kinokuniya.

—— 1981: *Essays on Technology, Employment and Institutions in Economic Development: Comparative Asian Experience*, Tokyo: Kinokuniya.

Ishiwata, S. 1975: Minkan kotei shihon toshi. In Ohkawa and Minami (1975), pp. 15–33.

Ishizaka, Y. 1965: Nihonshihonshugi seiritsu-shi. In Kajinishi et al. (1962), vol. 5.

Itagaki, Y. (ed.) 1970: *Nihon no Shigen Mondai*. Tokyo: Nihonkeizai Shinbun-sha.

Itoh, M. et al. 1991: *Sangyoseisaku no Keizaibunseki*. Tokyo: University of Tokyo Press.

Itoh, S. 1990: Jinko zoka, toshi-ka, shugyo kozo. In Umemura et al. (1988–1990), vol. 5, ch. 2.

—— and Kiyono, K. 1984: Trade and investment. In Komiya et al. (1984), ch. 5.

Itoh, T. 1989: Kokuze to kokusaku · tosei · keikaku. In Umemura et al. (1988–90), vol. 6, ch. 7.

—— and Watanabe, Y. (eds) 1987: *Shigemitsu Mamoru Shaki*. Tokyo: Chuokoron-sha.

Iwanami Shoten (ed.) 1984: *Kindai Nihon Sogo Nenpyo*, (2nd edn). Tokyo: Iwanami Shoten.
—— 1989: *Nihon Keizai-shi*. Tokyo: Iwanami Shoten.
—— 1991: (7th edn) Series Showa-shi. 14 vols.
Iwao, S. 1991: The quiet revolution: Japanese women today. *Japan Foundation Newsletter*, XIX (1), 1–9.
Jansen, M. B. 1975: *Japan and China from War to Peace, 1894–1972*, Chicago: Rand McNally.
Japan Culture Institute 1979: The bureaucracy: Japan's pool of leadership. In Murakami and Hirschmeier (1979), pp. 79–92.
JAPEC Group 1986: Seisan taikoku seikatsu shokoku kara dakkyaku-seyo. *Chuokokon*, Nov. 1986, pp. 78–90.
Jinushi, S. 1975–76: Welfare: social security, social overhead capital and pollution. *Japanese Economic Studies*, 4 (2), 59–82.
Johnson, C. 1982: *MITI and the Japanese Miracle: The Growth of Industrial Policy, 1925–1975*. Stanford, California: Stanford University Press.
—— 1988: Studies of Japanese political economy: a crises in theory. In *The Japan Foundation Newsletter*, 1 (3), 1–10.
Johnson, S. K. 1988: *Japan Through American Eyes*. Stanford, California: Stanford University Press.
Jones, L. Q. P. 1974: *Nihonno Keizaitosei, Senji Sengo no Keiken to Kyokun*. Tokyo: Nihonkeizai Shinbun-sha.
Jones, L. R. and Sakong, I. 1980: *Government, Business and Entrepreneurship in Economic Development, the Korean Case*. Cambridge, Mass.: Harvard University Press.
Kahn, H. 1970: *The Emerging Japanese Superstate, Challenge and Response*. Englewood Cliffs, NJ: Prentice-Hall.
—— and Peppa, T. 1978: *Soredemo Nihon wa Seicho suru*. Tokyo: Saimaru.
Kajima, M. 1968: *The Emergence of Japan as a World Power*. Rultand, Vermont, and Tokyo: Charles E. Tuttle.
Kajinishi, M. et al. 1962: *Nihon'niokeru Shihonshugi no Hattatsu*. Tokyo: University of Tokyo Press (Todaishinsho).
—— (ed.) 1965: *Nihonkeizaishi Taiku*. Tokyo: University of Tokyo Press.
Kanamori, H. 1966: Economic growth and the balance of payments. In Komiya (1966a), pp. 79–94.
—— 1968: Economic growth and exports. In Klein and Ohkawa (1968), pp. 303–25.
—— and Takase, Y. 1977: Keizai seicho to fukushi: GNP to NNW. In Okita and Uchida (1977), pp. 115–31.
Kaneda, H. 1969: Long-term changes in food consumption patterns in Japan. In Ohkawa et al. (1969), pp. 398–431.
Kato, M. 1987: The ongoing process of restructuring. *Economic Eye*, 8 (4), 4–7.
Kato, S. 1967: *Chusho Kigyo no Kokusai Hikaku*. Tokyo: Toyo Keizai Shinpo-sha.
Katzenstein, P. J. 1988: Japan, Switzerland of the Far East? In Inoguchi and Okimoto (1988), pp. 275–304.
Kawaguchi, H. 1970: Over-loan and the investment behaviour of firms. *Developing Economies*, 8 (4), 386–406.

—— and Kato (eds) 1970: *Nihon Nogyo to Keizaiseicho.* Tokyo: University of Tokyo Press.

Kawamura, M. 1990: *Ikyo no Showa Bungaku – 'Manshu' to Kindai Nihon.* Tokyo: Iwanami (*Shinsho* no. 144).

Kayo, N. (ed.) 1958: *Nippon Nogyo Kiso Tokei.* Tokyo: Norin Suisangyo Seisansei Kojo Kaigi.

Keizai Antei Honbu (Economic Stabilization Board), *see* (1) above.

Keizai Koho Center (Japan Institute for Social and Economic Affairs): *Japan: An International Comparison.* Tokyo (annual).

—— *Keizai Yoran* Tokyo (annual).

Kelley, A. C. and Williamson, J. G. 1974: *Lessons from Japanese Development: an Analytical Economic History.* Chicago: University of Chicago Press.

Kenneth, P. 1977: State and society in the interwar years. *Journal of Japanese Studies,* 3 (2) (Summer).

Kindainihon Kenkyukai (ed.) 1979: *Showaki no Gunbu.* Tokyo: Yamakawa Shuppan (Nenpo) 1.

—— 1980: *Bakumatsu Ishin no Nihon.*

—— 1982: *Taiheiyosenso.*

—— 1987: *Senji Keizai* (Nenpo).

Kinmonth, E. H. 1981: *The Self-made Man in Meiji Japanese Thought: From Samurai to Salary Man.* Berkeley Calif.: University of California Press.

Kirschen, E. S. et al. (eds) 1964: *Economic Policy in Our Time.* Amsterdam: North-Holland.

Klein, L. and Ohkawa, K. (eds) 1968: *Economic Growth: The Japanese Experience since the Meiji Era.* Homewood, Ill: Irwin/Nobleton, Ontario: Irwin–Dorsey.

Kobayashi, A. et al. (1981): *Gendai Nihon-no Zaisei Kinyu, Seifu to Kigyo.* Tokyo: Hakuto-shobo.

Kobayashi, H. 1975: *Daitowa Kyoeiken no Keisei to Hokai.* Tokyo: Ochanomizu-shobo.

Kobayashi, M. 1980: *Nihon no Kogyoka to Kangyo Haraisage.* Tokyo: Toyo Keizai Shinpo-sha.

Kodansha 1983: *Kodansha Encyclopaedia of Japan,* Tokyo, 8 vols plus index.

Kogane, Y. 1982: *Changing Value Patterns and their Impact on Economic Structure.* Tokyo: University of Tokyo Press.

Koh, B. C. 1989: *Japan's Administrative Elite.* Berkeley, Calif.: University of California Press.

Koike, K. 1978: Japan's industrial relations: characteristics and problems. *Japanese Economic Studies,* 7 (1), 42–90.

Kojima, K. 1958: *Nihon Boeki to Keizai Hatten.* Tokyo: Kunimoto Shobo.

Komiya, R. (ed.) 1966a: *Postwar Economic Growth in Japan* (translated by R. Ozaki). Berkeley, Calif.: University of California Press.

—— 1966b: The supply of personal savings. In Komiya (1966a), pp. 157–81.

—— 1966c: Japan. In National Bureau of Economic Research (1966), pp. 39–90.

—— 1975a: *Gendai Nihon Keizai Kenkyu.* Tokyo: University of Tokyo Press.

—— 1975b: Planning in Japan. In M. Bornstein (ed.), *Economic Planning, East and West.* Cambridge, Mass.: Ballinger.

—— 1984: Jo-sho. In Komiya et al. (1984), Introductory chapter.
—— and Itoh, M. 1988: Japan's international trade and trade policy, 1955–1984. In Inoguchi and Okimoto (1988), pp. 173–224.
—— and Iwata, K. 1973: *Kigyo Kinyu no Riron: Shihon Cost to Zaimu Seisaku*. Tokyo: Nihonkeizai Shinbun-sha.
—— and Yamamoto, K. 1981: Japan: the officer in charge of economic affairs. *History of Political Economy*, 13 (3), 600–27.
—— et al. (eds) 1984: *Nihon no Sangyo Seisaku*. Tokyo: University of Tokyo Press.
—— and Yokobori, K. 1991: *Japan's Industrial Policies in the 1980s*. Tokyo: Research Institute of International Trade and Industry, Studies in International Trade and Industry 5.
Kosai, Y. 1972: *Shiryo Keizaihakusho*. Tokyo: Nihonkeizai Shinbun-sha.
—— 1981: *Kodo Seicho no Jidai*. Tokyo: Nihon Hyoron-sha.
—— 1986: *The Era of High-Speed Growth: Notes on the Postwar Japanese Economy* (English translation by J. Kaminski). Tokyo: University of Tokyo Press.
—— and Ogino, Y. 1984: *The Contemporary Japanese Economy*. London: Macmillan.
—— 1984: Fukko-ki. In Komiya et al. (1984), ch. 1.
—— 1987: The politics of economic management. In Yamamura and Yasuba (1987), pp. 555–92.
—— 1989: Kodoseichoki no keizai seisaku. In Umemura et al. (1988–90), vol. 8, ch. 5.
—— and Harada, Y. 1988: Economic development in Japan: a reconsideration. In Scalapino et al. (1988).
Kosobud, R. and Minami, R. (eds) 1977: *Econometric Studies of Japan*. Urbana, Ill.: University of Illinois Press.
Krasner, S. P. 1988: Japan and the United States: prospects for stability. In Inoguchi and Okimoto (1988), pp. 381–413.
Krause, L. B. and Sueo, S. 1976: Japan and the world economy. In Patrick and Rosovsky (1976a), pp. 383–458.
Kubota, A. 1969: *Higher Civil Servants in Postwar Japan*. Princeton, NJ: Princeton University Press.
Kumagai, H. 1972: *Keizaiseisaku no Mokuhyo*. Tokyo: Nihonkeizai Shinbun-sha.
—— et al. (eds) 1979: *Keizaigaku Daijiten*. Tokyo: Toyo Keizai Shinpo-sha.
Kuznets, S. 1937: *National Income and Capital Formation*. New York: National Bureau of Economic Research.
—— 1955: Economic growth and income inequality. *American Economic Review*, 45 (1), 1–28.
—— 1958: Underdeveloped countries and the pre-industrial phase in the advanced countries: an attempt at comparison. In Agarwala and Singh (1958), pp. 135–53.
—— 1963: Notes on the take-off. In Rostow (1963), pp. 22–43.
—— 1966: *Modern Economic Growth: Rate, Structure, and Spread*. New Haven, Conn.: Yale University Press.
—— 1967: Quantitative aspects of the economic growth of nations: level and structure of foreign trade: long-term trends. *Economic Development and Cultural Change*, 15 (2), 1–140.

—— 1968: Notes on Japan's Economic Growth. In Klein and Ohkawa (1968), pp. 385–422.

—— 1971: *Economic Growth of Nations: Total Output and Production Structure.* Cambridge, Mass.: Harvard University Press.

—— 1973: Modern economic growth: findings and reflections. *American Economic Review*, 63 (3), 247–58.

Kyogoku, J. 1985: Modernization and national ethos: Japan in the twentieth century. *Japan Foundation Newsletter*, XIII (3), 1–8.

—— 1987: *The Political Dynamics of Japan* (translated by N. Ike from original text *Nihon no Seiji*, Tokyo University Press, 1983). Tokyo: University of Tokyo Press.

Kyoiku-sha (ed.) 1981: *Gyosei Kiko.* Tokyo: Kyoiku-sha, 22 vols.

Landes, D. S. 1965: Japan and Europe: contrasts in Industrialization. In Lockwood (1965), pp. 93–182.

—— 1969: *The Unbound Prometheus: Technological Change and Industrial Development in Western Europe from 1750 to the present.* London: Cambridge University Press.

Lehmann, J.-P. 1982: *The Roots of Modern Japan.* London: Macmillan.

Levine, S. 1958: *Industrial Relations in Postwar Japan.* Urbana, Ill.: University of Illinois Press.

Lewis, A. 1955: *The Theory of Economic Growth.* London: George Allen & Unwin.

—— 1958a: Economic development with unlimited supplies of labour. In Agarwala and Singh (1958), pp. 400–49.

Livingston, J. et al. (eds) 1973: *The Japan Reader, Imperial Japan: 1800–1945.* London: Pelican Books (first published in USA in 1973).

Lockwood, W. W. 1955: *The Economic Development of Japan: Growth and Structural Change 1868–1938.* Oxford University Press.

—— 1968: *The Economic Development of Japan: Growth and Structural Change,* (expanded edn). Princeton, NJ: Princeton University Press.

—— (ed.) 1965: *The State and Economic Enterprise in Japan: Essays in the Political Economy of Growth.* Princeton, NJ: Princeton University Press.

LTES, see *Choki Keizai Tokei.*

Ludz, T. 1972: The family: the source of human resources. In Berg (1972), pp. 177–97.

Macpherson, W. J. 1987: *The Economic Development of Japan, 1868–1941.* London: Macmillan.

Maddison, A. 1964: *Economic Growth in the West: Comparative Experience in Europe and North America.* New York and London: Twentieth Century Fund and George Allen & Unwin.

—— 1969: *Economic Growth in Japan and the USSR.* London: George Allen & Unwin.

Mainichi Daily News, 1975: *Fifty years of Light and Darkness: The Hirohito Years.* Tokyo: Mainichi Shinbun-sha.

Makino, F. 1980: 1930–Nendai no Rodoryoku Ido. *Keizai Kenkyu*, 31 (4), 362–7.

Marcewski, J. 1963: The take-off hypothesis and French experience. In Rostow (1963), pp. 119–38.

Marchal, J. and Ducros, B. (eds) 1968: *The Distribution of National Income*. London: Macmillan.

Marshall, B. K. 1983: *Capitalism and Nationalism in Pre-war Japan: the Ideology of the Business Elite, 1868–1941*. Stanford, Calif.: Stanford University Press.

Martin, A. 1973: Japanese mining labor: the Miike strike. In Livingston et al. (1976), pp. 489–94.

Maruo, N. 1972: A measure of welfare standards of the Japanese people. *Annals of the Institute of Economic Research*, 3, 101–34.

Maruyama, M. 1974: *Studies in the Intellectual History of Tokugawa Japan* (translated by M. Hane). Tokyo: University of Tokyo Press.

—— 1979: *Thought and Behaviour in Modern Japanese Politics* (expanded edn, ed. Morris I.). Tokyo, Oxford, New York: Oxford University Press (Asian College Texts).

—— 1986: *Bunmeiron no Gairyaku'o Yumu*. Tokyo: Iwanami (Shinsho), 3 vols.

Masamura, K. 1978: *Nihon Keizairon*. Tokyo: Toyo Keizai Shinpo-sha.

Masui, Y. 1969: The supply price of labor: farm family workers. In Ohkawa et al. (1969), pp. 222–49.

Matsubara, I. 1893: *Saiankoku no Tokyo*. Tokyo: Iwanami.

Matsuishima, H. 1973: Senji keizai tosei no seiritsukatei to sangyoseisaku. In Ando (1973), chapter 8.

—— 1990: Sekaishi no game-o nihon ga koerutoki. In Chuokoron-sha, May 1990, pp. 138–69.

Matsumoto, K. 1990: Sekaishi no game o Nihon ga koerutoki. Chuokoron, May 1990, pp. 138–69.

Maynard, G. 1962: *Economic Development and the Price Level*. London: Macmillan.

McLaren, W. 1973: A political history of Japan during the Meiji Era. In Livingston et al. (1973), pp. 203–21.

McRae, N. 1967: The rising sun. *Economist*, 27 May.

—— 1980: Must Japan slow? *Economist*, 23 February.

Meadows, D. H. et al. (eds) 1972. *The Limits to Growth: a Report for the Club of Rome's Project on the Predicament of Mankind*. New York: Universe.

Mikuriya, T. 1989: Senji sengo no shakai. In Umemura et al. (1988–90) vol. 7, ch. 5.

Minami, R. 1965: *Tetsudo to Denryoku*, LTES, vol. 12.

—— 1969: The supply of farm labor and the 'turning point' in the Japanese economy. In Ohkawa et al. (1969), pp. 270–99.

—— 1973: *The Turning Point in Economic Development: Japan's Experience*. Tokyo: Kinokuniya.

—— 1976: The introduction of electric power and its impact on the manufacturing industries: with special reference to smaller scale plants. In Patrick (1976), pp. 299–325.

—— 1977: Mechanical power in the industrialization of Japan. *Journal of Economic History*, 37 (4), 935–58.

—— 1981: *Nihon no Keizai Hatten*. Tokyo: Toyo Keizai Shinpo-sha.

—— 1986: *The Economic Development of Japan: a Quantitative Study*. London: Macmillan.

—— 1987: *Power Revolution in the Industrialization of Japan: 1885–1940*. Tokyo: Kinokuniya.

—— and Ono, A. 1981: Behaviour of income shares in a labor surplus economy: Japan's experience. *Economic Development and Cultural Change*, 29 (2), 309–24.

Mishima, M. 1990: High-tech automation for a labor shortage. *Economic Eye*, 11 (2), 29–31, summer 1990.

Miwa, R. 1979: Takahashi zaiseiki no keizaiseisaku. In *Tokyo Daigaku*, Shakai Kenkyu Kai (ed.). Tokyo: University of Tokyo Press.

—— 1987: *Nihon Keizaishi-Kindai* (3rd edn). Tokyo: Nihonhoso Shuppan Kyokai.

—— 1989: Sengo minshuka to keizaisaiken. In Umemura et al. (1988–90), vol. 7, ch. 3.

Miyamoto, M. 1990: Sangyoka to kaishasheido no hatten. In Umemura et al. (1988–90), vol. 4, ch. 5.

—— and Nakagawa, K. (eds) (1971–7): *Nihon Keiei-shi Koza*. Tokyo: Nihon Keizaishinbun.

Miyazaki, M. and Itoh, O. 1989: Senji sengo no sangyo to kigyo. In Umemura et al. (1988–90), vol. 7, ch. 4.

Miyazawa, K. 1964: The dual structure of the Japanese economy and its growth pattern. *Developing Economies*, 2 (2), 147–70.

Mizoguchi, T. 1970: *Personal Savings and Consumption in Postwar Japan*, Tokyo: Kinokuniya.

—— and Takayama, N. 1984: *Equity and Poverty under the Rapid Economic Growth: Japanese Experience*. Tokyo: Kinokuniya.

—— et al. (eds) 1978: Sengo Nihon no shotoku bunpu II, *Keizai Kenkyu*, 29 (1), 44–60.

Mizuno, A. 1973: *Chingin Kozo Hendoron*. Tokyo: Shinhyoron.

Mizuta, H. 1988: Historical introduction. In Sugiyama and Mizuta (1988), pp. 3–33.

Mochida, N. 1990: Toshino seibi to kaihatsu. In Umemura et al. (1988–90), vol. 5.

Morikawa, H. (ed.) 1977: *Sengo Sangyoshi eno Shogen, Kyo'daika Jidai*. Tokyo: Mainichi Shinbun-sha.

Morishima, M. 1982: *Why has Japan 'Succeeded'?* Cambridge: Cambridge University Press.

Morris, I. 1960: *Nationalism and the Right Wing in Japan: a Study of Postwar Trends*. Oxford University Press.

Morris-Suzuki, T. 1989: *A History of Japanese Economic Thought*. London: Routledge.

Moulden, F. V. 1979: *Japan, China and the Modern World Economy*. Cambridge University Press.

Murakami, H. 1982: *Japan; the Years of Trial 1919–52*. Tokyo: Kodansha International.

—— 1983: *Kuni Yaburete*. (Originally written and published in English in 1982 as *Japan: the Years of Trial, 1919–52*. Tokyo: The Japan Culture's Institute). Tokyo: Kodansha International.

Murakami, Y. 1987a: Gendainihon-no seiji keizai model. In NIRA (1987a), ch. 1, part 1.

—— 1987b: The Japanese model of political economy. In Yamamura and Yasuba (1987), part I.

—— and Hirschmeier, J. (eds) 1979: *Politics and Economics in Contemporary Japan*. Tokyo: Japan Cultural Institute.

Muramatsu, M. 1981: *Sengo Nihonno Kanryosei*. Tokyo: Toyo Keizai Shinpo-sha.

—— and Krauss, S. 1987: The conservation policy line and the development of patterned pluralism. In Yamamura and Yasuba (1987), 516–54.

Murphy, T. 1989: Power without purpose, the crisis of Japan's global finance dominance. *Harvard Business Review*, March–April.

Musgrave, R. A. and Peacock, A. T. (eds) 1958: *Classics in the Theory of Public Finance*. London: Macmillan.

—— 1969: *Fiscal Systems*. New Haven, Conn.: Yale University Press.

Muto, H. 1984: Jidosha sangyo. In Komiya et al. (1984), ch. 11.

Muto, I. 1970: The December 1969 election: an analysis – *AMPO* Interviews. *AMPO*, 3–4 March 1970, pp. 12–20.

—— (ed.) 1985: *Soft-ka to GNP Statistics*. Tokyo: Ministry of Finance.

Nagai, M. 1971: *Higher Education in Japan: its Take-off and Crash*. University of Tokyo Press.

—— and Urrutia, M. (eds) 1985: *Meiji Ishin: Restoration and Revolution*. Tokyo: United Nations University Press.

Nagamine, H. (ed.) 1981: *Nation building and Regional Development. The Japanese Experience*. Tokyo: Maruzen Asia.

Najita, T. 1987: *Visions of Virtue in Tokugawa Japan – the Kaitokudo Merchant Academy of Osaka*. Chicago, Ill.: The University of Chicago Press.

Nakagawa, K. 1981: Organised entrepreneurship in the course of the industrialization of prewar Japan. In Nagamine (1981).

—— 1985: Japanese shipping in the nineteenth and twentieth centuries: strategy and organization. In Nakagawa, K. (ed.), *Business History of Shipping Strategy and Structure*. Tokyo: Tokyo University Press.

—— et al. (eds) 1976–84 Proceedings of Fuji Conference: *Strategy and Structure of Big Business* (1976); *Social Order and Entrepreneurship* (1977); *Marketing and Finance in the Course of Industrialization* (1978); *Labour and Management* (1979); *Government and Business* (1979); *Overseas Business Activities* (1984). Tokyo University Press.

Nakagawa, Y. 1979: Japan, the welfare super-power. *Journal of Japanese Studies*, 5 (1), Winter.

Nakamura, J. I. 1966. *Agricultural Production and the Economic Development in Japan*. Princeton: Princeton University Press.

Nakamura, S. 1982: *Chuken Kigyo-ron, 1960 nendai to 1970 nendai*. Tokyo: Toyo Keizai Shinpo-sha.

Nakamura, T. 1966: The modern Industries and the traditional Industries at the early stage of the Japanese economy. *Developing Economies*, 4 (4), 567–93.

—— 1971: *Economic Growth in Prewar Japan*. New Haven, Conn.: Yale University Press.

—— 1981: *The Postwar Japanese Economy: its Development and Structure*. Tokyo: University of Tokyo Press.

—— 1983a: *Economic Growth in Prewar Japan* (translated by Robert A. Feldman). New Haven, Conn.: Yale University Press.

—— 1983b: *Senjinihon no Kahoku Keizaishihai.* Tokyo: Yamakawa Shuppan-sha.
—— 1984: *Nihon Keizai: Sono Seicho to Kozo* (2nd edn, 5th impression). Tokyo: University of Tokyo Press.
—— 1985: *Economic Development of Modern Japan* (in collaboration with B. R. G. Grace) Tokyo: Ministry of Foreign Affairs.
—— 1986: *Showa Keizai-shi.* Tokyo: Iwanami.
—— 1989: Gaisetsu 1937–54. In Umemura et al. (1988–90), vol. 7, ch. 1.
—— and Hara, A. 1972: Keizai shintaisei. In *Nihonseijigakkai Nenpo.* Tokyo: Iwanami.
—— and Odaka, K. 1990: Gaisetsu 1914–37. In Umemura et al. (1988–90), vol. 6.
Nakano, M. 1986: *Nihongata Seisaku Kettei no Henryo.* Tokyo: Toyo Keizai Shinpo-sha.
—— 1985: *Meiji Taisho-ki no Keizai.* Tokyo: University of Tokyo Press.
—— 1986: *Jiminto Seiken.* Tokyo: Chuokoron-sha.
Nakayama, I. 1960: The Japanese economy and the role of the government. *Hitotsubashi Journal of Economics,* 1 (1), 1–12.
—— and Shinohara M. (eds) 1969: *Nihon no Keizai Hatten: Kogyoka to Mirai.* Tokyo: Ushio Shuppansha.
Naramoto, S. 1982: *Ninomiya Sontoku* (14th edn). Tokyo: Iwanami (Shinsho).
—— 1979: *Edojidai no Political Economy.* Tokyo: Nihon Hyoron-sha.
National Bureau of Economic Research 1966: *Foreign Tax Policies and Economic Growth.* New York: Columbia University Press.
Natsume Soseki. 1988: Mankan Tokoro Dokoro (first published in 1909) Tokyo: Chikuma (Bunko) Soseki Zenshu, Vol. 7.
NIRA, see Sogokaihatsu Kenkyu Kiko.
Nishibe, S. 1975: Socio Economics. Tokyo: Chuokoron-sha.
—— 1990: Dai-sakkaku Jidai. Tokyo: Shincho-sha.
Nishikawa, S. 1979: *Edojidai no Political Economy.* Tokyo: Nihon Hyoron-sha.
—— 1980: Fukuzawa Momosuke, Kurosawa Shoemon to Okuheishoko. *Nihon Keizai Zasshi,* 156 (3), 60–76.
—— 1983: Wasurerareta Japanologist. *Economist (Tokyo),* 25 January.
—— 1985a: *Nihon Keizai no Seicho-shi.* Tokyo: Toyo Keizai Shinpo-sha.
—— 1985b: *Fukuzawa Yukichi to san-nin no Koshin-tachi.* Nihon Hyoron-sha, Econo Books, no 9.
—— 1988: The historical legacy in 'modern' Japan: competition, paper currency and benevolence. *The Japan Foundation Newsletter,* XVI (1), 1–8.
—— (ed.) 1980: *The Labor Market in Japan: Selected Readings* (translated by Ross Mouer). Tokyo: Japan Foundation.
—— and Abe, T. 1990: Gaisetsu 1885–1914. In Umemura et al. (1988–90), vol. 4.
Noda, T. 1979: Prices. In Ohkawa and Shinohara (1979), pp. 219–28.
Noguchi, Y. 1986: The development and present state of public finance. In Shibata (1986), ch. 2.
—— 1987: *Nihonzaisei no Chokisenryaku.* Tokyo: Nihonkeizai Shinbun-sha.
Noma, H. 1956: *Zone of Emptiness.* Cleveland and New York: World.

Norman, E. H. 1940: *Japan's Emergence as a Modern State: Political and Economic Problems of the Meiji Period.* New York: Institute of Pacific Relations.

North, D. C. 1955: Location theory and regional economic growth. *Journal of Political Economy,* 63, Feb.–Dec., 243–58.

Nurkse, R. 1953: *Problems of Capital Formation in Underdeveloped Countries.* Oxford: Basil Blackwell.

Obi, K. 1980: The theory of labour supply: some new perspectives and some implications. In Nishikawa (1980), pp. 41–66.

Odaka, K. 1982: An analysis of the personal consumption expenditures in Japan, 1892–1967. In *Essays in Development Economics in Honor of Harry T. Oshima.* Metro Manila: Philippine Institute for Development Studies, pp. 335–56.

—— 1989a: Niju kozo. In Umemura et al. (1988–90), vol. 6, ch. 3.

—— 1989b: Seicho no kiseki (2). In Umemura et al. (1988–90), vol. 8, ch. 4.

—— 1990: Sangyo no ninaite. In Umemura et al. (1988–90), vol. 4, ch. 4.

Ogura, M. and Yoshino, N. 1984: Zaisei to zaiseitoyushi. In Komiya et al. (1984), ch. 4.

Ogura, T. (ed.) 1967: *Agricultural Development in Modern Japan.* Tokyo: Fuji.

Ohkawa, K. 1968: Changes in national income distribution by factor share in Japan. In Marchal and Ducros (1968).

—— 1969: *Nihon Keizai Bunseki: Seicho to Kozo.* Tokyo: Shunju-sha.

—— 1972: *Differential Structure and Agriculture: Essays on Dualistic Growth.* Tokyo: Kinokuniya.

—— 1974: *Nihon Keizai no Kozo: Rekishiteki Shitenkara.* Tokyo: Keiso-shobo.

—— 1975: Keizai no hatten kozo: nihon no keiken no kokusaiteki igi. In Ohkawa and Minami (1975), pp. 178–209.

—— 1976: *Keizai Hatten to Nihon no Keiken.* Tokyo: Taimeido.

—— 1978: Past economic growth of Japan in comparison with the Western case: trend acceleration and differential structure. In Tsuru (1978), pp. 3–15.

—— 1979a: Aggregate growth and product allocation. In Ohkawa and Shinohara (1979), pp. 3–33.

—— 1979b: Product structure. In Ohkawa and Shinohara (1979), pp. 34–58.

——, Johnston, B. F. and Kaneda, K. (eds) 1969: *Agriculture and Economic Growth: Japan's Experience.* Tokyo: University of Tokyo Press.

—— and Minami, R. (eds) 1975: *Kindai Nihon no Keizai Hatten: Choki Keizaitokei ni yoru Bunseki.* Tokyo: Toyo Keizai Shinpo-sha.

—— and Hayami, Y. (eds) 1978: *Papers and Proceedings of the Conference on Japan's Development Experience and the Contemporary Developing Countries: Issues for Comparative Analysis.* Tokyo: International Development Center of Japan.

—— and —— (eds) 1973: *Nihon Keizai no Choki Bunseki, Kozo Hado.* Tokyo: Nihon Keizai Shinbun-sha.

——and Rosovsky, H. 1962: Economic fluctuations in prewar Japan: a preliminary analysis of cycles and long swings. *Hitotsubashi Journal of Economics,* 3 (1), 1–33.

—— and —— 1964: The role of agriculture in modern Japanese economic development. In Eichen and Witt (1964), pp. 45–69.

—— and —— 1965: A century of Japanese economic growth. In Lockwood (1965), pp. 47–92.

—— and —— 1973: *Japanese Economic Growth: Trend Acceleration in the Twentieth Century*. Stanford, Calif.: Stanford University Press.

—— and Shinohara, M. (eds) 1979: *Patterns of Japanese Economic Development: a Quantitative Appraisal*. New Haven, Conn.: Yale University Press.

—— et al. 1957: The Growth of the Japanese Economy since 1878. Tokyo: Kinokuniya.

—— et al. (1965–88). See LTES.

Ohkouchi, K. 1979: *Kurai Tanima no Jiden – Tsuiku to Iken*. Tokyo: Chuokoron (Shinsho).

Ohoka, S. 1957: *Fires on the Plain*. New York: Alfred A. Knopf.

Oka, Y. 1986: *Five Political Leaders of Modern Japan* (translated by A. Franson and P. Murroy). University of Tokyo Press.

Okayama, R. 1979: Industrial relations in Great Britain and Japan, from the 1880s to the 1920s. In K. Nakagawa et al. (1979), vol. 4, pp. 207–37.

Okazaki, H. 1966: *Nihon no Rodoryoku Mondai*. Tokyo: Kobun-sha.

—— 1977: *Koreika Shakai eno Tenkan*. Tokyo: Kōbunsha.

Okimoto, D. I. and Inoguchi, T. 1988a: Introduction. In Inoguchi and Okimoto (1988), pp. 1–20.

—— 1988b: Political inclusivity: the domestic structure of trade. In Inoguchi and Okimoto (1988), pp. 305–44.

—— 1989: *Between MITI and the Market: Japanese Industrial Policy for High Technology*. Stanford. Calif.: Stanford University Press.

Okita, S. 1983: *Japan's Challenging Years: Reflections of my Lifetime*. Canberra: Australian National University, Australia–Japan Research Centre.

—— and Uchida, T. (eds) 1977: *Kokusai Keizai Symposium: Atarashii Han-ei o Motomete*. Tokyo: Nihon Keizai Shinbun-sha.

Olson, M. 1965: *The Logic of Collective Action*. Cambridge, Mass: Harvard University Press.

Ono, A. 1973: *Sengo Nihon no Chingin Kettei: Rodoshijo no Kozo Henka to Sono Eikyo*. Tokyo: Toyo Keizai Shinpo-sha.

—— 1980: Comparative perspectives on labor's share. In Nishikawa (ed.) (1980), pp. 255–72.

—— and Watanabe, T. 1976: Changes in income inequality in the Japanese economy. In Patrick (1976), pp. 363–89.

Ono, G. 1922: *Expenditure of the Sino-Japanese War*. Oxford: Oxford University press.

Orchard, J. 1978: Government suppression of the labor movement. In Livingston et al. (1976), pp. 332–5.

Oshima, K. et al. (eds) 1983: *Jinbutsu – Nihon Shihon Shugi*. Tokyo: University of Tokyo, 4 vols.

Otsuka, K. 1986: Keizai hatten to kogyoka – nichigo no hikaku. In Ikema (ed.) (1986), ch. 3.

Ozawa, T. 1974: *Japan's Technological Challenge to the West, 1950–1974: Motivation and Accomplishment*. Cambridge, Mass.: Massachusetts Institute of Technology Press.

Passin, H. 1965: *Society and Education in Japan*. Columbia University, Teachers College Press.

Patrick, H. T. 1967: Japan 1868–1914. In Cameron (1967), pp. 239–89.
—— 1968: The financing of the public sector in postwar Japan. In Klein and Ohkawa (1968), pp. 326–55.
—— (ed.) 1976: *Japanese Industrialization and Its Consequences*. Berkeley, Calif.: University of California Press.
—— and Rosovsky, H. (eds) 1976a: *Asia's New Giant: How the Japanese Economy Works*. Washington, DC: The Brookings Institution.
—— and Rosovsky, H. 1976b: Japan's economic performance: an overview, In Patrick and Rosovsky (1976a), pp. 1–61.
Paukert, F. 1973: Income distribution at different levels of development: a survey of evidence. *International Labour Review*, 108 (2–3), 97–117.
Peacock, A. T. and Wiseman, J. 1960: *The Growth of Public Expenditure in the United Kingdom*, Princeton, NJ: Princeton University Press.
Peck, M. and Goto, A. 1981. Technology and economic growth: the case of Japan. *Research Policy*, 10 (3), 222–4.
—— and Tamura, S. 1976: Technology: In Patrick and Rosovsky (1976a), pp. 525–85.
Pempel, T. J. 1982: *Policy and Politics in Japan, Creative Conservatism*. Philadelphia: Temple University Press.
Phelps Brown, E. H. 1968: *A Century of Pay*. London: Macmillan/New York: St Martin's Press.
Pusey, M. 1991: *Economic Rationalism in Canberra: a Nation-Building State Changes its Mind*. Cambridge University Press.
Pyle, K. B. 1988: Japan, the world, and the twenty-first century. In Inoguchi and Okimoto (1988), pp. 446–86.
Ranis, G. 1955: The community-centered entrepreneur in Japanese development. *Explorations in Entrepreneurial History*, 8 (2), 88–98.
—— 1969: The financing of Japanese economic development. In Ohkawa et al. (1969), pp. 37–57.
Reischauer, E. O. 1954: *The United States and Japan*. Cambridge. Mass.: Harvard University Press.
—— 1977: *The Japanese*. Cambridge, Mass.: Harvard University Press.
Rekishigaku Kenkyukai (ed.) (1958–59): *Meijiishin-shi Kenkyu Koza*. Tokyo, 6 vols and supplementary volumes.
Reynolds, L. G. 1983: The spread of economic growth to the Third World: 1950–1980. *Journal of Economic Literature*, 21 (3), 941–80.
Ritschl, H. 1958: Communal economy and market economy. In Musgrave and Peacock (1958).
Rosenberg, N. 1972: *Technology and American Economic Growth*. New York: Harper & Row.
Rosovsky, H. 1959: Japanese capital formation: the role of the public sector. *Journal of Economic History*, XIX (3), 350–73.
—— 1961: *Capital Formation in Japan: 1868–1940*. Glencoe, Ill.: The Free Press.
—— 1966: Japan's transition to modern economic growth, 1868–1885. In Rosovsky (1966).
—— (ed.) 1966: *Industrialization in Two Systems: Essays in Honor of Alexander Gerschenkron*. New York: John Wiley, pp. 91–139.
—— 1968: Rumbles in rice-fields: Professor Nakamura vs the official statistics. *Journal of Asian Studies*, 27 (2), 347–60.

Rostow, W. W. 1960: *The Stages of Economic Growth: a Non-communist Manifesto*. London: Cambridge University press.
—— (ed.) 1963: *The Economics of Take-Off into Sustained Growth*. London: Macmillan.
—— 1978: *The World Economy: History and Prospect*. London: Macmillan.
Saito, O. 1988: Daikaikon Jinko Sho'no-keizai. In Umemura et al. (1988–90), vol. 1, chapter 4.
Sakamoto, T. 1971: *Japanese History*. Tokyo: International Society for Educational Information Press, publication no. 42.
Sakai, T. 1988: Jinsei-kara 'Minpu'-e' – keizaishiso no tenkan'. *Shukan Asahi Hyakka*, 91. Tokyo: Asahi Shinbun.
Sano, Y. 1989: *Kigyonai Rodo Shijo*. Tokyo: Yuhikaku.
Samsom, G. B. 1966: *The Western World and Japan*. London: Barrie and Jenkins.
Sato, K. 1977: A model of investment behaviour: fixed investment and capacity in Japanese manufacturing, 1952–1963. In Kosobud and Minami (1977), 75–113.
Sato, S. 1979: Response to the West: the Korean and Japanese patterns. In A. M. Carig (ed.), *Japan: a Comparative View*. Princeton, NJ: Princeton University Press.
—— and Matsuzaki, T. 1986: *Jiminto Seiken*. Tokyo: Chuokoron-sha.
Sawa, T. 1984: *Kodo Seicho, Rinen to Seisaku-no Dojidai*. Tokyo: NHK Books.
Sawamoto, M. 1982: *Kokyotoshi 100-nen no Ayumi*. Tokyo: Taisei Shuppan.
Scalopino, R. A. et al. (eds) 1984: *Asian Economic Development – Present and Future*. University of California, Berkeley, Institute of East Asian Studies.
Schumpeter, E. B. 1940: *The Industrialisation of Japan and Manchuko 1930–1940*. New York: Macmillan.
Sekiyama, N. 1942: *Nihon Jinkoshi*. Tokyo: Shikai Shobo.
Shakaihosho Kenkyujo (Social Development Research Institute) (ed.) 1973: *Shakaihosho Suijun Kiso Tokei*. Tokyo: Toko Keizai Shinpo-sha.
Sheridan, K. 1977: Understanding the Japanese economy: a review of the Japanese national economic plans: 1956–1986. *The Australian Quarterly*, 49 (3), 75–93.
—— 1984: Softnomisation – the growth of the service sector in Japan. *Journal of Contemporary Asia*, 14 (4), 410–30.
—— (ed.) 1992: *The Australian Economy in the Japanese Mirror*. University of Queensland Press.
Shibagaki, K. 1979: Keizai shintaisei. In University of Tokyo, Shakai Kenkyu-jo (ed.) (1979).
Shibata, T. (ed.) 1986: *Public Finance in Japan*. Tokyo: University of Tokyo Press.
Shimada, H. 1981: *Earnings Structure and Human Investment: a comparison between the United States and Japan*. Tokyo: Kogaku-sha.
—— 1990: Asset inflation and the strained social fabric. *Japan Echo*, XVII, Special Issue, 13–20.
Shinbo, H. et al. 1975: *Suryo Keizaishi Nyumon: Nihon no Zenkogyoka Shakai*. Tokyo: Nihonhyoron.

—— 1978: *Kinsei no Bukka to Keizai Hatten: Zenkogyoka e no Suryoteki Sekkin*. Tokyo: Toyo Keizai Shinpo-sha.
Shinbo, S. 1980: *Gendai Nihon Keizai no Kaimei: Stagflation*. Tokyo: Toyo Keizai Shinpo-sha.
Shinha, R. P. 1969: Unresolved issues in Japan's early economic development. *Journal of Political Economy*, XVI (2) (June).
Shinohara, M. 1961: *Nihon Keizai no Seicho to Junkan*. Tokyo: Sobun-sha.
—— 1962: *Growth and Cycles in the Japanese Economy*. Tokyo: Kinokuniya.
—— 1964: *Keizai Seicho no Kozo: Tanki Nihon Keizai no Bunseki*. Tokyo: Kunimoto Shobo.
—— 1967: *Kojin Shohi Shishitsu*, (Personal Consumption Expenditures) LTES, vol. 6.
—— 1968a: A survey of the Japanese literature on small industry. In Hozelitz (1968), pp. 1–113.
—— 1968b: Patterns and some structural changes in Japan's postwar industrial growth. In Klein and Ohkawa (1968), pp. 278–302.
—— 1969: Nihon no kogyoka: totatsuten no sho-tokucho. In Nakayama and Shinohara (1969), pp. 21–62.
—— 1970: *Structural Changes in Japan's Economic Development*. Tokyo: Kinokuniya.
—— 1972: *Kokogyo* (Mining and Manufacturing), LTES, vol. 10.
—— 1979a: Manufacturing. In Ohkawa and Shinohara (1979), pp. 104–21.
—— 1979b: Consumption. In Ohkawa and Shinohara (1979), pp. 159–76.
—— 1982: *Industrial Growth, Trade, and Dynamic Patterns in the Japanese Economy*. Tokyo: University of Tokyo Press.
—— 1986: *Nihon Keizai Kogi*. Tokyo: Toyo Keizai Shinpo-sha.
—— and Fujino, S. (eds) 1967: *Nihon no Keizai Seicho*. Tokyo: Nihon Keizai Shinbun-sha, pp. 139–78.
Shinotsuka, E. 1986: Women in labour force. Economic view from Japan (translated from *Ekonomisto*, 13 July 1982; selection from *Economic Eye*). Tokyo: Keizai Koho Center, pp. 157–65.
Shionoya, Y. 1964: Patterns of industrial growth in the United States and Sweden: a critique of Hoffmann's hypothesis. *Hitotsubashi Journal of Economics*, 5 (1), 52–89.
—— 1967: Kogyo hatten no keitai. In Shinohara and Fujino (1967).
—— 1968: Patterns of industrial development. In Klein and Ohkawa (1968), pp. 69–109.
—— and Yamazawa, I. 1973: Kogyo seicho to gaikoku boeki. In Ohkawa and Hayami (1973), pp. 331–63.
Shirai, T. and Shimada, H. 1979: Japan. In T. Dunlop and W. Galenson (eds), *Labor in the Twentieth Century*. New York: Academic Press.
Shiroyama, S. 1977: *Nezumi*. Tokyo: Bungei Shunju-sha (Bunshun Bunko).
Shoda, K. 1971: *Nihon Shihonshugi to Kindaika*. Tokyo: Nihon Hyoron-sha.
Shoji, H. and Miyamoto, K. 1977: Environmental pollution in Japan. *Japanese Economic Studies*, 5 (4), 3–40.
Shiozaki, H. 1979: Tōseiha no keizaiseisakushisō. In Kindainihon Kenkyukai (1979 Nenpo), vol. 1.
Shively, D. A. 1976: *Tradition and Modernisation in Japanese Culture*. Princeton, NJ: Princeton University Press.

Shoko-sho (Department of Commerce and Industry), *see* in (1) above.

Showa Dojinkai 1957: *Wagakuni Kanzenkoyo no Igi to Taisaku, Tokei kara Mita Koyo to Shitsugyo*. Tokyo: Showa Dojinkai.

Silberman, B. S. 1968: Structural and functional differentiation in the political modernisation of Japan. In Ward, R. E. (1968), chapter X.

Smith, R. J. 1983: *Japanese Society, Tradition, Self and the Social Order*. Cambridge University Press.

Smith, T. C. 1955: *Political Change and Industrial Development in Japan: Government Enterprise, 1868–1880*. Oxford University Press.

—— 1959: *The Agrarian Origin of Modern Japan*. Stanford, Calif.: Stanford University Press.

—— 1973: Pre-modern economic growth – Japan and the West. Berkeley: *Past and Present*, no. 60, August, pp. 127–60.

—— 1988: *Native Sources of Japanese Industrialisation, 1750–1920*. Berkeley: University of California Press.

Sorifu Tokeikyoku, *see* in (1) above.

Spaulding, R. M. 1967: *Imperical Japan's Higher Civil Service Examinations*. Princeton, NJ: Princeton University Press.

Storry, R. 1983: *A History of Modern Japan*. London: Penguin.

Stretton, H. 1987: *Political Essays*. Melbourne: Georgian House.

Sugihara, S. 1984: *Nihon no Economist*. Tokyo: Nihon Hyoron-sha.

—— et al. (eds) 1990: *Nihon-no Keizai Shiso 480-nen*. Tokyo: Nihon Keizai Hyoron.

Sugiyama, C. and Mizuta, H. (eds) 1988: *Enlightenment and Beyond, Political Economy Comes to Japan*. Tokyo: University of Tokyo Press.

Sugiyama, S. 1989: Kokusai kankyo to gaikoku Boeki. In Umemura et al. (1988–90) vol. 3. ch. 4.

Sumiya, M. 1969: *Nihonjin no Keizai Kodo*. Tokyo: Toyo Keizai Shinpo-sha, vols 1 and 2.

—— 1978: *Nihon Rodo Undo-shi*, (12th edn): Tokyo: Yushin-do.

—— and Taira, K. (eds) 1979: *An Outline of Japanese Economic History, 1603–1940: Major Works and Research Findings*. Tokyo: University of Tokyo.

Suzuki, N. (ed.) 1975: *Asian Industrial Development*, Tokyo: Institute of Developing Economies.

Suzuki, T. (ed.) 1962: *Zaiseishi*. Tokyo: Toyo-Keizai Shinpo-sha.

Suzuki, Y. 1980: *Money and Banking in Contemporary Japan: the Theoretical Setting and Its Application* (translated by John G. Greenwood). New Haven, Conn.: Yale University Press.

Tachi, M. and Okazaki, Y. 1965: Economic development and population growth: with special reference to Southeast Asia. *Developing Economies*, 3 (4), 497–515.

Tachi, R. 1964: *Meiji Zaisei-shi Kenkyu*. Tokyo: Aoki Shoten.

—— 1966: Fiscal and monetary policy. In Komiya (1966a), pp. 11–31.

—— and Moroi, K. 1965: Senzen sengo no kigyo kinyu. In Tachi and Watanabe (1965), pp. 83–105.

—— and Watanabe, T. (eds) 1965: *Keizai Seicho to Zaisei Kinyu*. Tokyo: Iwanami Shoten.

Takahashi, M. 1986: The public sector in the national economy. In Shibata (1986), ch. 1.

Bibliography 307

Takahashi, Y. (ed.) 1973: *Shiminshakai no Keizai Kozo*. Tokyo.
Takayama, N. 1980: *Fubyodo no Keizaigaku*. Tokyo: Toyo Keizai Shinpo-sha.
Takeda, T. et al. 1987: *Nihon Zaisei Yoran* (3rd edn). Tokyo: University of Tokyo Press.
Takemae, E. 1985: *Shogen Nihon Senryo-shi GHQ Rodo Ka no Gunzo*. Tokyo: Iwanami Shoten.
Takeuchi, Y. (ed.) 1967: *Nihon no Shakaishihon – Genjobunseki to Keikaku*. Tokyo: Kajima Shuppan.
—— 1990: *Senbatsu shakai, shiken, shoshinomeguru 'kanetsu' to 'Reikyaku'*. Tokyo: Recruit shuppan.
Takizawa, N. 1912: *Kohon Nihon Kinyu-shi Ron*. Tokyo: Yuhikaku.
Tanaka, Z. and Morita, A. 1991: Political science. In Toho Gakkai, op. cit., *Social Sciences 1986–87*, Vol. VII, Part 1, pp. 35–65.
Teramura, Y. 1987: Nicchusenso-ki no boeki seisaku. In Kindainihon Kenkyukai (1987), pp. 81–102.
Teranishi, J. 1972–3: A survey of economic studies on prewar Japan. *Japanese Economic Studies*, 1 (2), 47–98.
—— 1982: *Nihon no Keizai hatten to Kinyu*. Tokyo: Iwanami.
—— 1989: Fukinkoseicho to kinyu. In Umemura et al. (1988–90), vol. 6, ch. 4.
—— 1990: Kinyū-no kindai-ka to sangyo-ka. In Umemura et al. (1988–90), vol. 5, ch. 7.
Terasaki, F. 1957: *Bridge to the Sun*. Chapel Hill, NC: University of North Carolina Press.
Toho Gakkai (under the auspices of the Japan Foundation) 1974–1990: *An Introductory Bibliography for Japanese Studies*. Tokyo: Bonjin Co., vols I–VI.
Tominagi, K. 1990: *Noson no Kindai-ka to Shakai Hendo*. Tokyo: Kodansha (Gakujutsu Bunko).
Totten, G. 1966: *The Social Democratic Movement in Prewar Japan*. New Haven, Conn.: Yale University Press.
Toyo Keizai Shinpo-sha (ed.) 1935: *Nihon Boeki Seiran*. Tokyo: Toyo Keizai Shinpo-sha.
Toyota Jidosha Kogyo 1967: *Toyota Jidosha 30-nen-shi*. Tokyo. Toyota Jidosha.
Tsuchiya, T. 1954: *Nihon Shihonshugi no Keieishi-teki Kenkyu*. Tokyo: Misuzushobo.
Tsujimura, K. 1966: The employment structure and labor shares. In Komiya (1966a), pp. 107–30.
—— 1984: *Nihon no Keizaigakushatachi*. Tokyo: Nihon Hyoron-sha.
Tsuru, S. 1964: Survey of economic research in postwar Japan. *American Economic Review*, IIV (4) 79–101.
—— (ed.) 1978: *Growth and Resources Problems Related to Japan*. Tokyo: Asahi Evening News.
Tsuruta, T. 1982: *Sengo Nihon no Sangyo Seisaku*. Tokyo: Nihon Keizaishinbun-sha.
—— 1984: Kodoseicho ki. In Komiya et al. (1984), ch. 2.
Tullock, G. (ed.) 1980: *Toward a Theory of Rent-seeking Society*. Texas: Texas A & M University Press.
Uchida, H. 1990: Gijutsu iten. In Umemura et al. (1988–90), vol. 4, ch. 3.

Uchida, T. and Watanabe, T. 1959: Nihon keizai no hendo 1951–1956. *Kikan Rironkeizaigaku*, 9 (3–4), 9–20.

Uchino, T. 1983: *Japan's Postwar Economy, An Insider's View of its History and its Future* (translation by M. Harbison. original text Sengo Nihon Keizaishi, 1978. Tokyo: Kodansha) Tokyo: Kodansha International.

Uekusa, M. 1982: *Sangyo Soshikiron*. Tokyo: Tsukuma Shobo.

—— 1984: Sekiyukiki-ikō. In Komiya et al. (1984), ch. 3.

Ueno, H. 1976–7: Conception and evaluation of Japanese industrial policy. *Japanese Economic Studies*, 5 (2), 3–63.

—— 1988: *Kyoso to Kisei, Gendai no sangyososhiki*. Tokyo: Toyo Keizai Shinpo-sha.

—— and Teranishi, J. 1975: Choki model no kiso to kadai: 2-bumon model no rironteki framework. In Ohkawa and Minami (1975), pp. 369–98.

Umemura, M. 1979: Population and labor force. In Ohkawa and Shinohara (1979), pp. 241–9.

—— 1980: The seniority-wage system in Japan. In Nishikawa (ed.) (1980), pp. 177–87.

—— 1980: Bakumatsu no keizai hatten. In Kindainihon Kenkyukai (1980), pp. 3–30.

—— et al. 1966: *Noringyo*, LTES, vol. 9.

—— and Yamamoto, Y. (eds) 1989: Kaiko to ishin. In Umemura et al. (1988–90), vol. 3.

—— et al. (eds) 1988–90: *Nihon Keizaishi*. Tokyo: Iwanami Shoten.

Vol. 1, M. Miyamoto and A. Hayami (eds), 1988: *Keizaishakai no Seiritsu, 17–18th Century*.

Vol. 2, H. Shinbo and O. Saito (eds), 1989: *Kindai Seicho no Shido*.

Vol. 3, M. Umemura and Y. Yamamoto (eds), 1989: *Kaiko to Ishin*.

Vols 4 & 5, S. Nishikawa and Y. Yamamoto (eds), 1990: *Sangyoka no Jidai*.

Vol. 6, T. Nakamura and K. Odaka (eds) 1989: *Niju Kozo*.

Vol. 7, Nakamura, T. (ed.), 1989: *Keikaku-ka to Minshu-ka*.

Vol. 8, Yasuba, Y. and Inoki, T. (eds), 1989: *Kodo Seicho*.

University of Tokyo, Shakai Kenkyu-jo (ed.) 1979: *Senji-Nihon Keizai*. Tokyo.

Veblen, T. 1945: The opportunity of Japan. In L. Aidzrouni (ed.), *Essays in our Changing Order*. New York: Viking Press, pp. 248–66.

—— 1946: *Imperial Germany and the Industrial Revolution*. New York: Viking Press.

Vernon, R. 1966: International investment and international trade in the product cycle. *Quarterly Journal of Economics*, 80 (1), 190–207.

Vogel, E. V. 1979: *Japan as Number One: Lessons for America*. Cambridge, Mass.: Harvard University Press.

Wallich, H. C. and Wallich, M. I. 1976: Banking and finance. In Patrick and Rosovsky (1976a), pp. 249–315.

Ward, B. 1978: *The Home of Man*. New York: Norton.

Ward, R. E. (ed.) 1968: *Political Development in Modern Japan*. Princeton, NJ: Princeton University Press.

—— 1974: *The American Occupation of Japan 1945–1952: an Annotated Bibliography of Western Language Materials*. Chicago.

Watanabe, T. 1968: Industrialization, technological progress, and dual structure. In Klein and Ohkawa (1968), pp. 110–34.

—— 1970: *Suryō Keizai Bunseki: Seicho o Meguru Sho'mondai.* Tokyo: Sobunsha.

—— 1977: Price changes and the rate of change of money wage earnings in Japan, 1955–1962. In Kosobud and Minami (1977), pp. 178–97.

Wilson, R. A. 1957: *Genesis of the Meiji Government in Japan.* Tokyo.

Wray, H. 1983: Introduction to chapter VIII. In Wray and Conroy (1983), pp. 172–4.

—— and Conroy, H. (eds) 1983: *Japan Examined, Perspectives on Modern Japanese History.* Honolulu: University of Hawaii Press.

Yamada, S. 1967: Changes in output and in conventional and non-conventional inputs in Japanese agriculture since 1880. *Food Research Institute Studies,* 7 (3), 371–413.

—— and Hayami, Y. 1970: Kogyoka no shihatsukiniokeru nogyo no seisansei. In Kawaguchi and Kato (1970).

Yamaguchi, K. et al. (eds) 1982: *Nihon sangyo hyakunen-shi.* Tokyo: Nihon keizai Shinbun-sha (Nikkei-Shinshyo) vols 1 and 2.

Yamamoto, H. 1972: *Ishinki no Kaido to Yuso.* Tokyo: Hosei University Press.

Yamamoto, S. 1989: *Nihonjintowa-Nanika,* Tokyo: PHP, 2 vols.

Yamamura, K. 1967: *Economic Policy in Postwar Japan: Growth Versus Economic Democracy.* Berkeley, Calif.: University of California Press.

—— 1974: *A Study of Samurai Income and Entrepreneurship: Quantitative Analyses of Economic and Social Aspects of the Samurai in Tokugawa and Meiji Japan.* Cambridge, Mass.: Harvard University Press.

—— 1976: General trading companies in Japan: their origins and growth. In Patrick (1976), pp. 171–99.

—— 1977: Success ill gotten? The role of Meiji militarism in Japan's technological progress. *Journal of Economic History,* 37 (1), 113–35.

—— and Yasuba, Y. (eds) 1987: *The Political Economy of Japan: the Domestic Transformation, volume 1.* Stanford, Calif.: Stanford University Press.

Yamazawa, I. 1975a: Industrial growth and trade policy in prewar Japan. *Developing Economies,* 8 (1), 38–65.

—— 1975b: Strategy of industrial development: Japanese experience. In Suzuki, N. (1975), pp. 314–48.

—— and Kohama, H. 1978: Shosha katsudo to boeki kakudai. *Kikan Gendai Keizai,* 33, 176–91.

—— and Yamamoto, Y. 1979a: *Boeki to Kokusai Shushi,* LTES, vol. 14.

—— and —— 1979b: Trade and balance payments. In Ohkawa and Shinohara (1979), pp. 134–56.

Yanokota, Kinenkai (ed.), *Nihon Kokuzei Zue,* Tokyo (annual).

Yasuba, Y. 1976: The evolution of dualistic wage structure. In Patrick (1976), pp. 249–98.

—— 1980: *Keizai Seichoron.* Tokyo: Tsukuma-Shobo.

—— 1987: Pre-conditions to industrialization in Japan. *The Economic Studies Quarterly,* 38 (4), 289–371.

—— and Inoki, T. 1989: Gaisetsu 1955–80. In Umemura et al. (1988–90), vol. 7, ch. 1.

Yasuoka, S. 1978: Nakamigawa Hikojiro. In Yasuoka et al. (1978), vol. 1.

—— et al. 1978: *Nihon no Kigyo-ka,* vol. 1, *Meiji-hen.* Tokyo: Yuhikaku.

Yokoyama, G. 1898: *Nihon-no Kasokaikyu*. Tokyo: Iwanami.

Yonekawa, S. 1982: The development of Chinese and Japanese business in an international perspective: a bibliographical introduction. *Business History Review*, 56.

—— 1985: Recent writing on Japanese economic and social history. *Economic History Review* (February), 107–23.

Yoshitomi, M. 1977: *Gendai Nihon Keizai Ron*. Tokyo: Toyo Keizai Shinpo-sha.

Youngson, A. J. (ed.) 1972: *Economic Development in the Long Run*. London: George Allen & Unwin.

Appendix: Statistical Data

Table A.1 Gross Domestic Product (GDP) and Gross National Expenditure (GNE), at current prices

	1885	1897	1907	1912	1921	1926	1930	1935	1944	1955	1965	1975	1983	1986
A. GDP	714	1 589	3 202	4 116	12 407	13 669	11 265	14 455	56 772	7 087	25 722	120 519	217 577	224 936
1 Factor income by sector	714	1 589	3 202	4 616	21 407	13 669	11 765	14 455	56 772	7 087	25 722	120 519	217 579	243 360
2 Primary	384	579	1 210	1 609	3 675	3 415	1 983	2 858	10 104	1 634	2 882	7 012	6 971	7 031
3 Secondary	110	334	713	847	3 109	3 517	3 198	4 477	22 983	2 030	9 195	47 612	84 191	94 189
B. GNE	806	1 957	3 743	4 774	14 886	15 957	13 850	16 734	14 503	8 622	32 657	147 874	275 203	331 346
1 Personal consumption, C_p		1 545	2 787	3 657	11 171	12 359	10 572	10 833	26 554	5 529	19 123	84 568	163 343	191 657
2 Government consumption, C_g		164	408	450	1 549	1 332	1 624	2 637	2 599	8 894	12 690	14 890	27 942	32 571
3 Private investment, I_p		74	291	431	565	1 708	1 710	963	17 031	1 447	7 587	34 855	55 483	72 420
4 Government investment, I_g	16	58	133	212	731	953	492	510	3 624	677	2 890	13 655	23 134	22 596
5 Export, E	42	191	617	727	2 065	2 985	2 701	4 247	3 950	979	3 563	20 254	43 486	38 090
6 Import, M	45	292	633	837	2 338	3 364	2 502	4 092	4 328	904	3 197	20 349	38 159	24 791

C. Share in total factor income

1 Primary	39.8	36.4	37.8	34.9	17.2	24.5	16.9	19.8	17.8	23.1	11.2	5.9	3.2	2.9
2 Secondary	15.4	21.0	22.3	18.3	14.5	25.7	27.2	31.0	12.7	28.6	35.7	39.5	38.7	38.7
3 Tertiary	44.8	42.5	39.9	36.0	26.3	49.3	56.0	49.3	41.7	48.3	53.0	54.7	58.1	58.4
Total	100.0	100.0	100.0	100.0	100.0	100.0	100.0	100.0	100.0	100.0	100.0	100.0	100.0	100.0

D. Share in GNE

1 C_p	80.9	78.9	74.5	76.6	75.0	77.4	76.3	64.7	35.6	64.1	58.6	57.2	59.3	57.8
2 C_g	8.3	8.4	14.6	9.4	10.4	8.3	11.7	15.8	36.0	10.4	8.2	23.6	10.2	9.8
3 I_p	9.2	15.0	14.6	11.8	10.5	10.7	7.0	15.5	22.8	16.8	23.2	9.2	20.5	21.9
4 I_g	2.0	3.0	4.8	4.5	4.9	6.0	3.6	3.1	4.9	7.9	8.9	9.2	8.4	6.8
5 E	0.5	9.8	22.1	15.3	13.9	18.7	19.5	25.4	4.9	11.4	10.9	13.7	15.8	11.5
6 M	0.5	14.9	22.1	17.5	13.9	21.1	19.5	25.4	5.8	11.4	10.9	13.7	14.1	7.5
Total	100.0	100.0	100.0	100.0	100.0	100.0	100.0	100.0	100.0	100.0	100.0	100.0	100.0	100.0

Sources: for 1885–1940, Bank of Japan, Hundred-year Statistics of the Japanese Economy, and Ohkawa and Takamatsu (1974); for 1944–86, EPA, Annual Report on National Accounts, Kokumin Shotoku Hakusho and Kokumin Shotoku Tokei Nenpo, and Shinohara (1986, p. 278).

Table A.2 *Basic economic trends, 1874–1985*

	1874 to 1885	1885 to 1900	1901 to 1916	1917 to 1932	1933 to 1937	1941 to 1944	Second World War period 1938 to 1944	1946 to 1955	1956 to 1965	1966 to 1975	1978 to 1985	Postwar period 1945 to 1985
National product (current prices)	n.a.	3.00[a]	2.48	1.59	1.42	1.66	(2.78)	6.59	3.71	4.56	1.90	(241.64)
National product (constant prices)	n.a.	1.62[a]	1.43	1.45	1.23	0.96	(0.94)	1.46	2.42	2.25	1.48	(25.08)
Product – agriculture	1.24	1.25	1.33	1.06	1.19	0.85	(0.65)	1.66	1.24	1.19	1.10	n.a.
Product – manufacturing	1.31	2.44	2.30	1.82	1.65	1.01	(0.43)	5.53	3.71	2.26	1.52	n.a.
Price index – wholesale	1.48	1.64	1.60	1.31	1.16	1.72	(2.84)	98.00	1.05	1.74	1.33	n.a.
Real personal consumption per capita	1.09	1.38	1.12	1.20	1.09	0.73	(0.71)	2.00	1.92	1.62	1.27	(9.41)
Wages or salaries Nominal	n.a.	2.08	1.81	2.73	1.70	5.02	(3.38)	135.72	2.18	4.54	1.79	(2400.91)
Real	n.a.	1.37	0.70	1.71	0.99	1.28	(0.26)	5.93	1.46	2.04	1.15	(20.20)
Employment	n.a.	n.a.	n.a.	n.a.	1.22	0.56	(0.82)	1.72	2.23	1.09	0.98	(4.10)
Labour productivity	n.a.	n.a.	n.a.	n.a.	1.28[b]	0.79[c]	(1.17)[d]	1.36	2.03	2.45	1.79	(12.06)

[a] For 1887–1902; [b] for 1940–5; [c] for 1940–5; [d] for 1935–45; n.a. indicates 'not available'.

Sources: for 1874–1940, Ohokawa and Takamatsu (1974), Shinohara (1972) and Ando (1978), for 1944–86, EPA, *Annual Report on National Accounts,* Shinohara (1986, p. 278; 1987, p. 6), Ohokawa et al. (1965), and Gleason (1986, table 1).

Table A.3 *Indices for economic growth, 1887–1987*

	Growth factors	
	1887–1987[a] *(1887 = 1.0)*	*1935–87*[b] *(1935 = 1.0)*
GNP		
Nominal	336 470.0	16 450.0
Real	44.5	11.6
Wages and salaries		
Nominal	83 640.0	8 110.0
Real	17.6	5.3
Production	293.1	22.9
Labour productivity	n.a.	9.9
Employment	2.6	1.8

[a] One hundred years from the Restoration to 1987.
[b] Fifty-two years prior to the Second World War.
n.a. indicates 'not available'.
Source: Shinohara (1986, p. 278).

Table A.4 *Percentage proportion of total value of output in various manufacturing industries, 1875–1985*

	1875	1900	1915	1930	1935	1940	1950	1955	1965	1970	1975	1985
1. Steel	1.0	0.4	4.5	6.2	10.0	14.0	⎱13.0	9.6	9.1	9.5	8.9	⎱
2. Non-ferrous	2.2	2.2	3.8	2.5	2.8	2.4	⎰	4.2	3.9	4.4	3.1	⎬ 14.0
3. Metal products	n.a.	n.a.	n.a.	n.a.	n.a.	n.a.	3.0	3.2	4.7	5.4	5.2	⎰
4. Machinery	2.1	4.0	9.3	11.3	16.3	25.9	n.a.	n.a.	n.a.	32.4	39.7	⎱
5. Chemicals	19.0	n.a.	n.a.	n.a.	n.a.	n.a.	12.9	11.0	9.5	8.0	8.2	⎰ 12.5
6. Heavy industries (subtotal of 1–5)	(24.3)	(17.3)	(29.3)	(32.8)	(43.5)	(58.9)	(50.0)	(50.2)	(61.7)	(66.6)	(65.1)	(66.1)
7. Cement	2.1	2.0	2.4	2.6	2.6	2.4	3.3	3.4	3.5	3.6	3.8	3.3
8. Textiles	22.3	35.8	32.9	30.6	29.1	16.8	23.2	17.5	10.3	7.7	6.8	4.6
9. Food-processing	40.2	35.9	27.1	25.0	16.4	12.2	13.4	17.9	12.5	10.4	11.9	11.0
10. Light industries (subtotal of 7–9)	(75.7)	(82.7)	(70.7)	(67.2)	(56.5)	(41.1)	(50.0)	(49.8)	(38.3)	(33.4)	(34.4)	(33.9)
11. Total (1–5) + (7–9)	(100.0)	(100.0)	(100.0)	(100.0)	(100.0)	(100.0)	(100.0)	(100.0)	(100.0)	(100.0)	(100.0)	(100.0)

Note: Total and subtotal figures differ from simple aggregations of each item for some years due to rounding. n.a. indicates 'not available'.
Sources: For 1875–1970, Ando (1987, p. 11); for 1975–1985, MITI Kogyo-hyo (Industrial Statistics), 1985.

Table A.5 Imports and exports by product, 1874–1984

	Exports					Imports					
	Food	Raw material products	Light industry products	Heavy industry products	Others	Food	Raw material products	Coal and oil products	Light industry products	Heavy industry products	Others
1874	48.2	7.6	32.0	7.6	4.6	9.6	4.3	1.2	42.0	11.9	31.0
1880	36.9	8.6	41.0	10.4	3.1	10.1	2.0	3.2	43.3	14.5	26.9
1890	21.4	9.5	45.9	19.7	3.5	26.4	7.3	5.6	28.6	23.1	9.0
1900	11.2	10.8	58.4	13.8	5.8	17.3	21.9	5.3	17.8	37.1	0.6
1910	11.5	5.3	64.3	13.4	5.5	18.5	36.6	3.4	9.5	29.3	2.7
1920	8.1	3.5	65.9	15.3	7.2	18.2	36.6	2.2	4.7	35.1	3.2
1930	9.9	3.4	63.1	17.7	5.9	29.3	30.1	6.3	6.6	26.1	1.6
1939	11.7	3.5	50.1	33.1	1.6	20.7	23.9	8.0	3.7	37.8	5.9
1951	5.1	1.9	54.8	37.1	1.1	25.2	55.7	8.0	2.7	6.8	1.6
1960	6.6	2.6	43.0	46.5	1.3	12.2	65.7		1.4	20.5	0.2
1970	3.4	0.9	19.2	75.8	0.7	13.6	54.7		5.6	24.3	1.8
1980	1.2	1.0	12.2	84.4	1.2	10.4	66.8		6.2	15.5	1.1
1984	0.8	0.7	11.3	86.2	1.0	11.7	58.5		7.1	20.2	2.5
1987	0.7	0.7	10.0	87.6	2.0	15.0	40.9		13.8	26.7	3.6

Sources: Shinohara (1986, p. 285) and Yanokota Kinenkai, *Nihon Nokuzei Zue* (1985–8).

Table A.6　*Economic White Papers, 1947–89*

Report no.	Year	Title[a]
1	1947	A Report on Actual Conditions in the Economy – emergency economic policies: presenting the theoretical basis for new policies to fight inflation and to appeal to the population for understanding the co-operation
2	1948	A Report on the Economy – in retrospect and prospect: a plan for economic rehabilitation
3	1949	Economic Analysis of the Current Problem – the plan for economic stabilization: aiming at balance in the budget, reduction and elimination of subsidies, a fixed exchange rate and promotion of key industries
4	1950	The Economy under a Policy of Stabilization
5	1951	The Economy under a Policy of Stabilization
6	1952	Growth Capacity of the Economy after the Immediate Postwar period
7	1953	Economic Policy to Restore Economic Independence
8	1954	Preparation for Economic Independence
9	1955	Economic Growth and Modernization – with specific reference to technical progress, trade and investment
10	1956	Economic Growth and Modernization of Industries and Production Facilities
11	1957	Problems of Over-accelerated Growth – Industrial information facilities and the dual industrial structure
12	1958	Economic Cycles – the accumulation of unsold stocks and excessive investment for capacity expansion
13	1959	The Economy in Severe Depression – in search of effective policy measures for economic recovery
14	1960	Growth and Competitiveness in the Economy
15	1961	How is Economic Growth Generated? – rapidly increased demand, investment and trade surpluses; labour shortages and inflation
16	1962	The Changing Nature and Pattern of the Economy – an economic turning point?
17	1963	The Road Towards an Advanced Industrial Economy – a plea for balanced industrial growth and accumulation of social overhead capital
18	1964	The Liberalization of Trade and Capital – growth without (the feeling of) prosperity
19	1965	Towards Stable Economic Growth: increase in bankruptcies, lowering of profitability, highly geared corporate finance and the new role of public finance
20	1966	Towards Stable and Continuous Economic Growth
21	1967	Efficiency Versus Welfare – a high-growth economy and problems of inflation, land prices and environmental degradation
22	1968	Japan and the World – promoting capital liberalization and joint venture programmes with foreign enterprises

Table A.6 *(Continued)*

Report no.	Year	Title[a]
23	1969	Towards an Affluent Society? – further problems of pollution and environmental degradation
24	1970	The New Socio-economic Dimension – in search of growth without inflation and the establishment of a welfare economy
25	1971	The Balanced Economy – trade and domestic activity: 25 years of high-speed growth; retrospect and prospect
26	1972	Building a New Welfare State – expansion of the public-sector economy
27	1973	Increasing Welfare without Inflation – the expansion of public finance and the floating of the yen
28	1974	Beyond Economic Growth – towards balanced growth
29	1975	Towards Stable Economic Growth – changes in the economic conditions for growth and the problems of a decelerating economy
30	1976	Laying the Necessary Economic Foundations for Stable Economic Growth
31	1977	The Process of Adjustment – successful transition towards a stable and decelerated economy: problems of the lack of new investment activities, high savings and structural unemployment
32	1978	The Economy in Transition – the J-curve effect
33	1979	Vitalization of the Japanese economy – towards stable employment
34	1980	New Problems in Economic Development: the development of the Japanese Economy, its environmental changes, oil supply restrictions, international economic friction, utilization of private vitality and socio-economic changes
35	1981	Vitality of the Japanese Economy – its features and problems
36	1982	Basic Structural Conditions for Policy Selection: balance and growth, potential problems of the public sector and new types of international specialization and industrial adjustment
37	1983	Conditions for Lasting Long-term Development and Effective Business Adjustment Policies
38	1984	Changes in Industrial Structure and the Internationalization of Finance
39	1985	The New Age of Growth – ageing of the population and the loss of economic vitality
40	1986	New Currents of Industrial Development and Enrichment of Stocks
41	1989	Globalization of the Economy
42	1990	Towards Continuous Economic Growth and Expansion

[a] I have translated the original titles and sub titles so as to convey the basic gist of the content.
Sources: EPA, *Shiryo Keizai Hakusho 25-nen* (1972) and *Keizai Hakusho* (1979–89).

Table A.7 *National economic plans, 1956–90*

	Planning period and date of publication[a]	Planned and actual rates of growth[b]		Planned and actual increase in consumer price[b]	Planned and actual size of trade balance[b]	Major objectives of plan, and policy problems to be solved
		GNP (real)	Mining and mfg products (real)			
I. Five-year plan for Economic Self-support	1956–60 (Dec. 1955)	5.0 (9.1)	7.4[c] (15.6)[c]	None (2.0)	0 (−0.1)	(i) Modernization of productive capacity (ii) Development of international trade (iii) Increased domestic production and minimum use of foreign exchange (iv) Development of land and resources
II. New Long-range Economic Plan	1958–62 (Dec. 1957)	6.5 (10.9)	8.2[d] (13.5)[d]	None (3.5)	1.5 (−0.2)	(i) Promotion of exports (ii) Accumulation of capital (iii) Strengthening of industrial base (iv) Expansion of heavy and chemical industries (v) Modernization of agriculture sector

	Plan	Period (date)					Principal objectives
III.	National Income-doubling Plan	1961–70 (Dec. 1960)	7.2 (10.9)	10.5 (13.8)	None (5.7)	1.8 (23.6)	(i) Investment in social overhead capital (ii) Modernization of industrial structure (iii) International co-operation (iv) Advancement of science and technology (v) Mitigation of the 'dual' industrial structure
IV.	Medium-term Economic Plan	1964–8 (Jan. 1965)	8.1 (10.8)	9.9 (13.6)	2.5 (5.0)	0 (14.7)	(i) Modernization of low-productivity sectors (ii) Efficient use of labour force and encouragement of labour mobility (iii) Improvement in the quality of life

(continued)

Table A.7 (Continued)

| Planning period and date of publication[a] | Planned and actual rates of growth[b] | | Planned and actual increase in consumer price[b] | Planned and actual size of trade balance[b] | Major objectives of plan, and policy problems to be solved |
	GNP (real)	Mining and mfg products (real)			
V. Economic and Social Development Plan	1967–71 (Mar. 1967)				
	8.2 (12.0)	10.2 (12.7)[e]	3.0 (5.7)	14.5 (63.2)	(i) Price stability (ii) Economic efficiency (iii)[f] Advancement of social development
VI. New Economic and Social Development Plan	1970–5 (May 1970)				
	10.6 (6.5)[f]	12.4 (7.5)[g]	3.0 (20.7)	35.0 (83.2)	(i) Price stability (ii) Promotion of social development (iii) Maintenance of proper rate of economic growth
VII. Basic Economic and Social Plan	1973–7 (Feb. 1973)				
	9.4 (−0.6)	13.5 (−9.4)[h]	4.0 (20.7)	59.0 (−1.8)	(i) Creation of a rich environment (ii) Comfortable and stable civil life (iii) Price stability (iv) International co-operation

	Plan	Dates					
VIII.	Economic Plan for 1976–80	1976–80 (Spring 1976)	6.0 (5.1)	n.a.	6.0	40.0	(i) Price stability and full employment (ii) Stable life and betterment of civil life and environment (iii) International co-operation
IX.	New Economic and Social Seven-year Plan	1979–85 (Aug. 1979)	5.7 (4.1)	n.a.	n.a.	Roughly balanced	
X.	Outlook and Guidelines of Economy and Society in the 1980s	1983–90 (Aug. 1983)	4.0 (n.a.)	n.a.	n.a.	Interactively harmonious balance	

[a] Dates in brackets indicate the date of publication.
[b] Figures in brackets are actual.
[c] For 1955–60; [d] for 1957–62; [e] for 1966–71; [f] for 1970–4; [g] for 1970–1; [h] for 1974; n.a. indicates 'not available'.

Sources: Sheridan (1977, pp. 78–9) and material (in mimeo form) supplied privately to the author by the EPA in 1987.

	1948		1955	1957	1960	

Division of the economic plan

Economic rehabilitation plan — 5-Year plan for economic self-support — New long range economic plan — The National Income-doubling Plan — Mediu econo plan

(Period of rehabilitation)   (Period of self-support)   (First period of high g

International environment

The Peace Treaty   Admission into GATT   Acceptance of obli under Article 8 of the IMF Charter Admission into O (industrialization)

(Independence)   (Towards trade liberalization)
Admission into IMF and IBRU

Market liberalization

Lapse of Temporary Stabilization, Act of Balance of Commodities   Guidelines for liberalisation of trade and foreign exchange transactions   Abolition foreign e budget s

(Free-market systematization)

(Liberalization)

Development of industry

Electric Power Development Promotion Act   The 2nd Rationalization Plan for the Steel Industry   New industria construction promotion la
The First Rationalization Plan for the Steel Industry   5-Year Plan for Fostering the Petrochemical Industry   Conception of Pacific coastal belts

(Period of introduction of foreign technology)   (Period of enlargement

Land development and the build-up of social capital

Comprehensive National Land Development Act   Comprehensive land develop- ment near Kitagami River   The Capital Region Reform Act   The First Comprehens National Development (nodal system of devel

Establishment of Japan Telephone and Telegraph Corp.   Japan Highway Public Corp. Law

The first 5-year plan for roads   Start of construction of Mei-Shin Highway (Nagoya–Kobe)   Op Mei-Shin

The first 5-year plan of JNR (Japan National Railways (electrification and track doubling)   The second 5-year plan of (Shinkansen Railway plan)

Announcement of the plan for the Tokaido New Railway   Opening of New Railwa

(Full provision of foundations, reduction of various disparities)   (Shortage of social cap high-speed network)

Living environment

Hokkaido Comprehensive Development 5-Year Plan   Producer's price of rice through income compensation system   Nationwide Medical Care and Pension Law, Agricultural Basic Law   Mou Villa Dev Act

(Absorption of former military personnel and civilians returning from abroad)   (Income gaps, dual structure of the economy)   (Measures densely p regions)

Figure A.1   *History and background for the Japanese economic plan, 1948*

1970	1973	1976	1979	1983	1985	1990

ic   New   Basic   Economic   New economic   Outlook and   MITI policy
al   economic   economic   plan for   and social   guidelines of   in the 1990s–
nent   and social   and social   the second   7-year plan   economy and   towards
           development plan   half of   society in   creating
           plan   the 1970s   the 1980s   human

                            Long-term vision for 1974   MITI 'vision' for the 1980s   values in the
                                                                                                                    global age
period of high growth)   (Period of co-ordination)

ion of the US   Recovery of diplomatic   Iranian Revolution
convertibility   relations between   (second oil crisis)
Shock)   Japan and China

                    Return of Okinawa

                    First oil crisis

sic $1 = Y308   Yen moved to the   Enforcement of new   Establishment of
nes   (Smithsonian   floating system   Foreign Exchange   new Kansai Airport
              rate)   Control Act
zation
al   Agreement on special measures for foreign entry into public works
ent
                                   Introduction of various import promotion measures
tion for introduction of technology
                    (Floating system, internationalization)   Japan–US semiconductor agreement

tion of large-scale mills Law promoting   Act of Technopolis   In search of policy
akai, Fukuyama,   relocation of industries   measures to maintain
a)   industrial vitality

awata–Fuji Steel merger
tablish Shin-Nippon Steel   Promotion of intellectual property
   Ltd.)   protection and standardization

           (Period of knowledge-intensiveness)   (Period of new technology)

nd Comprehensive   Establishment   The Third Comprehensive
Development Plan   of National   National Development Plan
le project system)   Land Agency   (integrated residence system)

g of To-Mei Highway   Automation of the nationwide
–Nagoya)   telephone network,
                                           the elimination of customer waiting lists

           Opening of Sanyo Shinkansen Line   Opening of Tohoku and Joetsu Shinkansen lines
           (priority to region and quality of   (Progress to advanced information society)
           life)

Law of   Abnormal price increase   End of the 'post   'Paradox of
ation   (Act for emergency measures   World War II   prosperity'
Law of   to stabilize national life)   high-growth period'
n
                                                              Tightening of labour supply

                    (Diversifying sense of values)   Introduction of new industrial labour policy

es: Shinohana (1977), EPA (1972) and material (mimeo) privately supplied to the
   by the EPA in 1987 and 1990.

	1948	52	55	57	60	65
	Economic rehabilitation plan	5-Year plan for economic Self-support	New long-range economic plan	National Income-Doubling Plan	Medium-te economic plan	
(Period)	(rehabilitation)		(self-support)		(high growth no. 1)	
Procedure in planning	Target levels (regain the standard of living of prewar period) ↓ Study the conditions to achieve targets	Optimum growth rate ↑ Colm method	↑ Alternative growth rates approach	Growth rate predetermined ↓ Study the conditions and policies to achieve the target		
Policy measures	Control on quantities and prices of commodities and on foreign trade	Fiscal and monetary policy Control of imports (commodities, technology)				
Role of the plan	Standard for implementing the control	To give a basis for other specific plans and to guarantee consistency among them (JNR, Electric Power Company and so on)		1. To present guid 2. To show the g policy from a 3. To co-ordinate		
Method for projection	Accumulating method	Colm method	Alternative growth rates approach	Step-by-step approach		

Figure A.2 *Planning methods.*

Sources: Shinohara (1977), EPA, *Shiryo Keizai Hakusho 20-Nen* (1972) and material (mimeo) privately supplied to the author by the EPA in 1987 and 1990.

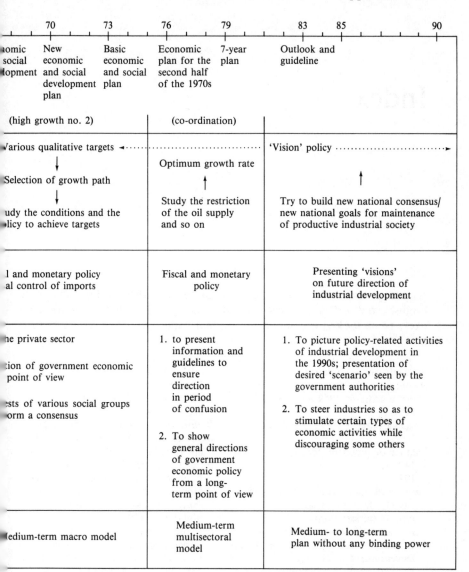

Figure A.2   *continued*

Index

As the general rule topics are given in forms either in Japanese or in English, and in full or abbreviated depending under which they are more likely to be looked up. Japanese personal names are given with surnames first.